A C
OF S

Brian Marriner

True Crime Library – No. 1
A Forum Press Book
by the Paperback Division of
Forum Design,
P.O. Box 158, London SE20 7QA.

An Imprint of True Crime Library

Typeset by T.S. Typesetting,
1 Park Avenue, West Wickham, Kent BR4 9JU.
Printed and bound in Great Britain by
HarperCollins Manufacturing, Glasgow.

ISBN No. 1 874358 00 1

To my son, Steven,
for the encouragement.
And for Mike James,
the inspiration

In the True Crime Library series:

An expert in criminology and forensic science, Brian Marriner has established himself as one of Britain's leading true crime authors. He is a regular contributor to the top non-fiction crime magazines; *True Detective, True Crime Monthly* and *Master Detective* – and has written editions of *Murder Casebook*. His book *Forensic Clues To Murder* was described by Colin Wilson as "the definitive text on forensic medicine, which is destined to become a modern classic".

What distinguishes Marriner's work is his uncanny knack of probing the motives and thinking behind the crimes, while introducing the most gruesome elements with calm scientific interest.

CONTENTS

Foreword

By Colin Wilson

John Addington Symonds's classic *Renaissance in Italy* contains an account of one of the most appalling tyrants known to history – Ibrahim ibn Ahmed, a ninth-century prince of Africa and Sicily. We would probably say simply that the man was an insane sadist. Symonds tells how on one occasion he murdered sixty youths 'originally selected for his pleasure' by burning them alive in a furnace or suffocating them in the steam chamber of his bath. Eight of his brothers and his own son were murdered in his presence.

But his fiercest fury was directed against women. He seems to have been darkly jealous of the perpetuation of the human race. Wives and concubines were strangled, sawn asunder and buried alive if they showed signs of pregnancy. His female children were murdered as soon as they saw the light; sixteen of them whom his mother managed to conceal and rear at her own peril were massacred upon the spot when Ibrahim discovered whom they claimed as a father.

There then follows an extremely curious passage:

Contemporary Arab chroniclers, pondering upon the fierce and gloomy passions of this man, arrived at the conclusion that he was the subject of a strange disease, a portentous secretion of black bile producing the melancholy which impelled him to atrocious crimes.

As to Symonds himself, he tried to explain Ibrahim's crimes by inventing a new word – haematomania, which simply means blood-lust.

But then we have to remember that Symonds was writing around 1870, and that at this time no one understood the nature of sex crime. What seems stranger still is that the very idea was unknown. Only a few years earlier, in 1867, a clerk named Frederick Baker approached a group of children near the town of Alton, in Hampshire, and persuaded an eight-year-old girl named Fanny Adams to go with him for a walk. A few hours later her disembowelled body was found in a hop garden, literally torn to pieces. Baker's diary had an entry: 'Killed a young girl today. It was fine and hot.' In reporting this story, and Baker's subsequent execution, the *Illustrated Police News* explained that Baker was the son of an alcoholic and was suffering from 'mania'. The fact the child's genitals were missing was not mentioned.

In discussing the case in my *Criminal History of Mankind*, I point out that even the account in the *Illustrated Police News* offers us a number of interesting clues to the psychology of the killer. When the child's mother encountered Baker soon after the abduction and asked him what had happened to her daughter Baker seemed perfectly calm, and assured her that Fanny had gone off to buy sweets. She saw no blood on his clothing. That would be impossible unless Baker had stripped himself naked before killing her child. And that suggests premeditation, as does his unperturbed manner – a man who has just surrendered to an overwhelming impulse would feel shaken and guilty. So Baker had thought it out in advance. In fact few sex killers commit their crimes 'out of the blue'; most of them have been brooding on rape for a long time, and many have a collection of pornography. Frederick Baker was a paedophile, and he had probably been indulging in sadistic daydreams, including decapitation – Fanny's head was the first part of her to be found – for months or years before he finally nerved himself to put his fantasies into practice.

Just over twenty years later, what I have called 'the age of sex crime' was launched by the unknown maniac known as Jack the Ripper. As everyone now knows, he killed five women in the Whitechapel area of London between August and November 1888, usually disembowelling them, and taking away certain inner organs. But one of the oddest aspects of the Ripper murders is that the Victorians did not recognize them as sex crimes. Sir Melville Macnaghten, Commissioner of Police soon after the murders, later described the Ripper as 'sexually insane'. Yet what he meant was almost certainly that the Ripper was a 'religious maniac' who hated prostitutes because of their immorality. In fact this was one of the most popular theories at the time – that he was a puritan driven to insanity by his hatred of immoral women.

Eleven years after the Ripper murders, in 1899, there appeared in England an edition of a strange German work called *Psychopathia Sexualis* by a German doctor named Richard von Krafft-Ebing, and it achieved instant wide circulation. This was the first major clinical work on 'sexual perversion', and it devoted its final chapter to a consideration of the problem of sex crime. This, says Krafft-Ebing, is on the rise, particularly the rape of children under the age of fourteen. And this comment itself offers us an important insight into the rise of sex crime. In the nineteenth century there was so much poverty that any 'gentleman' with five shillings in his pocket could pick up a working-class girl and take her to the nearest rooming house – 'Walter', the anonymous author of the Victorian sexual classic *My Secret Life*, describes dozens of such encounters, in many cases with girls who were virgins when he met them. This meant that it would have been pointless to commit rape on a teenage girl, when she would probably consent to intercourse for a few shillings. But children were still 'forbidden'. This explains why, in the mid-nineteenth century, 90 per cent of rapes that came to court were committed on children. It was not until the early twentieth century, when women began to work in factories and offices, that they ceased to be available to casual Don Juans like Walter – became 'forbidden' – and began to figure increasingly in the rape statistics.

But it is interesting to note that the few sex murders mentioned by Krafft-Ebing were all committed by idiots or 'degenerates': people with a history of alcoholism and mental illness. In fact, he cites far more cases of exhibitionism than of murder. And he obviously finds this just as difficult to explain, except in terms of insanity or 'degeneracy'. He explains that modesty is an ingrained characteristic in all civilized societies, and that therefore anyone who offends public decency by exposing himself must be mentally defective or degenerate.

Now obviously he is overlooking an important alternative: that a perfectly normal person may have such a high level of sex drive. and be so frustrated, that his 'civilized' inhibitions disappear, and he goes out and exposes himself to a schoolgirl, or makes an attempt to assault her sexually. Why did he overlook anything so obvious? The answer is, quite simply, because he was born in 1840, and grew up in a society in which sex crime was a rarity, except among drunks or degenerates.

It is not surprising that Krafft-Ebing failed to understand the real nature of the problem. Even today, with roughly a century of sex crime behind us, we are only just beginning to grasp what happened. And what happened is very odd indeed. In previous centuries there was very little sex crime in our modern sense of the word. *The Newgate Calendar* (1774) is one of the most comprehensive accounts of crime in the eighteenth century, and there are only three or four 'sex crimes' in the whole book – a lord who kidnapped and raped a Quakeress, a teacher who had sexual intercourse with a ten-year-old servant girl, and so on. The great majority of the crimes involve robbery. And that was because, in the eighteenth century, most people were so poor that their main problem was simply keeping body and soul together. Moreover, sex was so freely available that rape would have been superfluous.

Now, one of the great social revolutions of the century occurred in 1740, when a novel called *Pamela* appeared on the bookstalls in London. It was written by a printer named Samuel Richardson, and told the story of a pretty servant girl whose young master makes strenuous efforts to take her virginity, and ends by marrying her. *Pamela* was the first novel in our modern sense of the word. Dozens – in fact, hundreds – of novels had been written before then, but they were mostly old-fashioned tales of travel and adventure. *Pamela* was more like a soap opera, a novel with which every reader could 'identify'. And within a year or two, novels had become the great popular entertainment of the age. And many of them, like *Pamela*, contained a strong element of voyeuristic sex.

Seven years after the publication of *Pamela,* a penniless young adventurer named John Cleland wrote a sex-novel called *Memoirs of a Woman of Pleasure* – better known as *Fanny Hill*, the first pornographic novel. It tells the story of how a young country girl comes to London, takes a job as a maidservant in a place which she is too innocent to recognize as a brothel, is introduced to the delights of sex by a lesbian, then loses her virginity to a young gentleman who subsequently deserts her; after that she makes a living by selling her body. The government was so shocked by Cleland's novel that he was offered a life pension on condition he wrote no more, and he lived happily ever after. And it was another fifty years or so before pornography really 'caught on' – largely as a result of the underground popularity of the novels of the Marquis de Sade. By the year 1830 – shortly before the accession of Queen Victoria – England was flooded by pornographic novels (many printed in Amsterdam) with titles like *The Lustful Turk* and *The Bedfellows*. And devotees of pornography (like Keats's biographer Lord Houghton) would have noticed an interesting difference between *Fanny Hill* and *The Bedfellows*. *Fanny Hill* was quite unashamedly ribald and Rabelaisian; this new pornography was somehow furtive. A typical story might describe how a ten-year-old girl peeps in through the pantry window and sees the butler masturbating; curious to learn more, she takes the first opportunity to ask him what he was doing, and after swearing her to silence, he tells her about the birds and the bees . . . And in a day or so, he climbs into her little bed and 'makes a woman of her'. Sex was ceasing to be a hearty pleasure that could be described in the kind of cheerfully bawdy language Shakespeare would have used, and had become a matter of *imagination*. And there was something curiously overheated and feverish about the Victorian sexual imagination. Victorian pornography is full of incest and seduction of minors and men peeping through holes in lavatory doors. It was at about this time that an engineer discovered 'superheated steam', and it would not be inaccurate to say that Victorian pornographers discovered 'superheated sex'.

This is what Krafft-Ebing failed to understand: that a perfectly normal person could become so obsessed with sexual desire that he might become a kind of sexual criminal. And it is true that during Krafft-Ebing's lifetime this was still by no means obvious. The case of Frederick Baker – already discussed – was one of the first notable sex crimes to take place in England, and Krafft-Ebing included it in a later edition of *Psychopathia Sexualis*. But Baker was obviously mentally unstable. So was Eusebius Pieydagnelle, a French butcher's assistant who became so obsessed with blood that he finally went on a killing rampage, stabbing seven people to death and experiencing orgasm as he did so. So was Jesse Pomeroy, an American teenager with a sadistic streak who murdered two children in Boston. So was the Italian Vincenz Verzeni, who could only achieve orgasm while throttling women. So was the Frenchman Louis Menesclou, who lured a four-year-old girl to his room in Paris, then raped and dismembered her. So was the French Jack the Ripper, Joseph Vacher, who roamed around the countryside in the 1890s, committing murder and rape whenever he got the opportunity – a frightening anticipation of the modern 'serial killer'. When Krafft-Ebing died in 1902 it was by no means obvious that the sex killer might be, in many respects, a fairly normal individual.

But as the new century progressed, it became increasingly obvious. Even as early as 1895, a Sunday school teacher named Theodore Durrant lured two girls into a Baptist church in San Francisco, and raped them after killing them. A man named Hadley rented a house in San Francisco, lured a teenage babysitter to it, and left her naked body in the bed for weeks – he was never caught. In 1913 a teenager named Mary Phagan was murdered in a factory basement in Atlanta, Georgia; Leo Frank, the Jewish manager of the factory, was accused of the crime, and lynched. Many years later it was established that the actual killer was the negro caretaker. The most interesting thing about the Frank case is that it created such a world-wide sensation, demonstrating that sex crime was still a rarity.

But it was during and after the First World War that the age of sex crime really began. In a village near Budapest, a man named Bela Kiss lured women to his cottage and killed them for their money and possessions, concealing the naked bodies in oil drums. Kiss was a handsome Don Juan, much admired by women; he was also a 'satyr', a man with such a craving for sex that he often made love to several prostitutes a day. He used the money from his murders to hire more prostitutes. 'Satyrism' may or may not be abnormal, but it is certainly fairly common (in 1981 the novelist Georges Simenon admitted in his *Intimate Memoirs* that he had been a lifelong satyr, and that he had made love to some ten thousand women, mostly prostitutes). A number of German sex killers, including Fritz Haarmann, Karl Denke, Georg Grossmann, Adolf Seefeld, and the 'Düsseldorf vampire' Peter Kürten, operated during and after the First World War, and made the concept of serial murder – which had caused such universal panic in the days of Jack the Ripper – familiar to police forces all over Europe. Meanwhile in the United States, Earle Nelson, known as 'the Gorilla Murderer', wandered around from Seattle to Buffalo leaving a trial of raped and strangled bodies, while a violent rebel named Carl Panzram killed at random because he found life so awful that he felt he was doing his victims a favour by helping them out of it.

And now, as we approach the end of the twentieth century, sex crime has become – as Brian Marriner remarks – a growth industry. We do not fully understand the reasons for it, but one is fairly obvious. The level of sexual promiscuity has always been high in slums. In the Whitechapel of Jack the Ripper – where the average number to a room was seven – incest was common, and children played 'mothers and fathers' as a matter of course. A friend of Lord Salisbury was walking down a slum court when he saw a boy and girl of about ten attempting sexual intercourse on the pavement. He pulled the boy off the girl, and received the indignant rebuke: 'Why do you take hold of me? There's a dozen of them at it down there.' Many years later a zoologist named John Calhoun tried the experiment of overcrowding rats in cages, and found to his astonishment that, beyond a certain degree of overcrowding, he was breeding 'criminal rats' who roamed about in gangs committing cannibalism and rape. This obviously explains what is happening in a modern city like New York, where a gang of Harlem teenagers recently raped and sodomized a female jogger in Central Park, leaving her with serious permanent injuries. In our overpopulated world, we are witnessing the 'overcrowded rat syndrome' on a terrifying scale.

One of the major problems for policemen investigating rape is that the sex criminal is not easy to track down by the normal methods of scientific crime detection. He strikes casually and, unlike a burglar, seldom leaves behind clues in the form of fingerprints. This is why Jack the Ripper was never caught; this is why Joseph Vacher evaded the French police for three years; this is why the Yorkshire Ripper was able to remain at large for more than five years, until he was finally caught by chance. But the case of Colin Pitchfork undoubtedly marks a major turning-point in the history of crime detection. The discovery of 'genetic fingerprinting' means that – unless he takes the precaution of wearing a condom – every rapist now leaves behind his 'fingerprint' inside his victim. And even if he wears a condom, a single spot of his blood, or a fragment of his skin under the victim's nails, is enough to reveal his identity. Just as the discovery of fingerprints in the 1980s changed the history of crime detection, so the discovery of the genetic fingerprint could, potentially, make sex crime the easiest type of crime to detect. But this would require a considerable act of courage on the part of governments. In the early days of fingerprinting, the government of Argentina decided that it would be a simple matter to have a universal fingerprint register, by taking the prints of every baby when it was born. But the idea caused such a storm that it was soon dropped, and no government has dared to revive it since. Yet it is, on the whole, a simple and practical idea that would dramatically reduce the crime rate. If it became a matter of course for every sexual offender to be 'genetically fingerprinted', the same would apply to the sex-crime rate. And if *everyone* was genetically fingerprinted at birth, premeditated sex crime – of the type committed by Bundy, John Duffy and Michael Fairley ('the Fox') – would virtually disappear, for the rapist would know in advance that he was leaving his signature behind.

This is no place to examine the new problems posed by the 'serial killer' – Brian Marriner has done it adequately and powerfully in this volume. It is enough to point out that new techniques like 'psychological profiling' – as used in the Duffy case – and the widespread use of police computers, are proving to be as successful as 'Bertillonage' and fingerprinting in the last decade of the nineteenth century. After a century of sex crime, the odds are once again beginning to switch against the criminal and in favour of the police. So although the cases in this book are gruesome and horrific, there can be no doubt that its ultimate message is one of optimism: that in the present climate of scientific progress, sex crime is one day destined to become as obsolete as stage-coach robbery or cattle rustling.

Introduction

A Century of Sex Killers

I have been writing professionally on the subject of murder for many years now, recording the deaths of victims by every possible means, and it is sometimes difficult to preserve that all-important detachment, that splinter of ice, which every writer needs to shield himself from the horror of that which he reports. After a few years of this kind of diet everything around you begins to exude crime, and what comes across most powerfully after studying hundreds of such cases is a sense of tremendous *waste*.

To write a book devoted to sex murders is not a pleasant task. To immerse oneself in the minds of the most infamous sex killers means paying a price which may be perhaps too much in the sense of psychic damage, but such a book needs to be written. Sex crime is a growth industry, and to combat it we need first to try to understand the thinking-processes and warped motivations of the rapist and killer.

My basic thesis is that every sex killer is speaking to us in a kind of code, and it is our task to try to interpret those signals. It is a desperate kind of communication – William Heirens's 'For Heaven's sake catch me before I kill again' is typical of the death-wish inherent in most sex murderers. By comparing cases and noting the patterns which emerge we will be able to identify these killers that much more quickly.

The problem is urgent. In England, in 1938, there were 5,018 sex crimes. By 1951 this figure had increased to 14,633. In 1955 it was 17,078, and by 1961 it was over twenty thousand. Now it appears to be doubling almost every year. The statistics are truly frightening. What we are facing is a new twist in the old trade of murder.

If we look at murder as history, we find that the nineteenth-century murderer was typically a poisoner who killed for gain. Palmer the Poisoner, who poisoned his wife, children and several business associates and was publicly hanged at Stafford in 1855, fits into this category, as does Dr Pritchard (1865), Florence Maybrick (1889), Dr Crippen (1910) and Herbert Rouse Armstrong (1922). Here we can clearly see an economic motive.

Burke and Hare, the Edinburgh body-snatchers, sold corpses to medical schools, and when bona-fide corpses were not available they killed to obtain them – but again, the motive is clearly economic: it was simply a method of surviving the grinding poverty of the times. We have all heard of people being hanged for stealing a loaf of bread. Times were hard, and a certain amount of crime was a reaction to poverty. One felon protested to a judge that he was being hanged for stealing a horse. 'No', the judge corrected him, 'you are being hanged so that horses will not be stolen'.

Then, in our century, we had the rise of the sex killer. Sex has always been a potent motive for murder, usually because of an adulterous affair in which the wife or husband stands in the way – the 'eternal triangle'. Thus we had the 'Red Barn' murder of 1827, when William Corder murdered his mistress, Maria Marten, in the Red Barn at Bury St Edmunds.

But the new type of sex killer is qualitatively different. He hungers for sex as the old-time killer hungered for money. Perhaps the Jack the Ripper murders of 1888 were the first true sex-murders in England, unrecognized as such at the time – his contemporaries argued that he was 'morally insane'. My personal feeling is that Christie was probably the first true sex killer in this century. This psychopathic personality killed at least six women in his London home – 10 Rillington Place – between 1943 and 1953, rendering them unconscious – or dead – before having sex with them. He was a true necrophiliac, and the case still has the power to horrify and shock. Christie was followed by Heath, and the long line of sex killers down to the present day which includes such appalling examples as the Yorkshire Ripper, Dean Corll, John Wayne Gacy – killer of thirty-three boys – and Ted Bundy in the USA.

We think of the USA as being the origin of the sex killer, with Britain following the trend. But even Australia is beginning to display the same symptoms. In June 1987 five young Australians were jailed for life for the rape and murder of a former beauty queen. After abducting the 26-year-old nurse they repeatedly raped her and dumped her nearly decapitated body in a field. The public gallery at Sydney's Central Criminal Court erupted in wild cheering when judge Alan Maxwell said that the official files of the prisoners should be clearly marked 'Never to be released'.

Of all impulses – greed, fear, hatred – the sexual drive is the most human and understandable. It exists in all of us. But the sex-impulse can be either highly romantic, the stuff of poetry, or base and squalid. There are extremes in sex-killings, with the Everests represented by the tragic lover's triangle situation, and the ocean depths by the child-killers: the Moors Murderers and the like.

If we look at a sex-inspired murder in its highest form (the Rattenbury and Stoner or Bywaters and Thompson cases), then we see a kind of Greek tragedy; given those people in that time and circumstances, then there is a kind of grim inevitability about the resulting murder. Aristotle said the purpose of tragedy was to 'cleanse the heart by means of pity and terror', and the fates of Alma Rattenbury and Edith Thompson do just that. We get a kind of 'There but for the grace of God' feeling. Goethe probably meant this when he wrote that he had never read the details of any crime which he did not deem himself capable of committing. But that is taking it too far. None of my readers, I would hope, could ever bring themselves to contemplate committing the sort of cruel murders contained in this volume.

The basic problem seems to be that nature has gifted human beings with a sex-drive far too strong for its biological purpose of procreation. We are, in short, over-sexed. Yet we have always been so, and sex killings on the scale we have them are very modern phenomena. It is vital to ask the question why. Let us look at a typical case for a possible answer.

Robert Poulin was a Canadian youth, aged eighteen. In 1975 he lured a neighbour's seventeen-year-old daughter into his Ottawa home, then manacled her to the bed, raped and sodomized her, then stabbed her to death. He set fire to the house, then went to his school armed with a shotgun and began shooting fellow-students at random. He injured seven of them before turning the gun on himself and blowing his head off. When police searched his home they found a large collection of pornographic magazines and a blow-up rubber doll. His diary read: 'I've thought of committing suicide, but I don't want to die before I've had the pleasure of fucking some girl.' He recounts how he ordered the doll by mail-order. A later passage reads: 'Doll arrived. Big disappointment.' It was a sad, pathetic case of a youth with absurd, enhanced expectations about sex. The reality was such a let-down. .

But the sex hunger is plain. Perhaps because of the undue emphasis placed on sex in our society by the justly maligned media, young men are led to expect more than reality can deliver, and then kill out of a sense of frustration.

In 1824 Thomas De Quincey published his cele-brated essay *Murder Considered As One of The Fine Arts.* Supposedly a paper which was to be read to the 'Society for the Encouragement of Murder', it has often been misunderstood as gallows-humour. But De Quincey was using irony to point out psychological truths. Let us suppose that such a 'Society' existed, however. How would it go about encouraging sex murder? *By doing precisely what we do*: exploiting and packaging sex as a commercial product. To 'do dirt on sex', as D.H. Lawrence would have said. It may be that pornographic books and videos have done more to incite sex crimes and contributed more to our current 29 per cent increase in rape cases than any other single factor. . . The reader should be struck by the cases in this book in which the killer was found to possess an extensive library of pornographic magazines and video films.

Hunger was the title of a remarkable novel by Knut Hamsun, a vivid and impressionistic early study of alienation. Hunger is deprivation, the starving of an appetite, of a need, which if it gets out of control leads to antisocial behaviour. Hunger can take many forms – sexual or financial, for example – but its most interesting aspect is the hunger for recognition, for fame, to be *known*. We all have this innate need. In the criminal it simply looms abnormally large.

If you think about the Christie case, you remember the confession describing his feelings as he gazed down at the body of Muriel Eady, who he had just strangled and raped: 'Once again I experienced that quiet, peaceful thrill. I had no regrets.' Here we can clearly identify the mechanism of this hunger at work. It is as if for some people only the act itself – however monstrous – can give meaning to a torpid sense of reality. It is pointless to condemn this hunger. It is a fact of human psychology which cannot be either condemned or approved. It simply *is*. This hunger can be a positive or negative factor in the life of the individual. If positive it leads to the entrepreneur, the maker of empires. But in the criminal it is always switched to the negative pole.

We have witnessed the emergence of a new type of criminal whom I have called Reactive Man. In simple terms, Reactive Man refuses to accept life as he finds it. The old-style criminal wanted to steal an apple from the orchard; reactive man wants to burn the orchard down. He is the scavenger, the looter living in the wreck of a civilization. Freedom – the problem of what to do with it – is his disease. Boredom is his natural state. He feels stifled, trapped, viewing violence as the only means of escaping from the strait-jacket. He is the complete criminal, his life is a chain-reaction which can only end with his death or imprisonment for life.

Reactive Man reacts against what he feels to be the restraints and repressions of our society. He is never in the wrong, he is never sorry. He is breeding fast – faster than we can build cages to house him. He is the stranger among us, never of us. Many labels could be hung on him (and indeed are) but none tells us very much. Rebel. Psychopath. Terrorist. All are shorthand symbols for a state of mind. And that is hate. Freud said that if a baby had the power it would destroy the world from the rage born of the frustration of its infantile desires. Perhaps Reactive Man is simply immature. Certainly he feels superior to the rest of us.

That attitude of superiority comes across strongly in the Moors Murders case. Brady had corrupted Hindley with his mix of sex and de Sade. Both had come to feel that other people were simply insects, morons, maggots, cabbages. They *deserved* to be killed. . . Peter Sutcliffe murdered thirteen women in his five-year reign as the Yorkshire Ripper. When he was finally captured police found in his lorry a hand-lettered card reading: 'In this truck is a man whose latent genius, if unleashed, would rock the nations. . . ' Straight away the problem can be seen: how can any man consider that the murder of thirteen defenceless women constitutes genius? Sutcliffe was an example of the frantic ego-assertion which characterizes so many of today's killers.

So what are we to do? Continue throwing our undesirables into prison? It doesn't seem to work. It is impossible not to think of the sex-criminal as being sick, as intrinsically lacking in normal psychological vitamins. His whole life is an act of *hunger*. To treat him we would first have to know what he hungers for. Punishment is a useless expedient, like caging an animal demented by hunger and expecting it to reform.

A typical case from the USA occurred in the summer of 1980. Douglas Daniel Clark, thirty-four, and his girl-friend Carol Bundy, thirty-seven, took to driving along Sunset Boulevard picking up girls. Once inside the car Clark would force them to perform oral sex on him, while his plump girl friend watched. At the moment of climax he would shoot his victims in the head. He had murdered five girls ranging in age from fifteen to twenty-four. He kept the heads of his victims in the freezer at the home he shared with Carol Bundy, and in the evening they would take out the heads, and after Carol Bundy had made up the faces and neatly combed the hair they would play with them like 'Barbie dolls', as she expressed it. Clark was sentenced to death; the girl-friend got a life sentence. Significantly, Clark claimed that he had been inspired to kill after reading a book called *Ted Bundy. All-American Killer*. (The case of Ted Bundy is contained in this book.)

Here we see the basic 'throwaway' attitude common to sex killers, the total lack of identification with the victims, who remain 'objects'. In England we saw the resentment factor in sex killings in the case of Patrick Byrne, the Birmingham YWCA murderer who in 1959 cut off his victim's head with a knife and then amputated a breast. His excuse? 'I wanted to get my own back on women for causing my nervous tension through sex.'

We seem to be creating people with mental hang-ups about sex – because sex is basically a *mental* activity far more than a physiological one. The key phrase is: *we* are creating, because killers are made, not born. They are products of our society. We bore them, nurtured them, shaped them. We must accept some of the blame. We are a society lacking in values.

It is too easy to hide behind psychiatry and dismiss murder as being in some way an illness; to regard sex killers as being simply very sick people. It is time we faced up to it: they are our dragons whom we must slay – or perish ourselves. There are no easy answers to the problem. Locking sex killers away in prison is the worst possible answer, since a lengthy confinement only serves to incubate the perverse desires which will be displayed once again when the prisoner is released. Neither is castration the answer. There have been cases reported from those states in the USA which practise it of castrated offenders committing further sex attacks. We may be forced to take a long look at the death penalty – and I hope we are never forced into that situation. Simplistic solutions have never proved effective in the war against crime.

This compendium of sex killers is by no means comprehensive – sheer lack of space makes that impossible. But the major cases are here.

Chapter One

LOOKING BACK ON
JACK THE RIPPER

We must try to understand why Jack the Ripper has continued to exercise such a powerful hold on the imagination of the world. He remains the best-known of all sex killers, having inspired films, plays, novels and even operas – not to mention the 'Ripper industry' which has produced hundreds of books, each claiming to give the definitive answer to the enigma of exactly who the Ripper was. The bibliography of Jack the Ripper runs to an entire volume in itself, and the autumn of 1987 saw no less than seven major books published on the case, and a filming of a television series. 'Naming' the Ripper has become almost a parlour game, with a plethora of books giving us many ingenious and frankly preposterous theories as to his identity. No new books will tell us anything more than we already know. The facts should all be in: what is missing is the name of this infamous killer, and that we shall never know. In all likelihood he was a sad, mad nobody, an ordinary and unremarked individual whose name has never appeared in any book or any official police reports – the official Scotland Yard files will be released for public inspection in 1992.

It is quite obvious, for example, that had Peter Sutcliffe, the Yorkshire Ripper, stopped his murder-spree after his twelfth victim – having been killed in a lorry-smash, for example – we would never have known his name, and a century hence no doubt books would be written claiming to identify the Yorkshire Ripper as a pop-star, cricket captain or policeman. As it is, we have books claiming that Jack the Ripper was, variously, the Duke of Clarence, a mad doctor, a barrister, a Russian anarchist, 'Jill the Ripper', the artist William Sickert, condemned criminals Dr Neill Cream and George Chapman, and even Sir Arthur Conan Doyle.

From our vantage-point it is difficult to understand *why* Jack the Ripper continues to fascinate us. He killed five, possibly six, prostitutes in the late summer and autumn of 1888 in the cramped slum-area of Whitchapel in London. He killed them in a ten-week period, always in the early hours and always around weekends. He killed them in the midst of an area teeming with people and under the noses of special police patrols, and yet was never seen. He killed with incredible speed, with arrogant cunning and ease, in a savage and shocking manner.

Perhaps his longevity lies in the *manner* in which he killed. The French called him Jacques L'Evrentreur, Jack the Stomach-opener, and this is a far more accurate description of the Ripper. He disembowelled his victims in a mad frenzy to reach the womb. Despite claims made by many writers, it is not true that the period between each killing grew shorter, as if the killer were accelerating into homicidal mania. Let us examine the dates. The official file states that the Ripper 'killed five, and five only', with Mary Nicholls being the first in the series, but I am of the opinion that Martha Turner was a Ripper victim, so the chronology runs like this: 7 August, Martha Turner; 31 August, Mary Nicholls; 8 September, Annie Chapman; 30 September, Elizabeth Stride and Catherine Eddowes; 9 November, Marie Kelly. The pattern is remarkably regular: a murder after the first week of every month, with another murder at the month's end. The 'double event' on 30 September was because Jack was disturbed during the first murder and was unable to get the organs he wanted, and angry and frustrated went in search of another victim. A half-mile away he found Catherine Eddowes, and after disembowelling her took away one of her kidneys and her uterus. According to this chronology, we should have expected another Ripper killing around 30 November, but the Ripper killings had ceased.

And there lies much of the fascination of the Ripper case, precisely because he was never caught, and yet stopped killing. The fact is, as Professor Camps has pointed out: 'Sadistic killers of this type do not "burn-out" or retire.' The cases of Peter Sutcliffe and Dennis Nilsen bear this out: they would have gone on killing for ever if not apprehended. Only death, emigration or incarceration in a jail or an asylum could explain the cessation of the Ripper murders. Sir Melville Macnaghten, assistant commissioner of the Metropolitan Police shortly after the Ripper killings, left notes written in 1894 which referred to three suspects: these notes are practically the only real evidence we have. Much nonsense has been written about them. They are said to have surfaced in the 1950s, when Daniel Farson quoted from them in his book *Jack the Ripper*. He had obtained them from Macnaghten's daughter, Lady Aberconway. But in fact these private notes had been quoted by Major Arthur Griffiths, HM Inspector of Prisons, in his book *Mysteries of Police and Crime* (vol 1) published in 1898, just ten years after the murders. Major Griffiths quotes Macnaghten so exactly – he was a friend – that he must have had access to them. The notes read:

I enumerate the case of three men against whom the police held very reasonable suspicion. Personally, and after much careful and deliberate consideration, I am inclined to exonerate the last two, but I have always held strong opinions regarding No. 1 and the more I think the matter over, the stronger do these opinions become. The truth, however, will never be known, and did, indeed, at one time lie at the bottom of the Thames, if my conjectures be correct.

No. 1. MR M.J. DRUITT, a doctor of about 41 years of age and of fairly good family, who disappeared at the time of the Miller's Court murder, and whose body was found floating in the Thames on 31 December, i.e. seven weeks after the said murder. The body was said to have been in the water a month or more . . . From private information I have little doubt that his own family suspected this man of being the Whitechapel murderer; and it was alleged that he was sexually insane.

No. 2. KOSMINSKI, a Polish Jew, who lived in the very heart of the district where the murders were committed. He had become insane owing to many years' indulgence in solitary vices. He had a great hatred of women, with homicidal tendencies. He was (and I believe is) detained in a lunatic asylum about March 1889. This man in appearance strongly resembled the individual seen by the City P.C. near Mitre Square.

No. 3. MICHAEL OSTROG, a mad Russian doctor and a convict and unquestionably a homicidal maniac. This man was said to have been habitually cruel to women, and for a long time was known to have carried about with him surgical knives and other instruments; his antecedents were of the worst and his whereabouts at the time of the Whitechapel murders could never be satisfactorily accounted for. He is still alive.

The only thing wrong with the Macnaghten notes is that the 'doctor' was a barrister, Montague John Druitt; he was aged thirty-one; and there is no record of any PC in Mitre Square having seen anyone. Although the notes must reflect current thinking at the Yard when

Macnaghten took over, the fact is that every senior police officer involved in the case disagreed with each other as to the identity of the Ripper and the date of his death or incarceration, as we shall see later.

It is certainly conceivable that the Ripper did not commit suicide or become incarcerated in an asylum. He could simply have 'cured' himself of his impulses. If we accept the premise that in some cases the murderer kills 'for fear of something worse' – that is, only the act of killing keeps him from going insane – then it is possible that murder can act as a catharsis. Eric Ambler, in his book *The Ability to Kill*, advances the persuasive hypothesis that the Ripper was a schizophrenic and was in a fugue state during the killings. 'It is even possible that after the murder of Marie Kelly, Jack the Ripper never again knew of that passage in his life. There was something climactic and final about those incredible elaborations. Perhaps having achieved an apotheosis of horror, he had at last exorcised the evil that had haunted him.'

Of course, what is wrong with this theory is that whatever else he was, the Ripper was no schizophrenic. The word schizophrenia literally means 'split mind', but it is inaccurate to think of this condition as meaning two or more separate personalities, like Jekyll and Hyde. It is more a disintegrating mind with scrambled electrical activity and garbled thought processes, accompanied by visual and auditory hallucinations. Although schizophrenics can be dangerous to those around them, they do not commit serial murders. Schizophrenics are irrational and impulsive. They lack the thinking ability to plan cunning and sadistic crimes. They are incapable of premeditation.

The *psychopath* is the serial killer. Apparently normal, even charming, he is a ruthless but sane manipulator who feels that the normal rules of society do not apply to him. Often of above-normal intelligence, the psychopath is a clever killer who often manages to kill for years undetected. The Zodiac Killer, the Green River Strangler and Jack the Ripper fall into this category. Typically, the psychopath may play ego games with the police, sending them taunting letters, but psychopaths do not want to get caught and display extreme cunning to avoid detection even to the lengths of changing their *modus operandi* – like Peter Kürten, who admitted having changed from the use of a knife to that a hammer to fool the police. Significantly, when apprehended the psychopath will often feign insanity, as did Peter Sutcliffe, Manson, Bianchi, and Son of Sam – and may even be able to fool expert psychiatrists.

Whoever he was, Jack the Ripper was certainly a sexual psychopath. One who stopped killing after the murder of Mary Kelly.

But we still have not adequately described the fascination which the Ripper still exerts after a century. As a serial killer he has been left well behind in the league table. Peter Kürten killed nine; Dr Palmer fourteen; Fritz Haarmann twenty-seven; Petiot sixty-three; Henry Lee Lucas boasts of having committed 360 murders in the USA by every known method: stabbing, shooting, strangulation, mutilation and decapitation. To date the FBI have verified 144 of his murders. And even Mary Ann Cotton, back in the 1870s, poisoned fourteen or fifteen people in England. In our time, Peter Sutcliffe claimed thirteen women, and Dennis Nilsen fifteen young men. So why should an unknown man who killed five or six women remain the world's best-known killer?

The answer lies in the social conditions of his time, and the fact that he was the first true 'loner' sex killer. Men had killed for sex before, the solitary rape ending in death, but never in such a sustained and strange manner. I possess an old broadsheet which relates in bold black type:

THE AWFUL EXECUTION OF JOHN MEUX. A MOST HORRID MONSTER! Who Suffered at the City of Niemes for a most Brutal Rape and Murder on the body of Laura Vipont; after he had

Violated her Body, he plunged a knife into her breast, drank from her Blood, and ate a Particular Part of her Body! Sentenced by the High Court at Niemes to be strangled and afterwards hung in chains for rape and murder committed on Friday, November 5th 1824.

But Jack the Ripper was the first man to kill for killing's sake. He was a sadist who killed for pleasure, and out of a desire to cause shock.

It is recorded that a certain Mrs Mary Burridge collapsed and 'died of a fit' at her home at 132 Blackfriars Road, South London, on the afternoon of 8 September 1888. She had been reading a newspaper, the late Final edition of *The Star,* and it contained news of the 'latest horrible murder in Whitechapel', that of Annie Chapman, who had been found disembowelled that day. The killer – not yet known as Jack the Ripper – was shaking his fist at society, and Mrs Burridge's death was a kind of involuntary protest at a society in which such a horror could occur. A contemporary newspaper account, from the *Daily Telegraph* for Monday 10 September, reads:

Early on Saturday morning a ghastly murder was perpetrated near Spitalfields Market. The latest deed of ferocity has thrown Whitchapel into a state of panic. . . with so much cunning was the horrifying deed carried out that apparently no clue has been left. We are certainly led to imagine some baleful prowler of the East-end streets and alleys who. . . knows every bye-place well, who is plausible enough in address to beguile his victims, strong enough to overcome them the moment homicidal passion succeeds to desire, cunning enough to select the most quiet hour and the most quiet spot for his furious assaults, and possessed of a certain ghastly skill in using the knife. . . .

When Mary Burridge collapsed and died most crime was economic in nature. It is true that most of the famous

Victorian murders took place in middle-class surroundings, and involved jealousy or family conflict. But the majority of murders were still committed by people who were poor and desperate. The Ripper murders were so frightening because they seemed to involve deliberate *evil*. The unknown killer headed one of his letters 'From Hell', and the crimes makes him sound like a disciple of the Marquis de Sade. Yet now, a century later, this type of crime has become almost commonplace.

The murder of Charlotte Dymond illustrates how the mere suggestion of a sex-crime could cause huge crowds to turn out to witness the execution of her convicted murderer Matthew Weekes, and in fact it wasn't even a true sex-murder. It was what Victorians imagined a sex murder would be like. But the Ripper showed them the grim reality.

He literally exploded the issue of sex into Victorian society, forcing it to recognize and grovel in its own dirt. Matrons who were idealistic about sex were forced to acknowledge the perils of their 'fallen' sisters. The secret, morbid interest in sex was exposed when the Ripper committed in public deeds which many of those Victorian fathers and brothers, working in respectable offices, perhaps secretly envied. They read with shudders of horrified envy about the maniac who was committing what seemed like the ultimate rape. As with rape, so with sex murder: there is a great deal of rage displayed, the urge to impose total domination on the victim. Jack the Ripper was reminding his Victorian contemporaries that beneath the facade of the philanthropist, the polish of the capitalist and the idealistic adventurer or scientist, lay the brute. Lytton Strachey slew several sacred cows in his *Eminent Victorians*. The fact was that in a society containing Charles Darwin, the explorer Dr Livingstone, the heroines like Florence Nightingale, there also existed Jack the Ripper. He was reminding his society of that fact.

For our purposes – attempting to understand the mind of the sex killer – Jack the Ripper is practically useless.

We cannot hope to understand his motives because we lack that solid mass of biographical material that we have with Peter Kürten, for example. We know nothing about the Ripper precisely because he remained undetected. But at least we can use our modern knowledge and extensive case-histories of sex killers to try to penetrate the veils of time, interpret his acts, the clues he left behind, and to catch a glimpse of the shadowy figure who terrorized London a century ago.

First, let us examine the murders in some detail. They were not all committed in Whitechapel, but they all took place in the vicinity of the London Hospital. In the early hours of 7 August 1888, the body of Martha Turner, aged thirty-five (also known as Tabram) was found lying on the first-floor landing of a tenement house at 35 George Yard Buildings. She had last been seen at closing time by the Angel and Crown pub near Whitechapel Church the previous evening, talking to a soldier. The victim was a prostitute who had lodged at the Star Place, off the Commercial Road. At 3.30 a.m. Albert Crow, a cab-driver, saw the crumpled body, but thought it was a drunk sleeping rough. At 5 a.m. another tenant, John Reeves, left his room to go to work and discovered the woman lying in a pool of blood. He raised the alarm. Only when the body was examined during the post-mortem were the full extent of her injuries realized. She had been stabbed in the chest thirty-nine times by two different weapons, and also had nine stab wounds in the throat, as well as others in the breasts and abdomen. The doctor who carried out the post-mortem remarked: 'Whoever it was, he knew how and where to cut.' The soldier who had been seen with the victim was traced, but was able to prove that he had rejoined his friends at 1.30 a.m., and the victim had been seen returning alone to the Angel and Crown at about 1.40. But an identity parade of the soldiers was held, without result.

At 3.45 a.m. on the morning of Friday 31 August a cart-driver, George Cross, was walking down Bucks Row,

Whitechapel, when he saw what he thought was a tarpaulin lying in the gutter. He crossed the road to take a closer look, and saw that it was a woman lying prostrate. At first he thought she was drunk, but her skirts were around her waist, suggesting a rape victim. Just then another man, John Paul, came along the street. Cross asked him to help lift the woman, but Paul felt her hands and face and said she was dead. Both men set off to find a policeman. PC Neil was the first officer on the scene. By the light of his bull's-eye lantern, he could see that the woman's throat had been savagely cut. A nearby doctor, Dr Ralph Llewellyn, was sent for, and he ordered the body to be taken to the Whitechapel Mortuary. There he discovered the full extent of the woman's injuries. The abdomen had been ripped open, with loops of bowel protruding. There were bruise-marks on the jaw – suggesting that the killer had gripped his victim from behind, perhaps strangling her, before beginning his hideous mutilations. Apart from the incisions in the abdomen, there were two stab wounds in the genitals. The doctor reported at the inquest that the mutilations had been performed by a left-handed person using a long-bladed knife, that the killer had some knowledge of surgery, and that he had probably also been the killer of Martha Turner. (A view not shared by the police.) The victim was soon identified as being Mary Ann Nicholls, forty-two – 'Polly to her friends – a prostitute who lodged at 18 Thrawl Street, Spitalfields. She had last been seen alive at 2.30 on the morning of her murder, staggering drunkenly along Whitechapel Road in search of a client who would pay the fourpence a night her bed at the doss-house cost. At 3.45 she was found dead, and according to the doctor had been dead for no more than half an hour when he examined her. When her remains were formally identified by her husband, he was heard to say, 'I forgive you for everything now I see you like this.'

The third victim was also a prostitute, and also a resident of a doss-house, at 35 Dorset Street. Annie

Chapman, forty-seven, known as 'Dark Annie', had been turned away from the doss-house at 2 a.m. in the morning of Saturday 8 September, because she lacked the fourpence for her bed. She was drunk and argumentative, but asked the keeper to reserve her bed. 'Don't let my doss. I'll soon be back with the money.' Her mutilated body was found four hours later, at six o clock, in the yard behind 29 Hanbury Street, near Spitalfields Market – just half a mile away from Bucks Row. The body was discovered by John Davies as he left for work. He saw the slashed throat and ran to Commercial Street Police Station to fetch help.

Officers were soon on the scene, including Detective Inspector Frederick Abberline from Scotland Yard. The victim's wounds were hideous in the extreme. The head had been almost severed from the trunk; the woman had been disembowelled, and part of her intestines had been draped over her left shoulder. Dr George Bagster Phillips, a police doctor of long experience, examined the body and then had it removed to the mortuary. He then examined the crime scene and discovered part of an envelope bearing the seal of the Sussex Regiment with a post-office franking mark: 'London. 28 Aug 1988.' Close to the feet of the victim had been placed two brass rings taken from her fingers, together with some pennies and two new farthings. The careful way in which these items had been arranged suggested ritual. And all ritualization is a kind of message. More importantly, in the yard was also found a leather apron. This was to give the killer the initial name 'Leather Apron'.

The hunt began for 'Leather Apron', and a Polish Jew named John Pizer (known locally by that nickname) was arrested by the police, but cleared at the resumed inquest on Annie Chapman. The post-mortem on the victim found the usual bruises on the face, throat and chest, and the throat had been cut with two parallel incisions by a left-handed person. The woman had been disembowelled, and the uterus with its ovaries had been cut out and taken away by the killer. Dr Phillips stated at the inquest: 'Obviously the work was that of an expert – or one, at least, who had such knowledge of anatomical or pathological examinations as to be enabled to secure the pelvic organs with one sweep of the knife.' He thought the murder weapon was at least eight inches long, very sharp, and with a narrow blade.

The East End of London was now in a state of panic. The public were frightened not by murder (which was commonplace) but by the display of crazed, satanic intelligence, and it focused its outrage on the police. In particular it blamed the Commissioner, Sir Charles Warren, an ex-Army major-general who was more interested in boots, saddles and square-bashing than in catching criminals.

Vigilance Committees were set up after the *Star* suggested that the public should protect themselves. 'The people of the East End must become their own police.' The coroner who had presided at the inquests on three Ripper victims, Wynne Baxter, commented, 'There can be no question that had these unfortunate women been murdered with equal secrecy in the West End, rewards would not have been withheld.' (The Vigilance Committee had written to the Home Office asking for a reward for the killer to be posted, but the Home Office refused.)

Now, as if the previous murders had simply been an overture to raise nerves to straining-point, came the 'double event' which led to public hysteria. In the early hours of Sunday 30 September the Ripper struck twice. At 1 a.m. a hawker drove his horse and cart into the yard behind 40 Berners Street, which housed the International Workers Educational Club. Music was still playing loudly as Russian and Polish Jews danced inside, but the backyard was dark, and the horse shied away from something in the shadows. The hawker discovered the body of Elizabeth Stride, forty-five, a prostitute known as 'Long Liz'. She was 5ft 5ins tall, which must have been regarded as being unusually tall for the time. Blood was still pouring from the gash in her throat, but there were no mutilations of her stomach. The hawker had interrupted the Ripper in his work and he had slipped away in the darkness, furious and frustrated, seeking another victim urgently while the lust was on him.

Almost at the same time as 'Long Liz' was being murdered, another prostitute, Catherine Eddowes, forty-three, was released from Bishopsgate Police Station, where she had been held for being drunk and disorderly. Having proved that she could stand upright, she called out a cheery 'Goodnight, old cock' to the desk sergeant, and walked off in the direction of Houndsditch. Only five feet tall, with auburn hair, she was picked up by the Ripper and taken to Mitre Square in Aldgate. It had only three entrances, and was patrolled by a policeman every fifteen minutes. At 1.30 a.m. PC Watkins of the City Police found nothing amiss, but at 1.45 he discovered the body of a woman lying on the pavement 'ripped up like a pig in the market', in his own words. Officers at the scene of the first murder rushed to the second, just three-quarters of a mile away. The Ripper had killed twice in the space of an hour, but the location of the second murder put it within the jurisdiction of the City Police, and not the Metropolitan Police. Now both Forces were involved in the Ripper investigations.

Dr Phillips, the police doctor, had examined the remains of Elizabeth Stride. Catherine Eddowes was examined by Dr Gordon Burn. Eddowes lay on her back with her legs apart. Her throat had been cut and her clothing pushed up to her chest. Her abdomen had been ripped open, with the intestines pulled out and laid over her right shoulder. The face had been gashed across the nose and cheek. This crime provided the police with more clues than any other Ripper murder. One of the victim's kidneys was missing. Dr Burn's note read: 'The left kidney was carefully taken out and removed. . . I should say that someone who knew the position of the kidney must have done it.'

In his flight from the scene of the crime, the Ripper had paused to wash his hands in a public sink in Goulston Street, wiping his hands on a piece of apron taken from the victim. Major Henry Smith, Commissioner of the City Police, arriving in haste at the scene in a hansom cab, found bloodstained water still draining from the sink. . . . There was one more clue nearby. Scrawled in chalk was a message which the beat constable swore had not been there earlier. It read:

'The Juwes are The men That Will not be Blamed for nothing.' Major Smith wanted the message to be photographed, but Sir Charles Warren ordered it to be rubbed out, claiming it could lead to anti-semitic riots in the area. It was an incredible blunder, and emphasized the simmering conflicts between the City Police and the Met.

Then, for the first time, the Ripper had a name. He had christened himself with a name which would go down in history. Police released a letter he had sent to the Central News Agency two days before the double murder. It read:

Dear Boss, I keep on hearing the police have caught me but they won't fix me just yet. I have laughed when they look so clever and talk about being on the right track. The joke about Leather Apron gave me real fits. I am down on whores and I shan't quit ripping them till I do get buckled. Grand work the last job was. I gave the lady no time to squeal. How can they catch me now? I love my work and want to start again. You will soon hear of me and my funny little games.

The letter went on to say: 'The next job I do I shall clip the lady's ears off. . . Yours Truly, Jack the Ripper.' (This was important because an attempt had been made to cut an ear off Catherine Eddowes.)

A few hours after the double murder a postcard was received which was obviously a follow-up to the letter. It read:

I was not codding dear old Boss when I gave you the tip. You'll hear about Saucy Jack's work tomorrow. Double event this time. Number one squealed a bit. Couldn't finish straight off. Had not time to get ears for police. Thanks for keeping last letter back till I get to work again. JACK THE RIPPER.

The police took both communications seriously enough to reproduce them on posters on 3rd October, with the plea: 'Any person recognising the handwriting is requested to communicate with the nearest police station.' The 'double event' stunned London, as the contemporary account in the *Daily Telegraph*, published on Monday, 1 October 1888, shows.

Two more murders of the same cold-blooded character. . . were committed early yesterday. . . these new proofs of the continued presence in our streets of some monster in human form whose desperate wickedness goes free and undetected by force of its own terrible audacity and by as yet unrebuked contempt for our police. . .There is in truth reason enough for the public anger and even the public panic which cannot fail to arise when the details of these latest links in the frightful catena of slaughter have become known. . . Is the Home Office waiting for numbers seven, eight and nine of this ghastly catalogue of slaying? Is the Home Office contented to leave to the "regular methods' the search for this woman-killer who renders the midnight streets of the Metropolis dreadful with the footfalls of Death?

With public indignation at a new height the chairman of the Whitechapel Vigilance Committee, Mr George

Lusk, was again demanding a Government reward offer. The Lord Mayor had personally offered £500, but the Home Office would not budge. Mr Lusk did not get his demand met, but on 16 October he received through the post a small cardboard box containing half a kidney, and a letter reading:

> from hell. Mr Lusk, Sir, I send you half a kidne I took from one woman, prasaerved it for you, tother piece I fried and ate it it was very nice. I may send you the bloody knife that took it out if only you wate a whil longer. Signed Catch me when you can. Mister Lusk.

This letter was not signed Jack the Ripper, and the spelling errors are evidently those of an educated man trying to appear illiterate. But it is considered to be the most 'genuine' of the many Ripper letters, not least because the kidney was sent to Dr Openshaw, a pathologist at the London Hospital, and he declared it to be human and gave it as his opinion that it had come from the body of Catherine Eddowes. The kidney showed evidence of Bright's Disease, as did the victim, and an inch of renal artery was still attached to the kidney, with two inches remaining in the body, adding up to the normal length of three inches. Certainly Major Smith believed this letter to be genuine. An expert graphologist described the 'knife-edged and daggerlike strokes' in the word 'kidney' as displaying negative traits likely to lead to destructive outbursts.

As early as September the *Daily Telegraph* had complained: 'It is clear that the Detective Department at Scotland Yard is in an utterly hopeless and worthless condition. . . ' Now the entire Press joined in with attacks on Commissioner Sir Charles Warren. He displayed an insensitive and even ludicrous response to criticism when he hired bloodhounds to aid the hunt for the Ripper. At trials in Regent's Park on 8 October, Sir Charles acted as the hare – and the dogs promptly got lost! *The Pall Mall Gazette* and *Punch* had great fun at the expense of the unpopular Commissioner. James Monro, head of the CID, had resigned on 31 August, the day that Mary Ann Nicholls was found dead in Bucks Row, and he had been replaced by Sir Robert Anderson, who immediately went off to Switzerland on two months' sick leave. With the police apparently leaderless, Queen Victoria involved herself in the case, writing to Scotland Yard to voice her concern and make suggestions about catching the killer. On 8 November, Sir Charles Warren resigned his post – the news was greeted with loud cheering in the House of Commons.

The following day, Friday 9 November, was the Lord Mayor's Day, with the usual processions planned. On this same day the last of the Ripper's victims was discovered. There had been a five-week lull leading up to this dreadful climax. Mary Jeanette Kelly, twenty-four, was a prostitute who lived in a single room at 13 Miller's Court, which ran off Dorset Street in Spitalfields. She could not have been very successful at her trade, since she was in arrears with her rent to the extent of thirty-five shillings. The landlord's assistant, Thomas Bowyer, was sent to collect the money, and arrived at her ground-floor room at 10.45 a.m. Getting no answer to his knocking, he peered through a broken window and saw a butchered corpse lying in a welter of blood. Horror-struck, he ran back to the landlord, who in turn sent him to Commercial Street Police Station to raise the alarm. Officers were soon on the scene, and a telegram was sent summoning Divisional Superintendent Arnold, while Inspector Abberline at the Yard was also informed, and Dr Phillips sent for. One of the detective-sergeants at the scene was Walter Dew, later to gain fame as the policeman who arrested Dr Crippen.

Abberline arrived on the scene at 11.30, and had the room sealed off. The door to the room was locked, and Dr Phillips could see through the window that the victim was beyond any aid. The woman was barely recognizable as a human being, having been literally dissected to bits. Abberline sent a telegram to Sir Charles Warren asking for the famous bloodhounds to be brought to the scene: he was unaware that Warren had resigned the previous day. At 1.30 p.m. Superintendent Arnold decided that he could wait no longer. He had the window frame removed so that photographs could be taken, and then the door was forced open. The full extent of the horrific mutilations could now be seen. In a room twelve foot square, every inch seemed to be covered in blood and human flesh. Even the victim's entrails had been draped over a picture-frame. To add to the horror, she had been in the early stages of pregnancy.

The following description of the mutilations was published in the *Illustrated Police News:*

> The throat had been cut right across with a knife, nearly severing the head from the body. The abdomen had been partially ripped open, and both of the breasts had been cut from the body; the left arm, like the head, hung to the body by skin only. The nose had been cut off, the forehead skinned, and the thighs, down to the feet, stripped of the flesh. The abdomen had been slashed with a knife across downwards, and the liver and entrails wrenched away. The entrails and other portions of the frame were missing, but the liver, etc., it is said, was found placed between the feet of the poor victim. The flesh from the thighs and legs, together with the breasts and nose, had been placed by the murderer on the table, and one of the hands of the dead woman had been pushed into her stomach.

The murder-room was a wealth of puzzling clues. A candle in the room had not been used by the killer to illuminate his lengthy dissection – he was believed to have spend most of the night on his ghastly task – but a large fire had burned fiercely in the grate. Among the ashes were found rags and remnants of female clothing, yet the victim's clothing was still draped neatly over a chair. Had the killer dressed in female clothing to gain admittance to the room? (This was to lend credence to the 'Jill the Ripper' theory of a mad midwife.) The police had the eyes of the dead woman photographed, in the bizarre belief that the retina might retain the image of her killer.

Police traced witnesses who had last seen the victim alive, but these eye-witness accounts – like previous ones – were useless for practical purposes. A fellow-prostitute had seen Mary Kelly at 11.45 the previous night with a short, stout man with a carroty moustache. At 1 a.m. she heard Kelly singing. A Mrs Prater, who lived in the room above Kelly's, had returned home at 1.30 a.m. and fallen asleep immediately. Between 3.30 and 4 a.m. she was awoken by a cry of 'Oh, murder!' but went back to sleep. Sarah Lewis had called at 2 Miller's Court, opposite Kelly's room, at 2.30 a.m. on the Friday morning and noticed a man standing on the pavement staring at the Court. He was a stout man wearing a black hat. She had dozed in a chair, but had been woken at about 4 a.m. by a cry of 'Murder' but she too ignored it. Apparently such cries were common in the slums.

Perhaps the most important witness was George Hutchinson, a labourer, who lived in Commercial Street. In a statement to police he said he had seen Kelly at 2 a.m on the morning of her murder: she asked him to lend her sixpence, which he didn't have. Then, as she walked away, he saw a man stop and pick her up. The man was carrying a small parcel with a strap around it. He was aged about thirty-five, height 5ft 6in, complexion pale, dark eyes, slight moustache turned up at each end, dark hair, surly-looking. He was well dressed – a 'gent' – with a large gold chain across his waistcoat, and a tie with a distinctive gold horseshoe pin. Hutchinson ended his statement: 'Jewish appearance. Can be identified.'

But the statements of other witnesses served only to confuse the issue. At 8 a.m. a tailor claimed to have seen Kelly alive. At 8.30 a neighbour, Mrs Maxwell, claimed to have spoken to Mary Kelly. At 10 a.m. yet another neighbour claimed to have seen Kelly. Yet Dr Phillips placed the time of the murder at 2 a.m, which means the cries of 'Murder' between 3.30 and 4 a.m. were irrelevant.

There had been eye-witnesses at the other murders who had seen a man shortly before the discovery of the victim's body. and a 'composite' of all these descriptions indicates a man of about thirty years of age, medium height, with a small, fair moustache and wearing a deerstalker hat. The official police 'wanted' description, issued after the double event, reads: 'About twenty-eight, height five feet eight inches, complexion dark, small dark moustache. . . respectable appearance, carried a parcel wrapped in newspaper.' A later description in the *Police Gazette* has minor variations: 'Man aged thirty, height five feet seven inches, complexion fair, moustache fair, medium build, cloth cap with a peak. . . appearance of a sailor.'

Mary Kelly was buried at Leytonstone Cemetery on 18 November, and with her was buried the last of the Ripper murders and the last clues to his identity. The unknown murderer had ended the lives of five or six women, and the career of a police Commissioner – and had then stopped. Perhaps he had experienced his ultimate thrill and nothing else remained for him. Perhaps, as Ambler suggested, he had 'cured' himself of his mania. But the burial of Mary Kelly not only marked the end of the Ripper's reign, it left the field open for a century of wild speculation.

Now let us examine the various statements made by police officers who were in a position to know the facts, and had been involved in the Ripper inquiry – always remembering that the Ripper files had not been closed after the murder of Mary Kelly, since the police went on hunting the elusive 'Jack' late into the 1890s, and further murders of prostitutes were falsely attributed to Jack the Ripper.

We have already seen that Sir Melville Macnaghten suspected the 'doctor' whose body was found floating in the Thames at the end of 1888. This was failed barrister

Montague John Druitt, aged thirty-one. The *Acton, Chiswick and Turnham Green Gazette* for January 1889 reported the inquest on his death. The body, well dressed and with pockets weighted with stones, was recovered from the Thames near Chiswick on Monday 31 December 1888, and had been in the water 'about a month'. The dead man's brother, William, a solicitor from Bournemouth, testified that Druitt had been dismissed from his teaching post at a school in Blackheath, that his mother was insane, and Druitt feared he himself was going insane. He left a note reading: 'Since Friday I have felt I was going to be like mother and the best thing for me was to die.' His tombstone records that he died 'on 4 December 1888'. Macnaghten wrote, 'It is my belief that the killer committed suicide on or about the tenth of November'. He gives no basis for suspecting Druitt, other than his convenient suicide. What makes Druitt an unlikely candidate is the fact that he was playing cricket six hours after the death of Annie Chapman. However, Dan Farson based his book *Jack the Ripper* (1972) on Druitt as the Ripper. Evidence to support his theory came from Albert Backert of the Whitechapel Vigilance Committee. He stated, 'I was given this information in confidence about March 1989. It was then suggested to me by the police that the Vigilance Committee and its patrols might be disbanded as the police were quite certain that the Ripper was dead. . . He was fished out of the Thames two months ago.'

Watkins Williams, grandson of Sir Charles Warren, wrote, 'He believed the murderer to be a sex-maniac who committed suicide after the Miller's Court murder – possibly the young doctor whose body was found in the Thames on 31 December 1888.'

Macnaghten also claimed to know the identity of the journalist who had 'faked' the Ripper letters. Twenty years after the Ripper murders, Macnaghten published his memoirs in the *Sun*. He claimed that the Ripper killed five women only, dismissed Martha Turner as a Ripper victim, claiming that the soldier had killed her, but a frightened witness had refused to pick him out of an identity parade. He went on, 'Although the Whitechapel Murderer, in all probability, put an end to himself soon after the Dorset Street affair, in November 1888, certain facts pointing to this conclusion were not in the possession of the police till some years after I became a detective officer.'

Sergeant Ben Leeson was a CID constable at the time, and in his memoirs admits:

> I cannot throw any light on the identity of the Ripper, but one thing I do know and that is that amongst the police who were most concerned in the case there was a general feeling that a certain doctor, known to me, could have thrown quite a lot of light on the subject. . . He was never far away when the crimes were committed.

Inspector Frederick Abberline was convinced that the Ripper was George Chapman – real name Severin Klosowski. Chapman was a poisoner who murdered three women for gain. When he was arrested in 1902 Abberline told the arresting officers, 'I see you have caught Jack the Ripper at last!' Chapman was hanged on 7 April 1903. Inspector Neil, in his book *Forty Years of Manhunting* (1932), wrote: 'We were never able to secure definite proof that Chapman was the Ripper. . . In any case, it is the most fitting and sensible solution as to the possible identity of the murderer.' It seems hardly likely that a compulsive mutilator like Jack would have changed his method of killing to poisoning by arsenic.

Sir Robert Anderson declared in his memoirs that the Ripper's identity was known: he was a Polish Jew who was protected 'by his people' and was then incarcerated in an asylum. Sir Robert, who had been head of the Metropolitan CID, went into print three times – in 1907, 1910 and *The Police Encyclopaedia* (1920) – stating as a fact that the Ripper's identity was known. He was at pains

Victims of Jack the Ripper

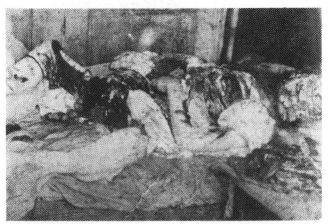

Mary Kelly as she was found in Miller's Court. The flesh from her thighs and legs, together with her breasts and nose, are on the bedside table

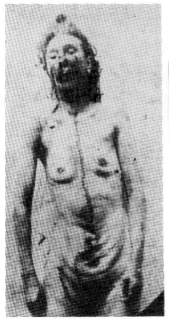

Left, mortuary photograph of Catherine Eddowes after post-mortem. Above, Elizabeth Stride

Kürten's flat at 71 Mettmännerstrasse where he lured Maria Büdlick

The corpse of Gertrude Albermann

Peter Kürten. The most horrific, the most frightening and the most puzzling

Ed Gein's kitchen. In a pan on the stove lay a human heart

A deputy shows the hook on
which the bodies were hung

Gein returns
to the murder scene

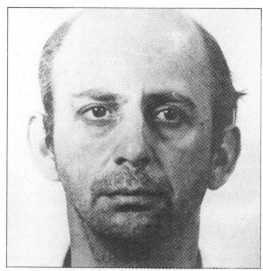

Joachim Kroll was also a cannibal

In the saucepan on the stove was a stew with a child's hand among the carrots and potatoes

to emphasize that the identity 'was an ascertained fact'. 'He and his people were certain low-class Polish Jews, for it is a remarkable fact that people of that class in the East End will not give up one of their number to justice.' After hinting that the Ripper was incarcerated in an asylum, he remarks in *The Lighter Side of My Official Life* (1916):

> I am almost tempted to disclose the identity of the murderer and the pressman who wrote the letter above referred to. But no public benefit would result from such a course . . . In saying he was a Polish Jew I am merely stating an ascertained fact . . . I will merely add that the only person who ever saw the murderer unhesitatingly identified the suspect the instant he was confronted with him, but he refused to give evidence against him.

Later he goes on:

> There was no doubt whatsoever as to the identity of the murderer, and if our London "detectives" possessed the powers and might have recourse to the methods of Foreign Police Forces, he would have been brought to justice.

Sir John Moylan, Assistant Under Secretary at the Home Office, wrote, 'The murderer, it is now certain, escaped justice by committing suicide at the end of 1888.' Sir Harold Scott, ex-Commissioner of Police, published the *Concise Encyclopaedia of Crime and Criminals* in 1961. The entry on Jack the Ripper reads, 'Five out of nine police officials involved in the case believed the killer was a doctor of either Russian or Polish nationality.' The entry then goes on to discuss various suspects.

> A Russian barber-surgeon known under various aliases: Alexander Pedachenko, Vassily Konovalov, and Mikhail Ostrog . . . worked at Walworth, within easy reach of London's East End at the time of the crimes, and assisted a doctor at a Camberwell clinic where, it is alleged, he treated four of the Ripper's victims.

The entry goes on to state that this suspect returned to Russia and was incarcerated in an asylum following the murder of a woman in St Petersburg in 1891. This theory formed the basis of Donald McCormick's book *The Identity of Jack the Ripper* (1959).

Among known, convicted criminals named as being candidates for the Ripper are Dr Neill Cream, the 'Lambeth Poisoner'; hanged at Newgate Prison on 15 November 1892. As he stood on the scaffold he called out, 'I am Jack the –' then the trap opened. These last words were verified by the hangman, James Billington. However, Cream was in prison during the Ripper murders – at Joliet in Illinois, USA – where he spent the years 1881 to 1891 serving a life sentence for murder. Frederick Deeming, hanged at Melbourne Prison, Australia, on 23 May 1892, was also said to have been Jack the Ripper.

We come now to the 'armchair detectives', which is to say the various theories as to the Ripper's identity which have been put forward in the numerous books about the case. Many of these theories accept a doctor as being the Ripper, and given the nature of the mutilations and the fact that all the murders took place in the vicinity of the London Hospital, and that three of the doctors who carried out post-mortems on the victims – Doctors Phillips, Llewellyn and Brown – spoke of the Ripper as having 'expertise and skill', this doctor theory is perhaps to be expected. Many theories also suggest a 'toff' – apparently an ordinary working-class nobody could not have been responsible for these artistic creations!

William Le Queux, in a book published in 1923, named the Ripper as Dr Alexander Pedachenko, claiming to have seen documents written in French by the monk Rasputin stating this as a definite fact. Unfortunately, Le Queux was an inveterate liar and a hack journalist short of cash. However, Donald McCormick accepted this as a basis for his book.

Leonard Matters, MP published the first classic book in 1923. His *Mystery of Jack the Ripper* was based on the revenge motive. A Harley Street surgeon named Doctor Stanley, whose son contracted syphilis from a prostitute named Kelly, goes around killing prostitutes until he comes to the right one. It is thinly veiled fiction.

William Stewart, in *Jack the Ripper: A New Theory* (1939) advances the Jill the Ripper theory, with a homicidal midwife as the killer. Aleister Crowley had suggested around 1930 that the Ripper had been a black magician, and indeed a man who dabbled in the occult, a certain Captain Roslyn D'Onston – real name Stephenson – wrote to Scotland Yard on 26 December 1888 naming a Doctor Morgan Davies, a house-surgeon at the London Hospital, as being Jack the Ripper.

Tom Cullen's *Autumn of Terror* (1965) names Druitt as the killer, as did Daniel Farson in 1972. Robin Odell's *Jack the Ripper in Fact and Fiction* (1965) suggested a Jewish *shochet*, or ritual slaughterman, as being the Ripper.

Richard Whittington-Egan's *A Casebook on Jack the Ripper* (1975) doesn't name anyone, but simply reviews the evidence. In that it differs from Stephen Knight in his *Jack the Ripper: The Final Solution* (1972), which advanced a conspiracy theory. This is basically the BBC TV series, televised as *The Ripper File* in 1973, suggesting that the Duke of Clarence, Victoria's grandson, son of Edward VII and heir to the throne, secretly married a shop-girl called Crook who bore him a child. The child was placed in the care of Mary Jeanette Kelly, and the Royal Physician, Sir William Gull, and other Masonic confederates went around killing prostitutes until they got to Kelly and retrieved the child.

Earlier, Dr Stowell had virtually named Clarence as being the Ripper in a magazine article which caused a sensation. To refute this Michael Harrison's 1972 biography *The Duke of Clarence* nominated Clarence's tutor, James Kenneth Stephen, as being the Ripper.

Harrison too has Sir William Gull conspiring to cover up the Royal involvement in the Ripper murders. It should be noted that Clarence died of syphilis.

The paucity of imagination – or perhaps the ripeness of it! – in writers is displayed by the fact that the painter William Sickert has been named as a possible Ripper, purely on the basis that he painted morbid subjects, including one entitled *The Camden Town Murder*.

Later books have shown more imagination and veracity. Martin Fido's *The Crimes, Detection and Death of Jack the Ripper* (1987) is based on exhaustive research, and reveals the Ripper to have been Nathan Kaminsky, twenty-three, a Polish Jew who suffered from syphilis and was treated for it at the Whitechapel Workhouse Infirmary during a six-week period. He lived at the centre of the murders, at Black Lion Yard, and was committed to Colney Hatch Lunatic Asylum in early December 1888 under the name of David Cohen. He died there in October 1889 of 'exhaustion of mania'.

Colin Wilson and Robin Odell collaborated on *Jack the Ripper: Summing Up and Verdict* (1987), a big book which covers all the ground and comes to the verdict that the killer was probably an ordinary, unsuspected person. Wilson gives an imaginative psychological profile of the likely killer-type.

But where do we stand at the end of this? On the basis of all the evidence we cannot put a name to the killer, but we are entitled to build up a portrait of the man who butchered some six women in the autumn of 1888. We have modern knowledge of sexual serial murderers, built up over the years. The FBI in the USA have done much work in this area, and have produced a psychological 'identikit' picture of a typical sex killer. It is strictly a male activity. Forty is the usual cut-off point: either the perpetrator is in prison by then or hopelessly insane. If he is young, there will be excessive frenzy-violence-mutilation. If older, the killings will be organized and cold-blooded. The basic personality types are:

disorganized, organized, mixed. Mixed is where the man can be 75% efficient in his normal job, and can function on a social level.

It is clear from our present-day knowledge of sex killers that they fantasize about sexual murder long before committing the act. Peter Sutcliffe, the Yorkshire Ripper, is a case in point. We know that he was a quiet, withdrawn adolescent with no history of aggressive behaviour. But he was morbidly fascinated by prostitutes, and used to sit in an old car simply watching them in the red-light district of Bradford, lacking the courage to approach them. Later on, as a man, he was cheated out of money by a prostitute, and felt humiliated. To get his own back he followed her and hit her over the head with a brick wrapped in a sock. A year later he was arrested under suspicious circumstances in the garden of a house with a hammer in his possession. Police charged him with 'going equipped for burglary' and he was fined £25. Later on, of course, that was to be his *modus operandi* in murdering thirteen women: first striking them on the head with a hammer, then stabbing them in the abdomen with a screwdriver. Sutcliffe was not insane or driven by an uncontrollable compulsion to kill. He was simply a quiet little man who felt victimized and wanted to get his own back. For Sutcliffe, stabbing women's bellies became an obsessive substitute for the sex-act.

We can summarize all this by saying that Jack the Ripper was a young man who lived in the Whitechapel area and was of normal intelligence. He probably mixed regularly with prostitutes and was known to many of them as a regular 'punter'. Nothing in his work or home life aroused any suspicion. That he stopped killing is the central puzzle. Either he moved – in which case he would have resumed killing in his new locality – he committed suicide or he was incarcerated in an asylum. The suicide theory is unlikely; no major sexual serial killer has ever committed suicide – apart from the rare possibility of the 'Jack the Stripper' killer in the mid-sixties (p.175).

Books will continue to be written about Jack the Ripper as long as there are writers to write them: the public demand seems insatiable. Other names will be advanced and future clues unearthed, but we will be no nearer that 'final solution' promised by so many writers. It was all a century ago, and the victims have long since been forgotten. The pub which Annie Chapman left to go to her death, the Ten Bells, has been renamed the Jack the Ripper. They serve red wine. . . American tourists are taken on guided tours of the murder sites and regaled with tales of missing ovaries. The search for the Ripper will continue for centuries to come; such is the fascination he still exerts.

Chapter Two

PETER KÜRTEN: 'A KING OF SEXUAL DELINQUENTS'

Of all the sex killers, Peter Kürten stands out as a unique gargoyle; at once the most horrific, the most frightening and the most puzzling. The address where he lived, 71 Mettmännerstrasse, has entered criminal folk-lore along with such other notorious addresses as 10 Rillington Place and 39 Hilldrop Crescent. No study of the sex killer would be complete without an examination of Kürten, described at his trial as 'king of the sexual delinquents'. This German monster is of special interest because in most cases we know very little about the inner workings of the killer's mind. In Kürten's case we know almost too much, thanks to the investigative work of Karl Berg, MD. Dr Berg spent the year between Kürten's arrest and execution talking to him and examining him, and his book *The Sadist* (1945) is a penetrating insight into the motives and reactions of a man who stands almost alone in the annals of twentieth-century murder: truly a man who could be termed a 'monster'.

Dr Berg, Professor of Forensic Medicine at Düsseldorf and Medico-Legal Officer of the Düsseldorf Criminal Court, was involved personally in the 'Düsseldorf Murders', and his book remains a milestone in forensic medicine, being the first detailed study of the mind of a multiple killer. He begins it with the words 'The epidemic of sexual outrages and murders which took place in the town of Düsseldorf between the months of February and November in the year 1929, caused a wave of horror and indignation to sweep throughout Germany and the whole world.' That is as good an introduction to the effect Kürten the killer produced as any. Dr Berg also reveals that the murders were variously called by the Press the 'Ripper Murders', 'Vampire Murders' and 'Werewolf Murders'.

It is important to understand the social background to the Kürten case, and the typical German murder of the time. Prior to Kürten, the three worst German murderers were Georg Grossmann, Karl Denke, and Fritz Haarmann. It was as if this trio were prophets, foretelling the appearance of Kürten, someone perhaps worse than themselves. Grossmann killed scores of girls and sold their flesh in the famine after the First World War, when meat was scarce. Following his arrest in 1921, he hanged himself in his prison cell before his execution could take place. Denke killed young men, pickling and selling their flesh. With typical Germanic thoroughness he kept a ledger in which he recorded the name, date and weight of each carcass as it was pickled. He killed between 1921 and 1924, and was known to have murdered at least thirty young men. He too hanged himself in his cell after arrest. Haarmann killed young men – at least twenty of them, and possibly as many as fifty – and he too sold the flesh as meat. He was arrested in 1924 and was later beheaded. The stage was set for the appearance of a super-monster. He duly arrived in 1929, although not without a long apprenticeship.

Peter Kürten was born on 26 May 1883, the son of a violent drunkard. One of a family of thirteen, he knew poverty early on, and was brought up in an atmosphere of overcharged sex – he had to sleep with his sisters, and listen to and even watch his parents having sexual relations. Kürten claimed that one of his sisters attempted to seduce him; what is certain is that his father was sentenced to three years' imprisonment for incest with his thirteen-year-old daughter. Kürten's sexual deviation was germinated by a dog-catcher who lived in the same house and taught Kürten to masturbate dogs. 'My youth was a martyrdom,' he told Berg.

Kürten's grandfather had served prison terms for theft, and there was a long history of feeble-mindedness in the family on the father's side. He can be regarded as proof of the hereditary factor in developing criminals, or conversely the belief of sociology that environment makes the criminal. Certainly his lengthy spells in prison did nothing to help him, and served only to incubate his perverse desires.

At the age of nine Kürten committed his first murder, according to his confession. He pushed a boy off a raft on the Rhine, and when another boy dived in to help the first one Kürten pushed him under the raft so that both drowned. At the age of thirteen he began practising bestiality with sheep, pigs and goats. His first ejaculation coincided with him stabbing a sheep while he had intercourse with it, and he discovered that the sight of blood gave him intense pleasure. From this moment on the link between sex and blood became firmly fixed in his mind.

At sixteen he ran away from home, stealing money to travel to Coblenz, where he lived with a prostitute with masochistic tendencies who encouraged him to torture her. Then he was arrested for theft and went to prison for the first time. It was to be the first of seventeen sentences that were to take twenty-seven years of his life. That first sentence was one of four years in harsh conditions, and Kürten was later to tell his judges: 'When I came out of prison I think I was a little crazy. . . it was too heavy a punishment, in my opinion. I was too young for it.' He served his first sentence at the Berger Gate, where he came under the influence of hardened criminals. He had himself tattooed – a typical act of prison culture. He was always to complain of having been over-punished for trivial offences.

When he was released from prison in 1899 he started to live with a prostitute of twice his age, who like the earlier one enjoyed being maltreated. This further increased his sadistic streak, confirming him in the belief that pain and sex were inextricably linked. In 1899, according to his own confession, he committed his first adult murder, strangling a girl while having sex with her in a forest. However, there is no police record of this incident. He spent the years between 1900 and 1904 in prison, serving two sentences – one for minor fraud, the other for trying to shoot a girl. During these two periods in prison Kürten admitted that he used to dream of revenge against the unjust society which had imprisoned him. He told Dr Berg:

> The long sentences I served when still quite young had a very bad effect on me. I did not masturbate. I got my climax of enjoyment when I imagined something horrible in my cell in the evenings. For instance, slitting-up somebody's stomach and how the public would be horrified. The thought of wounding was my peculiar lust, and in that way I got my ejaculation. . .That went on for years. If I hadn't had that I would have hanged myself.

Kürten even used to break prison rules deliberately, so that he would be put in solitary punishment cells where he could indulge his fantasies more freely.

After prison he was called up as a conscript to the army, but soon deserted. It was at this point that he began his acts of arson, setting fire to barns and hayricks, hoping that tramps might be sleeping in the hay. He told Dr Berg, 'I got sexual excitement from watching my fires, but I did not ejaculate.'

In 1905 he received seven years imprisonment for thirty-four thefts and twelve burglaries. He served his sentence in Münster Prison, where, he said, 'I had cell madness.' He once rolled himself in a bundle of silk, claiming he was a silkworm. If he was a chrysalis, he was to emerge as a terrifying killer. Kürten claimed that he was able to poison some convicts in the prison hospital, a claim which has never been substantiated. Here he refined his dreams of revenge. Imprisonment can break the weak – the majority of first-time convicts never reoffend – but with certain exceptional individuals it serves only to compress the psyche, to harden them. Kürten came out of prison in 1912 a cold and sinister man, determined to have his revenge on society.

He was soon back in jail, receiving a one-year term for maltreating a servant girl during intercourse, and discharging a firearm in a restaurant after trying to accost a woman and having a waiter attempt to throw him out. Following his release, on 25 May 1913, according to his own account – and he was able to recall details in amazing depth from previous decades – he had become a professional burglar, and one evening he entered a pub in the Wolfstrasse, Köln-Mulheim, when the family were out at a fair. In one of the bedrooms he found thirteen-year-old Christine Klein asleep. In his own words to the court which tried him:

> I was hunting round the bedroom by the light of a pocket lamp. . . I saw a girl of about nine years in bed. I flung myself on this girl in a state of great agitation and strangled her, and when she was lying there quiet I took out my sharp little pocket-knife and cut the child's throat. . . First I had only the intention of stealing. But when I saw the child there came on me, beside the other excitement, the remembrance of my terrible sufferings and humiliations during my years of imprisonment. . . The remembrance of those brutal punishments, which in my opinion were often unjust, combined with the strong sexual passions which I have inherited from my father, made me absolutely crazy.

He said the act of killing had made him feel 'free' for the first time. The child had in fact been strangled, had her throat cut, and her sexual organs penetrated with fingers. By pure chance Kürten left his handkerchief behind, and as it bore the same initials as the girl's father, Peter Klein, he was suspected of this terrible crime.

Also in 1913, Kürten attacked an unknown man and an unknown woman, knocking them unconscious with a hatchet and gaining sexual excitement from seeing the blood. He set fire to another hay wagon, and attempted to strangle two women.

Kürten spent the next eight years – 1913-21 – in prison, where he endured more 'terrible sufferings', thus increasing his mad desire for revenge. It had become a vicious circle: increased punishment led to increased revenge. In 1921 Kürten returned to Altenberg, telling everyone that he had been a POW in Russia. At this time he attempted to strangle a war widow. It was now that he met his wife-to-be. A peasant woman who looked prematurely aged, she herself had served a term in prison. Born in 1880, she had been engaged to a gardener for eight years, most of them as his mistress, when he jilted her. She was thirty-one, and felt that life had passed her by. She shot the cheating lover, and as a result she went to prison for five years. She was released in 1915, and perhaps as a result of her experiences she was always a stoical woman, accepting all life's burdens as just punishment for her former crime. She was later to say, 'I have taken all things as a punishment for my old life.' Why Kürten was attracted to her is difficult to understand, but she was to become his sheet-anchor, the one fixed solid rock in his existence. He never ill-treated her, but showed her great respect; and she was the only individual for whom he ever felt any genuine affection. He was later to feel more guilt over betraying her by his acts of infidelity than for any of his acts of murder. It may be that Kürten regarded her as a soul-mate; after all she too had suffered in prison. When Kürten proposed marriage she refused him; only when he threatened to murder her did she consent to a wedding.

For the next two years, following the marriage in 1923, Kürten lived a normal life as a married man in Altenberg, having a good job and becoming active in trade-union circles. He was twice charged for sadistic maltreatment of servant-girls, but managed to wriggle off the charges.

In 1925 Kürten moved with his wife to Düsseldorf. He walked the streets, fantasizing about blowing up the city with dynamite. With a fixed address – 71 Mettmännerstrasse – Kürten began with a few attacks widely spaced apart in time, as if in rehearsal for the main event. These attacks became more frequent and violent, following the typical pattern of a sexual psychopath. In 1925 there were three attempted strangulations of women; in 1926 one attempted strangulation, in 1927 five cases of arson and one attempted strangulation. In 1928 came eleven arson attacks, and 1929 began with six more cases of arson on barns and haystacks. Then on 3 February came the first attack on a woman, and Düsseldorf's 'Reign of Terror' had begun.

Frau Kühn was attacked on the evening of 3 February by a man who stabbed her twenty-four times, some wounds being in her temple. She survived, but Dr Berg noted that the wounds had been inflicted in rapid succession.

We have some confusion over the date of the first murder. Dr Berg gives 9 February and numbers the case 46. Cases 45 (Kühn) and 47 (Scheer) are also recorded as February crimes. But Margaret Wagner, in her book *The Monster of Düsseldorf* (1932), gives 8 March as the date of the Ohliger murder – a date followed by other writers. But as Dr Berg appeared as an expert witness at the trial of Kürten, I am inclined to accept his dating.

On 9 February, at nine o'clock in the morning, workmen found the body of eight-year-old Rosa Ohliger. She had multiple stab wounds in the chest, and had been strangled prior to the stabbing. An attempt had been made to set fire to the body with paraffin. The post-mortem examination revealed that the victim had injuries to her genitalia, the hymen being torn. Ejaculation had not taken place within the vagina, Dr Berg noted, but the killer had inserted into it a finger smeared with semen. The two separate crimes, the stabbing of Frau Kühn and the murder of the child, were not linked by the police at this time.

On 13 February Rudolf Scheer, forty-five, was found stabbed to death, many of the twenty wounds being in his temple. He was not robbed, and the killing appeared to be motiveless. With the benefit of hindsight Dr Berg tells us that the three crimes had the following factors in common: each had been a sudden attack in an isolated spot; each attack had been made at dusk; in each case a stabbing instrument had been used, and there was no apparent motive in each case – none of the victims was robbed, for example.

At this point, in April 1929, a local lunatic was arrested and questioned about the two murders – he had certainly attacked two women by trying to lasso them. He readily confessed to the murders, with a wealth of detail. Hans Strausberg, twenty-one, was an epileptic with a cleft palate and hare-lip, and had the mental age of an eight-year-old. Police accepted his confessions as genuine, and with him confined in a mental hospital for the criminally insane, police expected the murders to stop. They did not.

There was a long lull, then in the August of 1929 a spate of attacks and murders reawakened the fears of the local populace. On the evening of 21 August a Frau Mantel was stabbed in the back, her wounds not being serious. Shortly afterwards a girl named Anna Goldhausen and a man, Gustav Kornblum, were stabbed in a similar fashion. Both survived. It was as if the unknown assailant gained some kind of perverse satisfaction from the act of stabbing. Then on 24 August, a double murder stunned the city. The bodies of two girls, five-year-old Gertrude Hamacher and fifteen-year-old Louise Lenzen, were found strangled and stabbed in an allotment near to their homes. Their throats had been cut in an apparently motiveless act of murder, neither victim having been sexually assaulted.

Next day, in the afternoon, a domestic servant named Gertrude Schulte was accosted by a man calling himself Fritz Baumgart. The girl had been on her way to a local fair, but accompanied the man to nearby woods for a walk. Once inside the cover of the trees he attempted to have sexual intercourse with her standing up, but she refused, saying, 'I'd rather die.' 'Baumgart' replied coolly, 'Well, die then!' He stabbed her several times, so violently that the tip of the knife-blade broke off inside her spine. The stabbing had been in a rapid pattern. The girl survived, and was able to give police a good description of her attacker.

It was at this point that police began to think that they were looking for two killers, since it hardly seemed likely that the man who had killed *two* girls on Saturday evening would be seeking further victims on the Sunday.

In September came three more attacks on women, in one case the girl being thrown into a nearby river after attempted strangulation. But it was another murder, in late September, which caused a sensation. It signalled the start of a spate of hammer attacks. Ida Reuter, a servant-girl, set out for a Sunday walk and never returned home. The next day, 24 September, she was found in a meadow near the Rhine at Düsseldorf. The body lay with legs apart and the genitals exposed – as if deliberately. Sperm was found in her vagina, and her knickers had been stolen. Cause of death was a series of vicious hammer-blows to the head. Police now suspected that *three* killers might be operating in Düsseldorf, since a killer of this type was thought never to change his *modus operandi*, and therefore the stabber could not be the hammer-attacker.

On 12 October, at 6.30 a.m., missing servant-girl Elizabeth Dorrier was found gravely injured and unconscious near the river Düssel. She died without ever regaining consciousness on 13 October. She had been battered about the head with a hammer, and her vagina was injured, indicating a sexual motive for the killing. Her hat and coat were missing.

On 25 October came a double hammer-battering in two separate parts of the city. Frau Meurer, thirty-four, was knocked unconscious by a man with a hammer, and Frau Wanders, a prostitute, was also knocked unconscious with four blows from a hammer.

On 7 November, a five-year-old girl, Gertrude Albermann, went missing from her home in the city. Two days later her body was found near a factory yard, lying among nettles and brick rubble. She had been strangled and stabbed thirty-six times. She lay face downwards with her legs apart. Her knickers had been torn, and there were injuries to her vagina and anus.

By now the city was in a state of hysteria, with newspapers headlining each new 'Vampire Murder' The panic was increased when Kürten, imitating Jack the Ripper (whom he admired so greatly), began sending letters to the police and the newspapers indicating where the body of another victim might be found. He drew a little map. Police searched a meadow and dug up the body of Maria Hahn, a servant-girl. She had been dead since August, and police unearthed her body on 14 November. It was completely naked, and had twenty stab wounds inflicted on it – three to the temple, seven in the neck and ten in the breast. Dr Berg noted 'coitus per anum'. Thousands of morbid spectators flocked to the spot where the body had been found.

The panic in Düsseldorf led to Germany's greatest detective, Detective Chief Inspector Gennat of the Berlin Police, being assigned to the case. He had an excellent reputation as a meticulous man-hunter, having once followed up no less than 800 clues to track down a murderer. His first act was to hold a press conference at which he told reporters that the present case was unique in the history of criminology, and that the original 'Jack the Ripper' was a mere beginner compared to his new disciple. But he prophesied that the killer would make a mistake and be caught, as he had 'a yearning for publicity'. Inspector Gennat tried to organize the local police, who were in a dispirited state, convinced that they were hunting no less than four separate killers in the city. A stabber. A strangler. A hammer-killer. A homosexual killer who killed men only. So great was the interest aroused by the case that Edgar Wallace booked into a Düsseldorf hotel.

Inspector Gennat arranged for a tailor's dummy, dressed in the clothing of Elizabeth Dorrier, to be taken around the dance-halls of Düsseldorf in the hope that someone might recognize her and remember the girl's companion on the day of her death.

But unknown to the police and citizens of Düsseldorf, the murders had come to an end. There had been eight murders in ten months, and fourteen attacks. The attacks would continue for another six months, including the attempted strangulations of women in February 1930 (Hilda); two in March (Maria and Irma) three in April, followed by attacks on several girls and a hammer attack on Charlotte Ulrich. In May came the attempted strangulation of Maria Büdlick – or 'Butlies' – and finally the attempted murder of Gertrude Bell.

It was the attempted strangulation of Maria Büdlick on 14 May 1930 which was to lead to Kürten's arrest. He had at last made the mistake prophesied by Inspector Gennat. Maria was a servant-girl who came from Cologne to Düsseldorf looking for a job. When she arrived at the railway station she was accosted by a strange man who tried to persuade her to go with him. Kürten intervened, angrily denouncing the man as a 'pervert' and offering the girl his protection. The girl trusted him. He was a soft-spoken and gentle-mannered man.

Kürten took the girl to his apartment at 71 Mettmännerstrasse for some refreshment. He gave her a drink of mild and a sandwich and offered to take her to a hostel. But instead he took her for a walk in the woods, the Grafenbergerwald, telling her that the hostel lay in the 'Wolf's Glen'. Once inside the forest Kürten tried to have sexual intercourse with her while throttling her. For some reason he never completed the attack. Instead he released her and asked her if she could remember where he lived. She said no, so he let her go.

Later the girl wrote an account of this incident in a letter to a friend. It arrived at the wrong address, and was handed over to the police. They traced Maria Büdlick, and she was able to lead them to the Mettmännerstrasse on 21 May, although she was unable to remember the house. They stopped at a similar house to talk to the landlady, and at this point Kürten came downstairs and recognized her – and the police. He realized he was close to being arrested, and managed to slip away unseen.

Precisely why he gave up at this point is uncertain. The police could have charged him with attempted rape of Maria Büdlick, but could hardly have proved the murders against him. Whatever the reason, he suffered some form of spiritual collapse and decided that the game was over. That night when his wife returned home in the early hours from the restaurant where she worked – Kürten usually met her outside to protect her from the 'monster' – he confessed everything to her. At first his wife did not believe him, and he was forced to relate various details of his murders. He took her out for a last meal, but she was so upset that she could not finish her portion. Kürten ate his share, and then finished off what she had left. His appetite never deserted him at any point in his life.

Kürten persuaded his wife that she should turn him in to the police and thus collect the reward money. Eventually, on 24 May, Frau Kürten went to the police. She had known nothing of his double life – in fact, he had used her absences at night, at work, to commit his attacks. She told police, 'He frequently had sexual intercourse with me, even against my will. In the last two years he has been extremely keen on it.' She told police about the arrangements for her next meeting with her husband, and four armed officers kept the appointment and arrested Kürten. He submitted without a struggle, even wearing an ironical smile.

Nobody could believe Kürten was the killer who had been hunted for so long. His employers described him as a 'good worker', and to the neighbours he appeared to be a respectable man. They remembered that at the time of the murder of little Rosa Ohliger he had said that whoever did it ought to be handed over to the people to be torn to pieces.

For the police it was the end of a complicated inquiry. No less than 2,650 clues had been followed up; 200 people had falsely confessed to the murders; 250 accusations a day were received at police headquarters; 13,000 letters a day had poured in to Düsseldorf police; 9,000 people had been questioned, and a card-index file of 70,000 entries had been compiled. The same problems were later to be encountered by police hunting the Yorkshire Ripper: they found themselves buried under a mountain of paperwork.

Kürten immediately made a full confession to the murders, although he was later to withdraw it. But Gertrude Schulte picked him out of an identity parade. He was produced in court to be charged in June 1930, and was remanded in custody until his trial in April 1931. This was the year that Dr Berg spent examining him.

Dr Berg found Kürten to be 'frank and ironic'. He had a pocket edition of Lombroso, and used the hereditary factor as an excuse for his murders – that and the revenge-fantasies which prison had incubated in him. He told Dr Berg that he had become interested in his own perverse desires, and said, 'As regards the motives I gave for my actions. . . I had begun to think things over because of the criminal inspector who was so very interested in the psychological aspects of the case. But I must own up that in spite of this, I really always was in the frame of mind when I had the desire – or perhaps you would call it the urge – to kill somebody. The more people the better, and yes, if I had the means of doing so, I would have killed whole masses of people – brought about catastrophes. Every evening when my wife was at work I went prowling about for a victim. . . The sex urge was always strong in me, particularly during the last years. But it was increased by the deeds themselves. That was why I had to go out again and again to look for another victim. . .'

Asked how he managed to have normal sexual intercourse with his wife, he replied that it had been with great difficulty. He had to fill his head with sadistic fantasies before he could succeed. He said in the course of another interview, 'The main thing with me was to see blood. . . I felt sexually excited.' He confirmed that the act of stabbing brought about an ejaculation, saying:

> It was thus as I lay on the Albermann child, my member still in the child's vagina, while I continued to stab her breast. . . I had no satisfaction during the sexual act, only later on during the throttling. I became stiff again, and when, as I stabbed her throat, the blood gushed from the wound, I drank the blood from the wound and ejaculated. I probably drank too much blood, because I vomited.

Speaking again of his wife – he was delighted to learn that she had received some of the reward money – he said, 'I always got on well with my wife. I did not love her for any sensual motives whatsoever. It was respect for her noble character.'

The Hahn case had elements of necrophilia, the naked body had been sexually assaulted, both vaginally and anally; leaves and soil were found in the anus. Kürten admitted that after he had killed and buried her he decided to alter the location of the grave. He dug her up, kissing and fondling the corpse. He said he had wanted to crucify her body to a tree 'to stir up some excitement', but the body was too heavy. He reburied it, and later often visited the grave. He was able to ejaculate simply by fingering the earth that covered it.

The revelations of Kürten to Dr Berg still have the power to terrify. He emphasized that he always ejaculated when he heard the sound of gushing blood, and said that once while out looking for a victim in the Hofgarten, he decapitated a sleeping swan. 'In the Spring of 1930 I noticed a swan sleeping at the edge of the lake. . . I cut its throat. The blood spurted up and I drank from the stump and ejaculated.'

When he committed arson, or a murder, he would mingle with the crowds that gathered, and achieved orgasm by the uproar provoked in the spectators. Yet he insisted to Dr Berg, 'I am not mad.' He told Dr Berg about his fantasies of blowing up bridges and poisoning wells, of blowing up Düsseldorf with dynamite. Or he would save Düsseldorf from the 'monster' and be hailed by a grateful public with torch-light processions. At first he attempted to convince Dr Berg that he killed 'for revenge on society', but later admitted the sexual motive for his crimes. He told Dr Berg, 'When Professor X was here for the first time, he brought his lady assistant with him, and she had such a lovely white neck that I would have loved to strangle it.'

He also revealed that in his years in prison he had gained sexual pleasure from the written word. 'I always read the murder stories in the newspapers. They excited me sexually. . . I have read Jack the Ripper several times.'

Kürten's trial began on 13 April 1931 in the drill-hall at Düsseldorf police headquarters. Grisly exhibits produced in court included the skulls of some of his victims, and the weapons he used to kill – plus the spade used to bury Maria Hahn. In accordance with the German custom, the trial took place before three judges and a jury. Kürten stood in the dock smartly dressed, his hair neatly combed, his pleasant-looking face attentive. He was now almost forty-eight, and had spent over twenty years of his life in prison. The indictment against him included nine murders and seven attempted murders.

Dr Jansen, for the prosecution, asked several times for the press to be excluded because of the unsavoury nature of the evidence, but the judges refused. The presiding judge, Dr Rose, allowed Kürten to tell his autobiography from the dock. 'I was born in 1883. . . as a child I suffered much from my father's drunken brutality.'

Judge: 'Why did you write those letters to the press and police?'

Kürten: 'I hoped to achieve a sadistic satisfaction from them, and succeeded in doing so.'

Judge: 'What made you change the instrument of murder? [from knife to hammer]'

Kürten: 'I hoped to get more enjoyment from it. . . . but this did not quite give me the satisfaction I wanted.' Kürten was civil and soft-spoken in the dock, anxious to communicate his thoughts.

In later testimony Kürten said, 'In prison I began to think a great deal about revenging myself on society. I did myself a great deal of damage through reading blood-and-thunder stories; for instance I read the tale of Jack the Ripper several times. When I came to think of what I had read in prison, I thought what pleasure it would give me to do things of that kind once I got out again.' He spoke of his 'sexual tension', and of the great pleasure he derived from the shock and indignation his crimes caused. He also admitted that he had deliberately changed his choice of weapons 'to bring about the theory that there were several murderers at work'.

Professor Berg gave evidence, describing Kürten as 'King of the sexual delinquents'. Kürten, he said, could not be categorized. He had no *modus operandi*. Sometimes he robbed his victims, sometimes not. He attacked men, women and children, displayed every sexual aberration, yet lived a normal life as a husband to his wife, who never once suspected the grim truth about him. He was not weak-minded but strong-minded, and had an incredible memory of crimes committed over two decades. He was a pyromaniac, had delusions of grandeur, megalomania and sexual mania. Kürten differed from the normal sadist in that he pursued *different methods of violence* alternatively. Instead of following a set *modus operandi*, he deliberately changed his methods to fool the police – and succeeded. He had a great ability to lie and deceive, possessed great presence of mind and an ability to bluff.

Kürten had been a professional burglar in earlier years, and had simply extended his field of activity to murder, using his developed skills to avoid detection and capture. He was a vain and cunning criminal. His excuse of revenge against an unjust society was simply a mask for his sadistic sex-drive. Years of solitude in prison cells had developed in him the power of auto suggestion: 'the ability to achieve orgasm purely by his indulgence in sexual fantasies'. Shaking his head sadly, Dr Berg said, 'Kürten is perfectly sane.'

The defence was one of insanity at the time of the murders. Professor Rather gave psychiatric evidence for the defence, Professor Sioli for the prosecution.

Kürten's wife gave evidence. She said, 'I never connected my husband with the Düsseldorf murders. I never saw any marks on his clothes, because he was always so particular about cleaning them himself. He always slept soundly. Taken all round, he was good-tempered and kind-hearted. He often told me about the bad treatment he had had in prison, of being taken in fetters through the town when he was only a boy.'

Dr Hertel, the magistrate who had first examined Kürten and taken down his confession, told the court, 'Kürten was an inexplicable riddle. What was Kürten's spiritual state before and during the acts? Why did Kürten make his confession to his wife?. . . Kürten must have guessed that his hour had come. A deep spiritual depression forced him to lay bare his secret. . . . I had the immediate impression that he would retract his confessions . . .He retracted everything . . . The fight with Kürten lasted two months, the fight for the truth with a skilful, strong and intelligent adversary. In the end there came to be a certain bond between myself and the accused. . . . His confession came entirely of his own free will. He bowed to the majesty of the law. . . . He admitted premeditation in every case to his crimes.'

Dr Jansen, the prosecutor, asked Professor Sioli, 'Kürten has told us that if danger of arrest threatened, even in the midst of his passion he could stop the attack and flee. Is not that a proof that impulse was not irresistible?' Professor Sioli replied, 'It is a proof.'

Dr Wehner, the young defence lawyer, asked the witness: 'Another expert called Kürten the King of sexual delinquents because he unites nearly all the sexual perversions in one person. Can that not change your opinion?'

Professor Sioli: 'I cannot see in Kürten's case any borderland case of premeditation.'

Dr Wehner: 'That is the dreadful thing – that the man Kürten is a riddle to me – that I cannot solve it! Haarmann only killed men – Landru only women – Grossman women – but Kürten killed men, women, children and animals – he killed everything he found!'

Professor Sioli: 'And was at the same time a very clever man and quite a nice one.' (There was laughter in court at this sally.)

One witness, a girl who was assaulted by Kürten when she was sixteen, told the court how one day he stood in front of a waxwork display of murderers and burglars, and said, 'One day I shall be as famous as they are.' This 'desire to become known' has motivated many modern crimes – particularly the assassination of famous men – but this drive is present in most of us. James Berry, the former public executioner, tells us in his autobiography *My Experiences as an Executioner* that he was inspired to apply for the post of hangman after reading about his predecessor, Marwood, in a newspaper. 'To travel and become famous like him!' he thought.

Kürten's final remarks are of some interest. He declared that the real reason he confessed to his wife was because 'there comes a time in the life of every criminal when he can go no further. And that spiritual collapse is what I experienced.'

In his final speech the prosecutor said, 'The 48-year-old Kürten has spent more than twenty years in prison. His sadistic desires developed to a dreadful intensity when allowed full play in his imagination. . . . . But he has no reason for making imprisonment in itself the cause for his tendencies. When he came into the cells reserved for prisoners undergoing special punishment, it has been acknowledged that he deliberately brought this about to indulge his dream-desires in a more undisturbed way. . .

'Unappeasable sadist and egocentric indulger in delusions of grandeur, Kürten had nine victims to his account, butchered in the most gruesome manner only to satisfy his own appetites. He tortured his victims more and more bestially before he killed them as he became increasingly harder to satisfy. He began to consider killing whole sections of the population. Kürten absolutely deserves the title 'king of sexual delinquents'.

'In the opinion of expert psychiatrists, Kürten was fully responsible for his actions. He only murdered in his leisure hours when he knew himself to be free from the supervision of his wife. If he had murdered according to the dark urge or under some compulsion, he would never have chosen his times so carefully. As for the theory of expiation – that he sought a victim to appease his wronged sense of justice for evil done to himself – that was not a delusion but a creation of his own imagination. . . to defend his own actions to himself. Kürten believed he had the right to indulge himself at will at the expense of his victims. The true motive for all his criminal actions was sexual satisfaction. Kürten is a pyromaniac, a sadist, a fetishist and a masochist. . . . A man of high intelligence and penetrating mind, he is absolutely and entirely responsible for all his actions . . . . I demand for Peter Kürten the penalty of death nine times. . . .'

Kürten's counsel told the court, 'I too am convinced of Kürten's guilt. But a soul of this kind cannot be dissected, cannot be analysed like an ordinary psyche. Kürten is a psychological riddle.'

The jury was out for an hour and a half, returning with guilty verdicts on all the charges. Kürten was sentenced to death nine times. He refused to appeal against the sentence, telling Dr Berg, 'It would be the pleasure of all pleasures to hear my own blood gushing into the basket when my head is cut off.' He also revealed, 'I could never have stopped my attacks. If I were outside again today I couldn't guarantee that something of the kind might not happen again. I haven't felt any pricks of conscience up to now. I could not act differently.'

Kürten was eventually persuaded to apply for a pardon, which was duly refused. However, it was widely believed that he would not be executed, since the government of the day was considering the abolition of capital punishment. But the execution was arranged. Kürten, born a Catholic, left letters to the relatives of his victims expressing regret, but it is unlikely that he could feel genuine remorse. Following his conviction, he was bombarded with love-letters, and people asking for his autograph.

On the morning of 2 July 1931, at Klingelpütz Prison in Cologne, Kürten was executed by guillotine. He had enjoyed the condemned man's last meal so much – Wiener schnitzel, chips and white wine – that he asked for it again. He remained cheerful to the last.

During his trial Kürten had expressed the hope that the full details of his crimes would not be published in the newspapers, as he himself had been morally damaged by reading such accounts. It is a telling point, and one which deserves an answer to the question: if you believe that pornography and violent literature can influence a potential killer, why write about Kürten?

The answer, quite simply, is that the study of murder and the science of criminology is an attempt to find a *pattern* in what otherwise might be regarded as senseless and wanton slaughter. And an actual murder case can tell us more about the true motivation of a man stripped down to his basic drives than any novel. Sir Leslie Stephens, himself a judge, wrote a long time ago, 'The highwayman is often more interesting to the historians of society than the learned judge who hangs him.' Lombroso was the first man to attempt to find a pattern in the chaos of crime, even if his methods have long since been discredited. Conan Doyle's Sherlock Holmes personified this when he said to Watson, 'If only we could lift the roofs from all the houses in London, what incredible twists and turns we would see, what *patterns. . . .*'

The first thing to emerge from a study of Kürten is the grim effect of lengthy imprisonment on the human psyche. Albert Camus was remarkably perceptive when he wrote in *The Rebel* : 'Twenty-seven years in prison do not, in fact, produce a very conciliatory form of intelligence. Such a lengthy confinement makes a man either a weakling or a killer. . . . In prison, dreams have no limits and reality is no curb. Intelligence in chains loses in lucidity what it gains in intensity.' He was talking about the Marquis de Sade, a man whose savage intelligence remained unbroken throughout his years in the Bastille, and who poured out his sick fantasies in words – millions of them.

From personal experience I know that prison is a place where men are either broken or made harder. Imprisonment has the effect of compressing the soul, and there seems to be an optimum amount of imprisonment the individual can take. Just so much educates; too much erodes. Kürten spent his time in prison dreaming of revenge, of 'compensatory justice': that is, getting his own back on his tormentors by in turn tormenting the innocent. It is illogical, of course, but behind it one can see a kind of warped thinking-process.

Lacenaire, the convict writer-philosopher, is an interesting example of this. He was executed in January

1936 at the age of thirty-six. In his *Memoirs* he tells us of his suicidal state of mind at the time of his crime, his despair of society. But rather than kill himself he decided to 'have the blood of society'. He was the archetypal 'loner'; an intelligent man, he despaired of the social injustice he saw all around him, and retreated into the defeatism of crime. He claimed he wanted to 'cancel his relations with society', and the triangular blade of the guillotine granted his wish. The annals of crime are full of such types.

Chapter Three

LOVERS OF THE DEAD

It is impossible to write a book of this nature in chronological order – which is the ideal. Now and again, in order to make an important point, it is necessary to group together several cases which are separated geo-graphically and by time. In this chapter I intend to examine the link between sex murder and necrophilia – a crucial link which has been ignored by past writers in the field of criminology – and so I find it necessary to produce brief vignettes of some of the most notorious killers of this type.

Many of the cases mentioned undoubtedly deserve separate chapters to themselves, but the limitations of space make this impractical; however, where possible I have included a chapter devoted to a representative type: e.g. Peter Kürten, Ted Bundy *et al.*

In 1942 the crime-writer F. Tennyson Jesse gave us her six classic categories of motive for murder: Gain, Revenge, Elimination, Jealousy, Lust, Conviction. They remain valid for all time, and with a little mental effort we can enter into the mind of the murderer, the rapist, robber, or dedicated assassin.

But it takes a great deal of empathy to attempt to understand the crime of necrophilia, the desire to have sex with the dead, or more accurately, sexual desire directed towards death. Under what motive do we place this urge?

At first glance it appears to be a kind of mad lust, and the case-histories of the perpetrators make the mind reel with a kind of vertigo. It is a crime which appears to defy reason, negating every normal human impulse as it does.

The first theory or explanation which springs to mind is that the necrophile is a man who cannot face a living, mature woman. And there would appear to be some evidence to support this thesis of the sexually inadequate male. Christie, who killed his victims before intercourse, had been known as 'Reggie No-Dick' and 'Can't Do It Christie' in his home town of Halifax as a youth. But this answer does not satisfy me: it is too *obvious*. Most sexually inadequate males buy pornographic magazines or even inflatable rubber dolls. They do not kill. The psychological mechanism which inclines a man to have sex with the dead must lie buried much deeper than that.

To begin with, it is important to define what we mean by necrophilia. Medical opinion differs on this point, but theoretically it should mean a man who likes to have sex with a dead woman simply because she *is* dead. It can be seen that many of the cases in the medical literature are not true necrophiles in this sense. Most, for example, are morgue attendants who simply have more opportunity than anyone else, and can indulge their desire in secret.

The Los Angeles psychiatrist Paul de River in the book *The Sexual Criminal* (1956) gives an account of a typical case. The individual concerned is an unmarried man, aged forty-three, who said 'At the age of eleven, while a grave-digger in Milan, Italy, I began masturbating, and when alone would do so by touching the bodies of dead, young, good-looking women. Later, I began inserting my penis into the dead girls. I came to America. . . where I secured a job washing bodies in a mortuary. Here I resumed my practice of having intercourse with dead girls, sometimes in the caskets or on the table where the bodies are washed.'

That case would seem to support the theory of the sexually inadequate male – but does it? Perhaps as a foreigner in a strange land he found it difficult to meet live, willing sexual partners, and so took what was available. Yet other cases are much more perverse, and cannot be explained so simply. Dr de River gives another account, the case-history of a 21-year-old morgue attendant, 'D.W.' At the age of eighteen D.W fell in love with a girl. He had intercourse with her just once, before she died of tuberculosis. Her death shattered him: at the funeral he wanted to jump into the grave with her. Later he said, 'Whenever I masturbated I visualized having intercourse with my dead sweetheart.' He abandoned his plans to enter medical school, and instead enrolled at a school of undertaking. He worked hard at his new profession, and duly graduated. But the presence of dead females excited him, and he began masturbating over them, then violating the corpses. In a two-year period he violated hundreds of female corpses ranging from infants to elderly women. Then, de River writes:

> . . . on one occasion he was so impressed with the corpse of a young girl fifteen years of age that when alone with her the first night after death, he drank some of her blood. This made him so sexually excited that he put a rubber tube into her urethra and with his mouth sucked the urine from her bladder. . . he felt more and more the urge to go further. . . to chew part of her body. He was unable to resist this desire, and turning the body upon its face, he bit into the flesh of the buttocks. . . He then crawled upon the cadaver and performed an act of sodomy on the corpse.

This type of behaviour is bizarre. It is repulsive. It is also criminal – necrophilia being a criminal offence in all civilized societies – but it is not exactly what we are looking for. What we are looking for is the man who kills by choice for sex; who prefers his women to be dead, rather than alive and willing. We will not find our quarry in the psychiatrist's waiting room, but instead in the depressingly long list of sex killers.

One of the earliest cases we have details about is that of Sergeant *François Bertrand,* a young French soldier born in 1822, who was arrested in Paris in 1849 for a series of sex crimes. As a child he was unusually strong, with more than a hint of sadism in his character. He smashed things frequently, and at the age of eight was already masturbating. He joined the army and became a good soldier. By the age of twenty-four he was beginning to treat animals in a sadistic manner, killing dogs and tearing out their intestines with his bare hands. He became a necrophile at twenty-five, describing it in detail in his confession.

> At midday I went for a walk with a friend. It happened that we came to the garrison cemetery, and seeing a half-filled grave I made an excuse to my friend and left him, to return to the grave later. Under the stress of a terrific excitement I began to dig up the grave with a spade, forgetting that it was clear daylight and that I might be seen. When the corpse – a woman's – was exposed I was seized with an insane frenzy and, in the absence of any other instrument, I began to beat the corpse with the spade. While doing so I made such a noise that a workman engaged near the cemetery came to the gate. When I caught sight of him I lay down beside the corpse and kept quiet for a while. Then, while the workman was away to get the police, I threw some earth on the corpse and left the cemetery by climbing over the wall. Then, trembling and bathed in cold perspiration and completely dazed, I sat for hours in a small spinney. When I recovered from this paralysis I felt as though my whole body had been pounded to a pulp, and I felt weak in the head.

Later he dug up the corpse with his hands and tore open the abdomen.

Bertrand continued to commit acts of this nature, once digging up fifteen corpses in one night until he found one which satisfied him, and even swimming rivers to indulge his perversion. Of one corpse, that of a sixteen-year-old girl, he said, 'I did everything to her that a passionate lover does to his mistress.' He added, 'All my enjoyment with living women is as nothing compared to it.' He was eventually caught by an elaborate booby-trap: he tripped over a string attached to the trigger of a rifle and was shot and wounded. Following his trial he received a sentence of one year's imprisonment, and disappeared from the annals of crime.

The pace begins to quicken. In 1871 *Vincenz Verzeni*, twenty-three, committed two sex-murders. One was a fourteen-year-old girl, the other a 28-year-old woman. He attacked them in the fields, strangling them and tearing out their intestines and genitals with his hands. Under interrogation he admitted experiencing sexual pleasure when choking a woman. It was as if Verzeni was a fore-taste of Jack the Ripper a decade later.

France had its own Ripper at roughly the same time as ourselves. *Joseph Vacher* was tried in 1897, and sent to the guillotine on 31 August 1898, his severed head afterwards being examined by experts seeking some clue to his twisted personality. Born in 1869, his whole life expressed resentment of society. (He was later to blame all his troubles on being bitten by a mad dog at the age of eight.) His background was average for the period: one of fifteen children in a peasant family. From a very early age he suffered from acute boredom, as if life was permanently grey. He entered a monastery at one point, as if seeking some meaning to life, but was expelled after making sexual advances to other novices. During national service in the army he attempted to commit suicide when a young girl rejected his proposal of marriage. The bullet failed to kill him and left him with facial paralysis on the right side. For this he was committed to a mental hospital, being discharged as 'cured' in April 1894.

It was at this point, and in the same year, that he began to kill; leading the life of a tramp and wandering the countryside in search of victims. In May 1894 he killed twenty-year-old Eugénie Delhomme, his first victim. After strangling her, he cut her throat, severed her right breast and trampled on her belly, after which he had intercourse with the body. In the following three and a half years Vacher murdered seven women and four youths, most of whom he disembowelled.

For five months following his arrest he was studied by a team of alienists headed by Professor A. Lacassagne. It was perhaps the first time in history in which a scientific attempt was made to probe the mind of a killer. He confessed to the murders with the following statement: 'Yes, it is I who committed all the crimes with which I am charged – and I committed them all in moments of frenzy.' He had to be carried semi-conscious to the guillotine.

There is a strong element of the necrophile in the case of Bela Kiss, a Hungarian with a penchant for preserving the bodies of his victims, as a butterfly-collector preserves his specimens. In 1916 soldiers searching for petrol at his farm in Hungary found more than twenty petrol drums, each containing the strangled corpse of a woman pickled in alcohol. Kiss used to advertise in the newspapers regularly for female companions, and although press reports at the time attributed the motive for the murders to the theft of their belongings, the puzzle remains: why keep the bodies? Incidentally, Kiss was never arrested. It is believed that he switched identity papers with a dead soldier, and later emigrated to America.

England did not lack sex murderers. 1946 saw the case of Neville Heath (see p. 121) a 28-year-old sadistic killer who was hanged for the murders of two women.

In the case of *John Reginald Halliday Christie* (see p. 135) we can see that 'inner moral collapse' in detail. In 1953 six nude female corpses were discovered at a house at 10 Rillington Place, Notting Hill, London.

After he was arrested the resulting trial revealed him to be a necrophile. A woman had to be dead, or at least unconscious, before he could achieve an erection.

So far the cases examined seem to indicate a kind of ego-assertion: the desire to have total power over the victim. Sexual inadequacy no longer serves to satisfy as an explanation for necrophilia. Sergeant Bertrand was an extremely virile man, for example, who kept his wife and mistresses busy. Peter Kürten satisfied the prostitutes with whom he lived, and had his wife complain that he was sexually insatiable. It would seem that there is a vital clue missing. Sexual inadequacy or ego-assertion are not enough in themselves to explain this phenomenon. Some other explanation is required.

The Moors Murders gave us a clue. The clue lies in the fact that Myra Hindley allowed Ian Brady to take photographs of her kneeling on the grave of John Kilbride. Why? Was it some kind of weird, ritualistic act? Certainly we can expect to find an obsession with death at the root of any explanation for the behaviour of the lovers of the dead, as typified in the next case.

Ed Gein was a bachelor aged fifty-one when he was arrested in 1957 for the murder of Bernice Worden, owner of the local general store at Plainfield, Wisconsin, USA. Gein was a farmer whose early upbringing by a puritanical mother had made sex a taboo subject. Gein resorted to digging up female corpses to examine and experiment on, in at least one case taking the body home to have intercourse with it. He dug up a dozen or so middle-aged women, keeping the sexual organs and returning the rest of the body to the grave, explaining that he couldn't stand the thought of worms getting to them, as the sexual organs seemed to be 'like living things'.

Later, perhaps when he no longer had access to corpses, he took to killing to satisfy his lust. The missing store-keeper was found at Gein's farmhouse, decapitated and hung up by the heels. Gein admitted that he had also killed and laid-out Mary Hogan, who had been the town's tavern-keeper. The farm was found to contain a revolting collection of human remains. The refrigerator was stocked with human organs which accounted for fifteen bodies. He had eaten the flesh of some of his victims, and skinned others, using the skin to make personal items like belts and wallets. He had even preserved a complete female breast. It was reported that he had given his neighbours venison to eat, but Gein told psychiatrists: 'I never shot a deer. . . ' Gein was committed to the local insane asylum and his farm burned to the ground by horrified locals. Ed Gein was the inspiration for Alfred Hitchcock's film *Psycho*. He died aged seventy-seven, still in the asylum, in July 1984.

Between June 1962 and January 1964 *Albert DeSalvo*, the 'Boston Strangler' (see p.102), killed thirteen women. He was only identified as the Strangler because when he was an inmate at the Boston State Hospital he chose to confess to the horrific series of sex killings. Nobody believed him. He had to work hard to convince police of his guilt.

DeSalvo provides us with another clue: on one occasion he actually felt ashamed of killing a victim because she had 'treated him like a man' – i.e., a *human being*. He carefully covered the corpse before leaving the apartment, in an act of deep remorse. In other words, the lover of the dead cannot face having his victims 'personalized'. This came across particularly strongly in the case of Ted Bundy, the charming, handsome and well-educated killer of twenty-one women. He too said that the last thing a killer would want to do is to 'personalize the victim'. By 'personalize' Bundy meant the recognition of the victim as a human being. And, of course, to the killer they are not. They are cardboard cut-outs, *things* to be used.

Again, it may be argued that the examples I am using are not true necrophiles but simply sadistic sex-killers. But there can be no arguments about the next two cases. Ed Kemper (see p.109) and Herb Mullins, both sex-killers, were operating independently in the same small area of

Santa Cruz, California, during the period 1972-3. Between them they killed twenty-one people, often dumping the victims' bodies on each other's sites, thus confusing police investigators. In fact, when the pair were finally arrested and put in adjoining cells, they loudly abused each other, Kemper calling Mullins a 'creep with no class' for dumping bodies on *his* area.

Herbert Mullin was a psychologically disturbed young man – he was in the habit of burning his penis with a lighted cigarette. In October 1972, while driving along a quiet mountain road, he stopped to kill an old man pointlessly. Two weeks later he picked up a girl hitchhiker, stabbed her to death, and tore out her intestines with his bare hands. On 2 November he stabbed a priest to death in the confessional, and on 25 January 1973 he killed five people in one night. On 6 February he shot four boys to death as they camped in a state park. He was now completely out of control, locked into a killing-spree like a robot. A few days after shooting the boys, as he drove through the local town, a voice in his head said to him, 'Herb, I want you to kill me someone.' He stopped the car, leaned out of the window, and obediently shot to death an old man who was working in his garden. His licence number was noted by an alert neighbour, and Mullins was quickly arrested. At his trial he claimed that his acts of murder were committed to avert natural disasters, such as earthquakes. Found guilty of ten murders – he was not charged with all thirteen – he is eligible for parole in the year 2020.

Hans van Zon was a mass-murderer who appeared to kill totally without motive, and lived in a fantasy world. Born in 1942 in Utrecht, Holland, he grew up as a typical mother's boy, and appeared introverted to others, never joining in playground games and the like. The life he was really living was entirely within his head.

At sixteen he left home and went to live in Amsterdam, describing himself as a 'student' and living by petty crime. He borrowed money – which he never returned – to buy himself expensive clothes, and he capitalized on his good looks by having many love-affairs, some with men.

In July 1964 he committed his first murder. He had taken out a girl named Elly Hager-Segov for the evening, and then felt a sudden urge to kill her. He persuaded her to allow him to spend the night in her room, claiming to have missed the last train home, and made love to her. When she refused to make love a second time he strangled her, stripped her naked and cut her throat.

In 1965 he killed a homosexual film-director, Claude Berkeley, in Amsterdam. In April of the same year he killed his current girlfriend, Coby van der Voort, by persuading her to try a sex stimulant. It was in fact a knock-out drug, and once she was unconscious he clubbed her to death with a length of lead-piping, undressed her, stabbed her with a knife and tried to have intercourse with the body.

He made the mistake of boasting about the murder in the hearing of ex-convict Oude Nol, who blackmailed him into committing more murders, this time for gain. He killed a shop-keeper in May 1967, and a farmer in August. But when he attempted to kill a rich widow who Oude Nol had once courted he failed to kill her, and when she recovered she went to the police to report the murder attempt and the theft of a large sum of cash. Van Zon got life imprisonment, Oude Nol received seven years.

Wayne Boden was a young Canadian who became known as the Vampire Rapist. On 23 July 1968 he raped and killed Norma Vaillancourt, a 21-year-old teacher, in her apartment in Montreal. Her breasts were covered in bite-marks. In 1969 Shirley Audette was found raped and strangled in her apartment in West Montreal. Again there were teeth-marks on her breasts. On 23 November 1969 Marielle Archambault, a clerk in a Montreal jewellery store, left work with a well-groomed young man called 'Bill'. He was a new boy-friend. When she failed to arrive for work the following day her employer sent someone to her apartment. She was found dead, her breast badly bitten. There had been a struggle, and a crumpled photograph of 'Bill' was found at the murder scene, although it gave the police no clue as to his real identity.

Two months later the Vampire Rapist killed again. This time the victim was Jean Way, twenty-four. She was found nude in her apartment with the now familiar bite-marks on her breasts. The Canadian public were now in a state of some panic, and there was intense police activity to catch the killer. But when he struck again it was some 2,000 miles away in Calgary. Elizabeth Anne Porteous, a school-teacher, was found dead in her apartment on 18 May 1971. She had been raped and strangled, and there were bite-marks on her breasts. A man's broken cuff-link was found under the body. Friends of the dead woman had seen her with a new boy-friend, 'Bill', who drove a blue Mercedes with a distinctive sticker on the rear window advertising beef. The following day police spot-ted the car and arrested the driver, Wayne Clifford Boden, formerly of Montreal. He had moved to Calgary a year earlier. He admitted having been with Elizabeth Porteous on the previous evening, and that the cuff-link belonged to him, but he insisted he had left her alive and well.

Forensic evidence proved his guilt of her murder without any possibility of doubt. His underpants revealed seminal stains and pubic hair from the body of Elizabeth Porteous, and an orthodontist matched his teeth to the bite-marks on her breasts: there were no less than twenty-nine points of similarity. Boden was sentenced to life for the murder of Elizabeth Porteous, and later stood trial in Montreal for the three murders there. He collected another three life sentences. Although it seems certain that his murders were not premeditated, but resulted from an overpowering sadistic urge to bite women's breasts, I believe that the link with necrophilia – the coupling of sex with death – seems apparent in this case.

Joachim Kroll was a German cannibal killer who between July 1959 and July 1976 terrorized the Ruhr area of West Germany, and had a large police task-force hunting him. His method was to strangle and rape his victims, and then remove portions of their flesh to be taken home and eaten later. Manuela Knodt, sixteen, was found near the village of Bredeney, close to Essen. She had been strangled and raped, and had been a virgin prior to the attack. Slices of flesh were missing from her thighs and buttocks.

On 23 April 1962 Petra Grese, thirteen, was found dead in a forest near Walsum. This time both buttocks and the left forearm and hand were missing. On 4 June – just a couple of months later – Monika Tafel, thirteen, was found dead near Walsum. She had been on her way to school when she had been abducted. She too had been strangled and raped, and missing this time were large steaks of flesh cut from her buttocks and thighs.

By now the Press had labelled the unknown killer the Ruhr Hunter. On 22 December 1966 the Hunter strangled five-year-old Ilona Harke in a park in Wuppertal. He raped her and removed flesh from her buttocks and shoulders. Ten years later four-year-old Marion Ketter was playing with friends in the Duisburg suburb of Laar. A small, balding middle-aged man persuaded her to go off with him. When the mother reported the abduction police conducted a door-to-door inquiry. In one apartment house a tenant told them that his neighbour, lavatory attendant Joachim Kroll, had told him not to use the top-floor toilet as it was blocked-up. When the man asked 'With what?' Kroll had replied: 'With guts.'

A plumber was called to investigate the toilet. It was indeed blocked up with guts – the plumber found the internal organs of a small child, including the lungs. When police searched Kroll's apartment they found parcels of human flesh in plastic bags in the deep-freeze. And bubbling away in a saucepan on the stove was a stew, with a child's hand prominent among the carrots and potatoes.

Kroll was a mild little man, and obviously mentally retarded. When questioned at the police station (he actually believed he would be allowed to go home afterwards) he confessed to dozens of rape-murders, the first of which had occurred in February 1955. His flat was full of electrical sex-gadgets and rubber sex-dolls. Kroll said he liked to strangle the dolls as he masturbated. He talked quite freely about his perverse desires, and it appeared that he was a Christie-type, too inhibited to be capable of sex with a conscious woman. At the age of twenty-two he had begun killing for sex. He had led an aimless, rootless kind of life, and had plenty of time to study his victims in advance and make preparations. It seemed unlikely that he would not have killed in that ten-year period between Ilona Harke and Marion Ketter, and sure enough he was able to recall dozens of similar cases which had not been attributed to the Ruhr Hunter. Because he had struck over a wide area of Germany, many crimes had not been linked to him by the police, and so he was able to continue his killing-spree, mainly because Germany has many such killers – as apparent in the following chapter on German sex killers – and Kroll was simply one among many. And although mentally subnormal, his animal cunning had allowed him to operate unhindered for more than twenty years. He is currently detained in a hospital for the criminally insane.

William Miofsky, while not a true necrophile – in that his victims were still alive when he violated them – is characteristic of the genre. Dr William Miofsky was an anaesthiologist at the Sutter Memorial Hospital in Sacramento, California. His job was to administer anaesthetics to patients during surgery, but nurses noticed that he was doing more than his duty. He was slyly inserting his penis into the mouths of unconscious patients and moving it gently back and forth. On 7 January 1979 a team of nurses investigating his activities visited him performing the same act on a twelve-year-old girl. They informed the hospital administration, but no action was taken. It seemed inconceivable that a senior staff-member would indulge in such behaviour. The infuriated nurses then reported the matter to the County Medical Society, which did act. They confronted Miofsky with the evidence. He collapsed, resigned from the hospital, and attempted suicide. Then suddenly hundreds of former patients reported having bad dreams of a gagging sensation in the mouth. 155 women and 85 men subsequently sued the hospital for a total of $500 million in damages. Miofsky was sentenced to be detained in the state mental hospital.

The last decade in England has revealed more evidence of these freak killers. On 2 January 1981 Peter Sutcliffe (see p. 315), the 'Yorkshire Ripper', was finally arrested after a four-year man-hunt for the sex killer who had slaughtered and mutilated thirteen women. The pattern of his attacks was always the same: he bludgeoned his victim from behind with a hammer – often shattering the skull – and then stabbed them repeatedly in the area of the stomach and vagina with a screwdriver. Again, Sutcliffe was making an 'object' of a human being, symbolically entering his victim with the phallic screwdriver. At his trial Sutcliffe claimed that while working as a grave-digger he heard voices urging him to kill.

Dennis Nilsen (see p. 233) a former policeman, was tried in 1983 for the sex-murders of fifteen young men, killed in his London homes, then cut up and flushed down the drains. He often had sex with the corpses, masturbated over their remains in a symbolic farewell, and even kept one dead body sat in an armchair for a few days because: 'It was nice to have somebody to come home to.'

The literature of the criminologist and the psychiatrist is full of cases of sadism and necrophilia. Freud, Krafft-Ebing, Hirschfeld, de River – all have produced compilations of case-histories detailing every imaginable sexual perversion, and yet there is still no satisfactory explanation for necrophilia. In this brief study of sex-murderers we have noted various clues. Christie seemed to support the theory of the sexually inadequate male; but other cases – DeSalvo, Kürten, Heath, Bundy, Sutcliffe – all serve to contradict this idea, since they were all sexually virile men, and are in a sense the 'glamour boys' of murder. So ego-assertion suggests itself: the desire to dominate the woman totally by making her a mere 'object'. But is this a satisfactory explanation? I would suggest not. The concept of ego-assertion implies a person with drives and aims.

I think the real clue lies in the frequency with which the killer masturbated over his victims, as if performing a weird magical rite. Dr Francis Camps discovered semen in the welt of Christie's shoes, suggesting that he had masturbated while standing over his victims. Dennis Nilsen masturbated directly on the face of his victims, as did Albert DeSalvo. There is a funereal air about it all. It is indeed a magical rite – but one directed towards death, not life. These killers were not asserting their egos, but rather indicating that they themselves were somehow dead – despite Christie's 'quiet thrill'.

Necrophilia is basically *anti-life*. The German crimi-nologist H. von Hentig describes it as: 'The desire to tear apart living structures.' He cites the case of a man who stabbed thirty-six cows and mares to death, and then cut off various parts of their bodies. Kürten tore out dogs' intestines. Mullins did the same with the girls he killed. Vacher disembowelled his victims, as did Jack the Ripper. Fish butchered his; Gein cut them up and hung them up to cure like animal carcasses. Kemper preferred his women headless – that way there was no face to gaze at him, no eyes to observe him.

All these killers display the classic symptoms of alienation. They do not belong to the world; are non-participants who depersonalize their victims because they themselves have felt their own personalities leak away. Like schizophrenics, they have lost all contact with the real world, and march towards death like mechanical robots or zombies, locked into their own private nightmares. Look how eagerly most of them welcomed execution – Fish helped strap himself into the chair, and Kürten wanted to hear his own blood run out. Kemper demanded the death penalty.

If we study once more F. Tennyson Jesse's classic list of motives for murder – Gain, Revenge, Elimination, Jealousy, Lust, and Conviction – then the sex killings described here do not belong under the heading of 'lust' but rather 'elimination'. The lovers of the dead are eliminating life, just as de Sade dreamed of putting out the sun to deprive the universe of it. As human beings they are already dead. Even Charles Manson said at his trial: 'Now you want to kill me. I'm already dead, have been all my life.'

In one of his essays G. K. Chesterton wrote that he considered suicide to be the ultimate crime, worse than murder. The murderer kills one person, or a dozen or more. The suicide effectively kills all mankind, since they cease to exist for him. Perhaps Freud's 'death-wish' is an apt concept for the peculiar – and fortunately rare – individuals who choose to love the dead rather than the living. They have become zombies. Not creatures of legend, but all too true cases of the living-dead, stalking our cities as death-freaks. Perhaps they are even among the crowds who flock to gawp at gruesome and horrific traffic accidents. . . .

Chapter Four

THE GERMAN SEX KILLERS

It may seem presumptuous for an English writer, coming from a nation which has produced both Jack the Ripper and the Yorkshire Ripper, to state that Germany has the unenviable record of having produced more sex killers than any other European nation; but any reading of the annals of homicide reveals this to be a fact.

The *crime passionel* is typically French, as the term implies. The typical French murder is a crime of passion, or a poisoning or a gangster-killing. It is difficult to find a true sex killer among the French. Certainly they had Henri Landru – 'Bluebeard' – the infamous murderer of ten women and a boy between 1915 and 1919 – but with Gallic pragmatism he killed for gain, not sex. Dr Marcel Petiot was guillotined in May 1946 for the murder of twenty-seven people (although he admitted having killed sixty-three), but again the motive was profit not sex. Even Troppmann, killer of a family of eight people in 1869, murdered for profit. Joseph Vacher, the French 'Ripper', is the only notable true sex killer in that nation's modern history.

Why then should the German nation have produced so many sex killers – and not just 'ordinary' sex killers, but necrophiles and cannibals like Grossmann, Haarmann, Denke, Kürten, and Kroll? The answer would seem to lie buried deep within the German national psyche: a dark impulse which found its fullest expression during the Nazi era.

Fritz Haarmann, the homosexual 'Butcher of Hanover', murdered about fifty young men between 1918 and 1924, selling their bodies for meat, after sodomizing them. He claimed to have killed his victims by biting through their windpipes. He had a keen commercial instinct – selling his victims' clothing, for example. At his trial he insisted on conducting his own defence. When shown a photograph of one alleged victim he protested: 'I have my taste, after all. I could never have chosen such an ugly creature as the photograph depicts.' He told the court firmly, 'I want to be executed on the market-place. On my tombstone there must be put this inscription: "Here Lies Mass-Murderer Haarmann". The court acceded to neither request, and Haarmann was duly decapitated.

Adolf Seefeld was a sad and seedy character. A homosexual mass-murderer who was to continue killing during the Nazi era, and was duly executed by his new masters, his crimes were hushed up by the Nazi press, which tried to represent both a new order and a new morality. Born in 1871, Seefeld was first charged with the murder of a young boy in 1908, but the evidence was too thin to convict him. However, he was to spend some twenty-three years in jail for sexual offences against young boys.

Seefeld was a travelling clock and watch repairer by profession: in reality he lived the life of a tramp, often sleeping out in the open. He gained a reputation of sorts as a kind of warlock among simple country folk, and was believed to be capable of putting spells on sheep and cattle.

Seefeld had a rare *modus operandi* : he killed his victims by poisoning them with liquids which he concocted from wild plants and fungi. His twelve victims were all found in attitudes of peaceful repose, with no apparent evidence of sexual assault. It would appear that for Seefeld homosexual practices palled, and he found murder to be an even bigger thrill.

Among his victims was Kurz Gnirk, eleven, murdered on 16 April 1933; Ernest Tesdorf, ten, killed 2 November 1933; Wolfgang Metzdorf, seven, killed 22 November 1933; Alfred Praetorious, killed 22 November 1933, aged ten – this was a 'double event'. Then came Hans Korn, eleven, on 16 January 1934; two boys – Thomas and Newmann – were found on 16 February 1934; another two boys, Edgar Diettrich, six, and Arthur Dinn, four, were found together in a forest on 16 October 1934; and a boy called Zimmermann was murdered on 23 February 1935.

Seefeld was arrested after the murder of the last boy, Zimmermann, and his trial took place a year later. He was executed on 23 May 1936. His case is notable in that it fits the usual profile of the sex killer, with the intervals between murders decreasing as if spiralling into a final frenzy.

Paul Ogorzov was another killer operating in Germany during the Nazi era, becoming known as the 'S Bahn Killer' because of his habit of murdering women on trains or near the railway lines in the years 1939 to 1941. A sadist, he raped his victims after bludgeoning them to death. He was tried on 24 July 1941, aged twenty-eight. It was a short, one-day trial, the Nazis being anxious to keep the case under wraps – Ogorzov was a known Party member. He was found guilty of the murders of eight women, mostly around the Berlin area, and was speedily executed within two days of the verdict.

Bruno Lüdke was another wartime mass-murderer whose crimes were hushed up by the Nazis. Born in 1909, he was mentally defective, and began killing at the age of eighteen. The turmoil and confusion of wartime Germany made it easy for him to kill undetected for some time. He had been sterilized by the SS following a conviction for sexual assault, but the operation did nothing to curb his sexual appetite. He had a history of torturing animals, and the psychiatric background of the full-blown sadist. He worked as a laundryman, and once used his horse-drawn cart to run down a woman deliberately.

On 29 January 1943 the body of 51-year-old Frieda Rösner was found in a gravel pit on the outskirts of Berlin. She had been strangled. Near her body lay the small pile of firewood she had been collecting. The ensuing inquiry into her murder was headed by Kriminalkommissar Franz, a policeman with a high reputation for solving cases. He had all the known criminals in the area surrounding the village of Köpenick – close to where the body had been found – rounded up and brought into police headquarters. Lüdke was among them. When he was questioned he was asked if had known the murdered woman. He admitted that he had, and that he had last seen her in the woods. When accused directly of killing her Lüdke sprang at the throat of his police questioner, and had to be restrained by force. He then admitted having killed her, but added that under the provision of the law protecting mental defectives he could not be indicted for the crime. He then went on to confess to the murders of eighty-five women throughout Germany since 1928. His usual method of killing was stabbing or strangling, with rape as the chief motive. There is speculation that various local police chiefs were only too glad to blame Lüdke for all Germany's unsolved murders – he was a choice scapegoat – but it seems unlikely that his actual total of victims was as high as eighty-five, even though the information he provided was accurate about the circumstances of each case. Lüdke's belief that as a mental defective he could not be punished proved to be unfounded. In some cases men had actually been convicted of the murders to which he was now confessing, and his case caused such embarrassment that details were kept from the Press, and Lüdke became, in effect, a State secret. He was sent to a hospital in Vienna, where he was used as a guinea-pig for experimental drugs. He died following a lethal injection on 8 April 1944.

Albert Fish. He tortured and murdered dozens of children. He even admitted eating six of them

Ten-year-old Grace Budd. Fish feasted on her body for nine days

Albert DeSalvo, the Boston Strangler

Edmund Kemper liked to play and have sex with the headless bodies

Two victims of the Hillside
Stranglers, dumped in the
Los Angeles area

Hillside Strangler,
Kenneth Bianchi. Right,
his killing cousin, Angelo
Buono

Gordon Frederick Cummins, London's war-time Ripper. Victims were savagely mutilated, one slashed open with a tin-opener

Three of the four women Cummins murdered in as many days. Above, Evelyn Hamilton, right Evelyn Oakley and top right Doris Jouannet

Neville George Clevely Heath

His first victim,
Margery Gardner

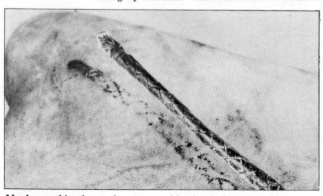

Marks on skin shows the severe whipping inflicted on Margery Gardner by Heath

The case of *Werner Boost* contained elements of the case of Caryl Chessman – the 'Red-Light Bandit' of the USA – and *folie à deux,* a weird psychological phenomenon which can be clearly seen in the Moors Murders case, and which will be seen again in other cases. The text-book definition of this condition is as follows: 'While they are conceived in isolation, paranoid reactions show a particular tendency to spread by psychological contagion. In the narrow circle of the family this tendency may be the cause of Folie à deux, as when a husband takes on and believes the paranoid delusions of his wife.' (From *Clinical Psychiatry,* by Slater and Roth.)

In simple terms, *folie à deux* is a madness shared by two people.

Boost preyed on courting couples in cars around the city of Düsseldorf, and killed five people between 1953 and 1956. When he was finally arrested and questioned by police Boost said that the sight of courting couples made him 'see red', adding, 'These sex horrors are the curse of Germany.' His first victim was a lawyer, Dr Serve, shot dead in his car near the Rhine on 17 January 1953. His young companion in the car – a male – was knocked unconscious, and was later able to tell police that the attack had been carried out by two men.

The next couple to die were a Herr Behre and Fräulein Küssmann, in November 1955. They were bludgeoned in their car, the vehicle then being pushed into a lake so that they drowned.

The Press were calling the murders the work of the 'Düsseldorf Doubles Killer', and the public were in a state of some panic. In February 1956 a couple courting in a haystack were attacked, the haystack being set on fire afterwards. The charred remains of Herr Falkenberg and Fräulein Wissing were recovered by police. The man had been shot, but the woman had been given an injection of cyanide.

On 6 June 1956 an armed forestry worker named Spath saw a man armed with a revolver spying on courting couples in vehicles. He arrested him and took him to the local police station, where it was discovered that the captive was named Werner Boost. A check on the files revealed that he had a long criminal record. His first recorded conviction for theft was at the age of six, and he had spent many years in an institution for juvenile delinquents. During the war he had been taken prisoner by the British, and in 1951 was jailed for stealing metal from tombs in cemeteries.

Boost was questioned about the 'doubles murders' by Chief Inspector Mattias Eynck, but refused to admit to any murders, although he did make the revealing remarks about courting couples making him 'see red'.

At this point a man named Franz Lorbach surrendered himself to police, telling them that he had been Boost's accomplice in the murders. A timid, slightly built man, Lorbach claimed that he had been 'hypnotised' by Boost into helping commit the murders. They had first met while out shooting, and Boost completely dominated the other man. He told Lorbach of his hatred for courting couples, and coerced him into joining in attacks on them. At first they confronted couples and demanded money. Later, when Boost got hold of a drug which he used to render the couples unconscious, he began to rape the women, persuading Lorbach to do the same.

Just prior to the murder of Dr Serve, Boost had talked about a unique method of murder : he would fill balloons with cyanide gas, which he would then release inside the cars of his chosen victims. He had killed Dr Serve with a pistol-shot, leaving Lorbach to kill his companion. Lorbach could not bring himself to do it: he whispered to the man to pretend to be dead, then hit him over the head, assuring Boost, 'He won't wake up again.'

Boost was charged with all the murders, his revolver having been identified by a ballistics expert as being the weapon which had fired the shot which killed Dr Serve. Investigations were then opened into a series of murders around Helmstedt in Lower Saxony in 1946, when many people attempting to cross the border between the Russian and British zones were shot. Boost had been living in Helmstedt at the time. . . Inspector Eynck stated 'The indictment will be one of the longest on record.'

In 1959 Werner Boost, then aged thirty-one, was sentenced to life imprisonment. Lorbach received six years imprisonment. The Press had compared Boost to Kürten, but the comparison was slight. Both had been motivated sexually, but Boost did not need to see or hear blood to become potent.

Rudolf Pleil liked to refer to himself as *der beste Totmacher* – the best death-maker – and boasted of having murdered fifty women. A small, chubby man, with a friendly face, he began his killing-spree in 1945. Like Kürten, he began his criminal career as a burglar and then progressed to murder. Also like Kürten, he used a variety of weapons in his killings: stones, knives, hammers and hatchets. He began by attacking women in order to rob them, but found the urge to rape his unconscious victims irresistible. He truly *enjoyed* murder, mutilating his victims' bodies. A vain killer, he wrote letters from prison to the authorities, offering his services as a public executioner, and now and again confessing to yet another murder, simply to get an outing from prison to some town where he had buried a body. But these were no idle boasts. He wrote to one mayor suggesting he look in the town's well: a strangled body was recovered from it. He described himself in letters as 'quite a lad', and said, 'Every man has his passion. Some prefer whist, I prefer killing people.' He committed suicide in his cell in February 1958, before he could be brought to trial.

Heinrich Pommerencke, twenty-three, was sentenced to six life terms of imprisonment on 22 October 1960, which amounted to some 140 years in jail. He had been found guilty of six rape-murders and twenty rapes.

Pommerencke was a small youth whom girls tended to ignore, and perhaps this induced a sense of sexual inferiority in him – although he boasted that he seduced his first girl at the age of ten. Born in Mecklenburg, close to Rostock, he began raping girls at the age of fifteen, waiting outside dance-halls to accost them. After his capture he told police that he had committed his first murder after going to see the Hollywood epic *The Ten Commandments*. The scene of harlots dancing around the Golden Calf filled him with disgust and with a certainty that women were the source of all the world's evils. He decided to teach them a lesson, he said. Immediately after the film he attacked and raped an eighteen-year-old girl in a local park, cutting her throat when he had finished with her. Although he claimed at his trial that he never intended to kill any of his victims, but simply to render them incapable of putting up any resistance, the evidence reveals an insane lust to kill. He once pushed one of his victims, Dagmar Klimek (aged twenty-one), out of a speeding train, then pulled the emergency cord and jumped out after her and stabbed her to death. A week later, on 8 June 1959, he strangled sixteen-year-old Rita Waltersbacher. Found guilty of six murders, Pommerencke told the court that he had wanted to kill seven women, as he felt that seven was a lucky number. He also blamed sex-films for his rape-attacks, claiming that they made him feel so tense inside that 'I had to do something to a woman.'

If Pommerencke was an example of the sexually inadequate male, then *Dieter Beck* was just the opposite. A handsome man with a succession of girl-friends, charming and well-spoken, he had no problem in getting women into bed. But although a sexual success in the town of Rehme, West Germany, he grew tired of pliant females and began hunting girls who would fight back. Through the 'swinging sixties' he raped and murdered three girls: Ingrid Kanike in 1961, Ursula Fritz in 1965, and Annaliese Herschel in 1968. At his trial a stream of former girl-friends followed one another into the witness box to testify to his sweet nature, though some recalled that he *did* have a penchant for fondling their necks during intercourse. In June 1969 he was found guilty of the three murders and sentenced to three life terms.

Klaus Grabowski, another German child-killer, had the rare distinction of being murdered in court by the mother of one of his victims. In 1970 Grabowski was convicted of child-molestation and given a light prison sentence, with a recommendation that he should receive psychiatric treatment. His sexual perversions with children consisted of removing their clothing and tickling their genitals – there was never any hint of violence in his offences. But his record of child-sex offences was a long one.

In January 1975 he lured a child into his flat and tried to remove her clothing. Panicking when the child began to scream, he attempted to strangle her, but recovered enough sanity to stop his attack and revive the girl with cold water. He then sent her home. This time the court sentenced him to be detained for a lengthy period in an institution for sexual psychopaths. But when Grabowski agreed to be castrated he won an early release.

Castration is supposed to remove the sexual impulses: it did not have this effect with Grabowski – proof that sex is in the head rather than the loins. He continued to lure little girls to his room with candy, and then sexually assault them. By January 1980 Grabowski was living in a two-room flat on the Wahmstrasse. He was now aged thirty-four.

On the morning of 5 May 1980 seven-year-old Anna Bachmeier vanished while out playing. Police were called to search for the missing child, and when they realized that Grabowski lived only a street away from the Bachmeier home they took him in for questioning. They discovered that he had been receiving hormone injections to restore his virility, and a girl-friend confirmed that the injections certainly worked. More importantly, a witness was found who remembered having seen Grabowski talking to a little girl at the relevant time. Grabowski finally admitted that he had killed the child. He had strangled her and buried her body just outside the town.

He took the police to the site of the grave.

His trial for the murder began on 3 March 1981, with the defence demanding that the charge should be reduced to manslaughter on the grounds that the murder had not been a sex murder, or premeditated – Grabowski had strangled her in panic – and that he had voluntarily allowed himself to be castrated. (The question of why he removed the girl's tights, which he used to strangle her, was not raised.) The general feeling was that he would receive a light sentence.

On 6 March Grabowski took his place in the dock as usual, and Marie Ann Bachmeier, mother of the murdered girl, crossed the courtroom swiftly and shot him with a Beretta pistol. Grabowski fell dead, and the mother dropped the pistol and waited to be arrested.

She was put on trial for manslaughter, with a good deal of public sympathy behind her. A defence fund raised a large amount of cash on her behalf. In early March 1982 the mother (who had herself been sexually molested at the age of nine, and was raped while pregnant at the age of eighteen) was sentenced to six years' imprisonment. She was released on bail pending an appeal.

Robert Wilhelm Stullgens, thirty, was a compulsive sex killer in the city of Düsseldorf. On 12 June 1980 the inhabitants of a block of flats at 12 Tussmannstrasse alerted the police to investigate the Deck family, who occupied a flat in the building. They had not been seen for two days. Police broke into the apartment and discovered the naked body of Margaret Deck and her two children, Thomas, two, and baby Christian, six weeks old. All had been strangled. The husband, Wilhelm Deck, was missing.

The police conducted door-to-door inquiries, and as a result of information from another neighbour broke into a flat occupied by a man named Stullgens. He was not at home, but in his flat was the body of Wilhelm Deck. He had been stabbed in the back.

Police records revealed that Stullgens had been released

from prison only five months previously, having completed a sentence for rape. He had raped a young mother in a park, and attempted to rape her child. Stullgens was traced to Essen, where he had fled to seek refuge with his mother. He was arrested and taken back to Düsseldorf. He confessed to the murder of the Deck family immediately. He told police that he had seen Margaret Deck in the basement of the block of flats and had felt an urgent need to have sex with her. But he was able to control his compulsion enough to concoct a cunning murder plan. He waited for the husband to return home from work, then asked him to come up to his flat to help him move some furniture. Once inside Stullgens's flat, the husband was stabbed to death.

Stullgens then took the dead man's keys and let himself into the Deck flat, where he forced Margaret Deck to strip naked and perform fellatio on him before he killed her and the two children. He was sentenced to life imprisonment.

This is not intended to be a comprehensive guide to all German sex killers, but simply to give a flavour of the *type*.

Chapter Five

SEX MURDER USA –
THE TOP TWENTY

America, land of affluence and liberty, is the ultimate dream of starving millions around the world. The USA is the most powerful nation in the world, and by extension the most influential. American styles are copied and reflected all over the globe. But there is a darker side to the American Dream. It has been called 'The Air-Conditioned Nightmare', but the modern Sodom and Gomorrah might be a more apt description. It is the land of excess, of conspicuous consumption, and along with that has come the disposable item: the toothbrush or cigarette lighter you use once and then throw away. But now human beings have become disposable items. They are murdered by the thousand every year in the USA, bodies used to satiate a perverted lust and then thrown away like so much garbage.

Historically, Germany invented the sex murder – or *Lustmord*. Then the USA took it over, refined it, and gave it back to us as the modern market-leader form of murder. From the nation which gave us the 'top twenty', here is a brief run-down on America's top-twenty sex killers.

H.W. Mudgett. Just as any survey of English sex murders would start with Jack the Ripper, so the American scene begins with Herman Webster Mudgett, alias H.H.Holmes. He began his career studying medicine, then found that if he insured non-existent people and stole their bodies from the dissecting room, he could claim money on them. In 1891 Mudgett had his 'Torture Castle' built at Chicago's 63rd Street. This large, rambling structure consisted of secret rooms, concealed doors, hidden staircases, and a large chute which led to the cellar. Here Mudgett lured his female victims, whom he seduced and then drugged. Then he would dissect them. During the Chicago Exposition of 1893 he is believed to have disposed of at least two hundred girls in this fashion. Eventually he was brought to justice in 1895 on an insurance fraud charge, his Castle was searched and some two hundred corpses recovered. Mudgett began a long and detailed confession to all the murders, but had only reached No. 27 when he was executed on 7 May 1896.

Albert Fish was sixty-six when he was electrocuted at Sing Sing Prison in January 1936. He commenced his career of perversion by molesting children, then progressed to castrating several boys. Altogether he tortured and killed dozens of children. Professor R.E.L. Masters, in his book *Perverse Crimes in History*, describes Fish as an eater of excreta and a urine drinker; a child-molester, a masochist who had driven twenty-nine needles into his body – most of them in the genital region – a vampire, cannibal and sadist. He admitted cannibalizing at least six children. The crime for which he was tried was the murder of ten-year-old Grace Budd, on 3 June 1928. He lured Grace off to a children's party, then strangled her and butchered her body. He took pieces of the corpse home with him and cooked them in a stew on which he feasted for nine days. He said later that this kept him in a state of continuous sexual fervour.

He was caught six years after the murder of Grace Budd, traced through a letter he sent to her parents. When arrested he was found to have a large collection of newspaper cuttings about the case of Fritz Haarmann. At his trial the defence claimed insanity, although Fish himself stated, 'I am not insane. I am just queer.' Fish seemed to have a religious complex, defending the castration of boys as symbolic of Abraham's sacrifice of Isaac. He had later discovered that he was God. His killings were an act of mercy to save his victims from the horrors of life. Raised in an orphanage, where he was badly treated, he once wrote, 'Misery leads to crime. I saw so many boys whipped that it ruined my mind.' The psychiatrist Dr Frederick Wertham studied Fish and wrote about him in *The Show of Violence*. He appeared as an expert defence witness at the trial, arguing that Fish was insane. The jury rejected this, finding the prisoner guilty.

When sentenced to death in the electric chair the 'Moon Maniac', as newspapers had dubbed him – most of his killings took place on or near a full moon – said he welcomed it as 'the supreme thrill'. He eagerly helped adjust the electrodes in the chair, and even strapped himself in. The first jolt of electricity failed to kill him, being short-circuited by the needles in his body. Witnesses reported seeing a puff of blue smoke above his head, before the second charge extinguished him.

Earle Leonard Nelson, the 'Gorilla Murderer', was so named because of his large strangling hands. Born in Philadelphia in 1897, he was brought up by an aunt who tried to beat religion into him. In his teens he was involved in a street accident which left him with brain damage. Following that his criminal career began. He started as a peeping-tom, was jailed aged twenty-one for attempted rape, and was released in 1919, when he changed his name to Roger Wilson. For seven years nothing was heard of him. Then in 1926 he exploded into a murder frenzy. Between February 1926 and June 1927 he strangled twenty-two women, all of them boarding-house landladies whom he raped after death. Moving from town to town, he was killing at the rate of one every three weeks. When apprehended he showed great remorse and began quoting from the Scriptures. He was hanged on 13 January 1928.

Gerald Thompson was born in Illinois in 1910. He was known as a quiet man and an industrious worker. When a workmate's daughter was raped and murdered in June 1935 Thompson gave towards a collection for her wreath. Then police discovered that dozens of girls in the area had been subjected to sex attacks. They had been induced to get into a car, where the driver held them captive and forced them to strip naked. Then he would make them pose in front of the headlights of his car while he took photographs. None of the girls had reported these attacks to the police for fear of the photographs becoming public, but following the murder they did come forward. Thompson was identified as the attacker, and was questioned about the murder of the girl Mildred Hallmark. He confessed immediately, saying the girl had attacked him with her sharp nails, forcing him to kill her. 'Afterwards I slept like a baby,' he said, smiling. Fragments of his skin were found under the nails of his victim. He confessed to sixteen photo-rapes and said his ambition had been to commit a rape a week for a year. He also admitted to over fifty rapes since the age of sixteen. He went to the electric chair on 15 October 1935.

Donald Fearn, twenty-three, lived with his wife and two children in Pueblo, Colorado, and became obsessed with the defunct religion of the Pueblo Indians, who were known as 'The Penitentes' and practised self-torture and flagellation. The quiet railway mechanic brooded over his fantasies. In April 1942 his wife went into hospital to have her second child, and Fearn took advantage of her absence to put his fantasies into practice. His victim was Alice Porter, seventeen, a student nurse. On 22 April he forced her into his car at gun-point, drove her to an old adobe church, and tied her naked to the altar. He spent the night slowly torturing her with various implements until she was nearly dead. Then he raped her, before smashing her skull in with a hammer. He disposed of her body down a well. But he had been seen at the death-site when his car got stuck in mud, and he was arrested. He went to the gas chamber on 22 October 1942.

William Heirens is the classic sex killer, often quoted in psychiatric case-histories. Born in 1929 in Chicago to a puritan mother who taught him that sex was dirty, he reacted by developing such an intense hatred of women that he would vomit merely by touching a girl. At nine he was stealing women's underwear from clothes-lines, and in his teens the tall, good-looking young man began dressing in women's clothing and masturbating in front of pictures of various Nazi leaders. The power-complex allied to deviant sexuality is evident here. At university he was a good scholar but he was leading a double life: by night he was committing robberies which provided him with sexual fulfilment. He would have an orgasm simply from entering a strange woman's home. After several robberies in which he assaulted women who caught him burgling their apartments, in June 1945 he killed Mrs Josephine Alice Riss when she disturbed him, stabbing her fourteen times and almost decapitating her. In December 1945 he shot Frances Brown, thirty-three, to death, afterwards stabbing her dead body. In lipstick on the wall in the bedroom he left police a scrawled message: 'For heaven's sake catch me before I kill more. I cannot control myself.' He went on to abduct a six-year-old girl for ransom, but killed the child almost immediately in a nearby basement, where he dismembered her body. Caught six months later, Heirens confessed in the name of his alter ego, 'George Murman.' He was given three life terms of imprisonment with no possibility of parole. The 'Lipstick Killer', as he was known, remains in Joliet Penitentiary.

Dr Arnold Axilrod was a respected member of Minneapolis society, having been a former mayor of the city. His dental practice brought him in a good income: it also provided him with an opportunity to rape girls, once they were unconscious in his chair. The first victim to complain did so in 1955. She was a seventeen-year-old girl who was unconscious in the chair for six hours, and woke to find Dr Axilrod bent over her in a suggestive manner. The girl's complaints were not taken seriously. In late 1955 a dead woman was found dumped outside the city. She had been strangled, and had had intercourse shortly before death. She was also three months pregnant – yet her husband could not be the father, he had been in Korea longer than that. Police investigated the background of the victim, Mary Moonen, twenty-one. Her dentist was Dr Axilrod. . . He was arrested, and immediately confessed, saying: 'I guess I did it.' He was sentenced to five to twenty years in jail.

Melvin David Rees was a jazz musician – he played saxophone, clarinet, piano and guitar – and he was also a sex-killer. On 26 June 1957 he held up a car containing a courting couple at Annapolis, Maryland. He shot the woman, Margaret Harold, allowing the man, an army sergeant, to flee. He then stripped his victim and raped her. After the search of the area police discovered a basement devoted to the worship of murder. The walls were covered with police morgue shots of women who had been murdered, and various pornographic photographs. On 11 January 1959 a car containing four members of the same family – Carrol Jackson, his wife Mildred, and their two daughters aged five and eighteen months – was stopped on a lonely road in West Virginia by another car. A tall, thin man with ape-like arms got out of the other car carrying a gun. He forced the family into the boot of his car and drove off with them. Later the Jacksons' abandoned car was found and a search for them began. It was too late – the entire family had been slaughtered. Two months later, on 4 March, Carrol Jackson's body was found in a ditch. He had been shot in the head. Beneath him lay the body of his 18-month-old daughter, who had suffocated. On 21 March boys out playing spotted freshly dug earth, and digging a little, uncovered blonde human hair. Police were called and dug up the bodies of Mildred and Susan Jackson. Mildred had a stocking around the neck, Susan had been bludgeoned to death. Both had been raped. The grave was just a few hundred yards away from the basement which had featured in the first murder, and inside it police found a button from Mildred's dress.

The investigation was stalled, but two months later the police received an anonymous letter denouncing Rees as the killer of both Margaret Harold and the Jacksons. The writer said he had confronted Rees with this, and Rees had not denied it. The police tried to trace Rees, without success. Then in early 1966 the writer of the letter went to the police. He had received a letter from Rees, who was now working as a piano salesman in Arkansas. FBI agents arrested Rees and raided his parents' home. Inside they found a saxophone case containing a .38 revolver and a journal relating various sadistic acts, including the murder of the Jacksons. In the journal Rees described forcing Margaret Harold to commit fellatio upon him, and commented, 'Now I was the master.' The entries revealed him to be a genuine sadistic sex killer. The psychic Peter Hurkos had been called in after the murder of the Jackson family, and was able to give police a remarkably accurate description of the killer. He also said that the killer had committed nine murders. This was confirmed when police found connections linking Rees to the sex murders of four other teenagers: four girls who had been shot and raped. Rees was tried and executed in 1961 for the murder of the Jackson family.

Albert DeSalvo strangled thirteen women to death in the city of Boston between June 1962 and January 1964, plunging the city into a state of panic, with the police seemingly powerless to stop the killings. The 'Boston Strangler's trademark was in the jaunty bow tied in the ligature around the neck of his victims, like an artistic flourish. For ten months after the last killing there were no more murders, and the police and public speculated as to what had happened to the 'Strangler'. On 27 October 1964 he struck again, but this time his intended victim fought him off and was able to give police a description. It fitted the 'Measuring Man' who had been arrested for indecent assault in 1960. (Albert DeSalvo had persuaded girls into letting him measure their bodies for a 'free' dress.) DeSalvo was arrested, and confessed to two rapes and over four hundred burglaries. He was sent to the Boston State Hospital for observation – he had threatened suicide, and there was a question about his sanity. He was not tried for the stranglings but for four cases of attempted rape where the victims had positively identified him. Sentenced to life imprisonment in 1967, he was stabbed to death by a fellow-prisoner on 26 November 1973.

Charles Howard Schmid, twenty-three, was an only child who was showered with love and money by doting parents. He spent his time impressing teenagers in Tucson, Arizona, with tall stories about being a Mafia hood and running a prostitution ring. Certainly the dark-haired, handsome man impressed the local girls and had many sexual conquests. Perhaps they came *too* easy. . . . One evening in May 1964 he was sitting with his friend John Saunders, and a girl named Mary French. Schmid suddenly announced, 'I want to kill a girl tonight.' He persuaded his companions to accompany him to the home of Alleen Rowe, fifteen, and then talked her into going for a ride. Once in a remote desert spot Schmid killed the girl with a rock, after raping her. He then kissed Mary French, telling her, 'Remember I love you.' The following year – on 16 August 1965 – Schmid strangled Gretchen Fritz, seventeen, and her thirteen-year-old sister, Wendy, dumping the bodies in the desert. But he could not resist boasting to a friend, Richard Bruns, about what he had done. Bruns, who thought Schmid was lying, said to him, 'If you killed them, let's go and bury them.' Schmid drove him to the murder site, where they found the two bodies and buried them, Schmid telling Bruns, 'Now you're in this as deep as I am.' Schmid was arrested in San Diego for posing as an FBI agent questioning girls on the beach. He was in a state of some tension, screaming 'God is going to punish me.' The case is remarkable in that practically every teenager in Tucson knew he had killed Alleen Rowe and the Fritz girls, but did not tell their parents – much less the police. It was Richard Bruns who finally went to the police, leading them to the bodies of the Fritz girls. Schmid, Mary French and John Saunders were arrested. Schmid received three life sentences, French only five years jail, while Saunders was given life. Another interesting facet to the case is the obvious condition of *folie à deux* that Schmid was able to induce in his followers.

Richard Speck will be remembered for his senseless killing of eight student nurses in a Chicago hostel on the night of 14 July 1966. Speck was a tall, pock-marked young man of pleasant appearance, with fair hair and blue eyes. Born on 6 December 1941, one of eight children, Speck was twenty-four when he committed Chicago's biggest-ever mass murder. Semi-literate and an avid collector of comic magazines, he was drunk and probably high on drugs at the time. At gunpoint he entered the hostel and took six nurses prisoner, tying them up and promising not to hurt them, explaining that he was only after money. When another three nurses entered the hostel he took them prisoner too, binding them with torn sheets. Then one by one he took each nurse into an adjoining room, where he killed them at roughly twenty-minute intervals. One nurse, Corazon Amurao, twenty-four, hid under a bed and thus saved her life. The last girl left was Gloria Davey, twenty-two. Speck raped her for some twenty-five minutes, asking her at one point, 'Would you mind putting your legs around my back?' He sodomized her with an instrument before killing her. Miss Amurao witnessed this last killing. At 5 a.m., when the killer left the scene, she raised the alarm, crying, 'All my friends are dead.'

Police found the hostel to be a charnel-house. Only Gloria Davey had been sexually assaulted. The other seven victims had been killed for no reason, as if Speck had been a shark in a feeding frenzy. One was killed by a single stab wound to the neck, another with stab wounds to the neck, heart and left eye. Three had been strangled and stabbed. One had been mutilated deliberately. Miss Amurao remembered one vital detail: a tattoo on the killer's arm reading: 'Born to Raise Hell.' Speck was identified from this – and from a photograph he had pinned on an application for a job on a ship. On the run from the police, who had published his photograph with an 'Urgent Wanted' tag, Speck booked into a cheap hotel under the name B. Brien. On 16 July Speck slashed his wrists – it was a fake suicide attempt, since he fell into a neighbour's room and was rushed to hospital. The admitting doctor noted the tattoo and informed the police. Speck gave his real name. His fingerprints were found at the hostel, and Miss Amurao positively identified him as the killer. Speck had a long record for sex offences and an insatiable sexual appetite. He was suspected of several more murders: of a woman in April 1966, of three girls in July, and another mass murder in Michigan, some fifty miles away, where several victims aged from seven years to sixty were stabbed to death. Speck had been in the relevant area at the time.

The jury took just forty-five minutes to find Speck guilty, and he was sentenced to the electric chair. By using legal appeals, he stayed alive until the death penalty was abolished. In 1972 he was resentenced to life terms totalling 400 years. In 1976 his appeal for parole was rejected. Despite having maintained his innocence all along, in 1978 he told a newspaper reporter, 'Yeh, I killed them, I stabbed them and choked them.' Speck died on 5 December 1991 of a heart attack.

Lloyd Higdon is another example of *folie à deux* in action. On 4 July 1963 he picked up the fourteen-year-old daughter of a neighbour and raped her, aided by his wife. When the girl told her parents, police in Ypsilanti, Michigan, arrested both husband and wife and Higdon served two years for rape. On his release from prison he set up home with another woman, Lucille Brumitt, twenty-eight. Again he and his new woman picked up a girl, Roxanne Sandbrook, thirteen. When she refused to give in to his demands Higdon strangled and raped her, dumping her body on a local garbage tip. Knowing Higdon's record, police arrested him. They soon broke his phoney alibi, and both he and Lucille Brumitt were sentenced to life.

John Norman Collins was labelled the 'Ypsilanti Ripper' by the Press. The 22-year-old was a model student at the Eastern Michigan University in 1969. He was good-looking, but tended to be morose. The only clue to his real character came in a remark he made to a class-mate: 'If a man has to kill, he kills.' He had reworded the Fifth Commandment. Between August 1967 and July 1969 the bodies of seven young girls were found around Ypsilanti. All had been raped and tortured before being killed with a knife. Psychic Peter Hurkos was called in to help, but the case was to be one of his failures. However, the body of the last victim revealed forensic clues which helped police develop a profile of the killer. State Police Corporal David Leik realized that it fitted his nephew, Norman Collins, who was questioned but released for lack of evidence. Corporal Leik checked his basement out carefully, and found bloodstained clothing which matched the blood group of the last victim, Karen Sue Beckemann, and hair-clippings which had been transferred to the victim's body – Corporal Leik used to cut his children's hair in the basement – and other clues which linked the dead girl indisputably to that basement. She had either been killed there or her body had been stored there after death. At his trial Collins pleaded not guilty, but he was convicted on the solid mass of circumstantial evidence and sentenced to twenty years. Collins was a good-looking young man who possessed great charm and was never short of girl-friends. He did not kill for sex – even though his victims had been mutilated, one having a branch from a tree thrust into her vagina – and although he had an excessive sex-drive, he satisfied this with his many willing girl-friends. True, he had been beaten as a child by an alcoholic stepfather – perhaps this had warped him.

Juan Vallejo Corona arrived in the United States in the 1950s as an immigrant fruit-picker, but always had an eye to the main chance. Through sheer business acumen he became his own boss, becoming a contractor hiring illegal Mexican immigrants to pick fruit on various farms around Yuba City, California. He housed his workers on the Sullivan ranch. He was thirty-eight years of age, and had apparently overcome a bout of schizophrenia suffered in his early years.

On 19 May 1971 a Japanese farmer became suspicious when he discovered a large hole dug in his orchard – especially when the hole had been filled in by evening, when he inspected it again. He had it dug up by the police, who found the body of a vagrant named Kenneth Whitacre. He had been stabbed, and his head battered with a machete, after homosexual intercourse. Police began a wide-scale search of the area. On 21 May a tractor driver on Sullivan's ranch discovered another grave – and then more. All the victims had been male, all had been sexually abused before being killed by knife and machete. In one of the graves was a receipt with the name Juan Corona on it. Digging continued until 4 June, when the last known victim – the twenty-fifth – was uncovered. In his pockets were bank deposit slips in the name of Corona. The names of all twenty-five victims were carefully recorded in Corona's ledger, just as the Nazis kept careful accounts of their victims. The evidence against Corona was circumstantial: there is a suggestion that he had an untraced accomplice. Be that as it may, a jury took forty-five hours to find him guilty of all the murders, and he was sentenced to twenty-five consecutive life terms. Since his victims were all alcoholic vagrants, or illegal Mexican migrants, the case did not arouse any great public revulsion. Incidentally, in 1973 Corona was involved in a jail fight in which he was stabbed thirty times and lost an eye.

Sherman McCray, forty-seven, was the head of an itinerant family who wandered across the USA leaving a trail of murdered women in their wake. In June 1972 the family, consisting of Sherman, his wife Carol, son Danny, daughter Gina and her husband Carl Taylor, arrived in Santa Barbara, California, and were quickly picked up by the police following a spate of supermarket robberies. For these armed robberies Sherman McCray and Carl Taylor were both sentenced to five years to life. The other three members of the family received nine-month sentences for harbouring felons. But with the family behind bars, the police started looking into their background and uncovered evidence that they had, between August 1971 and February 1972, been responsible for the abduction, rape and murder of at least twenty young women. The McCray men had carried out these deeds with the assistance and approval of their women-folk.

The nomad family had travelled widely, with both Sherman McCray and Carl Taylor serving time in jails for various felonies committed along the way. On 12 August 1971 Sheri Martin, seventeen, was abducted from Salt Lake City, her nude body later being found in Nevada. She had been raped and shot. So too was Lenora Rose, twenty, who had been taken on 20 August from Denver, Colorado. On 28 September Elizabeth Perryman, twenty-six, was abducted from a restaurant in Lubbock, Texas. In every case the girls had been waitresses, the tills in their workplaces had been looted, and the girls had been raped and shot. Three victims vanished from Texas, two in Florida, and so on. Danny McCray finally broke under police questioning and confessed that he, his father, and brother-in-law had committed the murders. It was a case where a family, like a tribe of Huns, had wandered around the USA picking up victims at random and disposing of them like trash.

Dean Allen Corll, thirty-three, was well-liked and respected in Pasadena, California, where he worked for the Houston Lighting and Power Company. But he was a homosexual with a penchant for murder.

He had never really grown up, and much preferred the company of teenagers to that of adults. Some of the teenagers who went to his apartment never came out alive. . . He had two young henchmen, Wayne Henley and David Brooks, who helped him in his trade of murder. Most of the victims came from the slum area of Houston known as the Heights. The first victim was murdered in 1970, followed by two more in December of the same year: James Glass, fourteen, and Danny Yates, fifteen. Corll often murdered two at a time, including two brothers in January 1971.

On 8 August 1973 Henley telephoned the police to say he had killed Corll. He told officers that Corll had tried to kill him, and he had been forced to shoot him in the back six times. Under questioning Henley admitted procuring boys for Corll, who paid 200 dollars a head, and revealed that many of the victims lay buried in a boat-shed rented by Corll. When police dug up the floor of the shed they found the remains of seventeen corpses wrapped in plastic. At another site four more bodies were recovered, and six from yet another dumping ground. The total was twenty-three bodies, but Henley claimed that Corll's true total was thirty-one. Henley admitted that he and Brooks helped Corll strap his victims to a 'torture board' where they were sodomized for days on end. Torture was also practised, with teeth-marks being found on the genitals of one of the victims. In July 1974 Henley and Brooks both received life sentences for their part in the murders.

Edmund Emil Kemper was a true freak, standing six feet nine inches tall and weighing twenty stone. He was born 18 December 1948, and his parents split up when he was a young child. Lacking a father-figure, he modelled himself on John Wayne. His mother ridiculed his fantasies and obstructed any independent decisions he might make. He grew up nurturing dreams of torture and revenge, mainly of sadistic acts committed against female corpses. At thirteen he cut the family cat in pieces, and the hands and feet off his sister's doll. Finally beyond his mother's control, this boy fuelled by the classic Oedipus Complex was sent to live with his grandparents. They tried to be strict with the boy. On 24 August 1964 he shot dead his grandmother, stabbing her body repeatedly. He then did the same to his grandfather. He was sent to a mental hospital for the criminally insane, where he was found to have an IQ of 136. After five years he was released as 'cured' and sent to live with his mother in Santa Cruz, California. He detested his mother. . . .

Kemper began killing because of strong sexual urges, and killing because he would have been impotent with a living woman. On 7 May 1972 he picked up two girl students from Fresno State College in Berkeley, hitch-hiking. He drove the girls to a remote spot, forced Anita Luchese into the boot, then handcuffed Mary Anne Pesce, putting a plastic bag over her head. He stabbed her in the back and the abdomen, before cutting her throat. He then killed the girl in the boot. He took the bodies home, decapitated them and dissected them. He played with them as if they were dolls. Later he buried the pieces in the mountains. On 14 September 1972 he picked up another girl, aged fifteen, and after killing her, raped her. She too went back to his home to have her head and hands cut off, and to be dissected. On 8 Jan 1973 came another victim: he kept this one at home, performing sexual acts on the body. On 5 February came two more victims, both of whom he decapitated, having sex with the headless corpse of one of them. He used an axe to dissect the remains. On Easter Sunday 1973 Kemper went into his mother's bedroom and hit her on the head with a hammer. Then he used the knife he called 'the General' to decapitate her. He cut out his mother's larynx and dropped it into the waste-disposal unit, telling police later that he did it 'Because it seemed appropriate after she had bitched me so much.' With his mother's headless body in the closet, he invited a friend of his mother's over for dinner and killed her too. He beheaded her and had sex with her remains. That night he slept in his mother's bed. After going on the run he surrendered himself to the police, saying he was afraid they might 'shoot first and ask questions later'. He confessed to eight murders and various acts of necrophilia and cannibalism. He was tried at Santa Cruz in April 1973 on eight counts of murder, having been adjudged legally sane. Kemper asked for the death penalty: instead he received eight consecutive life terms. The psychiatrist Donald Lunde said of Kemper, 'In his way, he avenged the rejection of both his mother and his father.'

Paul John Knowles was another petty thief who graduated to murder. From 1965, when he was aged nineteen, to 1972, he spent half of his life in prison. When he was finally released from Raiford State Penitentiary, on 14 May 1974, he was in a state of complete freedom: he could do anything he wanted. He chose to kill. The tall, handsome red-haired man, now aged twenty-five, got into a fight after a messy relationship with a woman, and was locked up in Jacksonville police station for his pains. He promptly picked the lock on his cell and escaped. That same evening, 26 July 1974, Knowles broke into the home of a 65-year-old teacher and gagged her while he burgled her home. She suffocated to death. There was a large police dragnet out for Knowles, but he escaped it mainly by luck. He stole a car and picked up two sisters aged seven and eleven and killed them, dumping their bodies in a swamp. The next day he drove to Atlantic Beach, broke into a woman's home and strangled her with her own stocking. A couple of days later he picked up a young girl hitchhiking and strangled her after raping her. On 23 August he broke into a house occupied by Cathie Pierce and strangled her with the telephone cord while her three-year-old child looked on. On 3 September, in Ohio, he got into conversation with an accounts executive in a bar. The man, William Bates, left with Knowles. His naked, strangled body was found later in woods. Knowles drove away in Bates's car.

Using his victims' money and credit cards, Knowles travelled across the USA, to California, Seattle, and then

Utah. On 18 September, in Nevada, he broke into a camping trailer and shot dead the elderly couple to whom it belonged. He took their money and credit cards. Three days later he dragged a woman out of a car and raped and strangled her. He was now completely out of control, killing on impulse. On 23 September he met a woman, Ann Dawson, in Birmingham, Alabama. For the next six days they travelled around together. When her money ran out he strangled her on 29 September. Her body was never found. In Connecticut, on 16 October, he rang a doorbell at random. When a fifteen-year-old schoolgirl answered he forced her back into the house and spent the next hour raping her. When her mother returned home he made her cook him a meal, and then forced her to strip naked, after which he raped her several times. He finally strangled both victims. On 19 October, in Woodford, Virginia, he shot dead Doris Hovey, aged fifty-three. There was no motive: he just felt like killing. . .

With a stolen tape-recorder, Knowles began taping his confession to fourteen murders, almost as if he sensed the end was near, and he wanted his deeds preserved for posterity. On 6 November, in Macon, Georgia, Knowles picked up a man in a bar. The man was gay, and presumably the handsome Knowles made some promise of sexual activity. Once inside the man's home he stabbed him to death, then strangled his fifteen-year-old daughter, attempting to rape her after death.

In Atlanta, Georgia, Knowles met English journalist Sandy Fawkes. They spent a lot of time together in various motels and she never saw the full murderous side to his nature, although once he did pull a gun on her. She wrote a book about her experiences with Knowles: *Killing Time*. She described Knowles as being sexually incapable in bed. Also in Atlanta, Knowles tried to abduct a woman, but she escaped and got the licence number of his car. A police patrolman tried to intercept him, but Knowles warned him off with a sawn-off shotgun. Back in Florida Knowles stole another car. When stopped by a patrolman he took him prisoner and handcuffed him with his own cuffs. Knowles then drove off in the patrol car, with the officer sitting helplessly in the back. Using his siren, Knowles stopped another car being driven by a businessman – he was not satisfied with the patrol-car, complaining of its poor suspension. Knowles handcuffed the businessman, transferred the patrol-car officer to the new car, and drove off with them. He drove into some woods and then shot both handcuffed prisoners in the back of the head. After crashing through a police road-block, he ran into woods to escape, hunted by two hundred police officers with dogs and helicopters. He was captured on 17 November 1974. In four months of freedom he had murdered at least eighteen people. After appearing in court he was placed in a police vehicle to transfer him to prison. He succeeded in picking the lock on his handcuffs and attempted to grab a sheriff's gun. An FBI agent riding escort in the vehicle shot him dead. In answer to the question 'What would you do if you had complete freedom?' Knowle's answer was that of a de Sade: 'Rape and kill. . .

Kenneth Bianchi was to become known as the 'Hillside Strangler' and his murders display yet another *folie à deux* relationship.

Between October 1977 and February 1978 ten girls had been raped and murdered in Bellingham, California, the bodies being dumped like trash in the hills around Los Angeles. The hunt for the killer was complicated by the fact that two separate law-enforcement agencies were conducting separate inquiries. This led to the confusion which was a feature of the hunt for the Yorkshire Ripper. The break-through came in January 1979 when two girls, Karen Mandic and Diane Wilder, vanished from the house they shared in Bellingham. Karen had told a friend that she had been offered a 'detective' job by a security guard named Kenneth Bianchi. The following day the bodies of the two girls were found in the back of Karen's car. They had been raped prior to death. Los Angeles detectives became very interested in Kenneth Bianchi. The 27-year-old was a police 'groupie'; that is, he hung around cops and studied their mannerisms. The Hillside Strangler was known to have used a fake police badge to lure his victims into his car. Bianchi was arrested at his home, where he lived with his girl-friend and their child. He at first denied all knowledge of the murders, but detectives discovered that together with his cousin, Angelo Buono – a man in his forties – Bianchi had been involved in procuring prostitutes.

Under lengthy questionings he finally broke, admitting the murders of the two Bellingham girls and five of the 'Hillside Strangler' killings, but when he stood trial for his crimes his defence counsel claimed that his was a dual-personality, and that the killings had been committed by his alter ego 'Steve'. Bianchi also admitted the involvement of Buono in the murders. Bianchi managed to convince experienced psychiatrists that he was a genuine case of dual-personality but it was all a clever charade, as secret video-recordings proved. At his trial in October 1979 he was sentenced to six consecutive life terms. Buono was convicted later. Like most sexual serial killers, Bianchi's background was that of a child who had been abused and rejected, and so became an emotional cripple.

John Wayne Gacy was born on 17 March 1942 in Chicago, son of a Danish mother and a Polish father. When he was eleven he suffered a head injury which left him with a blood-clot on the brain which caused blackouts. He went to business college and became a shoe-salesman, marrying a colleague. Later he ran a fried-chicken business and became a member of the Junior Chamber of Commerce. He seemed the perfect citizen. However, in 1968 he was sentenced to ten years in jail for handcuffing an employee and trying to sodomize him. His marriage did not survive his imprisonment: his wife divorced him, taking with her their son and daughter. A weak character, Gacy was a liar and a boaster, although an affable man. He was a model prisoner, and was released after serving only eighteen months of his sentence. In 1971 he was arrested for picking up a teenager and trying to force him to engage in sex, but the boy failed to appear as a witness and the case was dropped. In 1972 Gacy married for a second time and set up his own business as a contractor. But he had developed a violent temper, and since his sexual performance was woefully inadequate, in 1976 came another divorce. One of his wife's complaints was the peculiar odour which hung round the house. . . .

On 21 March 1978 a 27-year-old Chicagoan met a fat man – Gacy – and got into his car to smoke a joint. Gacy slapped a chloroform-soaked cloth over his mouth, and when the man woke up he was in a house, being flogged with whips, and raped for several hours. He was finally dumped by the side of a lake. In hospital it was found that he was bleeding from the rectum, and that the chloroform administered had permanently damaged his liver. He had practically to beg the police to arrest Gacy, but the case dragged on, with Gacy out on bail, the police feeling that the evidence against him was not strong enough to secure a conviction. On 11 December 1978 Robert Piest, fifteen, vanished while calling at a drug-store to apply for a summer job. The drug-store had recently been renovated, and the contractor had been Gacy. The police went to his house at 8213 West Summerdale Avenue, Des Plaines, and questioned him about the missing boy. Eventually they searched his house, lifting a trapdoor leading to the crawlspace beneath the house. There was a stench of decaying flesh, and rotting corpses were in plain view. At the police station Gacy (known as the 'Fat Man') admitted killing thirty-two teenagers for sex, and said that twenty-seven of them had been buried in or around his house. The rest, including Robert Piest, had been dumped in the Des Plaines river. The 'Fat Man' had simply run out of space. Twenty-eight bodies were finally recovered from Gacy's house. In 1980 the 'Fat Man' was sentenced to life imprisonment.

Randall Brent Woodfield was another handsome serial killer; tall, with black hair and a moustache. A natural athlete, he had been signed by the Green Bay Packers, and the magazine *Playgirl* chose a beefcake photograph of him for their centrefold. (It was never published. The magazine scrapped it when the truth came out that the handsome hunk was also a cold-blooded killer.) Woodfield was the leader of an organization of Christian athletes at Portland State University. Not only was he big and strong, he was also deeply sensitive, writing very moving and articulate letters to the women he dated, together with romantic cards and roses. But he liked killing women too. His victims were to range from nine years of age to forty. He was the only son in his family, but had two sisters, and was consequently brought up in a feminine atmosphere. His early years revealed him to be a disturbed child who began exposing himself at the age of thirteen. From that he graduated to rape, and finally murder. His first murder was a 'double event'; he spotted two girls cleaning a building in Oregon one Sunday evening in 1981, and forced them at gunpoint to perform various sexual acts on him. When he was finally satisfied he shot each girl in the back of the head. Incredibly, one of the girls survived to testify against him, and had to relive in court the terror of her ordeal. Like most American sex killers, Woodfield had killed over a wide area – in his case the entire length of the Pacific Coast. He is currently serving life plus 155 years in the Oregon State Penitentiary, having been convicted of murder, rape and sodomy. Hundreds of admiring women still write to him, and he replies to every letter with tender and moving sentiments.

Christopher Bernard Wilder was a spree-killer, as opposed to the classic serial killer. The FBI's Behavioural Science Unit has divided serial killers into two basic types. There are those who kill over a long time-scale, like Bundy and Bianchi; and there are those who erupt and have a sudden explosion of murder overcome them and go on a short-lived murder spree. Wilder was a spree-killer with style.

Born in Australia, he ended up living in Florida, where he became a genuine millionaire playboy. He had a large house, raced cars for fun, took his many girl-friends for trips on his yacht, and never forgot to send flowers. He was the old-fashioned romantic type, always standing up when a woman entered the room. But from February to April 1984 he rampaged across the USA, killing beautiful women by enticing them with promises of a modelling career.

His *modus operandi* was to go to shopping malls where amateur fashion shows were held, with an expensive camera around his neck. When he spotted a likely victim he would show her his portfolio of photographs, proffer a business card with a phoney name, and make promises of fame and success. His first victim died on 26 February 1984. She was Rosario Gonzales. 3 March saw Elizabeth Kenyon die, followed by Theresa Fergusson on 18 March. On 23 March came Terry Walden, then Suzanne Wendy Logan on 25 March. Sheryl Bonaventure died on 29 March, Michelle Korfmann on 1 April. Beth Dodge was the last victim, on 12 April. On 13 April Wilder was shot dead in a shoot-out with New Hampshire state troopers as he tried to cross the border into Canada. His death was officially listed as 'suicide', but the psychological causes which led an attractive millionaire to become a sex killer remain unknown.

What have we learned from these brief biographies of America's top-twenty sex killers? The list itself is by no means exhaustive, but it is representative, and what does emerge is that the sexual serial killer is extremely dangerous – the US Justice Department estimates that serial killers claim five thousand victims in America every year.

These more than twenty soiled and stained characters do not in fact represent the USA of films and books – the 'land of the free'. They are not the American Dream, but the American Nightmare.

Ted Bundy: All-American Serial Killer (see page 208)

Chapter Six

CUMMINS – HEATH – CHRISTIE

Gordon Frederick Cummins was a young airman who became known as the 'war-time Ripper' because he murdered four women in four days in 1942. At first sight it would seem difficult to find any occult motivation for these sex killings, and yet Cummins killed with such a compulsive – and even careless – greed that his crimes defy rational explanation.

Detective Chief Inspector Greeno of Scotland Yard's famed Murder Squad was faced with a frenzied killer on the loose in London in the middle of the black-out. It was not until the discovery of the body of the third victim, however, that he realized that he was hunting a serial killer. Margaret Frances Lowe, forty-three, was a working prostitute who lived in a cheap lodging-house in Gosfield Street in the West End. She had not been seen for a few days, but in the turmoil of a war, the movements of one individual were of little concern. On Saturday 14 February 1942, her fourteen-year-old daughter came to visit her and made a grim discovery. Her mother lay dead, having been strangled with a silk stocking. The naked body had been mutilated with a razor blade. Greeno later described his first sight of the corpse 'as like seeing a crudely butchered carcass'.

As the detective studied the body he became aware of the similarities between this victim and two others discovered that week in London's West End. The other two victims had also been strangled and then savagely mutilated – one had been slashed open with a tin-opener.

The pathologist who studied the mutilated body of Margaret Lowe was Sir Bernard Spilsbury. He was able to confirm the similarities with two previous killings, and established the time of death as being on the Wednesday, 11 February.

The first murder had been that of Evelyn Margaret Hamilton, a forty-year-old school-mistress found dead in an air-raid shelter in Montague Place, Marylebone, on 9 February. Her handbag containing £80 was missing. On 10 February came the discovery of another body, that of Mrs Evelyn Oakley (known as Nita Ward), a 35-year-old prostitute. She was found in her Wardour Street flat, her throat cut and her stomach opened with a tin-opener. Police recovered fingerprints from the tin-opener and a mirror.

Now Chief Inspector Greeno stood gazing down at the third victim, and even as he studied the scene of the crime a messenger arrived with news of yet another murder. The woman lay dead in a bedroom not far away from where Greeno now stood. Doris Jouannet lay in her two-roomed flat in Sussex Gardens, close to Paddington Station. She was thirty-two, her husband over seventy, and she was known to pick up soldiers in Leicester Square pubs. She had last been seen alive at ten o' clock the previous evening. On the morning of Saturday 14 February, her elderly husband had returned home from his stint as night manager of the Paddington Hotel to find the milk had not been taken in. He also found his wife murdered.

The body was still warm when Greeno arrived on the scene. It bore the usual sickening mutilations found on the three previous victims, and had been hacked so savagely that portions of flesh were severed. Sir Bernard Spilsbury examined the wounds with his usual care, and announced that the killer was probably left-handed.

Greeno was placed in charge of all the murders, once it was realized that they were all the work of one psychopath who was expressing his hatred and lust in such graphic fashion. The 'Murder Incident Room' was established at Tottenham Court Road police station, and detectives were instructed to go out and talk to prostitutes and find out whether any of them had been pestered by a sadist or knew of one. Greeno realized only too well that the opportunist sex killer who selects his victims at random is the most difficult killer of them all to catch. Only a tip-off could help, or perhaps a mistake by the killer in the course of yet another murder.

That mistake came shortly after the discovery of Mrs Jouannet's body. A report was received of an attack on a Mrs Heywood outside a pub near Piccadilly – the Captain's Cabin. A young airman had put his arm around her and forced kisses upon her. When she resisted he tried to strangle her. A deliveryman saved her; he heard the sounds of a scuffle and investigated, disturbing the would-be killer. The airman ran off into the darkness, but he left behind a vital clue: his gas-mask lay on the ground, with his service number stencilled on the inside of the case.

Even while police were reacting to this news they learned that the killer had not fled entirely, but had immediately picked up another woman and had taken her by taxi to her flat in Southwark Street, Paddington. Once inside he attempted to strangle Mrs Mulchay, known as Kathleen King, but she fought back so furiously that he ran off, leaving behind his Service belt. She remembered that he wore 'flashes' on his tunic, indicating that he was an officer cadet.

Some twelve hours after the attack on Mrs Mulchay he was traced through his serial number as being Gordon Frederick Cummins, a student-pilot aged twenty-eight and married. When confronted by detectives he claimed he was innocent of any attack, having been in bed in his barracks all night. As for the gas-mask, it certainly was his, but he said it was possible that he had accidentally picked up the wrong one in a pub, and some other fellow had walked off with his. He signed a statement to this effect with his left hand. Although he fitted the description given by both women who had been attacked, there was still no real evidence against him, and the log-book at his quarters showed that he had been in his billet all night – an NCO recorded all arrivals and departures.

However, his alibi was soon broken – a fellow-airman had seen him leaving the billet in St John's Wood by the fire-escape – his fingerprints matched those found at the scene of the murder of Nita Ward, and in his possession were found items stolen from the home of Mrs Jouannet.

Cummins had a long record of being a 'Billy Liar' character. Although well-educated and coming from a good family, he spoke with a fake Oxford accent and claimed to have the right to use the title 'Honourable' before his name because he was the bastard son of an aristocrat. He had been dismissed from several jobs for dishonesty.

He had a short trial at the Old Bailey and was duly hanged at Wandsworth Prison on 25 June 1942 during an air raid. Sir Bernard Spilsbury carried out the post-mortem on Cummins just as he had on his victims. . . .

Neville George Clevely Heath was far more a 'Walter Mitty' type than Cummins, and since Christie shared this trait, it is worth considering whether this is a common characteristic of sex-killers: the desire to adopt masks, to pretend. . . To adopt another persona because they don't like the 'me' they see in the mirror.

The intrinsic interest of the case of Heath is that it was the first modern post-war murder trial which put the century-old M'Naghten rules under examination; in short, psychiatry itself was as much on trial as was Heath. The decisions in the case were bench-mark rulings which were to be quoted in other similar cases. At the trial of the Yorkshire Ripper, Peter Sutcliffe, the prosecution posed the question: 'Is he mad or is he bad?' But that question had first been asked at the trial of Heath in September 1946.

Born in Guildford, Surrey, in 1917, Heath was a handsome man, tall with fair hair, blue eyes and a firm jaw. Women were attracted to him, and he used that attraction for all it was worth. His parents had made sure he had a good education. But Heath was a vain man: his crimes were a demand for *more life*. He felt that a man like him should not be expected to live at an ordinary, mundane level. He longed for the bright lights, the night clubs and expensive motor-cars, although he was not prepared to work for these things. He felt that homage was due to him by right. Whenever television or cinema wants a bounder or a cad in a drama they use Heath as the prototype, building the character on him.

When he left school it was to work as a packer in a London warehouse for £1 a week. He soon rebelled against this drudgery and won a short-service commission in the RAF. The glamour of the uniform of the fighter-pilot fell on him like a senator's cloak, but Heath was an inveterate liar, always 'shooting a line', and he was court martialled for fraud and cashiered aged twenty. Two months after his ignominious discharge from the RAF he was put on probation for petty fraud. He was living on his wits, mostly off women, and often posed as Lord Dudley, or some other nobleman.

In 1938 he was sent to Borstal for robbery. Released in 1939, he joined the RASC as a private. Commissioned the following March, he was sent to the Middle East. Fifteen months later he was again court martialled for fraud and dismissed the Service. However, instead of returning to England in disgrace he went to Durban as 'Captain Selway, M.C.' Later he changed his name to Armstrong and joined the South African Air Force.

He rose to the rank of captain and married in 1942. In 1944 he was seconded to the RAF. At the end of the war he returned to South Africa, only to be divorced by his wife. In 1946 he was court martialled and dismissed from the SAAF for fraud and falsely wearing decorations to which he was not entitled. Heath was the type of man who would award himself the Victoria Cross without a second thought. He was also the prototype sadist.

In June 1946 Heath, now back in Britain, met Mrs Margery Aimée Brownell Gardner, thirty-two, at the Panama Club in South Kensington. She was a bohemian type who lived in Chelsea and dabbled in the arts and earned some money as a film-extra. Heath had booked Room 4 at the Pembridge Court Hotel in Notting Hill the week previously, signing the register 'Colonel Heath'. He had previously stayed at the same hotel under the name of 'Armstrong', the pseudonym he had used in South Africa. He was familiar with the routine of the nineteen-bedroom hotel, and knew there was no night porter. He had a key to let himself into the hotel, and another for his room.

Heath took Margery Gardner back by taxi to his hotel room. It had twin beds. There can be no doubt that Mrs Gardner expected some kind of sexual activity to take place, and activity of a 'kinky' nature. She was a masochist, and enjoyed bondage and flagellation. In this context it can be argued that she invited her own death; that she provoked in Heath some dormant sadistic streak, and thus belonged to that sub-section of criminology known as 'Victimology'. That is to say, she was a victim going around looking for someone to kill her.

At 2 p.m. the next day, 21 June 1946, a chambermaid tried to gain entry to the room so that she could make the beds. When she received no reply to her knocking she got the assistant manageress to let her into the room with her pass-key. The room was in darkness, the heavy curtains still pulled across. Mrs Alice Wyatt pulled back the curtains, and as light flooded the room it illuminated a scene of horror. On one of the beds lay a naked woman, obviously very dead. There was blood, and there were obvious mutilations. Mrs Wyatt ran downstairs and phoned the police.

A police sergeant from Notting Hill police station arrived on the scene at 2.35 p.m., having walked to the hotel. Violent death was a familiar thing and no cause for hurry just a year after a war which had claimed so many lives. Sergeant Fred Averill examined the body in Room 4 with care, professional detachment overcoming his initial revulsion. The dead woman lay on her back, her right arm beneath her. Her ankles were bound tightly together with a handkerchief. Her face and chin were badly bruised, and her body had been savagely whipped. Blood had oozed from the vagina.

Professor Keith Simpson was the pathologist called to the scene, and he made a more detailed examination of the body. He found a total of seventeen lash marks – two of them on her face – which had left a distinctive diamond-patterned weave from a riding whip. 'Find the whip and you've found your killer,' he told waiting detectives. He also deduced that the woman's hands had been bound from marks on the wrist, although the ligature was missing. Presumably she had been gagged – the occupants of the bedrooms on either side of Room 4 had slept soundly and undisturbed by any screams – but the gag was also missing.

She had to have been gagged: her breasts had been bitten, the nipples nearly bitten off. Her vagina had been badly torn by an instrument being inserted and then rotated – probably by a poker. The injuries had been inflicted before death, and from the blood on both beds it appeared that she had been whipped on one, before being moved to the other. One curious fact was that her face had been washed by the killer – traces of dried blood in the nostrils and the lashes of the left eye proved that. Cause of death was from asphyxia, either from the gag or a pillow, and she had died between 12.15 a.m. and 1.30 a.m. It was quite apparent to Professor Simpson that this was a case where perverse pleasures had gone too far, and they were seeking a sadist who at this point might be guilty of manslaughter only.

Since Heath had left his name and fingerprints at the Pembridge Court Hotel, it was not too difficult for Detective Superintendent Thomas Barratt (who was placed in charge of the murder inquiry) to deduce the identity of the likely killer, and he lost no time in issuing a press statement to the effect that he wished to interview Heath in connection with the case. Meanwhile a taxi-driver, Harold Harter, had been traced who remembered picking up Heath and Mrs Gardner at 12.15 a.m. on Friday 21 June, and dropping them off at the hotel. The fare came to 1s 9d. Shown a pile of photographs of different men, he had no hesitation in picking out that of Heath. A nation-wide hunt for the fugitive was instigated.

A check on Heath's background was revealing. In May of that same year he had taken Mrs Gardner to the Pembridge Court Hotel, and to the same Room 4, where a flogging session had been halted by the intervention of the hotel detective. A few weeks earlier a similar episode had taken place at a hotel in the Strand, but the rescued woman, naked and bound, was married and refused to press charges. A week prior to the murder Heath had taken a young woman, Yvonne Symonds, nineteen, to Room 4, having persuaded her to sleep with him by the promise of marriage. He had signed the register 'Lt Col and Mrs NGC Heath'. No harm had come to the girl. While being sought by the police Heath frequently phoned her at her parents' home in Worthing.

While on the run, with typical effrontery, Heath sent Superintendent Barratt a letter in which he admitted having booked Room 4 at the hotel, but claimed he had loaned the key of the room to Mrs Gardner so that she could entertain a friend. The letter went on:

> She met an acquaintance with whom she was obliged to sleep. . . I returned. . . and found her in the condition of which you are aware. I realised I was in an invidious position. . . and left. I have the instrument with which Mrs Gardner was beaten and am forwarding this to you today. You will find my fingerprints on it, but you should find others as well.

It was a remarkably shrewd ploy, although of course he never did send the whip.

At this point police knew they were seeking a sadistic killer who might strike again. They were to be severely criticized for not allowing Heath's photograph to be published, and thus saving further life, but they justified the press black-out by saying that because identification by witnesses was vital in the case against Heath the publication of his photograph might prejudice any criminal prosecution. In the event, Heath did kill again.

Heath had ended his letter to Superintendent Barratt by describing Mrs Gardner's alleged male companion on the murder night, and told the detective, 'The personal column of the *Daily Telegraph* will find me, but at the moment I have assumed another name.' The letter was dated 22 June, the day after the murder, and had been posted in Worthing.

The morning after the murder Heath had gone by train to visit his 'fiancée' in Worthing. They had lunch together and he booked himself into a hotel. The following morning he told Miss Symonds that he had special knowledge of a murder mentioned in the morning papers, and said he would tell her about it later. That evening, during dinner at a restaurant, Miss Symonds reminded him of his promise. He told her an extraordinary story, one which illustrates how coolly he could think under pressure. He said the murder had taken place in his room at the Pembridge Court Hotel but he had lent the victim his keys since she had a man she wanted to entertain. Heath then told of being taken to see the body by Superintendent Barratt – 'it was a very gruesome sight' – and that the detective had said the victim had been suffocated, and had had a poker shoved up her. Shaking his head sadly, Heath commented that a man capable of such an act must be 'a sexual maniac'.

When the Sunday papers came out they were full of news of the murder, and said police were anxious to interview Neville George Clevely Heath. Distressed by this, Miss Symonds phoned Heath at his hotel seeking an explanation. He made soothing noises, saying there was some mistake, and he was going back to London to straighten matters out with the police. He promised to phone her that night. But she never heard from him or saw him again until his trial.

That same Sunday, 23 June, Heath travelled to Bournemouth, booking into the Tollard Royal Hotel as Group Captain Rupert Brooke. There Heath was to stay for the next thirteen days, during which time another young woman was to meet her death in the most revolting manner.

In this seaside resort Heath met and wooed Doreen Marshall, twenty-one, taking her to dinner at his hotel. She was staying at the Norfolk Hotel. When she vanished on the night of Wednesday 3 July the manager of her hotel waited a couple of days before he made inquiries about her whereabouts. Discovering that she had been taken by taxi to the Tollard Royal Hotel on the night she disappeared, he telephoned the manager there, asking him if he had seen anything of his missing guest. The manager of the Tollard recalled that Captain Brooke had enter-tained a young girl for dinner that night. He approached the ex-pilot and asked him if his dinner companion might have been the missing girl. Heath laughed at the idea. 'Good heavens, no. I have known that young lady for a long while.'

A porter at the hotel remembered the couple leaving together on foot, Heath saying he would be back in half an hour. He next saw Heath asleep in his room at 4 a.m. Puzzled, he asked him how he had got back into the locked hotel. Heath said he had climbed in a window by using a ladder as a joke. That same day Heath was observed to be wearing a scarf around his neck, only partially obscuring some deep scratches. He was also unusually affluent, producing crisp white fivers to pay for his drinks, when before he had been broke and owed the hotel quite a large bill. In fact, that morning Heath had pawned Doreen Marshall's ring and watch. . . .

Soon after being asked about the missing girl, and hoping to forestall any suspicion, with typical bravado Heath telephoned Bournemouth Police and said he might be able to help them in their search for the missing girl. They offered to send an officer to the hotel with a photograph of the girl, but Heath insisted on visiting the police station. He arrived at 5.30 p.m., Friday 5 July.

He was seen by Detective Constable George Souter, and after looking at a photograph of the missing girl Heath confirmed that he had indeed met Miss Marshall on the night she disappeared, but he claimed she had left him to return to her own hotel quite alive and well. Heath – still using the name Brooke – was about to leave the police station when the father and sister of Doreen Marshall arrived. He greeted them effusively and chatted about the mystery of the girl's disappearance, saying she had probably gone off somewhere and would doubtless soon return. He mentioned an American in whom the girl had seemed interested.

Meanwhile Detective Constable Souter had made a call to Scotland Yard asking for a quick check on 'Brooke'; he was suspicious. . . The call was taken by Detective Inspector William Dawes, who immediately alerted Chief Inspector Reginald Spooner at his office in Hammersmith. Spooner phoned Bournemouth police station and asked Detective Constable Souter to note whether 'Brooke' had a slight nick in his nose. When told that he had, Spooner said urgently, 'Detain that man. I am coming to Bournemouth immediately.'

When Spooner walked into his cell at 1 p.m. the next morning and said, 'I believe you are Neville Heath' the prisoner replied quietly, 'Yes, I am.' Heath was put in a police car and driven to London, where he was detained at Notting Hill police station. Meanwhile Bournemouth Police searched his room at the Tollard Royal Hotel and made some interesting discoveries. In his sports-jacket was found a cloakroom ticket and the return half of a first-class ticket from Bournemouth to London — subsequently proved to have belonged to Doreen Marshall. Also found in his room was a bloodstained and knotted handkerchief and a single pearl from a necklace.

Now Bournemouth Police launched a large-scale hunt for the missing girl, with vast acres being searched by teams of police officers. Back in London on 8 July, Heath appeared at West London Magistrate's Court to be formally charged with the murder of Mrs Gardner and was remanded in custody for a week. Four hours later in Bournemouth a woman out walking her dog came across the body of Doreen Marshall lying in bushes near the cliffs in Branksome Dene Chine, just one and a half miles from the Tollard Hotel. The woman, a Miss Evans, had been attracted to the spot by a swarm of flies.

At 8.40 p.m. on Monday 8 July, police officers who had been called to the scene cautiously examined the body. Doreen Marshall lay naked and dead, obviously having put up a desperate struggle for her life. Her pearl necklace had been broken, and beads from it lay scattered all round. One stocking was found twenty-one feet away, and a powder-compact over seventy yards distant, with a stocking high up in some bushes. Forensic examination revealed that the girl had been beaten several times on the back of the head with a blunt instrument, and then the killer had knelt on her with such force that a rib had fractured, piercing the lung. Her wrists had been bound with the handkerchief found in Heath's hotel room, and she had been gagged. The inside of both hands bore defensive wounds, indicating that she had still been alive and trying to fight off the knife when it was used to perform the terrible mutilation on her body.

Two deep knife cuts across the throat were the immediate cause of death, but a nipple had been bitten off, and the knife had been used to cut a large Y-shaped gash from each nipple leading down to the groin. A rough instrument, possibly a branch, had been used to tear open her vagina and anus, perforating the tissues. The knife was never found, but it was deduced that Heath must have stripped naked to perform his ritual savagery, since no blood was found on his clothing. He must have washed off the blood in the sea – presumably getting rid of the knife at the same time – before dressing.

Heath displayed an astonishing indifference to his fate. While on the run, wanted for the sex-killing of one woman, he had killed another. He had then walked voluntarily into a police station. These might have seemed the actions of a madman, but his other actions belied this. After murdering Doreen Marshall he had stolen a few pounds from her handbag, and removed her jewellery. The following day he pawned her ring for £5, and just half an hour before he walked into the police station he sold her watch for £3.

There was never any doubt about Heath's guilt, only about his sanity. The cloakroom ticket was redeemed by the police and found to be a suitcase in which lay the riding whip used to mutilate his first victim. The diamond-weave pattern of the whip matched exactly the weals on the body. At identity parades Heath was picked out by the receptionist at the Panama Club, by the taxi-driver who had driven him and Mrs Gardner to the Pembridge Court Hotel, by the pawnbroker with whom he had pledged Doreen Marshall's ring and the jeweller to whom he had sold her watch. That single pearl found in Heath's hotel room matched exactly the twenty-seven pearls found near the body, and the knotted handkerchief contained human hairs which were matched forensically to those from the scalp of Doreen Marshall. Never has a case been so well proved scientifically against a killer.

Heath was charged with both murders and was committed for trial at the Old Bailey. A large crowd, many of them young women, queued for fifteen hours to get seats to watch the trial of the handsome young killer. This phenomenon of 'murder groupies' was later to be seen in the trial of Ted Bundy. Heath did not disappoint them. Wearing a light grey suit, well-groomed, his fair hair pomaded, his blue eyes twinkling, he never lost his composure throughout the trial, while his youthful fresh complexion gave him the appearance of a matinee idol.

The trial began on Tuesday 24 September 1946 and ended at 5.45 p.m. on the Thursday. Mr Justice Morris presided, with Mr Anthony Hawke prosecuting, and Mr J.D. Caswell KC defending. Heath replied with a firm 'Not guilty' when the murder charges were put to him.

In his opening speech (which lasted thirty-eight minutes) Mr Hawke outlined to the jury of ten men and two women the discovery of the body of Margery Gardner and the flight of Heath to Worthing. While at Worthing Heath had met a young woman, telling her he was 'closely connected' with the murder at the hotel in Notting Hill. Over dinner he told her details about the murder. Mr Hawke said, 'The curious thing is that his conversation contained observations which were uncannily near the truth. . . which it is hard to see how he could possibly have known unless he had been there at the time.' Heath had told the girl that the killer must have been a 'sexual maniac' and that he had seen the body and that "she had a poker sticking up her".

Anticipating a defence of insanity, Mr Hawke said that although the acts of murder were of such a nature that they indicated a killer 'sexually perverted to the stage almost of monstrosity', that in itself did not excuse the acts. He said that the letter written by Heath to Superintendent Barratt the day after the murder proved that Heath knew he had done something wrong and punishable by law, and was attempting to cover his tracks and evade justice.

Although Heath was being tried solely for the murder of Mrs Gardner, in an attempt to show his diseased mentality the defence admitted into evidence his previous convictions and the details of the murder of Doreen Marshall. Mr Caswell said, 'Those of us acting on his behalf have come to the conclusion that it is only right the jury should know all the facts both of this case and the subsequent case, and I have done my utmost to bring before you not only this man's previous life but the details of the second crime.'

Heath's statement to the police was read out in which he denied murder, and said that Miss Marshall had gone off with an American named 'Pat' on the night of her murder. Describing it as an 'astonishing case', Mr Caswell went on, 'Why have the public taken such an interest in this case? Is it because two terrible and apparently motiveless crimes have been committed by the same man within the short space of a fortnight – not a man who is unintelligent but a man who has seen a good deal of the world, a man who has three times been commissioned?'

Mr Caswell said that the second murder, committed when Heath knew that the police were hunting him throughout Britain, was proof of a 'progressive mania'. He said he would not be calling Heath into the witness box to give evidence, telling the jury frankly, 'You probably would not believe a word he said if he was called.'

The case hinged on the testimony of psychiatric experts. For the prosecution, Dr Grierson, Senior Medical Officer at Brixton Prison, and Dr Young from Wormwood Scrubs – who had observed Heath over a period of weeks – testified that he was sane and realized the enormity of his sadistic acts.

For the defence, Dr Hubert (who had practised at Broadmoor) said that from his examination of Heath he was of the opinion that Heath did not realize that his behaviour was wrong or criminal. He felt justified in inflicting cruelty because that was the only way in which he could obtain sexual satisfaction. Mr Hawke asked him, 'Is that your answer, Dr Hubert? That in as much as he wished to satisfy a perverted lust he thought it was right to satisfy it?' – 'Yes' – 'And therefore he does not know that what he was doing was wrong? Is that accurate?' – 'Yes.'

Dr Hubert said that Heath was 'morally insane', had a

'deficient moral sense' and was a sadist of the worst type. He insisted that Heath was certifiably insane. Mr Hawke pressed him: 'Are you saying that a person who does a thing which he wants to do because it suits him at the moment to do it, if that is a crime, is entitled to be called insane and therefore free from responsibility?' – 'Yes, if the crime and the circumstances are so abnormal that they are unthinkable to a normal person.' 'Does that mean that every sexual pervert, in order to indulge his perversion, is entitled to say he is free of any responsibility for the consequences?' – 'No.'

Dr Hubert talked of a history of 'moral degeneracy'; Mr Hawke insisted that it was simply 'a history of dishonesty when it suited him'. It was a classic confrontation between the legal definition of insanity enshrined in the M'Naghten Rules, and the medical definition which has made considerable advances in the century or more since the M'Naghten Rules were first introduced. The confrontation has never been settled, and no wise psychiatrist would ever testify at a criminal trial. Ideally, such expert witnesses should be used after conviction in an advisory capacity in determining sentence. Dr Hubert was a very experienced criminal psychiatrist made to look a fool by a very experienced criminal lawyer. At the time of testifying at the trial he was a drug-addict and mentally sick. Within a year he had killed himself with an overdose.

In his closing speech to the jury Mr Caswell said he was not asking them for sympathy, purely a review of the evidence as 'men and women of the world'. He suggested that a war-time accident, when Heath had his plane shot down under him, might have contributed to the man's sadism. He said that the murders showed no premeditation, that Heath showed no remorse or fear, or made any serious attempt to hide. Plainly, he had to be mad.

For the prosecution, Mr Hawke said the defence of insanity was absurd and the term 'moral insanity' had no legal validity. Heath was plainly guilty, and his actions had proved that he recognized his guilt. He had tried to escape from the police by hiding under an assumed name. Mr Hawke went on, 'A wise man once was asked: "Where would be the best place to hid a pebble?" And he had answered, "On the beach." What better could a person do than to mingle with seaside crowds and behave as a perfectly ordinary person at a hotel?'

Mr Justice Morris, summing-up to the jury, stressed that the law of insanity 'is not to become a refuge of those who cannot challenge a charge when it is brought against them'. He added, 'A perverted impulse cannot be excused on the grounds of insanity.' The judge referred to Heath's glib lies, his concealment of Doreen Marshall's body, his denial of his true identity, as being proof of a mind working at full capacity to escape punishment for his crimes.

The jury retired for just one hour, returning with a verdict of guilty. Asked if he had anything to say, Heath replied, 'Nothing.' He showed no emotion as the death sentence was passed upon him. He did not lodge an appeal, show any remorse or make a confession. He wrote to his parents, 'My only regret at leaving the world is that I have been damned unworthy of you both.'

Neville Heath was hanged at Pentonville Prison by Albert Pierrepoint on 16 October 1946. He remained calm and debonair to the end, and just before he went to the scaffold he was asked if he wanted a whisky. He replied in the affirmative, adding, 'I think I'll make it a double.'

There never was any explanation for Heath's mental condition since he refused to discuss sexual matters with the doctors, although there is evidence that he indecently assaulted a girl in his youth. It appears to be a case where the sadistic impulse lay dormant until the 'right' victim came along, one who could provoke the ultimate act of murder. How else can one explain the late development of the violent impulse, and the fact that he behaved decently with Miss Symonds?

Heath remains an enigma; the nice young man with the predatory instincts of the tiger. He has replaced the age-old stereotype of the sex killer as the slack-jawed drooling monster. We now know, from painful experience, that sex killers tend to be young, intelligent and rather charming. . .

John Reginald Halliday Christie was the most physically unappetizing of this trio of sex killers. Heath and Cummins were good-looking men who were fun to be with, and had pleasant social graces; it was a shame about their penchant for murder. . . Christie was a thin man, bald, physically weak and a thoroughly neurotic and unpleasant character.

Born on 8 April 1898, he was brought up in Halifax, West Yorkshire, one of a family of seven children. Even as a child he displayed his incipient hypochondria, missing school on many occasions because of imaginary illnesses. Like Haigh – brought up a few miles away in Wakefield – Christie also sang in a choir. At school he was known as a cissy; later on, because of his lack of sexual prowess, he was called 'Reggie No-Dick'. There is no cruelty quite so pointed as that of children.

After leaving school he got a job with West Yorkshire Police in Halifax but was soon sacked for pilfering, and was sacked by his subsequent employers at a carpet mill for petty theft. Many murderers display early signs of thievery, reminding one of De Quincey's dictum: 'If once a man indulges himself in murder, very soon he comes to think little of robbing; and from robbing he comes next to drinking and sabbath-breaking, and from that to incivility and procrastination.'

Later Christie became a projectionist at the Gem Cinema in Halifax. Perhaps the flickering fantasies he watched night after night stimulated his murderous impulse, although he was later to say that the most important event in his childhood was viewing a dead body – that of his grandfather – when he was eight. This may be of prime importance, given the necrophiliac aspect to the case.

He was called up for service in the First World War and was injured in France by an exploding mustard-gas shell, was gassed twice and blinded for some months. After that he spoke in a low, apologetic tone and wore glasses for his short-sightedness. He was married in May 1920, the marriage fortunately being childless. He had a succession of jobs; variously, cinema operator, clerk and postman. In April 1921 he was sentenced to three months imprisonment for stealing postal orders. In 1923 he was bound over for obtaining money by false pretences, and in that same year he went to London, leaving his wife behind in Sheffield. Free from marital encumbrance, he drifted from job to job, and in September 1924 was given nine months hard labour for theft at Uxbridge.

After this he seems to have settled down, holding a clerical job for five years. But in May 1929 his basically criminal character surfaced again, when he received six months hard labour for attacking a woman with a cricket bat. In 1933 he again went to prison for stealing a car.

His abandoned wife visited him in prison, and on his release went to live with him in London, the ten years separation apparently forgiven. It was in 1938 that the couple rented the three-roomed ground-floor flat at 10 Rillington Place, an address which was to become notorious in criminal history. Within the next few years seven women were to be murdered in that house. . .

Christie became a War Reserve policeman in 1939 and used his authority as a 'special' during those wartime years to become officious and petty-minded. Perhaps the cloak of authority gave him power-feelings; certainly it led to his first murder. He was based at Harrow Road Police Station, and called at a snack-bar to inquire about a man wanted for theft. There he met Ruth Fuerst, twenty-one, a tall Austrian girl who had come to England in 1939 as a student-nurse. She was last seen alive on 24 August 1943 at her digs in Notting Hill, and since Christie was vague about the date of her murder – or even if she was his first victim – she must be presumed to have been killed at some time in late 1943.

The 45-year-old Christie, in his dark blue uniform and peaked cap, invited Miss Fuerst back to 10 Rillington Place for a cup of tea, his wife being away visiting relatives in Sheffield. Her remains, recovered some ten years later, gave no indication as to the cause of death. We have Christie's own statement about it to police.

> She was very tall, almost as tall as me and I was 5ft 9ins. . . She undressed and wanted me to have intercourse with her. I got a telegram while she was there, saying that my wife was on her way home. . . I got on the bed and had intercourse with her. While I was having intercourse with her I strangled her with a piece of rope. I remember urine and excreta coming away from her.
>
> She was completely naked. . . She had a leopard skin coat and I wrapped this around her. . . I put her under the floorboards. I had to do that because of my wife coming back. . . next day my wife went out. While she was out I picked the body up from under the floorboards and dug a hole in the garden, and in the evening, when it was dark, I put the body down the hole and covered it up quickly with earth.

Christie was sacked as a War Reserve constable because a soldier complained abut his association with his wife. Christie then got a job at Ultra Radio at Acton, and there met small, plump Miss Muriel Eady, thirty-two. She and her boy-friend used to visit the Christies at Rillington Place, but one day she arrived alone. She complained of catarrh, and Christie said he could help her because of his 'medical knowledge' – which was elementary first-aid training. Inside a large square glass jar he had a solution of Friar's Balsam, with two rubber tubes coming from holes in the lid. Muriel Eady was persuaded to inhale the fumes from one tube. What she didn't realise was that the other tube was connected to the gas supply. Once his victim was unconscious Christie strangled her with a stocking and had intercourse with her corpse. In his confession Christie said, 'I gazed down at her body and felt a quiet, peaceful thrill. I had no regrets . . .' She too was buried in the garden. The date of her death was shortly after 7 October 1944, when she was last seen alive.

It is apparent by this stage that Christie had developed a method of gassing women so he could indulge his necrophiliac sexual rites, possibly masturbating over the corpses of his victims – as did another and later necrophiliac, Dennis Nilsen. There may have been women who survived his gassing experiments, or participated willingly, or victims we do not know about, because after killing two women in 1943 and 1944 he did not kill again until five years later, when he killed Beryl Evans and her daughter.

One of the mysteries of the case, and one which complicates the narrative, is the matter of Timothy Evans. In August 1949 Timothy Evans and his young wife Beryl, who lived above the Christies, had a violent quarrel. Christie was later to claim that he found Mrs Evans lying in front of a gas fire, having attempted suicide, and that he revived her. The following day, he said, she again wanted to kill herself, begged him to help her, and offered him sexual intercourse in return. He had intercourse with her, strangling her with a stocking as he did so.

It was suggested that Christie offered to perform an abortion on Mrs Evans, who was pregnant at the time of her death, and killed her while she was inhaling his special gas mixture to render her unconscious. Evans mentioned the question of abortion to the police in his confession. He said his wife had been trying to abort herself with a syringe and tablets. 'Reg Christie' had approached him and offered to perform a safe abortion, claiming to have studied to be a doctor before the war and showing Evans various medical books. His statement went on: 'On the Monday evening [7 November]. . . my wife said that Mr Christie had made arrangements for the first thing Tuesday morning. I didn't argue with her.' In another statement he said, 'When I came home in the evening [Tuesday] he was waiting for me at the bottom of the stairs. He said: "It's bad news. It didn't work." Christie claimed her stomach had been 'septic poisoned'. Evans described how he found his wife lying dead on the bed. 'I could see she was dead and she was bleeding from the mouth and nose and lower part.' He said he and Christie had carried the body downstairs, Christie saying he would get rid of it later. Christie emphasized that Evans would be suspected of her murder, while he himself, as a former policeman, would be free of any suspicion. As for the baby, Geraldine, Christie said he had arranged for a couple to adopt her. The facts are that the bodies of Mrs Evans and her daughter were both found in the wash-house.

On Monday 14 November 1949, Evans went on the run, having sold his furniture for £40. But after a week or so he walked into a police station in Wales, and made a statement confessing to the murder of his wife. He said he had put her body down a drain – even though it was found in the wash-house. He was quite ignorant of the fact that his daughter was dead at this point. He did at one point accuse Christie of being the real murderer, but when told that the body of his daughter had also been found he withdrew the accusation. He was of low men-tality, which possibly explains why he did not immediately inform on Christie when he found his wife strangled. Possibly he did murder his child – he was alleged to have confided to a prison warder that he killed her because 'her crying got on my nerves'.

Evans was tried for the murder of his daughter at the Old Bailey in January 1950. One of the chief prosecution witnesses against him was Christie. Evans's counsel attacked his testimony, bringing out his past convictions and suggesting that Christie was the real murderer, and that having killed Mrs Evans in a failed abortion attempt he had to kill the child too.

When Evans went into the witness-box to claim that Christie had killed his wife in the process of aborting her,

and had helped him carry the body downstairs, prosecuting counsel asked him, 'Can you suggest why Mr
Christie should have strangled your wife?' Evans replied
lamely, 'Well, he was at home all day. . . .'

For his part, Christie, the virtuous ex-policeman,
replied from the witness box that he knew nothing of any
abortion, and said that at the time of the murder 'I was in
bed a lot of the time with the illness I had, which is
enteritis and fibrositis in my back.' His doctor confirmed
this, and said he doubted if Christie could have carried a
body downstairs: 'At the time I was seeing him he could
hardly get off the chair sometimes; I had to help him up.'
On Friday 13 January Evans was found guilty and
sentenced to death. Christie was in court and burst into
tears. Evans was hanged on 9 March.

This case rumbled on over the years as a blatant
example of injustice, with Ludovic Kennedy writing a fine
book on the case which challenged the verdict with one
compelling question to the readers: did they believe 'That
Evans and Christie, quite unknown to one another, were
both strangling females in the same house in the same sort
of way. . . ?' After Christie's eventual detection as a
strangler of females himself, there was a public outcry for a
review of the case against the long-dead Evans. This was
carried out by Mr Scott Henderson, and in his Report,
published just before Christie was executed, he declared
that there had been no miscarriage of justice in the Evans
case.

This verdict could never be accepted, and due almost
solely to Ludovic Kennedy, the government of the day
were forced to order a judicial review of the case of Evans
in public, headed by Mr Justice Brabin. The hearing took
place during the winter of 1965-6, at the end of which
the judge came to the astonishing conclusion that 'it was
more probable than not' that Evans did kill his wife – but
not his daughter. Since Evans had been hanged for the
murder of his daughter, on 18 October 1966 the Queen
granted him a free pardon, and his remains were

removed from Pentonville Prison to be reburied in consecrated ground.

Christie made a full confession to the murder of Mrs Evans, in which he described in detail how he made a pretence of aborting her and gassed her with a length of rubber tubing. She struggled, and he hit her about the face, then whipped out what he called 'my strangling rope' and strangled her. He then had intercourse with her corpse. All of which makes Mr Justice Brabin's conclusion even more incomprehensible.

After this detour into the Evans case – essential to grasp fully the extent of Christie's hypocrisy and glib manner – we return to Christie back in 1950, having had his brief moment of glory as a witness in the Evans trial (he kept newspaper accounts of the trial in his wallet). Life went on as normal for Mr and Mrs Christie. Having helped hang a man for his own murders, Christie seems to have displayed no overt remorse, although he was now frequently visiting his doctor with a string of complaints which included insomnia, headaches, diarrhoea, flatulence, amnesia, back-ache and fibrositis. He was now a clerk with British Road Services. After the war he had secured a clerical position with the Post Office Savings Bank, but when his past convictions came out he was sacked and forced to seek another job. But even that shows his effrontery. He had a conviction for stealing postal orders, yet thought nothing of applying to the Post Office for a job.

By December 1952 Christie, now aged fifty-four, was in a state of decline both mentally and physically. Earlier that year he had been advised to go into a mental hospital for treatment for an anxiety neurosis, but he had refused treatment. On 6 December he gave up his job at British Road Services. The decline had become a terminal breakdown.

The house at 10 Rillington Place had been bought by a Jamaican in 1950, and the upper rooms had become occupied by blacks. Mr and Mrs Christie made several complaints about alleged noisy behaviour of their fellow-tenants to the Poor Man's Lawyer Centre, to no avail. Both husband and wife were now taking sleeping pills and phenobarbitone as a sedative to counter depression.

In December 1950 Christie killed again – this time his wife. Why he should have killed his wife of nineteen years remains a mystery. Certainly there was no sexual motive. He was to tell police, 'She was becoming very frightened from these blacks. . . and she got very depressed. On 14 December [Sunday] I was awaked at about 8.15. I think it was by my wife moving about in bed. I sat up and saw that she appeared to be convulsive, her face was blue and she was choking. . . I couldn't bear to see her, so I got a stocking and tied it round her neck to put her to sleep.' Mrs Christie ended up beneath the floorboards in the front room.

What is interesting about this episode is that Christie's behaviour after the death of his wife bore a remarkable similarity to that of Timothy Evans after the death of *his* wife. Both sold their wives' wedding rings, both sold the household furniture to *the same dealer*.

Christie sold his furniture on 6 January 1953, keeping only a mattress and blankets, a table and chairs and some crockery and cutlery. For ten weeks of bitter cold he lived in the back room with only his mongrel dog and cat for company. Every day he poured disinfectant down the drains and around to disguise the smell of his wife's decomposing remains. In fact, the atmospheric conditions in the house led to a process of dehydration and there was very little smell.

Sunk in apathy and despair, literally at the end of his tether, Christie had become divorced from reality and was experiencing what psychiatrists term 'disassociation'. That is, he was not really conscious of what he was doing, but viewed his own actions as if he was a spectator. Unemployed, with no wife to care for him and only £2.14s a week dole money to live on, Christie might well have committed suicide. Instead, with what was left of his dwindling reserves of sexual energy, he murdered three prostitutes in this period.

They were Kathleen Maloney, twenty-six; Rita Nelson, twenty-five, who was six months pregnant – both killed towards the end of January; and the last victim, Hectorina MacLennan, twenty-six, killed about 6 March. All were stuffed into an alcove which had formerly been used to store coal, and Christie had wall-papered over this to conceal it and make the wall appear continuous. MacLennan was naked save for a brassière, which appeared to be hooked on to a nail, holding her upright in a squatting position with her head bowed. The other two were partly clothed and wrapped in blankets. All three prostitutes had had VD, all had been strangled with a ligature, all three had a cloth between their legs, tied like a diaper. Mrs Christie too had been diapered. Intercourse had taken place with all three prostitutes at about the time of death.

It was Christie's last fling; in a sense he was living posthumously. On Friday 13 March he illegally sub-let his three rooms to a couple, taking three months rent in advance. He then took his dog to a vet to be destroyed, and walked out of 10 Rillington Place for the last time on 20 March, carrying his few possessions in a cheap suitcase. He spent that first night at a doss-house at King's Cross. He was drifting now, rootless. . .

The new tenants enjoyed an occupancy of just one day before the landlord visited and threw them out. The landlord then invited one of his tenants, a Mr Beresford Brown, who was living in Evans's old room, to use the kitchen in Christie's quarters. It was the unfortunate Mr Brown who, wanting to put up a bracket on the wall to hold a radio, discovered the hollow spot. Pulling back the wall-paper, he uncovered Christie's cache of bodies.

The police were quickly summoned, and senior detectives watched as Dr Camps, the Home Office pathologist, supervised the removal of the bodies, after they had been photographed *in situ*.

The house was now thoroughly searched, and later that night the body of Mrs Christie was discovered under the floorboards. Next the garden was dug up. Bones were uncovered which made up two complete female skeletons – a human femur was propping up the garden fence. These were the remains of Ruth Fuerst and Muriel Eady. In the yard the police found a tobacco tin containing four sets of pubic hair.

By the next day the newspapers had gone wild with bold headlines about the 'House of Horror'. A photograph of Christie was published in all the newspapers with the usual euphemism that police believed he could 'help them in their enquiries'. Despite an intensive police hunt nationwide, Christie eluded the police for almost a week, wandering around London in a daze. At 9.10 a.m. on Tuesday 31 March PC Tom Ledger was patrolling the embankment near Putney Bridge. He saw what he took to be a tramp leaning on the embankment wall, staring out across the river. The man was scruffy, unshaven and hungry-looking. Once he had removed his hat at the constable's request, the PC recognized him instantly by his bald dome as being Christie. The officer arrested him and took him to Putney police station. Standing by that embankment, Christie must have looked a forlorn figure. He was in a state of spiritual suspension; an inner moral collapse had left him devastated.

He was to make a series of statements, at both Putney and Notting Hill police stations. He admitted the 'mercy killing' of his wife, and later the murders of the three prostitutes. He did not admit to gassing or strangling them, or to having intercourse with them, although the forensic evidence was positive on all three points. This was a peculiar trait of Christie's, a kind of mealy-mouthed puritan streak. He did not like to talk about anything 'dirty', and thought masturbation was wicked. And so in all his statements he attempted to keep out all references to those things which he could not face. Every murder had been an accident, following a struggle. It had been the victim's fault. . .

Kathleen Maloney had forced her way into his house, demanding money and threatening to create a scene. Rita Nelson had Irish blood – she started *fighting*. MacLennan struggled. Ruth Fuerst tried to *force* him to leave his wife. Mrs Evans had *asked* him to help her kill herself.

In his interviews with the police he was vague and wandering, by turns apologetic and weeping. Of the murder of Maloney, he said he had known her previously. She had watched as Christie photographed another prostitute in the nude. On the night of her murder she had been very drunk. She asked Christie for money. He took her to Rillington Place and sat her in a deck chair. Above her head hung a length of rubber tubing sealed by a bulldog clamp. Christie loosened the clamp and she became drowsy. Christie said, 'There was a piece of rope. . . hanging from the chair. I don't remember what happened but I must have gone haywire. The next thing I remember she was lying still in the chair with the rope around her neck.' He told of removing her knickers and having intercourse with her, then placing a diaper between her legs. 'I left her there. . . after that I believe I had a cup of tea.' He was always drinking tea; a strong brew kept him refreshed during his murders.

Rita Nelson came next. She had come to London three months pregnant and had made an appointment to be admitted to a hospital for unmarried mothers. She never kept that appointment. It may have been that Christie persuaded her that he could give her an abortion and introduced her to his gassing device. He said she struggled – he had to strangle her. Then he had intercourse with her, diapered her, and put her in the alcove with Maloney. After which, presumably, he had a cup of tea. . .

MacLennan was looking for lodging with her boy-friend. Christie let them look around his rooms at Rillington Place and even allowed them to sleep overnight. Then he made sure of getting her alone in the house while her boy-friend was at the Labour Exchange. 'I took her into the kitchen and poured out a drink for her . . . when I undid the clasp to release the gas she spotted me. She became uneasy and got up to leave. But I was determined she should not escape, and I followed her into the hall. I seized hold of her neck and applied just sufficient pressure to make her limp. I took her into the kitchen and I decided that it was essential to use the gas again. I made love to her, then put her back in the chair. I killed her.' She went into the alcove with some difficulty: it was now full.

After being charged with the murder of his wife, Christie was remanded to Brixton Prison. On 15 April he was also charged with the murders of the three women in the alcove. By now his defence counsel had informed him that the only possible defence was one of insanity. He was interviewed in prison several times by a defence psychologist, Dr Hobson. At first he denied killing Mrs Evans. It was not until 27 April that he admitted killing her – but not the baby, Geraldine. He remarked to the Prison Chaplain: 'The more the merrier!' He had now confessed to the murders of seven women.

By now the case was attracting the same kind of feverish national interest as did the Moors Murders, and already sick jokes were circulating – the traditional British response to any tragedy or catastrophe, as if to counteract the horror. A typical joke was: 'Poor Christie: six women in the house and nobody to make him a cup of tea.'

On 18 May Mrs Evans and her baby were exhumed and their bodies examined. Three leading pathologists took part in the post mortem, and one of them, Dr Keith Simpson, tells us in his book *Forty Years of Murder* that although Christie claimed ownership of the infamous collection of pubic hairs with the words: 'The pubic hair in the tin found at 10 Rillington Place came from the three women in the alcove and from my wife' – in fact none of the clumps of hair matched any of the victims –

and he had examined them under a microscope. Mrs Evans had not been gassed, although Christie said he had used gas on her. Dr Simpson is of the opinion that Christie's confession to the murder of Mrs Evans was false, and made to bolster his defence of insanity. Evidence that points again at Evans as the killer of his wife.

On remand in prison Christie put on weight and took part in games. He was good at chess and was called 'Chris the chess champion' by other prisoners, to whom he boasted of his murders, confiding that his aim had been to commit twelve. Doctors who interviewed him in prison described him as being 'insignificant and unattractive, full of snivelling hypocrisy'. He often spoke of himself in the third person and described the murders as 'these regrettable happenings'. But although Christie probably did suffer some kind of amnesia regarding the details of the murders – his self-love could not let him admit to himself that he was a strangler, a necrophile and probably a child-killer – he was in control of himself. It is perhaps significant that he boasted to other prisoners, 'I could always get Evans to do whatever I wanted.' His IQ was found to register 128, compared to Evans's 68.

The trial of Christie for the murder of his wife began on Monday, 22 June 1953 in the No 1 Court at the Old Bailey, before Mr Justice Finnemore. The Attorney-General, Sir Lionel Heald, prosecuted, while Mr Derek Curtis-Bennett QC led for the defence.

Although Christie admitted the offence, the prosecution still had to present its evidence. Witnesses were called to testify to the effect that Mrs Christie had last been seen alive on 13 December 1952. Her body, the court heard, was found beneath the floorboards in the front room. Pathologists testified that death was due to strangulation – and so it went on. However, the Attorney-General, aware of public unease about the execution of Evans, now tried to show that Christie was lying when he said he had killed Mrs Evans.

On the second day of the trial Mr Curtis-Bennett rose for the defence. He brought to the attention of the jury details of all 7 murders to which Christie had confessed, even though he was only being tried for one. Mr Bennett said that he would not deny for a moment that Christie had killed Mrs Christie. Indeed, the jury would hear from Christie's own lips how he had killed a number of people. The defence was simply that Christie was mad, so mad that under the M'Naghten Rules he did not know what he was doing was wrong. 'Now', Mr Bennett concluded, 'this man at this moment will go into the witness box and tell his terrifying story. . . .'

Christie walked jerkily from the dock to the witness box, and once there stood staring blankly for half a minute. He appeared to be weeping. Led gently by his counsel, the meek-looking man with the bald head and spectacles told slowly and hesitantly of killing seven women. He was taken through the murders in detail, one by one. Asked whether he had committed any murders between 1944 and 1949, Christie replied, 'I don't know' – 'You mean you might have done?' – 'I might have done. I don't know whether I did or not.'

The judge asked him why, in the first statement to the police on 31 March, he had omitted to mention the murders of Fuerst, Eady and Mrs Evans. Referring to the murder of Mrs Evans, Christie replied, 'Well, the case I just dismissed from my mind and never gave it a second thought.' The judge reminded him that he had testified at the trial of Timothy Evans – had he forgotten that? 'Yes, sir, it had gone clean out of my mind.'

Dr Hobson was called for the defence. He said Christie suffered from hysteria, and it was highly probable that at the time of the crime he did not know that what he was doing was wrong. 'He has an abnormal memory. . . I believe these tricks of memory, or avoidance of getting down to disturbing topics, is to preserve his own self-respect, rather than to avoid incriminating himself.'

The prosecution called two doctors in rebuttal, Drs Matheson and Curran. Dr Matheson described Christie as 'a man of weak character. He is immature and certainly in his sex-life. . . I would call him a man with a hysterical personality. . . '

Dr Curran said Christie was 'an inadequate personality with hysterical features. . . a very extraordinary and abnormal man'. He said he did not believe Christie's alleged loss of memory was genuine. 'He has, like other criminals and murderers, a remarkable capacity for dismissing the unpleasant from his mind. . . He is a man with a remarkable capacity for self-deception.'

In his final speech for the defence Mr Bennett stressed that Christie must have been insane to have committed such terrifying acts, and then he pondered aloud: 'One wonders about the probability of there being two stranglers living in the same tiny premises. . . '

The jury retired at 4.05 p.m. on the fourth day of the trial and returned at 5.25 with a verdict of guilty. Mr Justice Finnemore donned the black cap, and pronounced the death sentence. Christie was resigned to his fate in the condemned cell, and in a funny sort of way was happy to be facing oblivion. On the morning of 15 July 1953 Albert Pierrepoint hanged him by the neck until he was dead – just as he had done to Timothy Evans three and a half years earlier.

Men cannot become monsters simply by committing monstrous acts. Christie came close. The absence of knickers on the corpses suggests a fetishism; certainly he was a necrophile. It is suggested that he would have gone on killing compulsively if not apprehended when he was, but on the evidence it seems that Christie had entered a mental twilight. He was a burnt-out case who had embraced death, as opposed to life, and probably went to the scaffold with a sense of relief.

Chapter Seven

SEX KILLERS OF THE ANGRY FIFTIES

The era of the Fifties is remembered as being the 'Angry' decade. It was a time when young writers questioned the accepted values of their society and sought an elusive 'truth', rejecting authority and claiming the right of the individual to assert himself, to proclaim his existence, at a time when individuality was increasingly being crushed by the weight of a massive technological society, and people were simply small cogs in the machine. The movement – such as it was – left us with a handful of provincial writers mainly from working-class backgrounds. It spawned the hippies and beatniks, and could be seen marching in the columns of CND, protesting against the Bomb.

It was all part of the continuous process of the 'youth-war', of course, which occurs in most generations. But perhaps the demand *for more life*, more freedom, led also to a rise in sex murder. Perhaps liberation led to licence.

From the viewpoint of the study of homicide, the Fifties was an interesting decade in that in the first half of it all murderers were subject to being hanged. But with the passing of the 1957 Homicide Act sex killers who might well have paid the ultimate penalty received life imprisonment instead.

Alfred Charles Whiteway Sex killers rarely confess to

their crimes, or tell us frankly about the dark urges which drove them to kill. Whiteway, twenty-two, was no exception. The few words of excuse he did utter – 'It must be mental. . . I can't stop it' – were to be retracted and hotly disputed at his trial.

On the morning of 1 June 1953 the body of an unidentified girl was found floating in the Thames a mile from Teddington Lock, near Richmond. She had been battered about the head, stabbed several times and raped. Police under the command of Detective Chief Superintendent William Rudkin searched the river-bank and discovered the spot where the attack had taken place, the grass being trampled and bloodstained. However, two pairs of women's shoes were found at the scene. . . .

The girl in the river was identified that evening by her mother. She was Barbara Songhurst, sixteen, an assistant in a chemist's shop in Teddington. She had gone out cycling the previous day with her friend Christine Reed, aged eighteen. Five days later the body of the other girl was recovered from the river. She had been raped and killed in a similar fashion, and both murders were obviously the work of the same man. Detective Superintendent Herbert Hannam of Scotland Yard – dubbed the 'Count' by the Press because of his natty clothing – was placed in charge of the investigation.

Witnesses were found who had seen both girls cycling homewards at about 11.30 a.m. on 31 May. Forensic evidence suggested that both girls had been murdered shortly afterwards by a killer who had lain in ambush for them. There was a large police inquiry, with a questionnaire directed at members of the public. This led to one vital clue: a week prior to the double murder, a schoolgirl had been raped on Oxshott Common, only eight miles from the murder site, and she had given a description of her attacker which included the fact that he had a cleft chin.

The inquest on the two girls heard that 'In both cases the sexual assault was of the most violent type. Both girls were *virgo intacta* before the assault.' Despite the large police inquiry it led to no conclusion. One of the cycles was missing – it was not found, and neither was the killer. The only hope for the police was that he would attack again, and make a mistake next time.

He duly attacked again almost a month after the murders, attempting to assault a 56-year-old woman sexually in Windsor Great Park. He seized her by the throat, but when she said she had just had a serious operation the attacker said, 'Give us a little kiss.' The woman handed over her purse containing 17s and the killer then warned her not to tell anyone or call out, because he had a knife and knew how to throw it. He then cycled rapidly away.

The description given by the victim fitted Alfred Charles Whiteway, a builder's labourer who had a record for sex-offences. He was arrested on the assault charge and questioned by Scotland Yard detectives about the towpath murders. Detective Superintendent Hannam was very interested in Whiteway. Here was a man with a cleft chin, a bicycle and knife. A man with a record for sex-offences who lived close to the Thames towpath. . . .

A week after being charged with the assault – the victim had picked him out from an identity parade – Whiteway was charged with the rape of the schoolgirl at Oxshott. She gave evidence before the magistrates, telling them of the attack on her by Whiteway. She said she had been attacked from behind by a man on a bicycle. He struck her on the back of the head and dragged her into some bushes. He had asked her how old she was. When she replied, 'Fourteen' he raped her. He had been carrying an axe. Whiteway had made a statement to the police admitting the rape, saying, 'I did assault her. . . I don't know what made me do it.'

On Thursday 20 August, Whiteway was brought from Brixton Prison to the magistrate's court at Richmond, to be charged with the murders of the two girls. At his Old Bailey trial in October for the murder of Barbara

Songhurst, Mr Christmas Humphreys prosecuting said that the girl had lived near Whiteway's home.

She would have recognized him; hence Whiteway's need to silence her. The evidence in the case was startling – not least of which was the fact that the axe used by Whiteway to kill had been hidden by him in a police car taking him to the station, and was found by a policeman who took it home to chop wood. The name of the unfortunate constable was PC Cosh. Later, realizing its importance, he had taken it back to the police station.

Whiteway had a large collection of knives and used to practise throwing them at trees. He was also known to carry a small axe at times. The axe returned by PC Cosh showed a strong reaction for blood, although the quantity was too minute to match for blood-grouping.

There was no real evidence linking Whiteway positively to the murders, apart from his confession, produced on the third day of the trial. Detective Superintendent Hannam said the statement had been made voluntarily by Whiteway, and began: 'It's all up. You know bloody well I done it. . . What a bloody mess. I am mental. Me head must be wrong. I cannot stop myself. I am not a bloody murderer. I only see one girl. She came round the track where I stood and I bashed her and she went down like a log. Then the other screamed out loud down by the lock. Never saw her till then, I didn't. I nipped over and shut her up. Two of 'em, and then I tumbled the other one knew me. If it had not been for that it would not have happened. Put that bloody chopper away. It haunts me. . . .'

There was a fierce courtroom duel between Mr Peter Rawlinson, defending, and Superintendent Hannam, with defence counsel suggesting that the entire statement had been fabricated. 'I suggest that the statement was invented by you?' Although Superintendent Hannam denied this, Mr Rawlinson certainly believed it, and was never to forgive Hannam for 'swearing away a man's life'.

Whiteway went into the witness-box to swear that his alleged statement was false, and that he had been forced to sign blank statement forms by trickery. He denied both murders.

The jury of ten men and two women took only forty-five minutes to find Whiteway guilty of murder. On Tuesday 22 December 1953 he was executed at Wandsworth Prison. He was a dull and uninteresting character who was basically a rapist forced to kill. It is significant that at the time of the rape and the double murders his wife was heavily pregnant. It may have been sheer sexual frustration which led to Whiteway's crimes.

Peter Thomas Anthony Manuel Peter Manuel was a petty crook who was also a serial killer. Although there is no direct evidence that his many murders were sexually motivated – none of the victims was raped – the inescapable conclusion is that Manuel derived some non-specific sexual pleasure from the mere act of killing. He is unique in Scottish criminal history, having been found guilty of seven murders, and remains a unique character. Hugh C. Rae used him as the basis for his absorbing novel *Skinner* (1965).

Manuel is a typical representative of the character born too strong for his environment – or too weak, depending on one's viewpoint. He was a little man of extreme arrogance who was determined to impress himself on the world, even if it meant talking his way to the gallows. He was a classic 'in-betweener'; too intelligent for his surroundings, but not talented enough to channel his intelligence into legitimate means of expression. As a result, his only opportunity to demonstrate his 'superiority' came when he conducted his own defence at his trial for murder, and it was a very impressive if futile performance. The trial judge referred to his defence as being 'conducted with a skill that is quite remarkable'.

Manuel was born in Manhattan, New York, on 15 March 1927. At first his family lived in Detroit, but when times got tough his family – who had emigrated to the USA in the hope of a better life – decided to return to the UK. Manuel was now a six-year-old boy. The family settled first in Coventry, but the dark-haired boy with the American accent did not fit in at his school. He began playing truant. At eleven he was put on probation for shop-breaking, and soon after was put in a remand home as being out of control.

From eleven to eighteen, Manuel spent most of his time in approved schools and borstal. Seven years in which authority attempted to crush the boy's innate sense of superiority and rebellion. They failed. In those precious few adolescent years he might have begun writing poetry; instead he turned to crime to give himself a sense of identity. He broke out of various approved schools a total of ten times, committing housebreakings and thefts all around the country. At fifteen he broke into a house and after taking a sleeping woman's purse struck her over the head with a hammer. There was no motive for the vicious assault, which might well have caused death, beyond the fact that Manuel *liked* inflicting pain.

When recaptured he was remanded to Leeds Prison for a spell in the hope that it might contain his raging spirit. But when he was returned to a Yorkshire approved school he broke out and attacked a woman on a lonely road just before Christmas 1942, stealing her purse and indecently assaulting her. This was his first recorded sex offence.

At sixteen he was sent to borstal for two years, managing only one escape. Released in 1945, he rejoined his parents, now living in Lanarkshire. After a brief spell trying to earn a dishonest penny in Blackpool, Manuel settled down in Lanarkshire, and soon afterwards there was an epidemic of housebreaking in the area. He appeared in court on fifteen counts of housebreaking, but was bailed. While on bail he attacked an expectant mother close to a hospital, raping her. Specks of soil found in his trouser turn-ups convicted him. He was sentenced to twelve months on the housebreaking charges but eight years for the rape, which he served at the notorious Peterhead Prison. If ever there was a place designed to break men's hearts and spirits it is Peterhead. It failed to break Manuel. He twice attacked warders.

On his release he had one aim: to join Glasgow's underworld and become accepted on his own terms. He failed. Experienced safe-breakers laughed at the young man who bragged of having won the American Golden Gloves championship. They viewed him as a petty crook with a big mouth. Manuel was now living with his parents in a council house in Birkenshaw, a village just outside Glasgow.

Manuel was working as a dustman by day, and in the evenings he tried to write short stories on a typewriter he owned. He also began sketching, showing some talent as an artist. This was his last chance to channel his frustration into creative outlets, but he decided his destiny lay in crime.

In July 1955 he was arrested on a charge of assaulting a girl who was taking a short-cut home from a dance. His family attempted to have him certified unfit to plead, but Manuel shrugged off legal aid and conducted his own defence. The girl testified that Manuel had seized her, threatening to cut her throat with a knife, and then forced her to a lonely spot and indecently assaulted her. She said, 'Afterwards he told me he had been watching TV that night when he had a sudden impulse to cut someone's head off and bury them.' The jury found the charge not proven. For the first time Manuel had taken on the forces of the law on its own terms and beaten it. It was to breed an unhealthy self-confidence in him which would ultimately destroy him.

From this time onward police kept Manuel under special observation. They knew he was a bomb waiting to explode. He had begun writing anonymous letters to the police, by turns offering false information about crimes, and at other times insulting various CID officers.

On 2 January 1956 Anne Kneilands, seventeen, vanished after leaving her home at East Kilbride on her way to a dance. Her body was found two days later on a local golf-course. She had been battered to death with extreme ferocity. Although she had not been sexually assaulted, her knickers were missing. Police suspected that Manuel was the killer, but they could not touch him. They had to abide by the rules and wait for sufficient evidence to warrant an arrest. They searched his home and found nothing. Questioned about scratches on his face, he said he had been in a fight in Glasgow. The fact that he was working near the spot where the girl was found was pure coincidence.

On 17 September 1956 three members of a family were found murdered in a bungalow at High Burnside. Mrs Marion Watt and her sister, Mrs Margaret Brown, lay in bed shot through the head. Mrs Watt's daughter Vivienne, sixteen, lay dying in another room. She too had been shot, after putting up a fight. All three women had died through bullets fired from a .38 Webley revolver. Adjoining properties had been burgled by someone who had walked on beds wearing muddy boots, and had chewed on stolen food. The husband, William Watt, had been away on a fishing holiday and arrived home to be met with the tragic news. Mr Watt, an ex-policeman, was arrested a few days later and charged with the murder of his family. An innocent man, he was to spend sixty-seven days in Barlinnie Prison.

Manuel was questioned about the murders. At the time of the killings he had been on bail on robbery charges. His home was searched yet again, but no firearms were found. He too duly arrived in Barlinnie, having been sentenced to eighteen months on the burglary charges. Manuel made a point of contacting Mr Watt once he was inside the jail, telling Watt he knew he was innocent, as he knew the identity of the real killer. Manuel even sent for Mr Watt's solicitor, Mr Laurence Dowdall, and related details of how each room in the bungalow had been left, as told to him by the 'real' murderer. When his detailed information about the bungalow was checked out by the solicitor it matched exactly. Only the real killer could have known the position in which victims lay.

Manuel was questioned in prison by detectives and his home searched once again, but the revolver had long since been dumped in the Clyde and there was no evidence against him. In November 1957 he walked out of prison a free man, contacting newspapers with offers to sell them his story.

Eight days later a Newcastle taxi-driver, Sidney Dunn, was murdered in Durham. He had been shot, and had his throat cut. He was known to have picked up a fare who spoke with a strong Scottish accent. On 28 December Isabelle Cooke, seventeen, disappeared while on her way to a school dance. Her route would take her close to Manuel's home. A large team of police searched for the girl; items of her clothing were recovered from the river Calder.

It was an incredible situation. For two years the police had known that Manuel was a killer; it was known to the Press; hundreds of members of the public were aware of it, yet he was allowed to walk free, although closely watched. People in a large area around Glasgow lived in fear of the unknown killer, keeping their daughters safely locked away at home, escorting them to school, at a time when the police knew full well who he was. Yet they could not touch him. The rule of law forbade it. Manuel dis-played an animal cunning and could not be broken under questioning.

On Monday 6 January 1958 Peter Smart, his wife Doris, and their son Michael, eleven, were found dead in their beds at Sheepburn Road, Uddington. They had been shot with a Beretta automatic pistol. They had actually been killed on New Year's Day – only four days after Isabelle Cooke – but their bodies had lain waiting to be discovered. Detective Superintendent Alex Brown, leading the murder inquiry, did not interview Manuel. He was certain that Manuel was the killer, but he felt that silence was the best weapon against him. If he was ignored he might be forced to show his hand. It was noted that he was spending freely, whereas before he had been broke. . .

Meanwhile, William Watt, an innocent man, had come out of prison determined to track down the man who had slaughtered his family. He talked to many people in Glasgow's underworld, and received definite confirmation that Manuel had bought a gun. Eventually a formal meeting took place between Mr Watt, his solicitor, and Manuel. Mr Watt listened grimly as Manuel spoke of things he had 'been told' about the murders, hoping that Manuel would slip up and incriminate himself. He did not.

On Tuesday 14 January 1958 a large team of CID officers arrived at Manuel's home and arrested him in the early hours of the morning. He was still asleep. In the house police found a camera and gloves stolen in burglaries; it was enough to keep him under lock and key. In an effort to force him to confess to the murders, police also arrested his mother and father. Faced with this, Manuel cracked and promised to make a statement on condition that his parents were freed.

He subsequently took detectives to a field in Mount Vernon, saying, 'This is the place. In fact I think I'm standing on her now.' Police dug and found the almost naked remains of Isabelle Cooke. Manuel also confessed to the two triple murders and the murder of Anne Kneilands. He told his story with a callous detachment which shocked hardened detectives.

In his statement he referred to the various murders in detail. Of Anne Kneilands, he described meeting her and offering to walk her home.

> We walked along a curving country road. . . About halfway along this road I pulled her into a field gate. She struggled, ran away and I chased her. In the wood she started screaming and I hit her on the head with a piece of iron I had picked up.

Of the Watt family he said:

'I entered the house by breaking a front-door panel made of glass. I opened the bedroom door. There were two in bed. I went into the other room and there was a girl in the bed. She woke up and sat up. I hit her on the chin and knocked her out. I tied her hands and went back in the other room. I shot the two people in this room and then heard someone making a noise in the other room. I went back in and the girl had got loose. We struggled and I flung her on the bed and shot her too.'

Of Isabelle Cooke:

I met a girl walking. I grabbed her and dragged her into a field. . . I tore off her clothes and tied something round her neck and shoulders. I then carried her up a lane into a field and dug a hole with a shovel. . . I covered her up and went back the way I came.

Of the Smart family:

I did it about six-o-clock in the morning of New Year's Day. . . I went into the bedroom and got £18 or £20 in new notes and four or five ten-shilling notes. . . I shot the man first, and then the woman, and then I shot the boy. . . I then went into the living-room and ate a handful of wee biscuits from a tray.

Every page of his statement was signed by himself.

Peter Manuel was to go on trial for eight of his known murders; the murder of the taxi-driver could not be dealt with as it had occurred in England. The trial began on Monday 12 May 1958 before Lord Cameron in the Justiciary Building in Glasgow. People queued for fourteen hours for seats, as if they were attending a premiere, and in a sense they were. It was to be a drama in which Manuel was to be the principal actor, the hero of his own biography. He was dressed for the part in a smart blazer, with blue trousers, a grey shirt and tie. His coarse good looks, with his dark hair hanging over his eyes, made him appear like an embryonic Presley-type. A jury of fifteen – nine men and six women – were duly sworn. Manuel pleaded not guilty to all charges and had a 'special defence' (peculiar to Scottish law) to some of the matters.

His special defence to the money and articles stolen from a house near the Watt bungalow and found in his possession was that he had received them from the original burglar, whom he named. His second special defence was one of impeachment: he alleged that the murders had been committed by William Watt. There were to be some 280 witnesses, and the forensic evidence was damning. Both murder guns had been recovered from the Clyde where Manuel said he had dumped them. The trial lasted sixteen days, and the testimony given ran to well over half a million words.

The first day was taken up with the murder of Anne Kneilands. A bullet had been found in the house by its new owner : it came from the same .38 Webley used to kill the Watt family. The man Manuel had named as the burglar had to appear in court to deny the charge.

On the fourth day William Watt testified about the murder of his family and his meeting with Manuel. He said Manuel had shown him a snapshot of Anne Kneilands, which he had then torn into small pieces. Various unsavoury characters testified about the illegal selling of guns in Glasgow, one telling of how Manuel had collected a 'package' from his house.

Halfway through the trial Manuel's counsel submitted that his confession should be excluded as it had been obtained under duress. Lord Cameron ruled that Manuel's admission had been made without pressure. The confession was allowed into evidence. Police officers testified as to how Manuel had made his admissions to the murders, and had led them to the spot where Isabelle Cooke lay buried. They insisted that Manuel had refused to have a solicitor present when he wrote his statement.

On the tenth day of the trial came the drama. Manuel sacked his counsel and announced that he would be conducting his own defence. It was the high-point of his life; now he was the focus of attention, with the chance to demonstrate his cleverness. He recalled Detective Inspector Tom Goodall of Glasgow CID and subjected him to a gruelling cross-examination. He spoke fluently and without reference to notes. Using the legal terminology to which he had become well used, he tried to trap the Inspector into damaging admissions. When Goodall described how Manuel had led officers to the spot where Isabelle Cooke lay buried, Manuel established that it had been dark at the time. 'In which hand were you holding your torch?' he asked. 'I had no torch', the Inspector replied. 'Then how could you see, if it was dark?' Manuel demanded triumphantly.

He suggested that the police were lying; that they had known where Isabelle Cooke lay buried before leading him to the spot, and that his statement had been made under duress, with threats made against his family.

On the twelfth day came the 'trial within a trial' when he recalled William Watt. Now he accused Mr Watt directly of killing his own family. Mr Watt replied, 'That is an atrocious lie.' When Manuel recalled ex-Superintendent James Hendry he asked him, 'Did you feel confident when you arrested Watt you had arrested the man who had shot his wife?' The judge would not allow the ex-detective to reply to this question. His opinions were not relevant.

The following day Manuel called his own mother and father as witnesses. While his mother agreed that he had been in the house all night at the time of the killing of the Smart family, she persisted that she had not heard him say in the police station, 'I don't know what makes me do these things.' She denied that any police officers had forced her to lie. His father, however, agreed that the police had prompted him.

Then Manuel himself went into the witness-box to give

a virtuoso performance. He denied being guilty of any of the murders, claiming that Mr Watt had admitted to him that he had shot his wife. Speaking fluently, with the odd joke here and there, he tried to persuade a hard-headed Scottish jury of his innocence. He had an answer for every allegation. He claimed that he had sold Mr Smart a gun which Mr Smart had then used to kill his family and himself. Manuel had gone to the house, found the family dead, and had taken away the gun because it might link him to the murders. It was all a conspiracy against him, and he had made a false confession only to save his family.

Cross-examined by the prosecution, he described the evidence against him as being 'ridiculous' or 'just coincidence'. He said that Mr Watt was a 'very arrogant man', and Detective Superintendent Brown was a 'rat of a man'. He claimed that he simply could not have done the murders: 'There was ten policemen watching my house every night.'

The prosecution made its closing speech, then Manuel made his. It was an inspired and articulate performance. The judge began his summing up, first directing the jury to find Manuel not guilty of the murder of Anne Kneilands. Despite Manuel's confession to the murder, there was insufficient corroboration to find him guilty. Referring to the prisoner's mental condition, the judge said a man 'may be very bad without being mad'.

The jury retired, taking two and a half hours to find Manuel guilty of all seven remaining murders. Lord Cameron sentenced Manuel to death with the traditional formula, then placed the black cap on his head and announced the peculiarly Scottish sentence: 'This pronounced for doom.' Manuel's appeal was rejected and on Friday 11 July 1958, after a glass of whisky, he walked to the execution chamber at Barlinnie Prison.

Before his execution Manuel confessed to three more murders. They were of Helen Carlin, a prostitute found strangled in Pimlico in September 1954; Anne Steele, fifty-four, found battered to death in Glasgow on 11 January 1956; and Ellen Petrie, stabbed in Glasgow in June 1956.

Peter Manuel undoubtedly obtained a morbid sexual satisfaction from the act of killing. He was a small, insignificant criminal who longed for the limelight, to be a star. Andy Warhol once said that in the future everybody will be famous – for just fifteen minutes. Manuel had his fifteen minutes and more.

Michael Douglas Dowdall On Monday 15 December 1958, a prostitute was taken home in a taxi by a young man she had met while she was plying her trade. Veronica Murray, thirty-one, was subsequently found dead in her room at 58 Charteris Road, Kilburn, London, on Christmas Eve 1958. She had been dead for about a week. She was naked, a pullover drawn up over her head, and the cause of death was the battering of her skull – she had been hit six times with a bloodstained dumb-bell which was found near her body, and her skull had been fractured. It was a routine killing of a prostitute; what made this one different was the series of small circular marks found on her body. They had been made after death, possibly by someone pressing a bottle-top into the flesh with great force. Fingerprints were found in the room, but a prostitute's room can be expected to bear the impressions of many strangers.

On 10 October 1959 a Mrs Hill was celebrating her birthday. She met a pleasant, good-looking youth in the West End and invited him back to her flat at Ismalia Road, Fulham. When she refused to have sex the youth partially strangled her with a silk stocking, and when she recovered she found circular marks all over her body. From the description she gave to the police, and from fingerprints found in her flat, police were able to link this attack with another, that on a 65-year-old woman who had been battered with a poker as she slept in her home near Sloane Square. She had been robbed of money and whisky. The prints also linked the mystery attacker with a series of burglaries over the previous year, including three in Chelsea, one in a Fulham pub, and another in the Westbury Hotel, Mayfair. The burglar had broken into a suite occupied by actor George Sanders and had changed his shoes, going away in a pair he found in the suite, after consuming a quantity of whisky. The badly worn shoes recovered by the police had 'W.G.' crudely nailed into the sole.

On 19 November 1958 Scotland Yard issued a public appeal for information about the killer, publishing a photograph of the shoes. It brought no response. The police and the public were unaware that 'W.G.' stood for Welsh Guards.

A week later, after another housebreaking expedition in which he robbed four or five houses in Chelsea, the killer broke through a police cordon of over a hundred officers. He had left behind his now-familiar fingerprints on whisky bottles and glasses. But he had also stolen an unusual cigarette-lighter bearing a distinctive emblem. The owner, an Australian businessman, had a replica. Police issued a fresh appeal with a photograph of the lighter, and this time a guardsman in the Welsh Guards camp at Pirbright reported to his CO that the man in the next bed to his had a lighter exactly like the one shown. His name was Michael Douglas Dowdall, eighteen, and he was a drummer.

Detective Chief Inspector Bob Acott and Detective Inspector Peter Vibart had been leading the investigation. They saw Dowdall at Woking police station. He had got rid of the lighter, but showed the detectives where he had hidden it. He then made a statement concerning the murder of Veronica Murray.

'Everybody has been against me. It is when I have been drinking I do these things.' Telling of how he took his victim home in a taxi, where they had sex and then went to sleep, he went on: 'When she woke me up we had a row over something and she called me a filthy little Welsh bastard. She threw a vase at me. . . She came at me with something and hit me on the back of the head. . . I rushed at her and knocked her down. . . I remember chucking some clothes over her. I took a bottle of whisky and then I left the place.' He said that only when he read of the death of the prostitute, a day or so later, did he realize that he had killed her. Attempting to explain his criminal activities, he told police: 'My Army mates think I'm queer; I've tried to show them they're wrong. . . My mates made me feel a nobody. So I have a drink, and then I feel better and more important.'

Dowdall, now aged nineteen, stood trial at the Old Bailey on 20 January 1960, before Mr Justice Donovan. The trial was to last only two days. Dowdall's defence was the new one of 'diminished responsibility', and for once the psychiatrists were in agreement. Dr Brisby, Principal Medical Officer at Brixton Prison, described Dowdall as 'a psychopath and a social misfit.' Dr Leigh, a psychiatrist at Bethlehem Hospital, confirmed that Dowdall was a psychopath, adding: 'He is a sexual pervert.'

Dowdall's father had been killed in the war in 1943, his mother died in 1948, and he was brought up by an aunt in Wales. He joined the Welsh Guards as a drummer boy at the age of fifteen, and began drinking heavily soon afterwards.

The jury retired for three hours before returning to request advice on 'diminished responsibility' and took another eight minutes to find him guilty of manslaughter. He was sentenced to life imprisonment. He was released on licence from prison in July 1975, suffering from a fatal illness from which he died in November 1976 aged thirty-six.

Patrick Byrne Quite the worst sex-killer of the Fifties was Patrick Byrne, a man who might have gone on to become another Kürten had he not been apprehended when he was. He brought an atmosphere of terror to Birmingham which was reminiscent of the Jack the Ripper killings. In fact, just prior to the murder of Stephanie Baird, a book by Donald McCormick – *The Identity of Jack the Ripper* – had been published. The police were to try to trace every person who had borrowed the book from public libraries, since the killing bore a striking resemblance to those described in the book. Byrne is a rare creature in the annals of the sex killer – one who admitted and told in full detail his motives and methods. His statement is of prime importance to any study of the mind of the sex killer.

It began on the evening of Wednesday 23 December 1959. Stephanie Baird was occupying Room 4 at the YWCA hostel in Wheeley's Road, Edgbaston, Birmingham. She was busy packing, intending to spend Christmas with her mother, when an intruder broke into her room. The man grabbed her, felling her with such force that her skull was fractured as her head hit the floor. He was kissing her passionately even while his hands were around her throat, strangling the life out of her.

The limp, dead body of his victim perhaps left the killer feeling frustrated and empty.

He had sex with the corpse, but that was not enough. She still remained an enigma. With a table knife he cut off her right breast. Then he attempted to cut open her stomach and mutilated her back and legs with the blunt knife. Then he cut off her head, holding it up by the hair to look at it in the mirror.

Police had been called to the hostel to investigate an attack on a twenty-year-old Mrs Margaret Brown. She was in the laundry room when the man walked in, fresh from killing Stephanie Baird. He struck her with a piece of rock wrapped in a brassière, but ran away when she started screaming.

The officers searched the grounds and found footprints in the earth outside an open window, then they discovered that Room 4 was locked. The door was forced open. The sight that met the first officer to walk into the room left him off work sick for months. The headless corpse lay on the floor, but standing on the bed, upright on its stump, was a human head, with a breast placed beside it. The only clue to the killer was a note he had left scribbled on an envelope. It read: 'This is the thing I Tought would never come.'

So began one of the biggest police man-hunts up to that time; 20,000 men were interviewed, and a large-scale search mounted for a bloodstained man. Every man within a three-mile radius of the hostel in the right age bracket was seen and his movements accounted for. There were many reports of a bloodstained man having been seen on a bus that night, but nobody was ever traced. Police appeals to the public included the suggestion that the killer might have some medical knowledge, or be a butcher, since the amputations seemed to display some basic knowledge of anatomy. This was far from accurate – the killer was a builder's labourer.

Two Home Office pathologists called in to examine the remains of Stephanie Baird disagreed on the case. Dr Frederick Griffiths was of the opinion that the killer had used the blunt table knife, with its handle broken off, to commit all the mutilations and the decapitation. He was certain that a killer would not change knives during such a grisly ritual. Dr Francis Camps, however, was of the opinion that the killer had used a sharp knife for some of the cuts, switching to the blunt knife found at the scene for others. He also felt that the killer might have some knowledge of dissection. As a result hundreds of medical students were interviewed, as were some four thousand butchers.

Detective Chief Superintendent James Haughton, head of Birmingham CID, personally headed the hunt for the killer and appeared on TV to make urgent appeals to the public. He was frank about the task which faced him. Every man in the area had to be traced and eliminated from the inquiry, and that meant questioning some hundred thousand people. Another difficulty was that many people had left the area to travel home for Christmas. Each would have to be traced by a laborious door-to-door inquiry.

John Reginald Halliday Christie with his wife Ethel in the garden at 10 Rillington Place

The body of Ethel Christie under the floorboards in the front-room, and below, after removal

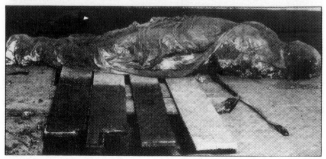

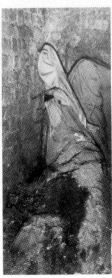

Christie had stashed three bodies in a recess in his kitchen. After removal of the nearly-naked one (left) two more shrouded figures (below) can clearly be seen

Patrick Byrne was quite the
worst British sex killer of the
Fifties

Stephanie Baird
was strangled then decapitated

The killer was caught almost by accident, not unlike the capture of the Yorkshire Ripper. Seven weeks after the murder a routine request was sent to Warrington Police asking them to interview Patrick Byrne. He had been lodging close to the hostel in Birmingham, but had left just before Christmas to go to live with his mother in Warrington, Lancashire. He had given notice to his landlady and his employer before the murder. A fellow-Irishman said that Byrne had been drinking with him on the evening of the murder, and as that had taken place between 6.20 p.m. and 7.15 p.m., this seemed to put Byrne in the clear. However, he had not been interviewed, and it was just a matter of tying up loose ends.

When Byrne called at Warrington police station on 10 February, he was seen by Detective Sergeant George Welborn, who asked him to account for his movements on the night Stephanie Baird was murdered. He answered the questions satisfactorily and agreed to have his fingerprints taken. But then the detective asked him, 'Have you anything else to tell me about your stay in Birmingham?' Either he had a penetrating gaze, or Byrne thought he could see into his soul. He blurted out: 'I want to tell you about the YWCA. I have something to do with that.'

That night he was driven to Birmingham, where he made a full confession to Superintendent Haughton which is unique in the literature of the sexual sadist. Byrne told the truth – as Dennis Nilsen would do later – and although it sickened his listeners, it remains an invaluable document.

The trial of Patrick Byrne began at Birmingham Assizes before Mr Justice Stable on Wednesday 23 March 1960. His defence counsel stated from the outset: 'The accused tells me he does not dispute the terrible details of this case. The defence is one which concerns the mental responsibility for the act. . . None of the facts will be challenged.'

Mr John Hobson QC, prosecuting, told the jury, 'The story you will hear is one of horror and bestiality such as one would ever hope not to dream about in one's worst nightmare.' He then read the long statement made by Byrne confessing to the murder.

I worked at Tarmacs in Hagley Road, facing St Chad's Hospital, until about ten o clock that Wednesday and then went to the Ivy Bush pub in Hagley Road. We had a drinking session there. . . I remember finishing up in Wheeley's Road, near the YWCA. I know the hostel there because I don't live far away.

I thought I would like to have a peep through a window. I have done this a few times before. . .The night I killed that girl in the cubicle I went in through the front drive and into the grounds. There was only one light on in the bedrooms. . . I looked through the window of the bedroom which had the light on in the block of cubicles and I saw a girl in there. . . She was combing her hair. I only watched for a few seconds. . . I decided to have a better peep from the inside. I went round the back and found a little window open a bit.

After describing how he got into the block, and placed a chair outside the door to Room 4 so that he could watch the girl through the glass panel above it, hoping she would undress, she heard the chair squeak and opened the door, confronting him.

I didn't speak and she asked me again what I was doing. I told her I was looking for somebody. She said: 'Let me get the warden.' We were standing quite close together then and I was just going to run and as I turned my arm touched her breast. This got me excited and I got hold of her breast. I said 'Give me a kiss' and before she could say no, I kissed her. She tried to shove me away but couldn't and for a second I got her round the waist. She only had her underskirt on and I felt her very close. I was feeling her all over and kissing her but she screamed and then I put my hands around her neck.

She went over backwards inside the room with me squeezing her throat and then fell backwards. Her head bounced on the floor and I was lying on top of her kissing her and squeezing her neck at the same time. I heard a couple of small noises in her throat and kept on kissing her. I was lying on top of her alongside the bed with our heads near the dressing table. After a while I knelt up and had a strong urge to have a good look at her. I was fully sure she was dead then because I had the whole power of my back squeezing her throat. I pulled her towards me and pulled the red jumper off her and threw it to one side. I lay on top of her . . . I did various things after that, I seemed to be in a hurry to do everything to her and hadn't the patience. I got up then panting and moaning. . . I bolted the door. I took my trousers and jacket and shirt off and I was naked apart from my shoes and socks. I rolled all over her. Her underclothes were all around her waist.

The next few sentences, in which Byrne describes his necrophiliac acts on the body of his victim, were never disclosed. The statement went on:

I got tired of that and looking up I could see the dressing table cupboard door open. There was a table knife in there. . . I looked at it for a couple of seconds. . . I got the knife in my right hand then and caught hold of her right breast and carved the knife around it. It was hard to cut round the skin but in the end I got it off. I was very surprised and disappointed it came away flat in my hand. I just looked at it and then flung it towards the bed. I scored her round the chest with the knife. . . [More unprintable details follow.]

I started on the back of the neck then, catching hold of her hair and pulling her head close to my bare chest. I kept on cutting away. I remember now the knife broke off close to the handle when I was cutting down her stomach and I carried on afterwards with the blade. This part seems a bit blurry, but I think I had something wrapped round part of the blade while I used it. It surprised me how easy the head came off. It's been puzzling me since why I took the head off. It's not connected with sex in all the books I've read. I can understand the breast. I remember when the head came off I had it by the hair and I stood up.

. . . I held it up to the mirror and looked at it through the mirror. . . I'd forgotten to tell you that just after I had done some of the mutilations I stood up and wrote a note with a biro on some paper on the dressing table. I can't remember the words I used but *I wanted everybody to see my life in one little note.*

The other times I had been definitely satisfied with peeping, but this time was different somehow.

He then tells of getting dressed and leaving the murder scene, still feeling consumed with lust. He saw another woman in the laundry room and attacked her. He described his mood in these terms: 'I was pretty frantic. . . I was very excited, breathing heavy and thinking that I ought to terrorise all women. I wanted to get my own back on them for causing my nervous tension through sex. . . I felt I only wanted to kill beautiful women.'

When he got back to his lodgings he started to write a confession, describing himself as having two personalities. 'I stood by the mirror in the bathroom talking to myself and searching my face for signs of a madman but I could see none.' He thought of committing suicide, then tore his note up.

Dr Percy Coats, senior medical officer at Birmingham Prison, said that Byrne was slightly below average intelligence, and from his own conversations with the man he had concluded he was a sexual psychopath. 'I think he knew what he was doing and that what he was doing was wrong. . . I think his sexual emotions took complete control of him at that time.' He said he believed Byrne was suffering from an abnormality of the mind and had impaired mental responsibility.

The judge asked: 'Would it be fair to say that when you get such a marked degree of depravity that individual cannot be guilty of murder?' The reply was: 'No, sir.' The judge continued, 'Are you saying there was nothing wrong with his mind except these depraved desires to which he surrenders?' – Dr Coats: 'Yes.'

Dr James O'Reilly, medical superintendent of All Saints Hospital, said Byrne had a long history of gross sexual abnormality. Byrne had told him that over the last five years and possibly from the age of about seventeen he had dreams and thoughts about sexual things towards women which had frightened him. He had fantasies which included putting a woman on a circular saw and putting her body through it and getting excitement from it. He considered Byrne to be suffering from an abnormality of the mind.

In his final speech to the jury defence counsel asked for a verdict under Section Two of the Homicide Act, saying, 'In my submission there has been called before you medical evidence – most compelling evidence – which you cannot possibly shirk from accepting that this is a case of a man who comes clearly within the terms of that particular section of the Homicide Act.

'This means, in terms of your verdict, that he would be guilty of manslaughter, not murder.'

The prosecutor reminded the jury that they were not bound to accept the medical evidence. 'After all, they can only give their opinions, the ultimate decision is yours.'

In his summing up the judge said that the evidence was that Byrne knew what he was doing and that what he was doing was wrong. There was no room for the application of the M'Naghten Rules, and no room for a verdict of guilty but insane. The summing up was later to be overturned by the Court of Appeal.

The jury took forty-five minutes to find Byrne guilty of murder and the judge sentenced him to life imprisonment. On appeal the Lord Chief Justice and two other judges decided that the judge's summing up had been wrong in law, and quashed the conviction for murder, substituting a verdict of manslaughter. The life sentence was not changed.

Byrne's background was that he had three convictions for housebreaking in Dublin, and convictions for drunken assault on the police in Birmingham. He had a long record as a Peeping Tom. His work-mates had nicknamed him 'Acky', and on the wall of his old lodgings police found scribbled the words: Acky the Window Peeper. But the 28-year-old labourer had graduated to sex murder. . . .

Chapter Eight

JACK THE STRIPPER

Between February 1964 and February 1965 six prostitutes were murdered in London, these slayings coming to be known as the Hammersmith nude murders. The killer, never apprehended or publicly identified, was labelled by the Press: 'Jack the Stripper.' An attempt to make sense of the details of the case and to probe the often obscure connections between these murders makes one realise just how difficult the task was which faced the police of 1888 hunting the original and elusive Jack. Just as there remain arguments about exactly how many women Jack the Ripper killed, so in the present case it is not clear that all the murders were the work of the same man, and the generic name given to the killings – the Nude Murders – is also misleading: not all the victims were naked.

It is difficult, almost impossible, for the reader to transport himself back to the ambience of 1888 and visualize the scene: always the case will be viewed from the modern standpoint. But it ought to be possible to immerse ourselves in the recent past.

In fact, for all the help the case provides to the modern researcher it might just as well have happened a century ago. The clues are as muddy and silted as the bed of the Thames, which played such a central role in the case. Nothing is clear, nothing certain, and the issue remains in as much doubt as the real identity of Jack the Ripper.

At 4.42 a.m. on 17 June 1959, the dawn of another hot day, a police patrol car from Chiswick police station spotted the body of a woman at Duke's Meadows at the side of the Thames, close to Chiswick Bridge. The woman sat propped against a tree-trunk as if contemplating the river. She wore a blue and white striped dress which had been torn down the front – and that was all. There were no underclothes, shoes or handbag. Pathologist Dr Teare examined the body and reported that she had been manually strangled not later than 2 a.m. Scuff-marks on her heels and abrasions to her back suggested that she had been dragged out of a vehicle and across the ground to her final resting place. She had engaged in sex recently, and had had a tooth removed not long before her death, the gum not yet being healed. Her stomach contents consisted of champagne.

Chief Detective Superintendent Edward Greeno was placed in charge of the case, and his first task was to establish the identity of the victim. A death mask was made, and a picture of sorts published. It was recognised by a friend of the dead woman, who immediately contacted the police. The victim was Elizabeth Figg, twenty-one, originally from Cheshire. Although a prostitute, and often using the alias Ann Phillips, she had never been arrested for soliciting and had no police record. She lived in a bedsitter in Duncombe Park, Upper Holloway, at a rent of 48s weekly. On the day she vanished, 16 June, she had gone to Ascot with a friend to ply her trade – hence the champagne.

The last person to see her alive (apart from her killer) was a client who picked her up in his car at 11.30 p.m. on Tuesday 16 June. She left him saying she had an appointment at Holland Park, and the taxi-driver who dropped her there was traced. He had dropped her off at 1.10 a.m. on the Wednesday. In the space of less than an hour she had been murdered and dumped. It was a fairly routine murder. A woman had been murdered –

presumably by a client – and the trail was cold. The case got pushed into the backlog of files awaiting attention.

Then on 8 November 1963 a man operating a mechanical digger at a rubbish tip at Mortlake, near the Thames, uncovered the headless body of a dark-haired woman. She was naked apart from one stocking. The remains were examined at Guy's Hospital, and from the recovered skull it was possible to establish that she was missing five teeth from the upper jaw and two from the lower, but if she wore a dental plate it was never recovered. From a tiny fragment of skin on one hand, the pathologist was able to get a match with the fingerprints of Gwynneth Rees, twenty-two, alias Georgette Rees, Tina Dawson and Tina Smart. She was originally from Wales, but her last known address was in Hague Street, Bethnal Green. Investigation into her background revealed that she had moved from there to a basement flat in Warriner Gardens, Battersea, in the August prior to her discovery at Mortlake rubbish tip in November. The rent had been £5 a week. She had eleven convictions for prostitution, and an inquest jury recorded that she had died from unknown causes.

Two dead prostitutes. The oldest profession is known to be a dangerous one, fraught with hazards. That two whores should die over three years apart seems unremarkable. Yet at one stage Scotland Yard were to link these two murders to the Jack the Stripper series. Later they were to admit that they did not belong, and were separate issues. Yet at the time they served to confuse the main issue, which was: were prostitutes being systematically murdered? And were they all being murdered by one individual?

When a third nude prostitute was found by boatmen floating in the Thames at Hammersmith on 2 February 1964 the police and the Press immediately recalled the deaths of the first two prostitutes and linked them as part of a series: the Nude Murders. This only served to confuse the issue further, since only Elizabeth Figg had definitely been murdered, and she had been wearing a dress.

This third body was confirmed by fingerprints to be that of Hannah Tailford, thirty, alias Ann Tailor, Theresa Bell and Hannah Lynch. Dr Teare reported that she had died from drowning – there was water in her lungs, proving that she had been alive when she entered the water. She was 5ft 2in in height, with long brown hair. The only items of clothing found were her stockings, around her ankles, and her panties, which were stuffed into her mouth. She had been in the water for a couple of days.

Hannah Tailford was a Geordie from Northumbria. She gave birth to a baby girl on 7 April 1961 at St George's Hospital, Westminster, and kept the child. She took barbiturates heavily, and was known to be severely depressed – one of the hazards of the drab life of the whore – and had often threatened suicide. Suicides have been known to gag themselves prior to death to prevent any involuntary cries. Dr Teare did not think this was a case of suicide. He had found a large and undigested meal in the stomach of the dead woman, and in his experience people who intend to commit suicide do not first have a feast. The inquest jury recorded an open verdict.

Then, just over two months later, at 8.30 on 8 April 1964, another nude prostitute was found floating in the Thames. She was five feet tall with blonde hair. There was a tattoo on her right arm. It depicted a tombstone on which was inscribed 'John in Memory'. An autopsy revealed that she had been four months pregnant. She was later identified as Irene Lockwood, twenty-six, alias Sandra Russell, who had lived in a flat at Denbigh Road, Notting Hill. Neighbours had heard her having a violent row with a man on the Friday night, and Tuesday morning she was dragged from the river. There was no evidence that Irene Lockwood had been murdered. She was simply a drowner.

Then sixteen days later, on 24 April, just a mile from the Thames, an assistant groundsman found a dead nude beside Beecham's sports ground at Acton, between Swyncombe Avenue and Boston Manor Road. The girl was lying face downward, head resting on her arms, her black hair spread out as if she was sleeping. But she was lying on rubbish and she had been choked. Commander George Hatherill was quickly on the scene. An examination of the body revealed only a tattoo on the forearm inscribed 'Loving You'. Fingerprints identified her as being Helene Catherine Barthelemy, 22, alias Helene Thompson and Helene Paul, originally from Scotland, last known address a flat in Talbot Road, Harlesden. She had been dead for some forty-eight hours.

Helene Barthelemy provided the police with the first positive clues they had yet received in the 'Stripper' inquiry. Dr Teare established that she had been stripped after death, and samples taken from her body showed under the microscope tiny particles of metallic paint – both primer and top-coat – as used in car-spraying. So the unknown killer had stored the body for forty-eight hours close to a garage of sorts. Furthermore, peculiar heat-marks on one side of the body showed that she had been kept close to a heat-source, something like a large transformer. Four teeth had been dislodged from her mouth with some force, and a broken tooth was still lodged in her throat, where there were also sperm traces. Why had the killer removed the teeth? Perhaps to delay identification or for some obscure pleasure of his own. . . A special squad of detectives from Shepherd's Bush police station were given the task of tracing all paint-spray operations in London, of which there were hundreds, if not thousands.

Then came one of those incredible true-life absurdities which was to bedevil the inquiry into the case of the Hammersmith Nude Murders. Kenneth Archibald, fifty-four, the caretaker at Holland Park Tennis Club, was facing a court appearance on a theft charge. He had been questioned about the Irene Lockwood murder, since a card had been found in her flat bearing the telephone number of the tennis club and the name 'Kenny'. In a fit of depression he walked into Notting Hill police station on 27 April and made a false confession to the murder, saying he had pushed her into the water. His statement could not be disproved because of its very simplicity, and he duly stood trial at the Old Bailey, where he promptly retracted his confession, saying he had made it in a fit of despair. The jury took under an hour to find him not guilty of the murder of Irene Charlotte Lockwood. Afterwards Archibald told reporters, 'That's the last time I'll confess to anything – especially to a murder I have never committed.'

At this point, in fairness, it is necessary to point out that it is this writer's opinion that the death of Helene Barthelemy was the first in a series of four murders committed by 'Jack the Stripper' – although some senior police officers still maintain that Elizabeth Figg was the first victim, back in 1959.

Now the pace quickens. On 14 July 1964, at about 2.30 a.m., a car was heard reversing from Acton Road into Berrymede Road. At 5.30 a.m. the nude body of a girl was discovered sitting propped up against a door on a garage forecourt next to a private house. The man who found it thought at first that it was a tailor's dummy. Her legs were crossed, and her trunk slumped forward as if she were contemplating her navel. She must have been posed deliberately to cause shock and outrage to whoever found her.

The victim was Mary Fleming, alias Mary Turner, born in Scotland, last known address a flat in Lancaster Road, Notting Hill, where she had lived with her two children. An autopsy revealed that she had been strangled, and forensic examination showed the same tell-tale specks of car-paint on her body. Under the spectrometer the paint specks matched exactly in size, composition and colour with the samples taken from the body of Helene Barthelemy. Mary Fleming had not been manually strangled, she had been asphyxiated – that is, her air supply had been cut off. Her false teeth were missing, and she had vanished three days previously. Again sperm was found in the back of her throat.

Now the killer's *modus operandi* became evident. He killed his victims during the act of fellatio by literally choking them to death with his penis, holding the head firmly by the hair to prevent escape. So great was the pressure that he dislodged their teeth in the process. It was a unique method of killing, although still technically asphyxia. Du Rose hints coyly at the method of killing by comparing the effect of a small apple stuffed into the back of the throat, but the meaning is plain. Then he kept bodies hidden until it was convenient to dump them, or perhaps to prevent the police from discovering that a murder had taken place until it was too late.

Margaret McGowan, alias Frances Brown, Anne Sutherland, Susan Edwards, and Frances Quinn, was the next victim. The 21-year-old vanished on 23 October 1964. Her body was kept hidden close to a spray-paint operation for almost a month, before being dumped on 25 November on waste land behind a car park in Horton Street, Kensington. She lay naked among rubbish, her face covered with a dustbin lid. She too was small – 5ft 1in – and had a tattoo on her forearm. Originally from Glasgow, she had moved to London where she was to mix with Dr Stephen Ward, and thus became involved in the Profumo scandal. She was a defence witness at Ward' trial; it was her brief moment in the limelight. And to muddy the water even further, investigation into her background revealed that she had been a friend of Helene Barthelemy and Mary Fleming.

Dr Teare certified the cause of death as being due to pressure on the neck, or asphyxia. One tooth had been dislodged by some force, and there was sperm in the throat. Again the paint-specks were present. Her clothing and jewellery were never found. Perhaps the killer kept them as a grim souvenir. He obviously dumped his victims at night, in previously chosen public places, and might well be a night-worker.

On 16 February 1965 the body of what was to prove to be the last victim was found in undergrowth on the Heron Trading Estate in Acton. She had last been seen alive on 11 January in a Shepherd's Bush hotel. The corpse was partly mummified by being stored close to a heat-source; there were the same trade-marks of teeth missing and sperm in the throat – and those paint specks.

By now the Press had whipped up the public into a state verging on panic, and Detective Superintendent John Du Rose was placed in charge of the case. Du Rose had a reputation for never taking more than four days to solve a murder case, and had been involved in such cases as Haigh the acid bath murderer, and the smashing of the Kray gang.

His first task was to go and examine the body *in situ*. The woman was 5ft 2in with dark hair and a tattoo on her forearm. Her earrings had been taken, possibly as a trophy. She was identified as Bridget Esther O'Hara, twenty-seven, alias Bridie Moore, a native of Dublin currently living at Agate Road, Hammersmith. Du Rose had to ponder over the killer's motive for storing the body for over a month. What did he do with her? Did he play with her like a doll? Or was it to delay any murder inquiry?

A squad was formed with orders to do nothing but talk to prostitutes and discover any clients with a perverse taste for violent oral sex. Another squad was still checking on all paint-spray operations. The Murder Squad had been expanded to two hundred detectives, with another four hundred officers assigned to the case on the ground. The task facing Detective Chief Superintendent Du Rose was to establish whether all the deaths, from Elizabeth Figg on, were linked. Certainly the last four were – but what about the other four? They had a superficial similarity. All had taken place in a particular area of London, though over some twenty-four square miles. All had been prostitutes.

Not all had been naked. Elizabeth Figg had been manually strangled shortly before her body was discovered – but this was not the case with Gwynneth Rees or Hannah Tailford. Helene Barthelemy and Mary Fleming died from asphyxia, with no apparent marks on the neck. Margaret McGowan had been strangled, and from the marks on her neck Dr Teare was firmly convinced that this was the work of a separate killer. Bridie O'Hara had been asphyx-iated without any marks.

Simple deduction leaves us with three true and certain 'Stripper' murders: Barthelemy, Fleming and O'Hara. Du Rose, however, accepted at least six murders as being down to 'Jack'.

Du Rose was lucky, or the killer was very desperate. The disposal site of the last body, on the Heron Estate, was on the killer's own doorstep. Tests revealed that at a transformer site on the estate spray-paint was carried on the air from a nearby spray-shop. All seven thousand employee's who worked on the estate were questioned about their movements. Du Rose was certain that the killer worked on the estate or had legitimate access to it. The detective had to decide how to flush out the killer, and decided on a policy of psychological warfare. He would use the Press and media in general to make the killer feel threatened. At press conferences he would announce that there was a list of twenty suspects. Later it would be halved to ten. Finally it was announced that the list had been narrowed down to three. It was all make-believe, of course, since Du Rose had no suspects at all. But it worked.

Within a month of the murder of Bridget O'Hara a security guard who patrolled the Heron Estate at night in a van committed suicide by gassing himself – ironically, this too would be recorded as asphyxia. He left a note saying: 'I cannot stand the strain any longer.' He was an unmarried man in his forties. Du Rose, in his memoirs *Murder Was My Business* (1971), states '. . . the man I wanted to arrest took his own life. . . Because he was never arrested or stood trial he must be considered innocent and will therefore never be named.'

The only real proof for the security guard being the killer is that following his suicide there were no more murders. . . Scotland Yard announced that the killer was dead. He had been executed by publicity.

Du Rose goes on to detail the killer's method of murder. 'In obtaining satisfaction he became utterly frenzied and at the moment of his orgasm, the girls died.' He goes on to speculate that the first murder – he refers to Hannah Tailford – might have been an acci-dent, a case of manslaughter, but that after he went on killing he must have known what he was doing. Perhaps it added an extra piquant thrill. . . Du Rose goes on: 'When he continued to indulge in his particular perversion, well knowing that the girls concerned would die, he must have recognised that he was fulfilling him-self as a murderer.'

We shall never know just who Jack the Stripper was, and we shall never be sure of exactly how many women he killed. He remains as elusive as the killer after whom he was named.

Chapter Nine

NEW LIGHT ON THE MOORS MURDERS

G.B. Shaw wrote: 'We judge an artist by his highest moments, a criminal by his lowest.' Shaw recognized a vital psychological truth: that there co-exists within some of us the artist and the killer, and the relationship between the two can set up a tension which leads to murder. Both artist and killer refuse to accept the limitations of reality, of *life as it is*. Both want to change the world; both want fame and recognition; both tend to live in a fantasy world where the distinctions between reality and fantasy become blurred. Creative men are notoriously self-willed, refusing to be bound by any rules – a trait they share with criminals. The difference between them is that the artist sublimates his rebellion into creativity. For those in whom the channels of creativity are blocked the psychic energy turns inward and poisons the inner life, producing murderers who kill in a curious trance-like state.

Such killers have retreated from reality into a world of fantasy. Life becomes a cinema-screen on which they are the principal actors. They become the heroes of their own imaginings, and if life is reduced to a cinema-screen, then the 'bit' actors become disposable. In our own century – the age of the cinema – we have witnessed a dramatic increase in these fantasy killings, with couples acting in *combination* to play out their deadly scripts. The French have a term for this situation: *folie à deux,* meaning a couple who support one another's fantasies and delusions. Two disturbed people come together by accident. Separately they would probably live out harmless lives. But when they come together it is like mixing glycerine and nitric acid: the result is explosive.

It has often been remarked that it was a 'million-to-one chance' which brought together Ian Brady and Myra Hindley. But in fact *folie à deux* is not that rare. The annals of murder contains many examples of deadly duos, including Bonnie and Clyde, Leopold and Loeb, Bywaters and Thompson, Snyder and Gray, Fernandez and Beck, Hulten and Jones – and the infamous Moors Murderers, the most notorious example of the genre.

What links these deadly couples together is that most basic of impulses, the sex drive, this even in the case of Leopold and Loeb. And sex can be a fatal will-o'-the-wisp. With some couples, after that first flush of passion has cooled and grown stale, 'kinky' sex takes over in an attempt to stimulate the fading passion, but even that becomes jaded. Wilder and weirder deviations are tried, but all lead to satiation and boredom. The fact is that sex is an illusion. Every man has experienced that same baffling dilemma: you can make love to a woman a hundred times – a thousand times – but you never totally possess her. Only for that brief moment are you joined in embrace; afterwards you must always separate.

Never has the *illusion* of sex been more cruelly exposed than in the case of the Moors Murderers. Just as Jack the Ripper pawed frenziedly with his bare hands into the entrails of women, as though seeking to discover the secret of sex, so Ian Brady and Myra Hindley practised murder as a method of divination. But in their case there was no frenzy. A witness to the murder of Edward Evans described Brady as 'showing as much emotion as a butcher working in a shop. . . He was very calm indeed. There was no frenzy.' Brady and Hindley were heavily involved in the *idea* of sex. They read de Sade, studied pornographic photographs, and even made their own. They were obsessed with the illusion of sex, and tried to penetrate the veil. They ended up killing children almost as an act of magic, to see if the reality of an actual corpse would bring some ultimate truth. In fact the act of murder was not so important to them. Far more important were the after-images. They derived a salacious satisfaction from the effects of their crimes, the grim souvenirs. Listening to the tape-recorded cries of the victims, looking at photographs of the graves – there was a voyeuristic madness here.

That madness is in us too, in the public fever for sensational sex-cases, the dirty-minded gloating which crimes like the Moors Murders foster. We too chase that will-o-the-wisp illusion of sex, hoping to learn its secrets from those devotees who go further than we dare. The sad fact is that national daily newspapers sold on average fifty thousand extra copies for every day of the trial of Brady and Hindley. Nobody wanted to miss the revelations.

There have been at least a dozen full-length books devoted to this case, which was called 'the crime of the century'. What justifies a fresh look at it is the new evidence which has come to light – notably the recovery of the body of Pauline Reade – and the subsequent confessions of both Brady and Hindley to other murders. This evidence throws a new light on the character of Myra Hindley and the old question of who was the dominant partner in the duo. I met the mother of Lesley Ann Downey during a television debate, and was humbled by the fact that even after all these years her grief is so palpable that I feel a genuine reluctance to write about the case for fear of opening old wounds; but a brief study of the case is essential to any study of sex killers. It is one of the most important English cases this century. My personal interest in the case is the enigma of Myra Hindley. I find it interesting that most women feel that Hindley was the dominant partner, infecting Brady with the lust to kill. Men tend to blame Brady. The truth must lie somewhere in between.

Ian Brady was born illegitimate in Glasgow to tea-room waitress Maggie Stewart on 2 January 1938. He did not live with his mother, but spent his childhood with another family, the Sloans, in the Gorbals district of the city. He grew up to be tall, with fair hair and grey eyes. At school he proved to be a better than average scholar, but was useless at sports and was teased for being a 'big lassie'. He retreated into a fantasy world of domination and sadism, torturing animals. Soon in trouble with the law – for housebreaking, for which he received probation – he was later convicted of nine similar offences and received two years probation on condition that he went to live with his natural mother in Manchester. In effect, he was 'deported'.

In 1954, at the age of seventeen, Ian Stewart arrived in Manchester, taking the name of his stepfather, Patrick Brady. In 1956 he was convicted of theft and spent two years in Hatfield borstal. Released in 1958, he went back to live with his mother, and eventually got a job at Millward's Chemicals Ltd, as a stock clerk earning £12 a week. It was at this point that he began dressing smartly, in three-piece suits, and started buying books on the Nazis, and pornography for his 'special collection'. He wrote off for tapes and records of Nazi marching songs and the Hitler speeches. In his lunch-break he studied German grammar. The secret fantasy life of sadistic domination was developing along sinister lines: he was reading de Sade avidly. He was a sullen, withdrawn figure, always an outsider, but he might have remained a reluctant law-abiding person had he not met Myra Hindley.

Myra Hindley was born on 23 July 1942, in the Manchester suburb of Gorton, a district of back-to-back houses with outside toilets. She was the elder of two daughters, and in infancy went to live with her grandmother, Mrs Ellen Maybury, a widow. The house she grew up in with her Gran was at 7 Bannock Street, Gorton. At school she too was a loner, a school report describing her as 'not sociable'. She was a day-dreamer, good at writing essays, but she did not have the disposition one might expect of the type. She was tough, aggressive, almost masculine, and enjoyed contact sports. She was captain of the school netball team, was a good swimmer, and took judo lessons. The death of her boyfriend, Michael, when she was fifteen devastated her. She did not sleep for days, and finally sought solace in the Roman Catholic Church. She took her first Communion on 6 November 1958, and was presented with a white-covered prayer-book by her aunt, Kath Maybury. That book was to play a significant role in subsequent events. In fact, seven years later it was to gaol her for life.

She was engaged for six months, but broke it off because she said her fiancé was 'too childish'. In 1961, aged nineteen, she dressed in the fashion of the times: tight pencil-skirts and sweaters. A tall girl, she missed being pretty because of a hooked nose and pointed chin. And she was still a virgin. After several jobs – and curiously enough, toying with the idea of serving with the NAAFI in Germany – she finally answered an advertisement for a typist at Millward Chemicals at £8.10s a week. Here she met and worked closely with Ian Brady. He often dictated letters to her in his nasal Glasgow accent.

From the start Myra Hindley was fascinated by the tall, slim man with the high, intelligent forehead and swept-back hair. His sallow face was set in the brooding expression of a James Dean type. He was withdrawn, a man of secrets, and spoke with a strange accent. To her he seemed a romantic Heathcliff figure, the ideal man. He was *different.* Even the act of smoking a cigarette he managed to invest with drama. He seemed like a man living out his own biography, as if conscious of some movie-camera focusing on his every move. She was nineteen and impressionable. He was twenty-one and rode a motor-bike. Hindley's diary entries reveal her fascination. 'The pig. He didn't look at me today.' But eventually he did.

Brady was living in Westmorland Street, Longsight, two miles away across the city from Gorton. He spent his spare time in his bedroom playing his Nazi tapes and reading books on sexual perversions. Gradually he began to talk to Hindley, revealing a little of the inner man. He loaned her books on Nazi atrocities, and talked in a sophisticated manner about sexual perversions. At Christmas she asked him to go out with her. He agreed. Her diary entry read: 'Eureka! Today we had our first date. . .' Eventually, she was no longer a virgin. A later diary entry reads: 'Jan. 1st 1962. I have been at Millwards for 12 months and only just gone out with him. I hope Ian and I love each other all our lives and get married and are happy ever after.'

Then, in June 1963, Brady moved in with Hindley, sharing the house with the grandmother, whose name was on the rent book. Brady introduced Hindley to German wine and Teutonic culture, persuading her to bleach her hair blonde and wear tight leather skirts and high boots. He nicknamed her 'Hessie' and she called him 'Neddie' because of his imitations of the Goon Show character. At this point Brady certainly dominated Hindley, teaching her his newly discovered philosophy of lust and cruelty. He bought a camera and took crude pornographic photographs of her, and of themselves in the act of intercourse and flagellation. Some of the photographs showed her with the weal-marks of a whip across her buttocks. There was a marked change in Hindley after she began cohabiting with Brady. She never again went to church, stopped baby-sitting, and became secretive and hard. Her grandmother was a frail woman who slept most of the time, and Brady and Hindley could do virtually as they liked. And they liked to kill.

We know now, from the new evidence, that their first victim was Pauline Reade, sixteen, who vanished on her way to a dance on the evening of 12 July 1963. As with the other victims, the cause of death remains unknown, but she too found a grave on the lonely Saddleworth Moors which rise high above Manchester. It is a bleak area, with rocks standing like twisted gargoyles, buried in the soft, peaty earth. With only the earth and sky for company, it is a perfect Wagnerian setting for any Nazi superman – or woman. Brady and Hindley had started putting their fantasies into practice.

That date for Pauline Reade – 12 July 1963 – is important. Because Hindley did not pass her driving test until the fourth attempt, on 7 November 1963, which raises the question of how the couple transported their victim to a moorland grave. (Brady *could not drive*.) Pauline Reade had lived only a short distance away from the couple. On 23 November 1963 – the day after the assassination of President Kennedy – Hindley hired a Ford Anglia from Warren Autos in Manchester. That same day John Kilbride, aged twelve, disappeared from a market at Ashton-under-Lyne. When Hindley returned the car it was covered in peaty mud. John Kilbride lay on the moors in a shallow grave. There was a big police search for the missing boy while the couple snickered quietly.

In May 1964 Hindley bought her first car, a white Mini van. On 16 June 1964 Keith Bennett, aged twelve years and six months, vanished near the home of Brady's mother. He too lies on the moor. At around this time, on Brady's orders, Hindley joined a rifle club at Cheadle, and from members she purchased a Webley .45 revolver for £8, and a Smith and Wesson .38 for £5. Brady, in a black shirt and with a gun in a shoulder-holster, often had 'Hessie' run him up to the moors so that he could practise target-shooting, and also visit the graves. They liked to visit the graves, and photographed each other kneeling on them. Later police were to use these photographs to locate some of the graves.

On 26 December 1964 Lesley Ann Downey, aged ten years and four months, vanished on her way to a fair with a friend. Her body was to be found ten months later, in a grave on Saddleworth Moors. Her murder had been recorded on tape by Brady and Hindley, and when it was played in court at the subsequent trial it caused even hardened crime-reporters to blanch.

Brady now felt that the time had come to expand his empire of evil by recruiting able lieutenants. Hindley's sister, Maureen, had been going out with a sixteen-year-old youth named David Smith. When he got her pregnant Smith married her in the summer of 1964. Smith had also been born illegitimate, and was a tough, cocky character with a criminal record. Now he was Myra Hindley's brother-in-law. Brady began to groom David Smith as a disciple, feeding him on wine and de Sade and talking of 'bank jobs' and other armed robberies, impressing the youth with his two guns and his air of sophistication. The young David Smith, sixteen, and his wife Maureen, eighteen, lived in the slums like Brady and Hindley. When these slums were demolished Brady and Hindley, together with the grandmother, were rehoused in the new overspill estate at Hattersley. The new, three-bedroomed house was at 16 Wardle Brook Avenue. On 23 July 1965 David and Maureen Smith moved to a flat in Underwood Court, just a few hundred yards away from Brady and Hindley's home. The four became constant companions, visiting one another's homes and travelling in Myra's new Mini Countryman on trips to the moors. And all the while Brady was loaning Smith books, and preaching to him the mad philosophy of de Sade and talking to him of committing armed robberies. After all, if as de Sade had declared 'God is dead', then why should one not rob?

In the words of the prosecution at the trial, the then Attorney-General, Sir Frederick Elwyn Jones QC., MP., said, 'Brady's interest in Smith went far beyond ordinary friendship. The association was one of the steady corruption of a youth by a man. . . Brady was interested in murder and wanted to make Smith a student of murder.' David Smith had begun to copy into an exercise book quotations from de Sade which interested him. 'People are like maggots, small, blind worthless fish-bait.' 'Murder is a hobby and a supreme pleasure.' David Smith might not have been a model citizen, but he was not prepared to commit murder. Brady's mistake, motivated by the fact that he was arrogant and corrupt, was to imagine that he could induce *anyone* to enter into and share his fantasies.

On 25 September 1965 Brady had an important conversation with David Smith, now seventeen. He told him, 'I have killed before. Three or four. The bodies are buried on the moors. I have photographs to prove it.' They had been drinking at the time, and Smith did not take the remarks seriously, thinking it was simply idle, drunken boasting. On 2 October 1965 Brady insisted, 'I'll do another one. I'm not due for another one for three or four months, but this one won't count.' It didn't 'count' in Brady's scheme of things because it was to be simply a demonstration murder designed to impress Smith and recruit him to the murder-team.

At midnight on Wednesday 6 October 1965 Myra Hindley called at the Smiths' flat at about midnight, and asked Smith to walk her home. The visit was a pretext to involve Smith in murder. When they got to 16 Wardle Brook Avenue Myra Hindley invited Smith in, saying that Brady had some miniature wine bottles for him. At the precise moment that Smith walked into the lounge, Brady began to kill the 'demonstration' victim, Edward Evans, aged seventeen years and nine months, whom Brady and Hindley had picked up in their car earlier that evening. The murder Smith witnessed was intended to make him an accomplice, and tie him in firmly to future murders.

As Smith entered the house there was a cry and Myra Hindley said urgently, 'Help him, Dave.' Smith rushed into the lounge and saw Brady standing astride Edward Evans with an axe held aloft, which he brought crashing down on the youth's head. In Smith's own words, given in evidence, 'I ran in and nearly had a stroke. I just stopped dead. My first thought was that it was a life-size doll, sort of half screaming and half groaning. Ian stood over him with an axe in his right hand.' Brady hit the victim at least fourteen times with the axe, then throttled him with a length of flex, all the while muttering in a dull monotone, 'The fucking bastard. The fucking bastard.' Then he looked up at Smith, smiled, and said: 'This one was the messiest yet.' He handed the axe to Smith, asking him to feel the weight of it – and thus ensuring he got his prints on the murder weapon – and Smith, dumb with terror, helped Hindley clean up the blood, and then helped Brady truss the body up in polythene sheeting. Then in a grotesque parody of domesticity that Joe Orton would have admired, Myra Hindley made them all a pot of tea. Her eyes were glittering with excitement as she commented to Brady, 'You should have seen the look on his face. The blow registered in his eyes!' She then reminisced fondly about previous murders.

David Smith left as soon as he could, promising to return next day with a pram to wheel the body out to Myra's car – but in reality he was terrified that if he showed any sign of dissent, he would be the next to die. Once back at his flat he was violently sick, and told his wife everything. At dawn the couple went to a nearby phone-box and dialled 999, saying, 'There's been a murder. . . ' That call was logged at 6.07. A patrol car arrived to pick up the couple, finding that David Smith was holding a knife and screwdriver to protect himself. Smith virtually threw himself into the police car. Once at Hyde police station Smith poured out his incredible story to Detective Superintendent Talbot. At 8.40 a.m. on 7 October 1965 Superintendent Talbot, wearing a borrowed baker's roundsman's coat with a basket of loaves over his arm, knocked on the door of 16 Wardle Brook Avenue. He was unarmed, despite being warned by David Smith that Brady had two guns.

At first Superintendent Talbot thought he was the victim of a practical joke. Myra Hindley seemed normal enough when she opened the door to him; a smart woman whose age he guessed at about thirty. But eventually the trussed-up body of Edward Evans was found in the locked back bedroom, and the couple were arrested. David Smith's statement about Brady talking of 'other murders' had aroused police interest, and different Forces and other senior officers became involved in the questioning of Brady and Hindley, including Detective Chief Inspector Joe Mounsey, the new CID chief of Ashton-under-Lyne. He was interested in any connection with the missing boy John Kilbride.

Under questioning both Brady and Hindley showed remarkable toughness. Brady admitted having killed Edward Evans, 'following a row', and did everything he could to implicate David Smith in the murder. Myra Hindley was questioned by woman detective Margaret Campion, thirty-seven, a very experienced officer. To all questions Hindley replied, 'My story is the same as Ian's. . . ask Ian. Wherever he went, I went. Whatever he did, I did.' The detective noted that Hindley did not have a hair out of place, and expressed concern only that her dog, Puppet, should be fed. Later police had to take the dog to a vet to have its teeth X-rayed to determine its age – this would have served to date the photographs found – but the dog died under anaesthetic. When told of the death of her dog Hindley screamed, 'You fucking murderers!' It was almost the only emotion she was ever to display.

Detective Chief Superintendent Arthur Benfield, chief of Cheshire CID, headed the inquiry. On 13 October he told a press conference, 'We have discussed the files of eight people who have disappeared without trace during the past three or four years.'

Brady's story was that there had been an argument with 'Eddie' leading to his death in the course of a struggle. But police found a coded list in Hindley's car. It was a carefully designed plan for the removal of all clues to the murder. Brady was later to claim that he and David Smith drew up the plan *after* the murder. GN stood for gun, and Det for detail, but PB was a puzzle. Brady said it stood for 'Pennistone Burn', but there was no such place. It actually stood for 'prayer book' and Chief Inspector Tyrrell was to find a ticket hidden in the spine of Myra Hindley's prayer book. It was a railway left-luggage ticket, number 74843. Two suitcases were recovered from Manchester Central Station. They contained letters, wigs, coshes, books on sexual perversions, two reels of tape, and nine photographs of Lesley Ann Downey in the nude, a gag around her mouth. When the tapes were played detectives listened in growing horror to the last moments of the little girl. Her death had been taped for posterity. Now the full cunning of Brady and Hindley was revealed. Before the murder ten months before, incriminating items had been packed into suitcases and placed in the left-luggage lockers until after the successful completion of the deed. It was proof of cool, calculating premeditation.

A vital witness in the case proved to be a local girl, Patricia Hodges, twelve, who lived a couple of doors away from Brady and Hindley. The couple had befriended her, and often took her up to the moors to picnic. She was driven in a police car to Saddleworth Moor, with instructions to tell officers when she recognized the spot where the picnics had taken place. She stopped the car at Hollin Brow Knoll, close to Wessenden Head. Police were able to match up photographs found in Wardle Brook Avenue with the actual sites where they had been taken. Including the picture of Myra Hindley kneeling, with a sinister smile on her lips, looking down at the earth. An army of policemen began digging on the moor. On 16 October the body of Lesley Ann Downey was found. On 21 October the body of John Kilbride was recovered, 373 yards away from the grave of Lesley Ann. But by December of 1965, with the coming of winter, digging ceased on Saddleworth Moor.

Brady and Hindley were formally charged with three

murders, but still refused to talk of any other missing children and possible murders. Hindley insisted that David Smith had killed Lesley Ann Downey, and Brady said it had been Smith who had brought the child to the house to be photographed. Even now, when all was lost, they were trying to implicate Smith, displaying their manipulative traits which they were never to lose.

The 'trial of the century' began at Chester Assizes – held at Chester Castle on 19 April 1966 – and was to last fourteen days. Before the trial, during the long remand in custody, Brady and Hindley had sought Home Office permission to be married: this was refused. When they appeared in the dock it was as bachelor and spinster. The court-room was packed with some 150 pressmen from all over the world, including authors and playwrights. There were few seats for the ordinary members of the public. The trial testimony was to reveal much about the perverse sexual streak which bound Brady and Hindley together. For example, the pathologist's examination of Edward Evans revealed that his fly-buttons were undone, and there were traces of dog hairs around his anus. The body of John Kilbride was found with trousers and underpants down around his knees. It is likely that Hindley derived sexual pleasure from watching Brady perform homosexual acts on his victims.

The Attorney-General, Sir Elwyn Jones QC, outlined the charges and the evidence to the all-male jury, the details of the perverted sexual murders of three children.. He emphasized that Myra Hindley was also firmly implicated in the murders. 'She was not merely clay in the hands of the potter, but an active, and some might even think leading, participant in all that transpired.' Brady looked bored, examining his well-manicured nails. The prosecution went on, 'You will be wondering why this man did this to a fellow human being. You might be wondering what Evans was doing in that house at all, what Hindley was doing there, and why Smith was there. To answer these questions it is necessary to go back to the beginning and piece together the history of events.' He told of the grooming of David Smith to be a murder disciple, ending with the night of the murder of Edward Evans, when Hindley called for David Smith and asked him to walk her home.

Sir Elwyn Jones said, 'We say this was a trick devised and executed by Hindley for one particular purpose: to get Smith back to Wardle Brook Avenue to witness the murder of Edward Evans. . . . The murder was pre-arranged by the two accused and they lured Edward Evans to the house that night for the express purpose of killing him, which they did.' He referred to the fact that the victim's trousers were down, saying, 'In association with his killing, as with the other two, there was present not only a sexual element, but an abnormal sexual element, a perverted sexual element.'

Maureen Smith, heavily pregnant, gave evidence against her sister, telling of how she had changed since meeting Brady, and of trips to Saddleworth Moor. (Maureen was to divorce David Smith, and died young from a brain tumour.)

David Smith, now eighteen, was the next witness. He told of Brady's talk of robbing banks and of murders. 'He said he had killed three or four people. I thought it was the beer talking.' He told of the horror of having to witness the murder of Edward Evans, and being forced to help parcel up the body. 'I just froze . . . My first thought was that Ian had hold of a life-size rag doll and was just waving it about. The arms were going all over . . My stomach turned over. It was half-screaming and groaning. . . He was making a gurgling noise like when you brush your teeth and gargle with water. . .' Prosecution: 'Will you tell us what kind of impression Brady created upon you as you watched him?' Smith: 'Well, I have seen butchers working in shops showing as much emotion as he did when they were cutting up sheep's ribs. He was very calm indeed. He was not in a frenzy – no frenzy at all.'

Both defence counsel – Godfrey Heilpern QC, for Hindley, and Emlyn Hooson QC, for Brady – cross-examined David Smith with some ferocity, trying to discredit him with his criminal record, suggesting that he was motivated by a newspaper contract to secure a conviction, and insinuating that he was as closely involved with the murders as were the two accused. Mr Hooson questioned Smith about opinions he had written in his exercise book. Mr Hooson: ' "Every man and woman is one of two things, a masochist or a sadist" – are these your views?' Smith: 'They were my views about people.' Defence counsel pursued: 'You were indoctrinated by murder, you were infected by it. Is it not the truth that you joined in?' Smith: 'No, sir.'

The high-point of horror during the trial came on Tuesday 26 April, when the sixteen-minute tape recording of the last minutes of Lesley Ann Downey was played to the jury, after the Attorney-General had read out the transcript of the tape. The victim was heard screaming, crying out. That tape-recording was the most damning piece of evidence in the case.

Brady in the witness box was careful always to try to protect Hindley as much as possible and implicate David Smith. Asked by Hindley's counsel, 'What are your feelings for Myra?' He replied. 'They are as man and wife.' Question: 'If you had different views about matters, whose views would prevail?' Brady: 'Mine. She was my typist.' He admitted the killing of Edward Evans, but denied any involvement in the murders of Lesley Ann Downey and John Kilbride. The photographs of Myra Hindley either kneeling over or gazing down at the graves was 'pure coincidence'. He was cross-examined for a total of nine hours by the Attorney-General, who suggested that the photographs were 'trophies of murder'. When questioned about his collection of pornographic books Brady snapped back, 'You'll find much worse collections in lords' manors all over the country!'

Detective Chief Inspector Tyrrell in his evidence made an interesting comment. He had asked Myra Hindley about the changes in her behaviour since meeting Brady, possibly seeking to suggest that he had corrupted her. Hindley had replied, 'I made all my own decisions. People go through several stages in their lives. After discussions they change their mind. Ian never made me do anything I didn't want to do.'

When Myra Hindley went into the witness box she was asked about her feelings for Brady. She said, 'I love him. I still love him.' Her voice was hoarse. Asked about her involvement in the taking of photographs of Lesley Ann Downey – she could hardly deny her voice on the tape – she replied, 'I have no defence. It was indefensible. I was cruel.' The Attorney-General was to call her remorse 'counterfeit shame'.

Brady had made a revealing slip of the tongue when describing the photographic sessions with the little girl. He had said, 'Afterwards, we all got dressed and went downstairs.' It was a slip that the trial judge, Mr Justice Fenton Atkinson, was to elaborate upon in his summing-up. 'It possibly casts a flood of light on the nature of the activities that were going on.'

The Attorney-General in his closing speech said, 'As in any sphere of activity, people who commit more than one murder or other crimes tend to leave their identifiable trademarks in each case. There were eight factors in common in these cases.' He listed them. The victims were all young. Had disappeared from public places. Had vanished from places in the same general area where Brady and Hindley lived. There was abnormal sexual activity with each victim. A motor vehicle had been an essential requirement in all the murders, to dispose of the bodies. The method of killing had been identical. Records, in the form of photographs and tape-recordings, had been kept of each murder. And in each case the burial place was a lonely moorland grave.

In his summing-up, the judge told the jury, 'If what the prosecution say is right, you are facing here two sadistic killers of the utmost depravity.' At 4.46 p.m. on Friday 6 May 1966 the jury returned with their verdicts. Brady was guilty of all three murders. Hindley guilty of two murders, not guilty of murdering John Kilbride but guilty of harbouring Brady knowing that he had killed the youth. Brady was sentenced to three life terms of imprisonment, Hindley to two life sentences with an additional seven years for the harbouring charge. Brady did not appeal, but Myra Hindley did. The Court of Criminal Appeal firmly rejected her appeal against conviction and sentence, describing the evidence against her as 'overwhelming'.

It should have been the end of the story, but it was simply the prelude to a long saga. The Moors Murders were to remain lodged in the public mind as a symbol of supreme wickedness. Had Brady and Hindley been hanged, it would indeed have been the end of the tale, but capital punishment had been abolished on 8 November 1965, just a month after the murder of Edward Evans.

Brady was now in Durham Prison, where he was frequently assaulted, and was scarred with boiling water by child-killer Raymond Morris. Brady asked to go on Rule 43, to be segregated in isolation for his own protection. He was to remain in solitary confinement for most of the years which lay ahead. No doubt he saw himself as some kind of Rudolf Hess figure. Just as Hess languished in Spandau Prison, refusing to be broken, so Brady would hold out, proud and aloof from the enemy which surrounded him. Hindley was in Holloway Prison, where she was assaulted by women prisoners until she too asked to go on Rule 43. The couple wrote to each other every week, the deadly partnership still intact. They started taking O Level German together, Brady passing the examination within six months. Brady wrote frequent petitions to the Home Office, demanding to be allowed visits from Myra – the right of common-law husbands and wives. Permission was always refused, and as a consequence Brady went on hunger strike for twenty-eight days. The couple were never long out of the headlines.

After five years in prison Myra Hindley became impatient. That bond between her and Brady could not survive separation behind steel bars and stone walls. She longed for freedom. In December 1970 she wrote in a letter: 'I feel so mashed-up mentally. . . The truth is that after only five years of a life sentence I am obsessed with an inordinate desire to be free.' She was having frequent visits from Lord Longford, the prison reform campaigner, and it was reported that she had rejoined the Catholic Church. She wanted freedom at any price and even now was displaying her extraordinary manipulative powers. She realised that being linked to Ian Brady reduced her chances of being released on licence, and decided to finish with him. In 1972 she wrote her last letter to him, renouncing him.

Brady was enraged by her defection, and cynically commented that her conversion to religion was a public relations exercise designed to enable her to 'work her ticket'. He was determined that Hindley would never escape his clutches, and at this point he began to play a cruel chess-game with her, one that seemed destined to last the rest of their lives. Every time there was an item in the Press suggesting that Hindley was perhaps being considered for release Brady would let slip another bit of poison to damage her chances of freedom.

The years passed. Myra Hindley despaired of ever being released. She had a lesbian affair with a prison officer at Holloway. An escape was planned and keys made, but the plot was foiled. The prison officer received six years imprisonment, and Myra Hindley, prisoner 964055, was taken to court and given an additional one year's imprisonment for her part in the plot.

Myra Hindley continued to write to influential people. She wrote to John Trevelyan, the film-censor, in 1974, 'Something is slowly dying inside me, and it's the will to live. . .' On 8 May 1975 she wrote again, 'What is life for? To die? Then why not kill myself at once? No, I'm afraid. Wait for death until it comes? I fear that even more. Then I must live. But what for? In order to die. I can't escape from that circle.' After being assaulted by a fellow-prisoner and having her nose and jaw broken, Myra Hindley was given plastic surgery and had her name changed by deed-poll to Myra Spencer. When this leaked out to the Press there was again speculation that the Home Office was preparing Hindley for release. Brady read the newspapers and took appropriate action. He was determined to end his days behind bars, like some Nazi martyr, and he was determined that *Hindley should too*.

Hindley got her BA Degree in Humanities from the Open University, but she could not escape from Brady. He was in Parkhurst Prison, making books in braille for the blind. Hindley had taken his place at Durham. In January 1978 Brady wrote an open letter saying, 'I have always accepted that the weight of the crimes both Myra and myself were convicted of justifies permanent imprisonment, regardless of expressed personal remorse and verifiable change.' Ian Brady, prisoner number 602217, was making sure that Myra would be damned with him forever.

Myra Hindley continued to have visits from Lord Longford and other personalities. When Lord Stonham was Under-Secretary at the Home Office he visited Hindley in prison and was so impressed by her demeanour that he said afterwards that he was worried that a person like her could be in prison. William Mars-Jones, who had been a junior counsel at the trial, retorted that he would be worried if she were not in prison. Lesley Ann Downey's mother vowed passionately on a television programme that if ever Myra Hindley were released she personally would kill her. Patrick Kilbride, father of victim John Kilbride, made the same promise.

Myra Hindley once again petitioned the Home Secretary, pleading for her release, saying, 'I feel I have more than paid my debt to Society. . . ' Angered by attempts to have Hindley released as a 'reformed character', Brady again wrote to the Press. The *Sunday Times* published his letter on 16 May 1982. He declared that he had no wish ever to be considered for release: 'Since the weight of our crimes justifies permanent imprisonment.' Now aged forty-four, Brady wrote to the Parole Board informing them, 'I will not wish to be freed in 1985 or even 2005.'

Things had not gone too well for David Smith in these years. He had been made a social outcast because of his association with Brady and Hindley, and was frequently assaulted and driven out of local pubs. He spent two years in gaol – 1969-71 – for stabbing a man in a brawl, and was divorced from Maureen in 1973. In his own way David Smith too had been a victim of the evil duo.

Myra Hindley was moved to Cookham Wood, an open prison in Rochester, Kent, in 1983. It was like a high-class hotel, each inmate having her own 'room' with carpets and curtains. There was colour television, and frequent escorted walks into town. Such a move, to a minimum-security gaol, usually means that a prisoner is nearing the end of the sentence imposed. Brady, the masochist, was still in segregation in Parkhurst. He told those people who talked to him, 'I want to die in gaol.'

The Home Secretary had announced in the Commons that Brady and Hindley would not be considered for release until 1985 – this statement had prompted Brady's letter to the *Sunday Times*. Police officers had visited Brady in Parkhurst; now it was announced that he was about to be moved to another prison. Gartree in Leicestershire was mentioned. There was now heavy Press speculation that Brady was ready to talk to the police about other murders. Myra Hindley wrote to a friend about these rumours, saying, 'I couldn't make statements about something I know nothing about. . . My conscience is clear. . . Regardless of any allegations he might make.'

At the age of forty-two and after seventeen years in prison, Myra Hindley again wrote to the Home Secretary requesting to be considered for release by the Parole Board. On 23 May 1985 Home Secretary Leon Brittan announced the recommendations of the Parole Board, 'That neither Ian Brady nor Myra Hindley should be released. The case of Ian Brady will be reviewed in ten years' time. Myra Hindley's will be reviewed in five years' time.' Lord Longford denounced the decision as 'brutal, revolting, astounding and disgusting'. Myra Hindley attempted to commit suicide with a pair of stolen scissors. When this failed she went on hunger strike. Now, after nineteen years in prison, she was finally broken.

In cell 4 at Parkhurst Prison, Brady was now thin and gaunt, and he was hearing voices. Slowly but surely he was going insane. But not *that* insane. When he read in newspapers that Myra Hindley had instructed her lawyers to take her case to the Court of Human Rights at Strasbourg, he let fall another drip of poisoned information. He told a reporter, 'If I revealed what *really* happened, Myra would not get out in one hundred years.'

In November 1985 Brady was certified insane and moved to the top-security mental hospital at Park Lane, Liverpool. Doctors had diagnosed acute paranoia and schizophrenia. In March 1987 Brady offered doctors at the hospital a bizarre deal. He would reveal the full list of victims he and Hindley had killed if the doctors would let him die – give him the means to commit suicide.

The race was on between Brady and Hindley as to who would be first to 'confess'. In March 1986 Brady agreed to meet Anne West, mother of Lesley Ann Downey, following an emotional letter from the bereaved woman. And Hindley was apparently moved by a letter written to her by the mother of Keith Bennett. Mrs Winifred Johnson, fifty-three, took five years to compose that letter, in which she begged Hindley to tell her what had really happened to her son.

Detective Chief Superintendent Peter Topping of Manchester CID had always been determined to solve the riddle of the missing children. He visited Hindley in Cookham Prison more than once, urging her to confess. Finally she told about the killings of Pauline Reade and Keith Bennett. She was taken on a highly publicized visit to Saddleworth Moor, tramping across the peat with police officers to point out likely sites for digging. Brady had refused to go back to the moor, describing Hindley's trips there as a 'public relations stunt'. But an army of policemen were once again digging on the Moors.

On 1 July 1987 police found the body of Pauline Reade. Her mother, Joan, is an in-patient at a psychiatric hospital because of what happened to her daughter. Nobody has remained untouched by this case. Policewoman Margaret Campion was ill with nerves after the Moors Murders trial and resigned from the Force in May 1967, just one year later.

In July 1987 Brady agreed finally to go back to his old-killing grounds on the moors to try to pin-point the grave of Keith Bennett. He failed, complaining that quarrying had altered the landscape since he had last used it as a cemetery over twenty years previously.

In August 1987 Brady told a BBC television reporter that he had given information to Manchester Police about five more killings. Police acknowledged having received this information, but could not treat the confessions as genuine until the details were substantiated. But dusty old files were reopened. . . There will be further developments in the Moors Murders case; the saga will not be over until the deaths of both participants.

Of all the books written about the Moors Murders, the most prominent was *Beyond Belief* (1967) by the eminent playwright Emlyn Williams. He attempted to 'fictionalize' the case in an attempt to get inside the mind of Ian Brady. He failed: you cannot enter into the mind of a murderer simply by an act of will. But Emlyn Williams does contribute to the old arguments of environment versus heredity – and at times seems to give comfort to both sides. Like most romantics, he ignores the real issues. Talking of Brady's background, the slum-environment of Manchester and a young man starved of culture, Williams writes, 'It is a level at which a starved young spirit cannot stay. If it refuses to rise from there, then there is only descent.' But he promptly dooms Brady as having been 'born bad' by asking the question: could Brady have ever, at any point, have chosen the right path in life? 'No,' Williams answers bleakly. 'It is not even a question of its having been too late. From the day of his birth, the spell had been woven. And nothing could have changed it. Nothing.'

I personally find such a response nonsense. Had Brady been the son of a millionaire, would he have killed? Brady *could* have lived out his life as a sullen outsider, had he not met Myra Hindley. He could not have accomplished what he did without a willing and active partner.

In retrospect, it is obvious that Brady was very much a Peter Kürten-type figure, who would have gone on raping and killing for years had he not been caught when he was. Like Kürten, he too returned to the graves of his victims, like a dog returning to its vomit. It now seems likely that since they had no vehicle, the couple must have persuaded Pauline Reade to walk up on the moor with them, and then cut her throat after Brady had raped her; and this throws new light on Brady. He was not simply a social rebel, a misfit shaking his fist at society out of pure resentment. Sex, pain and torture must have been closely linked in his mind, and he had probably been fantasizing over torture for years before that fatal meeting with Hindley. I suspect that his private fantasy was of being a concentration camp guard and being able to rape and torture his prisoners at will.

It seems unlikely that the public will ever be content to see either one of this couple walk free.

Chapter Ten

TED BUNDY: ALL-AMERICAN SERIAL KILLER

Theodore Robert Bundy was a handsome student, brimming with self-confidence and style. The man with the looks of a Robert Redford and a charming articulate manner to match, a product of the American Dream. Success was his for the choosing. Instead he chose to pursue a four-year orgy of destruction across the USA which left dozens of young women maimed or dead. Police believe Bundy killed twenty-one women, but the real figure may be as high as forty.

And in the manner of his passing Bundy brought out all the worst aspect of the American character. New President George Bush had promised a 'more kindly America'. When Bundy went to the electric chair on 24 January 1989, after some ten years on Death Row, Americans celebrated by holding parties, wearing T-shirts bearing the slogan 'Burn, Bundy, Burn'. And a local disc jockey urged listeners to turn off their coffee pots so that 'Sparky can have more juice'.

At the moment of his death thousands of spectators outside the prison roared their approval, drivers hooting their horns gleefully. A nearby bar was serving Bundy 'fries' and Bundy 'toast' with a sign above reading 'Roast In Peace.'

Looking for a psychological motive for the Bundy murders is almost useless. There are some men whose minds are unfathomable. Like giant squid, they lurk in the icy ocean depths, rarely showing their wreathed arms. All we can do is to examine his murders and try to discover some kind of pattern.

A narrative account of the Bundy killings is difficult to construct, since he killed in so many different locations across the USA, and along a diffuse time-span. Time and geography are important elements in the equation, as are the identities of the victims. The true total is not known, but Bundy once boasted to the police that an accurate figure would be 'in three digits'.

For our purposes, the first murder in his long series was that of Kathy Devine, fifteen, who vanished from Seattle, Washington state, on 25 November 1973. Her remains were found in a forest on December 6. Kathy had been strangled and sodomized. Most writers on the career of Bundy do not mention this case or attribute it to him, but the *modus operandi* fits.

Certainly Bundy attacked Sharon Clarke, eighteen, in her basement bedroom in Seattle on the night of 4 January 1974, bludgeoning her with a crowbar as she lay asleep in bed, and thrusting a speculum, or vaginal probe, deep inside her, causing internal injuries. She survived after spending some months in a coma, but even under hypnosis could remember no details of the attack.

In the early hours of 1 February 1974 Bundy was again on the prowl in Seattle. He found an unlocked door in a student's rooming house leading to a basement bedroom where Lynda Ann Healy, twenty-one, was asleep. Battering her unconscious, he carried her out to his Volkswagen car. (When 'hunting' victims, he removed the passenger seat to enable him to load bodies more easily.)

He drove her to Taylor Mountain, some twenty miles away, and forced her to undress. Then after raping her repeatedly he killed her. Police were baffled by the reported disappearance. All they had were bloodstained sheets and a pillow, nothing to indicate what had really happened. The victim, an attractive psychology student from the University of Washington, who did part-time ski reports for the local radio station, had simply vanished, and some officers tended to think she was just another runaway.

On 12 March 1974 Donna Gail Manson, nineteen, disappeared while on her way to a jazz concert in Olympia. Her body was never found. Susan Elaine Rancourt, eighteen, another university student, disappeared on 17 April, 120 miles from Seattle. On 6 May, Roberta Kathleen Parks, twenty-two, disappeared from Corvallis in Oregon, and twenty-six days later, on 1 June, Brenda Carol Ball, twenty-two, also vanished from the town of Burien.

It was unnerving. The killer was like the invisible man. He had the power to abduct his victims, often in broad daylight, and yet was never seen, or left a single forensic clue.

It was not until 11 June, when Georgina Hawkins, eighteen, vanished, and the decomposing body of missing girl Brenda Baker, fifteen, was found in a State Park that police began to suspect that one man might be responsible for all these crimes. That most feared animal the sexual serial killer was on the loose.

But before the police had time to study the evidence the unknown killer struck again, and this time he took two victims within a couple of hours of each other from the crowded Lake Sammammish Park, twelve miles from Seattle. It was 14 July when Janice Ott, twenty-three, and Denise Naslund, nineteen, were plucked out from a crowd of 40,000 people, and amazingly, Denise was accompanied by her boy friend, who saw nothing.

But other people had been more observant. For the first time police had witnesses. Young women told of having been approached by a handsome young man with an arm apparently in a cast, who asked them to help him put his sailing-boat up on the roof of his Volkswagen car.

He introduced himself as 'Ted'. Now the police had a definite lead and newspapers bore the headline: POLICE SEEK 'TED' IN MISSING WOMEN CASE.

Then, inexplicably, the killings in Washington state stopped. There had been at least one girl abducted, attacked or killed per month. Sharon Clarke in January, Lynda Healy in February, Donna Manson in March, Susan Rancourt in April, Roberta Parks in May, Brenda Ball in June – along with Georgina Hawkins – and a 'double event' in July: Janice Ott and Denise Naslund.

The unknown killer's appetite was sharpening, and if the pattern continued he should have killed again in August, but unknown to local police he had done just that.

Carol Valenzuela, twenty, disappeared on 2 August in Vancouver. Her body was to be discovered in October a few miles from Olympia, along with the remains of an unidentified female.

The forensic indications were that Carol had been strangled. But before that grim find another girl had vanished without trace. She was Nancy Wilcox, sixteen, who was last seen alive on 2 October. Her body was never found.

On 7 September a construction worker found the bodies of Janice Ott and Denise Naslund just two miles from the park from which they had been taken. At that site police found the remains of yet another unidentified female. Now for the first time police knew with certainty that they were seeking a solitary serial killer, and informed the Press of this fact.

If Bundy had any 'genius' – and one judge was later to call him a 'diabolical genius' – it was for moving on at just the right time, leaving the police following a cold scent. Bundy moved to Salt Lake City in Utah in September, to study law at the university there, having switched from psychology. The police back in Seattle were left to try to fit the pieces together of what was becoming an enormous puzzle. They did note that there were striking similarities between the victims, as if the killer was picking a *type* of girl. All had long hair parted in the middle and were white, slender and attractive. Each one vanished from or near colleges, all were single and had been wearing jeans or slacks when taken.

This was the signature of Ted Bundy, despite the fact that he was careful never to leave any clues – police were never to find a single fingerprint. By his selection of victims, Bundy was signing his ghastly work.

Detectives did receive some help when Bundy's long-time lover 'Elizabeth Kendall' (not her real name, but the one she used to write a book: *The Phantom Prince: My Life with Ted Bundy*) had phoned the 'Ted' hotline to give Bundy's name as a likely suspect. So had *True Detective* crime reporter Ann Rule. Both knew that Bundy fitted the description and the photofit, and that he drove a Volkswagen. More importantly, he spoke with a clipped, almost British accent, which witnesses had noticed.

Both women had agonized over naming Bundy, Elizabeth because she loved him, Ann because she liked and trusted him.

Ann Rule, former policewoman and now a crime reporter, had signed a contract to write a book about the string of unsolved murders in the area. She had first met Ted Bundy in 1971 when she was forty and he was a handsome 24-year-old psychology student. They were both working on the crisis-line at Seattle's Crisis Clinic, taking calls from would-be suicides and the like.

She was struck by his charm and kindness. Later she discovered to her horror that her 'friend' was the man she was writing about. In her book *The Stranger Beside Me* she explains: 'To write a book about an anonymous suspect is one thing. To write a book about someone you knew and cared for for ten years is quite another.'

But the fact that 'Elizabeth' and Ann had separately named Bundy did not help the police much. Lots of 'Teds' drove Volkswagens. Bundy was simply one of 3,500 suspects. The police were using the computer in the hunt for the killer, and had fed in 200,000 details including the names of 41,000 Volkswagen-owners, thousands of men with sex-records, and every student who had ever shared a class with one of the victims.

Programmed into thirty-seven categories, the computer was asked to isolate the suspect using different criteria. The results were interesting. There were 1,600 names on three of the categories, 600 on four categories. Asked for names which appeared on twenty-five of the thirty-seven categories, the computer printed out the names of just ten suspects. Bundy was seventh on that list. It took a long time to investigate each name thoroughly and police were working on number six when the break-through came.

In Utah Ted Bundy had been busy. On 18 October 1974 Melissa Smith, seventeen, vanished from the small town on Midvale, just south of Salt Lake City. She was the daughter of the local police chief. Her body was discovered nine days later in a canyon. She had been bludgeoned and sodomized, then strangled. Keeping to the two-a-month schedule, on 31 October seventeen-year-old Laura Aime disappeared. Her body was found in the Wasatch Mountains on 27 November. She had been bludgeoned and strangled.

Then 'Ted' made his first mistake when he attempted to abduct Carol DaRonch, nineteen, on 8 November in the town of Murray in the Salt Lake City area. Posing as a police officer and giving his name as 'Officer Roseland', he persuaded her to get into his VW car. When he attempted to handcuff her, clubbing at her with an iron bar, she fought him off and fled screaming. Carole would be able to recognize him if ever he was apprehended, for she had the enviable distinction of being the only living witness.

Angry and frustrated, that same night Bundy drove seventeen miles to snatch another girl, Debra Kent, seventeen, from a high school at Bountiful where a late-night play was being performed. Her body was never found. The only clue was a handcuff key found in the school car-park. Ted celebrated the new year of 1975 by snatching Nancy Baird, twenty-one, from a service station in Farmington on 12 January. Her body was never found.

Once again Bundy made the decision to shift his killing-grounds, and this time it was the turn of Colorado. While police in Seattle and Utah were still piecing together the threads, Caryn Campbell, twenty-three, disappeared from a hotel in the short walk from the hotel lobby to her room. Her nude body was found a month later, bludgeoned and raped.

In March 1975, back in Washington state, some of Bundy's handiwork was beginning to surface. A grim discovery was made on Taylor Mountain, when the skeletal remains of Brenda Ball, Susan Rancourt, Roberta Parks and Lynda Healy were found. For some crazy reason the killer appeared to have been driving long distances just to dump bodies in his own favoured funeral site. Roberta Parks, for example, had been transported 250 miles from Oregon to be dumped on Taylor Mountain.

More killings followed in Colorado. On 15 March Julie Cunningham, twenty-six, vanished from a street in Vail, and Denise Oliverson, 25, vanished while riding her bicycle in Grand Junction on 6 April. Neither body was ever found. Melanie Cooley, eighteen, vanished in mid-April, and her body was found two weeks later. Shelley Robertson vanished on 30 June, and her body was found in a mine-shaft in August.

Bundy was leaving a paper-trail which one day would kill him. A record of his credit-card transactions proved that he had bought petrol at these places and dates for at least the first three victims. Then came a dramatic arrest.

Back in Utah, on 16 August, a police patrol car stopped Bundy's car 'on suspicion' as he was cruising the streets of Granger, twelve miles from Salt Lake City, in the early hours of the morning. He had tried to out-run the patrol car, but lacked the speed. Asked what he was doing driving around, Bundy said he had just come from a drive-in movie where he had seen *Towering Inferno*.

The cop radioed in and found that that movie was not being shown. Inside Bundy's car were found burglary tools, an ice-pick, crowbar, a ski-mask made from a pair of tights, and a set of handcuffs. The mass killer was taken to Salt Lake City gaol and locked up, after having his 'mug-shot' taken and being fingerprinted.

He was held over the weekend on the minor charge of 'trying to evade a police officer'. On the Tuesday, when detectives at police headquarters held their regular weekly meeting, among the items on the agenda was the case of Theodore Robert Bundy, a law student from the university, in possession of what seemed to be burglary tools.

One detective pricked up his ears, remembering a memo Salt Lake City police had received from Seattle police the previous October alerting them to the possibility of Bundy being a murder suspect.

By 19 August Seattle had whittled the initial list down to a 'top one hundred' suspect list and were working their way through each name methodically.

When Salt Lake City police phoned to say they had arrested Bundy, his was the next name on the list to be checked. It was pure coincidence, but even the police need a little luck now and again.

Now a closer look at Bundy was taken by police in four states, with Seattle having priority.

Bundy was born illegitimate on 24 November 1946 in Philadelphia, the young mother moving to Seattle and later marrying a cook in the Veteran's Hospital.

As a young child Bundy was a daydreamer, thief and habitual liar. The discovery of his illegitimacy obviously had a severe effect on his already damaged personality. Shy and immature at school, where he was known as Ted Cowell – his mother's maiden name – he was raised in Tacoma, later going to the University of Washington to study psychology.

Despite his IQ of 124 he was a poor student who bit his nails and stuttered when he was nervous. The turning-point in his life seems to have come when he met Stephanie Brookes in the spring of 1967. He was instantly impressed by her air of sophistication. Rich, elegant and beautiful, with long hair, as all his victims were to be. . .

Through Stephanie he had a glimpse of a world to which he could never hope to aspire. He was poor, socially inept, awkward and emotionally immature. To impress Stephanie he transferred briefly to Stanford University to study Chinese, but felt lonely. The affair lasted a year and then Stephanie finished with him, complaining that he wouldn't grow up.

The rejection was shattering, and the blow to his ego enormous. He took a job in a hotel as a waiter in the dining-room and began drifting, mixing with thieves, drug-addicts and shoplifters. Bundy once walked out of a greenhouse with an eight-foot plant in a pot, putting it in his car where it stuck out of the sun-roof, and he often boasted of this theft as if it were a feat.

The rejection did not in fact destroy him, but just made him lose his hearing temporarily. Then be became filled with an icy resolve to better himself, and applied to transfer from the study of psychology to that of law.

His professor wrote a recommendation declaring 'Mr Bundy is undoubtedly one of the top undergraduate students in our department, exceedingly bright and personable. Our loss is your gain.'

Bundy started an affair with a divorcée he met in a bar and who helped pay his way through college. He then got involved in politics, on the campaign staff of Nelson Rockefeller. He began dating a typist who worked under him, Cathy Swindler. She described him as 'Kennedy-like, terribly charismatic, someone with a great deal of compassion, a champion of causes, blacks, the poor. He was unhappy with the injustices of society.'

Bundy taught her to play chess, and she said he was always 'the perfect gentleman'. It was ironic that Cathy's father should have been Captain Herb Swindler, chief of the homicide and robbery detail of Seattle Police, the man who was to lead the hunt for Bundy.

Stephanie Brookes had rejected Bundy in 1968, and since then he had worked on himself and become very charming and self-assured, radiating self-confidence. He had become a full-time worker for Art Fletcher, the black Republican candidate for Lieutenant Governor of the state. Fletcher lost, and for a time Bundy became a salesman in a shoe-shop. It was at this point that his interest in pornography began, along with his peeping-tom activities.

He began working for the Crime Commission for a month and became noted as an active and bright political campaigner. Many top politicians held him in high regard. Now a success, Bundy flew to San Francisco to renew his wooing of Stephanie Brookes. She fell in love with the new Ted Bundy, and they spent Christmas 1973 together as lovers, becoming formally engaged. Bundy had chased the woman who had jilted him for six years. Now he exacted his revenge. He deliberately and callously dropped her. All along he had wanted to reject her on *his* terms; it was the only way he could repair the psychic damage he had suffered. When Stephanie telephoned him in January 1974 to ask what was wrong, what had she done, he hung up on her.

There is a tendency to make too much of Stephanie and her rejection – she with the long hair – as having somehow inspired Bundy's killings. In fact, he had committed at least one murder before ever meeting her. However, since all the victims resembled Stephanie, it was as if he were symbolically killing her over and over again.

With Bundy in custody and handcuffs in his possession, Salt Lake City police began linking him with the attempted abduction of Carol DaRonch. She did pick him out of a police line-up, but the evidence seemed very circumstantial. Bundy could explain his possession of all the items found in his car as being either necessary for car repairs, or in the case of the mask, for skiing. As for the handcuffs, they came from his time on the Crime Commission. . . .

The police got a warrant to search his apartment and found clues linking Bundy to Colorado, although he denied ever having been there. He was cool and arrogant to the police, yet his answers to questions were foolish and self-incriminating. From his apartment police picked up credit-card slips for petrol he bought, purchases he made in the state of Colorado.

He was given bail, but kept under close surveillance. There was nothing concrete to link him to any killings, yet police were still certain he was their man. Aware of the surveillance, Bundy carefully cleaned out his VW, destroying forensic evidence as police watched helplessly, then sold the vehicle. He then had his hair cut very short and parted it on the opposite side as a precaution.

After a few weeks Bundy was served with a subpoena to attend a line-up at police headquarters. He was picked out by three witnesses, including Carol DaRonch, and was immediately placed in custody charged with attempted kidnapping. Bail was set at $100,000.

Friends, stunned by the news of his arrest, rallied round, including 'Kathleen' and Ann Rule. Everyone who knew Ted said he couldn't have done it, he was just too clean and wholesome. While in gaol Bundy wrote to the Press, who were obviously interested in the fact that Bundy had moved from Seattle, where murders had taken place and then ceased, to Utah where they had begun again. In the letters Bundy thanked his friends for their support, saying:

> I think of you constantly. I think of our beautiful State and the incomparable loveliness of Seattle. . . The law is a curious animal. To a law student it becomes highly abstract and impersonal. To a defendant it offers incredible new perspectives. I have great confidence in its ultimate product: justice. God Bless You.
>
> Ted Bundy.

Bail was eventually reduced to $15,000 and Bundy walked free.

Typically, he postured before TV cameras, bragging to the Press of his innocence. Then he flew to Seattle and played hide-and-seek with the police there, who attempted to trail him. Behind the scenes detectives from Washington, California, Utah and Colorado held a meeting to compare evidence which would link Bundy to all the known killings. The VW car he had sold was retrieved and carefully vacuumed by the FBI's laboratory experts. Samples of human hair were recovered. The FBI had become involved because of the likelihood that Bundy had transported victims across state lines.

Seattle police interviewed 'Kathleen', who had been his lover for six years and who had ended the affair, giving his name to the police when she realized that he was a habitual thief. Bundy telephoned her from Salt Lake City police headquarters after his arrest, and detectives wanted to know the substance of the conversation, and details about Bundy's private life.

In her book *The Phantom Prince* Elizabeth claimed that in her relationship with Bundy from October 1969 to September 1974 he had never been violent towards her and was always the perfect gentleman. He did have a hang-up about being illegitimate, she conceded.

Now she told detectives about Bundy's petty thefts, the fact that he had a fake moustache, that she had seen him bring home plaster of Paris and making a cast, and that he kept a lug-wrench in his car. She also revealed details of their sex-life, saying, 'He read about anal sex and insisted on trying it. I didn't like it but I went along with him.'

She told how Bundy had insisted they try bondage sex. He had tied her to the bed and had sex with her, but on the third occasion he tried to throttle her, and she refused to do it any more.

She also said, 'Sometimes, after I was asleep at night, I'd wake up to find him under the covers. He was looking at – at my body. . . with a torch!' She went on, 'When I talked about cutting my hair he got very upset. He really likes long hair.'

The trial on the kidnap charge began on 23 February 1976. The prosecution did not have a very strong case. In 29-year-old Bundy's apartment they had found a map of Colorado, from where five girls had disappeared that year. Strands of hair found in his VW matched those of Melissa Smith and Caryn Campbell, but a hair-match is nowhere as good as a fingerprint. All they really had was the identification by the victim, Carol DaRonch. Bundy, she insisted, was the man who'd tried to kidnap her.

Bundy waived his right to trial by jury, thinking that a judge would not be influenced by circumstantial evidence and would judge only on solid fact. In court Bundy looked clean-cut and handsome, the least likely sex-fiend. Polite and well-spoken, he said he could explain how it had all been a mistake. It just happened to be a coincidence that he was in the area at the same time.

This was to be the pattern of Bundy; he would never admit to any of his crimes. With a boyish shrug he would say yes, the circumstantial evidence looks bad, but it was all a pure coincidence. 'Sorry, guys, but you've got the wrong man.'

The defence managed to damage the testimony of Carol DaRonch and the reliability of her eye-witness evidence. Initially she had said her kidnapper had a moustache, then changed her mind, then changed it back again. It sounded weak, as the following extract from the trial testimony shows.

O'Connell: 'And you say he was wearing a moustache?'
DaRonch: 'Yes.'

'Shortly after the incident you said you had thought it over and decided the man didn't have a moustache, didn't you?'

'Yes.'

'And some time later you decided he did – right?'

'Yes.'

'When did you make that decision?'

'Right after I decided that he didn't have one.'

(In fact, Bundy had been wearing a beard at the time.)

The case seemed thin until Bundy himself took the stand. He could not resist showing how clever he was, and his contempt for prosecuting counsel. But the law student was a disaster under cross-examination. Witty and articulate as he was, his answers as to his movements on specific dates sounded flimsy and contrived. He claimed that he had tried to outrun the police car because he had been smoking pot, for example.

On 30 February, after careful deliberation, the judge found Bundy guilty of aggravated kidnap and sentenced the sobbing prisoner to a period of one to fifteen years in gaol. It meant Bundy would be eligible for parole in under three years.

The police were not satisfied with this result. Again they reviewed their evidence. Hairs found in Bundy's car matched those of Caryn Campbell, Melissa Smith and Carol DaRonch – too great a coincidence. On 11 March 1976 Bundy was interviewed in Salt Lake City gaol by detectives about the murders in Seattle, Utah and Colorado. He was also examined by Dr. Carlisle, a court-appointed psychiatrist, who asked Bundy what he thought about death. Bundy replied, 'I don't fear death. I don't believe in life after death.'

The interview revealed him to be a loner, feeling inferior when mixing with a higher social class. Dr. Carlisle's report noted that he was 'A private person. . . . evasive. . . fearful of women.'

On 22 October 1976 police served an extradition warrant on Bundy in Utah State Penitentiary. He was to be taken to Aspen to stand trial for the murder of Caryn Campbell. He was moved to Garfield County Jail at Glenwood Springs, forty miles from Aspen, where he was visited by Richard Larsen, a newspaper reporter who had known Bundy for years and believed in his innocence. He was then to reflect on the term 'Sociopath' – defined as: 'Lying, manipulative, prone to take chances and seek thrills. Clever at deception. . . '

From his meetings with Bundy, Larsen wrote his own book on the case: *Bundy the Deliberate Stranger*.

Bundy sacked his lawyers and elected to defend himself. He was granted special privileges, including the use of a typewriter, telephone and access to a law library. He grew friendly with the judge and with his gaolers. He escaped from court on 6 June, jumping from a two-storey window, but after five days in the Aspen Mountains he was recaptured. Asked why he had escaped, he replied, 'It was just too nice a day to stay inside. . . .'

At the murder trial the prosecution intended to introduce evidence of 'similar transactions' – the murders in Seattle and those in other states. (In England lawyers can introduce evidence of 'system'.) The judge refused to allow this, however, even though it was permissible under Colorado law. The prosecution had discovered two new witnesses who had seen Bundy with Laura Aime. She was exhumed so that her hair could be matched with samples found in Bundy's car. It was all academic, however, as Bundy wasn't there to be tried!

He had been busy planning another escape. On 30 December 1977, he climbed though a hole he had made in the ceiling of his cell, crawled along the loft, and emerged into the sheriff's living-quarters. Helping himself to a change of clothes, he walked out, drove to Denver in a stolen car, and was on a plane to Chicago before he was even missed.

Then he made the fatal decision to go to Florida. It was far away: there he could change his name and begin a new life, and as 'Chris Hagen' he began living in Tallahassee, near the campus of Florida State University. He liked being around universities; there were always plenty of vulnerable girls with long hair. He had planned to get a job, but found himself drifting, stealing the things he needed. Television sets, cars, credit cards.

On 15 January 1978 Bundy's inner demon, which had been dormant, came snarling alive. That night he attacked four girls at the Chi Omega sorority house, frenziedly bludgeoning them in their beds as they lay asleep. He left two girls dead, two more terribly mutilated.

Lisa Levy, twenty, had been raped and strangled, her right nipple almost bitten off, and she had been bitten savagely on the right buttock, the final indignity being a hairspray can jammed up her anus. Margaret Bowman, twenty-one, was also dead, having been violently strangled with her own tights. She had received a crushing blow to the right forehead, there was massive bleeding from her head and ears, and her neck had been broken. Although she had not been sexually violated, her panties had been torn off with such force that a burn mark was visible on her thigh.

Karen Chandler, twenty-one, was found rocking back and forth, moaning, blood pouring from her mouth. Her jaw, right arm and one finger were broken. Her skull was fractured, as was the orbit of her right eye and both cheekbones. Kathy Kleiner, twenty-one, had been bludgeoned in her sleep. Her jaw was broken and she had many deep gashes on her head and face. After she had been taken to hospital several of her teeth were found in her bedclothes.

Police arriving on the scene were shocked by the ferocity of the attacks; it looked like the work of an animal. But the animal wasn't satisfied. Within minutes he struck again, just a couple of blocks away in Dunwoody Street, battering Cheryl Thomas, twenty-one, in her sleep. She was found unconscious, covered in blood, her jaw broken. The only clue was a large semen stain on her bedsheet. It was to take her months to recover from her ordeal, and today she remains totally deaf in one ear and has lost her sense of balance. She wanted to be a dancer. . .

It was time for Bundy to move on, but he did not leave immediately. He left Tallahassee in a stolen white Dodge van headed for Jacksonville. His credit-card purchases of petrol, and eye-witnesses, placed him a hundred miles east of Tallahassee on Interstate 10 between 11 a.m. and noon on Tuesday 7 February. He was seen three hours later and seventy-five miles farther on, being served petrol. It was the same van, same licence plate. Later that night he used the stolen credit card to pay for a meal at a Holiday Inn near Jacksonville, where on 8 February, after buying petrol, he accosted the daughter of a Jacksonville detective outside her school and both he and his van were positively identified.

On Thursday morning, 9 February, he was in Lake City. There he abducted Kimberley Diane Leach, twelve. Her body was to be found on 7 April thirty-two miles away in a State Park. She had been sexually violated and strangled. The forensic indications were that her throat had been cut and she had been mutilated with a knife around the genital area. Bundy had now become a 'baby-raper', as convicts call them.

Returning to Tallahassee, Bundy loaded all his stolen belongings into a stolen orange VW car and drove away. On 10 February the FBI put Bundy on their 'Ten Most Wanted' list for questioning about thirty-six sex murders. He was described as 'Height 6ft Weight 145 to 175 pounds, slim athletic build, physical fitness enthusiast.'

An FBI spokesman said that if Bundy were convicted of all thirty-six murders he would become 'the most prolific mass-murderer in American history'.

On 15 February Bundy had been free for just forty-six days, during which time he had murdered three more women. On that day he was arrested in Pensacola, driving erratically in his orange VW. He fought the arresting officer, asking him to shoot him. Once in custody he gave his name as Kenneth Misner, the name on his stolen credit card. Then, after three days, he cracked, admitting his real identity. When local police realized they had a celebrity in custody, they got him to autograph his photograph on the FBI poster.

The police taped a statement by Bundy in which he refused to admit to the Chi Omega killings but hinted, 'The evidence is there. Keep digging.' In his long, rambling statement he gave clues to his condition. He said, 'Years ago I saw a girl on a bicycle. I saw her and knew I had to have her. I had to possess her.'

It was then, he said, that what he called his 'problem' began. Later in the interview he remarked, 'Sometimes I feel like a vampire.'

Because of the paper-trail of credit-card transactions he left behind him, pinpointing his movements and proving his guilt of Kimberley Leach's murder beyond doubt, one detective admitted later, 'If Ted had learned not to use credit cards and to drive better, we'd never have caught him.'

The police traced witnesses who had actually seen Bundy leading Kim Leach away, and realizing the importance of those bite-marks on Lisa Levy's buttocks, they had them photographed and took a dental impression of Bundy's teeth.

In those last days of freedom the mass-murderer's actions seem to have been those of a man deliberately tempting fate, almost as if he *wanted* to be caught, and feared freedom.

Now it was all over, the running done. The police had a damning case against him. They could link him to the Chi Omega murders and the Jacksonville killing.

Prior to his trial Bundy was once again examined by a psychiatrist to ensure that he was competent to stand trial.

In his report the psychiatrist stated: 'In a certain sense Mr Bundy is the producer of a play which attempts to show that authority can be manipulated. Mr Bundy does not have the capacity to recognize that the price for this "thriller" might be his own life.'

And again before his subsequent trial in Dade County Court in Miami the prosecution offered Bundy a plea-bargain. If he would plead guilty to the Chi Omega murders and the killing of Kimberley Leach, the prosecution would not seek the death sentence. Despite the urging of his counsel to accept the deal, Bundy contemptuously rejected it, and so forfeited his life.

When the sheriff of the local gaol refused him special privileges Bundy sued him in a $300,000 civil suit, and it cost the sheriff $7000 of his own money to defend himself.

On 29 June 1979 Bundy went on trial in Miami, a trial which was televised live across the nation. Now the evil killer was on stage; it was everything he had ever wanted: he was the cynosure of every eye, acting out his role as folk hero. He sacked his counsel and announced that he would be defending himself, which meant he could force his surviving victims from the Chi Omega sorority house into court and cross-examine them, making them relive their ordeal.

This is precisely what he did. Some 40 million viewers found the trial compulsive viewing. The attraction lay not so much in the horrific nature of the killings as in the personality of the man in the dock, immaculately dressed, eloquently arguing his own case, clashing angrily with the judge at times, making witty asides to the Press, and flashing smiles at the Bundy-groupies who crowded the front seats; women who gazed at him with adoration, tossing him little love-notes.

Bundy had been dubbed the 'Love-Bite Killer' by the Press, which was appropriate in view of the fact that his bites were to convict him, but why women – and there were many of them, from the young and pretty to the matronly – should be fascinated by a man who killed women so cruelly defies the imagination. It was a mass act of masochistic homage. In the dock the arrogant Bundy was convinced that he could literally get away with murder.

The twelve jurors were eventually chosen. Seven men (four black, one white, two Hispanic) and five women (three black, one white and one Hispanic). Judge Cowart had ruled Bundy's taped statements inadmissible, since he hadn't had his lawyer with him when he made it, and he also ruled out the evidence from Utah (the items found in Bundy's car). It was a blow to the prosecution, but not a major one.

In the course of his opening address the prosecutor laid great stress on the bite-marks found on the buttocks of Lisa Levy, saying, 'The State will show with a remarkable degree of dental certainty that the defendant in this case, Theodore Robert Bundy, was responsible for leaving those bite-marks.'

The most important expert witness was Dr Richard Souviron, an expert in forensic orthodontry. Using a large blown-up photograph of the bite-marks, he demonstrated to the jury each point of comparison, tooth by tooth. He proved conclusively that Bundy's teeth matched the bite-marks exactly, evidence which was confirmed by Dr Levine of New York University, adviser on dentistry to the New York Medical Examiner.

The case went to the jury on the afternoon of 24 July, at 2.57 p.m. At 9 p.m. the jury returned. They had been expected to be out all night, but seven times the jury announced guilty verdicts.

Shaking and trembling, Bundy told the judge, 'I will tell the court that I am not really able to accept the verdict.' It was a strange choice of words, but Bundy would still not admit his guilt to himself.

At the sentencing hearing Bundy's mother, Louise, told the judge, 'I consider it, the death penalty, to be the most primitive and barbaric thing that one human being can impose upon another.' The judge was not impressed. Before sentence was passed on 31 July Bundy told him, 'I find it absurd to ask for mercy for something I didn't do.'

Judge Cowart told Bundy, 'This court finds that the killings were indeed heinous, atrocious and cruel in that they were extremely wicked, shockingly evil, vile, and the product of a design to inflict a high degree of pain and with utter indifference to human life.'

After sentencing Bundy to die in the electric chair, Judge Cowart told him, 'Take care of yourself, young man. I say that to you sincerely. It's a tragedy to this court to see such a total waste of humanity. You're a bright young man. You'd have made a good lawyer. I'd have loved to have you practise in front of me.' They were strange words of comfort indeed.

Bundy was taken from the court and placed on Death Row in Raiford Penitentiary, Florida, in 1979 as convict 669063. It is the longest Death Row in any American prison, with hundreds of men waiting to keep their appointment with 'Old Sparky', as convicts call the chair.

On 7 January 1980 Bundy again stood trial for murder. The first trial had been for the Chi Omega killings, the second, held in Orlando, was for the murder of Kimberley Leach. The prosecutor reminded the jury that this was the anniversary of Kim's death, and quoted from the Bible: 'He that offend one of these little ones, it were better for him if a millstone were hung about his neck and he were cast into the sea and drowned.' He demanded the electric chair for Bundy, saying, 'Any other penalty would be a mockery of the system of justice.'

The prosecution presented formidable forensic evidence against Bundy, and there were eye-witnesses who had seen him in Jacksonville on the day Kim died, and one who actually saw him leading Kim away. There was also the physical evidence which linked him to the white Dodge van.

Bundy again acted as his own counsel and managed to pull off one piece of theatre. While examining his girlfriend Carole Boone in the witness box, Bundy proposed to her, was accepted, and thus legally married her in the presence of witnesses. This marriage took place on 9 February 1980, and appeared to have no effect on the jury. They voted the death penalty for him.

Three days later Judge Jopling sentenced Bundy to die in the electric chair, and again Bundy returned to Death Row.

Bundy had always been a careful killer, never leaving a single fingerprint, but each murder had borne his stamp. After his final capture he had telephoned 'Kathleen' again from the police station and told her about a force within him. "I just couldn't contain it,' he said. 'I've fought it for a long time. It got too strong. I tried to suppress it. It was taking more and more of my time. That's why I didn't do so well in school. My time was being used up trying to make my life look normal. But it wasn't normal. All the time I could feel the force growing within me. I have a sickness. I just can't be around and I know it now.' It was the nearest he was to come to a confession, until the moments before he faced the chair, of course. . .

It is clear from the internal psychological evidence that Bundy was not a split-personality in the classic sense, where each personality is unaware of the existence of the other. Bundy was a double-personality. He knew his other evil side existed, just as Ronald True, for example, was well aware of the existence of the *other* Ronald True who was going around impersonating him and trying to ruin him.

But some component of Bundy's make-up would never allow him to admit to himself his true nature. Like a child, he played the game of keeping his head buried in the sand in the hope that the horror would go away. But it could not, it was *inside* him.

But he did reveal a little of himself to two investigative reporters who interviewed him over a long period while he was on Death Row. They persuaded him to speculate in the third person as to what the killer might have thought and done. This device allowed Bundy to talk without having to say, 'I did it.' The tape-recorded interviews form the basis of the book *The Only Living Witness* by Michaud and Aynesworth.

Bundy told the reporters, 'I'm the most cold-hearted son of a bitch you'll ever meet.' He told them that he received no gratification from causing pain, and what really fascinated him was the hunt, the adventure of seeking out his victims. 'And to a degree, possessing them physically as one would possess a potted plant, a painting, or a Porsche. Owning, as it were, this individual.'

But he was not insane, just incredibly cunning, with lust for power over others driving him. There were signs that towards the end he began to realize that the monster within him was out of control. He wanted to help, even to die, but it was too late for that. Too many young women lay dead in his trail. . .

During his 'speculations' Bundy was asked if there would be any conversation between the killer and his victim. Bundy replied, 'There'd be some. But since this girl in front of him represented not a person but a thing, the last thing we should expect him to want to do would be to personalize this person.' In other words, the victim wasn't a person but a *thing*.

Bundy had admitted having been interested in pornography and violent movies since early childhood, long before he started killing. He had developed into a typical psychopath, a man entirely without conscience. He told the two reporters that he had forgotten what he had done in the past, claiming his ability to forget was a 'gift'.

He explained, 'A lot of people are encumbered with a mechanism called guilt. I don't feel guilty for anything. I feel sorry for people who feel guilt.'

Examining the clues, it is easy to pinpoint Bundy's perverse drives. What he really enjoyed was having power over his victims. When he was 'hunting' he shifted into his other personality; he was on stage, performing, but afterwards he remembered what he had done.

The experience of meeting and talking with Bundy left its mark on the two reporters – even frightened them. Bundy's friends, including Ann Rule, were horrified by the discovery that he was a sex killer. He seemed too normal, too ordinary, too much a good guy to be capable of such atrocities.

Nowhere in his outward appearance is there anything to help us detect other killers of his type. Ann Rule said 'Ted Bundy fits no pattern at all. You could not look at this record and say, "See, it was inevitable that he would turn out like this." In fact, it was incomprehensible.'

After all the blood which had been shed, after his two trials, Bundy remained on Death Row for almost ten years. Just putting him there had cost an immense effort. The long police investigation, involving officers from four different states, had seen the investment of over 100,000 man-hours to catch him.

On 24 January 1989 Bundy finally went to the electric chair. He was aged forty-two. He declined the traditional last meal and went to his death bearing a look of controlled anger. His appeals against his sentence had cost the American taxpayers over four million dollars. The night before his execution, in an attempt to stave off the inevitable, Bundy confessed to many more murders with full horrific details. He said he blamed pornography for his sick obsessions.

A panel of forty-two witnesses saw Bundy die at dawn, a one-minute surge of 2000 volts passing through his body. They reported that he had gently arched his back and clenched his fists as the current hit him.

Outside the prison demonstrators cheered and set off fire-crackers. Many wore T-shirts bearing a picture of the electric chair with the legend 'Burn, Bundy, Burn.'

The deceptively wholesome-looking man with the engaging smile and film-star looks was finally gone. He had confessed to murdering twenty-three women and young girls, but police suspected he had killed at least another fifteen. Even at the end Bundy couldn't bring himself to tell *all* the truth.

At the end Bundy's cockiness had deserted him as he spent his last few days helping detectives from Washington state, Utah and Colorado clear their books on unsolved sex killings. America's most infamous son had been written about in hundreds of newspaper and magazine articles, and in half a dozen best-selling books. A television film about him, *Deliberate Stranger*, had been made, starring Mark Harmon as Bundy. Many young American women still cherish romantic notions about Bundy, and Ann Rule still gets calls and letters from girls who want to move to Florida to be near 'Ted'. Ann Rule says, 'I have to tell them: "You're not in love with Ted

Bundy, you're in love with Mark Harmon." '

There really was nothing romantic about Bundy. Dr. James Dobson, a psychiatrist who saw him the night before his execution, said that only after the first killing had Bundy felt any remorse. 'But then the sex frenzy overcame him and he killed again, and as each crime passed, he grew desensitised. He could not feel any more. . .'

Bundy himself felt embarrassed at his bloody career, at being what one judge called 'the most competent serial killer in the USA today'. He refused to allow prison guards to overhear him confessing to detectives, and wrote the names of his victims on scraps of paper. One detective said, 'From what he's told us, I'd say he's the mass-killer of all time. There's not another man like him.'

The crowds outside the prison cheered their joy when Bundy was executed, displaying the ugly mood of a lynch mob. Just hours before he died his mother, Louise, told him in a phone-call, 'You'll always be my precious son. We'll always love you.' At her home in Washington she said, 'He sounded wonderful and at peace with himself. He said: "I'm sorry for causing you so much grief, but a part of me was always hidden." '

Now that part has gone along with the rest of him. Let us not make Bundy the stuff of legend or romanticize his deeds. He was rather the epitome of evil.

Let us remember instead his victims.

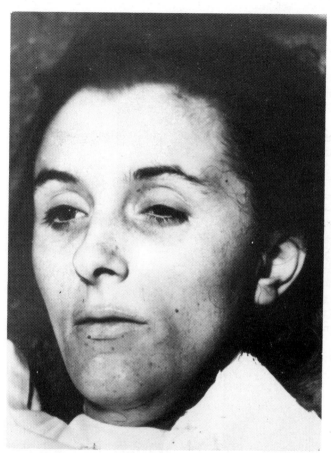

Elizabeth Figg. Believed to be Jack the Stripper's first victim

Victims in the Hammersmith nude murders

Gwynneth Rees

Hannah Tailford

Irene Lockwood

Bridget O'Hara

Margaret McGowan

Helene
Barthelemy

Mary Fleming

The towpath at Chiswick where the body of Elizabeth Figg
was found

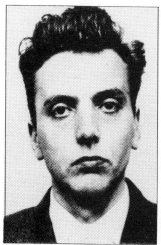

Ian Brady

Myra Hindley

The grim hunt on the moors

Chapter Eleven

DENNIS NILSEN –
THE DEADLY SCAVENGER

Dennis Andrew Nilsen was a very rare killer indeed, and that on a number of levels. One might almost be tempted to call him unique – were it not for the precedents. No other serial killer has told us so much about himself. In his fifty prison notebooks, which he handed to author Brian Masters so that he could write his incisive book on the case *Killing for Company,* Nilsen attempts to analyse his own motives. He was highly intelligent and articulate, and is all the more frightening for that.

As for the precedents: Lacenaire was the first murderer of what might be termed modern times to write his *Memoirs*; Kürten told his story in graphic detail to Dr Berg, who duly published *The Sadist*; Reginald Sidney Buckfield wrote a fictional account of his crime while in custody, but since he included details which could only have been known to the killer, he *wrote* his way into the dock. And more recently, Ted Bundy speculated to two journalists about the state of mind of the killer for whose crimes he was incarcerated for life.

Nilsen is also rare for the methods he employed to kill and for the number of his victims. Over a period of some four and a half years, in the heart of London, he lured fifteen young men to their deaths – and with two exceptions *nobody missed them*. This was because he chose his victims from among the young and dispossessed, the poor, homeless and hopeless, the natural losers. Young men who were homosexuals or drug-addicts, young men who were lonely, hungry, and who trusted the tall, slim man with the bushy brown hair and spectacles. He preyed upon the weak stragglers of any society, scavenging like a jackal.

There is an ancient Zen aphorism which asks: if a tree falls in the middle of a dense and remote forest, does it make a sound? The question brings in philosophical notions about *intentionality*: the fact that we impose meaning on events by the act of observing. The case of Dennis Nilsen forces us to reflect on moral, philosophical and sociological grounds. If fifteen young men could simply vanish and not be missed – then what does it say about us, about our society?

Nilsen stands almost alone in this century as a true gargoyle, his crimes eclipsing those of other murderers not simply by numbers, but by the impassive, implacably cruel nature of his killings, and the sheer arbitrary and irrational choices behind them all. The odd thing is that any close study of this man leaves you with the feeling that he was a person you might have valued as a friend – were it not for his odd penchant for murder. . . . Nilsen was a nice man; he was also a killer of intense ferocity, with dirty little motives which scabbed his soul. He masturbated over his victims. Took them out from under the floorboards periodically to fondle them and 'have sex with them' by placing his penis between their thighs. He sat them in the opposite armchair to watch TV with him or listen to music or simply join him in conversation. He kept one corpse in an armchair for a week because 'It was so nice to have someone to come home to.'

Lonely, shy, friendless, Nilsen truly killed for company. At one period he had six bodies under the floorboards of his flat and was not alone any more. He lived a fantasy obsessed with death, imagining his own and that of others, and had a necrophiliac streak which drove him to destroy living things, to be a destroyer not a creator.

He also loved poetry and music. He was all these things, but above all else – so low was his self-esteem, so insignificant his own life – he determined to create his own legend. If he was insignificant, then he would impose himself upon the consciousness of society, of other people. And the ultimate method of imposing oneself is to have total power over another human being. Nilsen's murders were committed not primarily for sexual needs, but for power-needs, for domination, to restore his humiliated psyche.

Nilsen succeeded only too well. When he stepped into the dock at the Old Bailey he was the legendary killer of the 'House of Horror'; murderer of fifteen young men and the attempted killer of seven others. Yet since he created his own legend – this clever, manipulative psychopath – even the legend is not true. Any attempt to view objectively the real Dennis Nilsen is a difficult task.

However, the task is well worth undertaking, since Nilsen presents us with the classic psychiatric model of the serial killer, and the quest for his real identity and motives can lead to valuable insights into the drives of all sex killers. Such an examination is not without its hazards, since there is a real risk of psychic contamination. Nilsen was very sick, his murders stomach-churning, and simply reading about them is very much like stepping into an abattoir.

Nilsen was born on 23 November 1945 in the Scottish village of Fraserburgh. Son of a Norwegian father and a Scottish mother, the most important episode in his early life came at the age of seven, when he viewed the dead body of his grandfather. He could not believe that something which had once been so vital was now dead, beyond all feeling or sensation. He wrote later that the sight of the corpse had a profound effect on him (Christie made the same claim), and that the experience had blighted his personality permanently.

At fourteen he joined the Army Cadets and revelled in the uniform: it made him feel important. He joined the Regular Army in September 1961, aged fifteen, to train as a chef in the Catering Corps. He was taught the skills of butchery. He later served in Aden, the Persian Gulf and Germany. During this period, surrounded by the young men, he discovered his own homosexuality but repressed his feelings.

In 1971 he was posted to the Shetland Islands, where he developed an interest in film-making. Corporal Nilsen took many films of a young private whom he instructed to lie still and 'play dead'. This was the first manifestation of his necrophile streak, and was an important clue to his later development. When he left the Army, in 1972, his conduct was recorded as being 'exemplary'.

In December 1972, aged twenty-seven, he joined the Metropolitan Police and was posted as a probationer to Willesden Green police station as Constable Q287. During the course of his duties he came across London's gay scene and visited many gay pubs. He gave expression to his homosexuality by having an affair with one man, and smuggling another back into his Police Section room for anal sex. After a year, to the surprise of his colleagues, he resigned from the Force. It lacked the camaraderie he had known in the Army.

For a time he wandered from job to job, working as a security guard until he got fed up with that. Putting on a uniform no longer conferred a sense of identity. Finally he was forced to sign on the dole, where he was persuaded to apply for a clerical post with the Department of Employment. He was appointed to the Denmark Street Job Centre in London's West End. Here he stayed for the next few years, having many homosexual affairs and contacts, picking up young men from the many gay pubs he frequented and taking them back to his flat at 195 Melrose Avenue in Cricklewood. Some never left alive. . . .

To his colleagues Nilsen was a prickly and hostile character who made it painfully clear that he wanted to be alone. He made no friends at work, and remained reclusive. Outside work he was different. He had moved into Melrose Avenue with a lover who eventually betrayed him and left him. This final humiliation pushed him over the edge, especially as he had been passed over for promotion because of his attitude. He was considered 'bolshie'. He began drinking himself into a stupor every night, listening to pop music over headphones with a manic intensity.

By 1978 Nilsen was using make-up to give himself the appearance of a corpse – dark eyes and dead white flesh – and masturbated while looking at himself in a mirror. He had become totally obsessed with the idea of death. He spent Christmas of that year alone in his flat, with only his dog Bleep for company. He was feeling acutely lonely and depressed. He picked up young men and took them home – *but they always left afterwards*. The next one would not leave him on his own.

His first victim, picked up in the Cricklewood Arms, was an unidentified Irish youth in his teens. They slept together that night – 30 December 1978 – and when Nilsen awoke in the morning he found he had strangled his sleeping companion during the night with one of his collection of fifteen ties. He washed the body in the bath, put it back in bed and attempted to have sex with it. Later, before putting the body under the floorboards, he masturbated over it. He said later, 'I took possession of a new kind of flat-mate.' He added that he had been determined to have company – 'even if it was only a body'.

That first killing shocked Nilsen: he said he shook uncontrollably for hours afterwards, wondering if he should give himself up to the police or commit suicide. The reason he gave for not following either course of action was that there would be nobody to take care of his dog.

That first victim remained under the floorboards at Melrose Avenue for seven and a half months, until Nilsen burned the body on a bonfire in the garden on 11 August 1979.

But there had been an earlier clue to Nilsen's homicidal nature. In 1976 he had attacked a young man he had brought back to his flat, attempting to strangle him with a tie. The young man fought him off and fled, reporting the incident to the police. Nilsen found himself being questioned at the police station at which he had once served. But since there was no obvious injury to the young man – who didn't want to press charges anyway – and since Nilsen had said he was drunk and could remember nothing, the matter was dropped.

On 31 October 1979 Nilsen picked up a young Chinese student in a pub near Trafalgar Square. He took him back to Melrose Avenue, and after a few drinks attempted to strangle him. The intended victim, Andrew Ho, fought him off, knocking him unconscious with a brass candlestick. Mr Ho reported the incident to the police because he feared he might have killed Nilsen. Again Nilsen pleaded drunkenness, and again the matter was dropped.

The second victim was a young Canadian tourist, Kenneth Ockenden, twenty-three. He was not a homosexual, but was delighted when a polite Englishman took an interest in him. Nilsen met him on 3 December 1979 in the Princess Louise pub in High Holborn. He took the young man on a guided tour of London, then took him back to Melrose Avenue for a meal and some drinks. After a bout of heavy drinking Nilsen persuaded the young man to listen to pop music on the headphones. Then he strangled him with the headphone cord. Nilsen said later, 'I kept him with me for the rest of the night. There was no sex, just caressing etc.' He sat the body in an armchair and made the face up with cosmetics. He watched TV with the corpse and held conversations with it. Eventually Nilsen put him under the floorboards, but took him back out at least four times in the next fortnight. He had sex with the corpse via the thighs. He washed the corpse, as he was to do with most of his victims. This ritual washing of the corpse was a demonstration of his total power over the victim, a ritual of symbolic importance.

Nilsen said he felt remorse after the death of Kenneth Ockenden, especially when he saw TV news about the young man's disappearance. He was bewildered and frightened by his own actions and again wanted to give himself up to the police.

But after two murders Nilsen said he came to feel 'less emotional' about it all, and accepted the fact that he was a compulsive killer. So unconcerned did be become about the act of murder that he kept small items belonging to his victims around his flat. He wore a watch belonging to one victim, and a pair of spectacles belonging to another. He told police, 'I did not feel that it was theft as the owners hadn't really gone away.' Indeed they hadn't, they were still under the floorboards.

In May 1980 Nilsen picked up his next victim, Martyn Duffey, sixteen, a Liverpool youth who had a record for petty theft and drug-addiction. Once at Melrose Avenue Nilsen strangled him unconscious and then drowned him in the bath. Afterwards he washed the corpse and placed it on the bed, masturbating over it. He too went under the floorboards. To cover the smell of putrefaction Nilsen was using air-fresheners and disinfectant. When the 'smell problem', as Nilsen termed it, became too strong to ignore, Nilsen took the bodies up and dissected them on the kitchen floor. The heads went into plastic bags, the bulky parts into two suitcases which he stored in the garden shed. Duffey's arms and hands were buried in a hole in the garden, and the internal organs of both men were just dumped in the street. A man found a plastic bag full of entrails and reported it to the police: they dismissed it as being simply refuse.

Billy Sutherland, twenty-seven, was a hard-case from Edinburgh. He was picked up in a pub near to Piccadilly Circus, and, having nowhere to sleep, agreed to accompany Nilsen back to Melrose Avenue. There Nilsen strangled him. He left him sitting dead in an armchair for two days before putting him under the floorboards. Nilsen liked to keep his victims as long as he could, bathing them and changing their underwear so he could fondle them.

The next four victims were never identified, but all were young men. No. 5 Nilsen called the 'Mex' because of his Latin appearance. No. 6 was Irish, picked up in the Cricklewood Arms. No. 7 was a pathetic creature, a young man, of emaciated looks who Nilsen said reminded him of a Belsen victim. Nilsen took him home and fed him, then, when he fell asleep in the chair strangled him with a tie. He was later to describe how the young man's legs had cycled frantically in the air as he fought for life. Nilsen said that this murder 'was as easy as taking candy from a baby'. That body too went under the floorboards.

By the end of 1980 Nilsen had six corpses on his hands – two dismembered in the garden shed, and four under the floorboards. With a grim touch worthy of Hitchcock, he would often forget about his bodies, leaving them lying on the floor or stuck in the wardrobe. Once he went to get a shirt from the wardrobe and had a body fall out on him. With a sigh of exasperation he decided he would have to do something about all the bodies littering the place. . . .

He took the bodies out from under the floorboards and dissected them. He said later, 'The flesh looked just like any other meat one could see in a butcher's shop, and having been trained in butchery I was not subject to any traumatic shocks.'

In September 1980 Nilsen burned all six bodies on a huge bonfire at the bottom of the garden, putting car tyres on the blaze to disguise the smell of burning flesh. Children gathered round to watch as the fire burned all day. Next day Nilsen used a roller to crush skulls and bones into small fragments. With a sense of relief – the bodies finally out of the way – he went out that night to a pub and picked up a young man, taking him back to the flat for sex. He did not kill this one: he left next morning unharmed.

But on 10 November 1980 he picked up Douglas Stewart, twenty-six, a fellow-Scot. He agreed to go back to Melrose Avenue for a drink and fell asleep in the chair. He woke to find his ankles tied and Nilsen trying to strangle him with a ligature. He managed to fight Nilsen off and grabbed a carving knife to make good his escape. He reported the attack to the police, but the two officers who responded to his call concluded that it had been a homosexual lovers' quarrel and took it no further.

Five more people died in 1981. Nilsen's murderous lust had not died with that fire. He had been turned down for promotion, and had also been mugged in the street and robbed. With his self-esteem at rock bottom he needed to kill again. *He killed for fear of something worse.* Murder was a safety-valve, it served as a catharsis and stopped him from going insane. 1981 had been a bad year all round for Nilsen. On 8 June his flat had been vandalized and he had called in the police. Detectives stood in his flat, unaware of the bodies under their feet.

The next victim, No. 8, was a tall young hippy with long fair hair. Nilsen picked him up in the West End, and his strangled body went under the floorboards. Victim No. 9 was another Scot, picked up in a Soho pub early in 1981. His strangled body went under the floorboards. Victim No. 10 was Irish. Nilsen could not remember strangling him, but woke up one morning to find him dead on the floor. Victim No. 11 was an aggressive Cockney skinhead with a dotted line tattooed around his neck with the inscription: 'Cut along dotted line.' Nilsen did just that. Nilsen had picked him up in Leicester Square, took him back to the flat and plied him his drink. When he passed out Nilsen strangled him. Of this victim Nilsen wrote, 'I went to bed thinking: end of a day. End of the drinking. End of a person.' He too went into the crowded space beneath the floorboards.

The next victim literally fell into Nilsen's lap. Malcolm Barlow, twenty-four, was an orphan from Rotherham. Of low intelligence, he suffered from epilepsy. On 17 September 1981 he had a fit in Melrose Avenue, and Nilsen found the vagrant slumped against a wall, sitting on the pavement. He telephoned for an ambulance. The following day Barlow had himself released from hospital and went in search of the Good Samaritan. He found Nilsen's flat and waited for him to arrive home from work, then invited himself in for a drink. Nilsen was seriously concerned about him, warning him not to mix alcohol with the tablets he was taking because of the possibility of an adverse effect. Barlow insisted on a drink. Later, Nilsen admitted that he had strangled Barlow because he was a 'nuisance' and for no other reason. He was hidden under the sink, later to be placed intact on the going-away bonfire.

Nilsen had been offered another flat at 23 Cranley Gardens, and was promised £1,000 by his landlord if he would agree to move. Nilsen arranged to move into the new flat in October, but first he had to get rid of the embarrassing four bodies under the floorboards. He dissected them, cutting along the dotted line on the skinhead's neck, and then had another huge bonfire, burning the bodies and throwing the entrails over the garden hedge for vermin to dispose of, before moving out on 5 October 1981.

It was the move to the new flat which was to prove Nilsen's downfall. There was simply no back garden for bonfires. Any future victims would have to be disposed of in a different manner, and Nilsen began cutting them up into small pieces and flushing them down the toilet. But the drains were to become blocked with chunks of human flesh. . . .

Cranley Gardens is a long and pleasant road in the Muswell Hill suburb of north London, lined with large semi-detached houses. It was into one of these – number 23 – that Nilsen moved. Managed by a local estate agent for an Asian owner, the house had been converted into six flats, and Nilsen moved into the very top flat in the attic, an apartment consisting of two rooms and a kitchen and bathroom. Here he lived with his dog, Bleep.

By now Nilsen had been promoted to executive officer and was working at the Job Centre in Kentish Town, where he was known to his colleagues as 'Des'. He had also become branch officer for the civil service union, CPSA, and seemed to delight in tweaking the nose of authority, battling against the system. The tall, thin, stooping figure of Des Nilsen, wearing the spectacles of victim Martyn Duffey, was a man of mystery to the people who shared the house. He hardly ever spoke, and made friends with none of them. He lived alone in his dingy flat, making no attempt to clean it or to clean the grease-covered stove.

Between January 1978 and September 1981, Nilsen had killed twelve men at Melrose Avenue, of whom only four were ever identified – Ockenden, Duffey, Sutherland and Barlow. At Cranley Gardens he was to begin killing again. In 1982 he killed twice, but before that he attempted to kill Paul Nobbs, nineteen, a student he met in a West End pub on 23 November 1981. He took him back to Cranley Gardens and cooked him a meal, after which they went to bed together for sex-play. Paul Nobbs woke at six in the morning to find that he had a raging headache, and when he looked in the bathroom mirror he was astonished to see that his eyes were bloodshot and his throat badly bruised. Nilsen told him that he had probably caught his neck in the zip of the sleeping bag. The fact was that he had attempted to strangle the youth during the night, but for some reason desisted from killing him. When Paul Nobbs left that morning a solicitous Nilsen advised him to see a doctor and gave him his telephone number, expressing the hope that they would meet again.

The first victim to be murdered at Cranley Gardens was known to Nilsen only as 'John the Guardsman'. He was later to be identified as being John Howlett, twenty-three, from High Wycombe. He was a drifter who lied that he had been in the Guards. They had met casually in December 1981, but they met again by chance in March 1982 in a pub. Nilsen invited him back to the flat for a drink, but was annoyed when his visitor made himself too much at home. Nilsen remarked acidly, 'I didn't know you were moving in.' When he fell into a drunken stupor Nilsen put a ligature around his neck, saying viciously, 'I think it's time you went!' He throttled him unconscious and then placed him in the bath to drown.

Nilsen dissected Howlett quickly: a friend was due to visit the next day. He boiled the head in a large pot on the stove and flushed the internal organs and some flesh down the toilet. The rest he packed into a tea-chest which stood in the corner of the flat. He later told police, 'I put all the large bones out with the rubbish for the dustmen.'

In April 1982 Nilsen met Carl Stottor, twenty-one, a six-foot-tall male dancer known professionally as 'Blondie', in the Black Cap pub in Camden Town. He took him back to Cranley Gardens and they went to bed together. In the middle of the night Stottor awoke to a living nightmare. He was being strangled, and was too weak to resist. He felt himself being lifted and carried, then plunged into a bath of water. Several times his head was pushed under the water, while he tried to beg for mercy. He then lapsed into unconsciousness.

He woke to find himself back in bed with the dog licking his face. In actual fact Nilsen thought he had succeeded in killing him, and was surprised when he revived. But he made every attempt to bring Stottor round once he realized he was alive, turning on all the bars of the electric fire to warm him. He persuaded Stottor that he must have got his neck stuck in the zipper of the sleeping bag and almost choked himself. Much was to be made at the subsequent trial of this strange episode. Why had Nilsen spared Stottor? How had he been able to snap out of his killing state? It seemed to suggest that there were two Nilsens, a Jekyll and Hyde in real life.

The next murder was that of Graham Allan, twenty-eight, from Glasgow; the exact date of his death is unknown, but it was some time in mid-1982. Allan, a drug-addict, was strangled and then dissected in the bath. He was later identified from an X-ray plate of his skull which bore a distinctive fracture.

On New Year's Day 1983 Nilsen attempted to strangle Toshimitu Ozawa, a young Japanese student. Ozawa managed to fight Nilsen off and fled the house in terror. Because there was no obvious physical injury, police dismissed the matter.

Nilsen was to tell police that he never went out looking for a victim to kill. He simply went out looking for company, and never knew when the urge to kill might come on him. Sometimes he could not remember having killed. On 27 January 1983 he woke to find a dead man in the armchair with a tie around his neck. A piece of string had been attached to the tie to make it long enough to function as a noose – this suggested premeditation, since the ligature must have been constructed *in advance*.

This time the victim was Stephen Sinclair, twenty, a punk and drug-addict. He had a borstal and prison record and suffered from hepatitis. Something of a social misfit, Sinclair had been a foster-child. Nilsen had picked him up in The George off Charing Cross Road on the evening of 26 January. Back at the flat Nilsen strangled him, then lay naked beside the body with an erection.

Nilsen later told police of how he had attempted to dispose of Sinclair. 'I put the head in a pot, popped the lid on and lit the stove. When the head was coming to the boil I turned the pot down to simmer, then I took the dog out for a walk. . . . Later I watched TV as the head was simmering.' Most of Sinclair's dissected corpse was in two black bags in the wardrobe. Nilsen tried to flush pieces of flesh down the toilet, but the toilets became blocked.

In February 1983 the residents of the other flats reported the blocked toilets to the landlord, who arranged for a plumber to call on Saturday 5 February. But on the night of 4 February Nilsen was busy cutting up Sinclair's body. On the Saturday the plumber decided the job was too big for him and advised the estate agent to call in DynoRod. On Sunday Nilsen finished dismembering the body, placing the various bits in his wardrobe.

On Monday 7 February Nilsen went to work as usual. The DynoRod engineer arrived at 6.15 p.m. on Tuesday. The engineer, Michael Cattrann, lifted a large manhole cover and climbed down into the sewer. There was a revolting smell, and he noted what looked like lumps of flesh blocking the outlet pipes. It was getting dark, and since he had not been long with the company and did not want to make a fool of himself, he packed up for the night, saying he would return the following day. However, he reported his grim find to his boss by telephone. That night Nilsen went down into the sewer and removed most of the flesh into plastic carrier bags, throwing them over the back garden hedge. But his neighbours had seen him at his midnight task.

Nilsen knew that the next day would be crucial: his luck was running out. Again he thought of suicide, but the thought of his dog Bleep deterred him. He went to work as usual, and before leaving at the end of the day he left a note in an envelope in his desk. The note said that if he were to be arrested there would be no truth in reports that he had committed suicide in his cell.

While Nilsen was at work the plumber and his boss returned to the manhole at Cranley Gardens with police officers. Portions of flesh were recovered from blocked pipes and were taken to a pathologist who declared them to be human tissue. When Nilsen returned home on the evening of 9 February he found three large men waiting for him. They were Detective Chief Inspector Peter Jay, Detective Inspector Stephen McCusker and Detective Constable Jeffrey Butler. They had checked Nilsen's background, and knew that he had been a policeman and might therefore prove 'tricky'.

Mr Jay said to the 37-year-old Nilsen: 'I've come about your drains.'

Nilsen replied, 'Why should the police be interested in drains?'

Mr Jay went on, 'The reason I'm interested in your drains is that they are blocked with human remains.'

Nilsen said, 'Good God! That's terrible. Where did it come from?'

'Don't mess about,' Mr Jay said. 'Where's the rest of the body?'

Nilsen confessed immediately, all resistance gone. 'In a plastic bag in the wardrobe,' he said. He took the officers up to his flat and showed them the bags. He was immediately charged on suspicion of murder.

In the police car taking them to Hornsey Police Station, DI McCusker asked Nilsen idly, 'Are we talking about one body or two?'

Nilsen replied, 'Fifteen or sixteen since 1978. I'll tell you everything. It's a relief to be able to get it off my mind.' Once at the police station an incredulous Mr Jay asked Nilsen, 'Let's get this straight. Are you telling us that since 1978 you have killed sixteen people?'

'Yes,' Nilsen replied. 'Three at Cranley Gardens and about thirteen at my previous address, 195 Melrose Avenue in Cricklewood.'

The human remains recovered from Nilsen's wardrobe were examined at Hornsey Mortuary by pathologist Professor Bowden. He found several plastic carrier bags inside the two large black plastic bin-liners. In one shopping bag was the left side of a man's chest including the arm, in another a torso, in a third a heart, lungs, spleen, liver, gall bladder, kidneys and intestines. Dissection had been skilful, the pathologist noted. Slowly he was able to reassemble the body of Stephen Sinclair.

The questioning of Nilsen began on 11 February at Hornsey Police Station, led by Mr Jay. It was to last thirty hours spread over a week, and the story which emerged chilled the listening detectives. With dispassionate calm, like the civil servant he was, Nilsen dictated a precise and detailed account of his many murders. He said that of the three people murdered at Cranley Gardens he knew only Stephen Sinclair by name. He said he was relieved he had been caught now, because 'If I had been arrested at sixty-five years of age there might have been thousands of bodies behind me.'

While telling detectives about how he had cut up bodies and flushed the remains down the toilet, he asked for an ashtray to stub out his cigarette. When a young constable told him to flush it down the toilet Nilsen replied drily, 'The last time I flushed something down the toilet I got into trouble.' He co-operated fully in the in-terrogation, as if anxious to have all his deeds recorded. While in custody he wrote a document entitled *Unscrambling Behaviour* in which he attempted to explain his motives. He displayed no signs of remorse at any time and admitted, 'I can't weep for my victims.'

The detectives tried to establish if the murders had been premeditated, if Nilsen had lured young men to his flat with the express intention of killing them. 'No,' said Nilsen, 'it just happened.' He said that far more people had visited his flat and left alive than had remained dead.

Asked how he could have cut up bodies and dabbled in flesh without feeling sick, Nilsen replied simply, 'The victim is the dirty platter after the feast and the washing-up is a clinically ordinary task.' He also told detectives about the seven attempted murders.

The detectives noted that there had been a gap of a year between the first and second killings, and then ten victims had been strangled within eighteen months, in 1980-1. Was there any reason for this? Could Nilsen supply any motive for the murders? Nilsen said he could not. He wasn't a sex-maniac or a robber or a sadist. 'What I am is totally irresponsible,' he said.

When his solicitor had finished reading his terrible confession he raised his eyes to Nilsen and asked, 'Why?' Nilsen shrugged. 'I was hoping you would tell me that,' he said. Within a day or so after his arrest, newspapers had begun headlining the case as 'The House of Horrors.' Nilsen saw those headlines and commented, 'The only House of Horrors I know is Number Ten, Downing Street.'

Nilsen was remanded to Brixton Prison, from where he sent a letter to the detectives handling his case, complimenting them on the professional way they had handled the inquiry. He was very conscious of the media interest in him, conscious that he had at last become a *somebody*. Once in prison Nilsen was made a Category A prisoner and was surprised at the hostility shown against him by fellow-prisoners. He made a bad prisoner. He tried to fight the system, going on hunger strikes and once assaulting prison staff: he got a black eye and lost a tooth as a result.

Convinced that he was being treated unfairly, he complained bitterly to the governor, and ended by sacking his legal counsel. At this time he also fell in love with a fellow-prisoner, David Martin, a tragic transvestite who eventually committed suicide in prison. Nilsen had begun writing his own account of his crimes in his many notebooks in an attempt at self-analysis. Like Kürten, he wrote he would welcome being executed and complained that he had been 'used' by a power to which he had surrendered control. He seemed convinced he was a victim of demonic possession, no doubt explaining his cryptic words written after he was convicted. 'They think they have the real me safely locked away here, but the real me is hundreds of miles away . . .'

The trial of Nilsen began at the Old Bailey on Monday 24 October 1983, with Mr Justice Croom-Johnson presiding. Mr Alan Green prosecuted, with Mr Ivan Lawrence for the defence. Nilsen was charged with six murders and two attempted murders. He pleaded not guilty to murder but guilty to manslaughter on the grounds of diminished responsibility.

The prosecutor told the jury of eight men and four women the facts relating to the arrest of Nilsen. He said that seven victims had now been identified, although only six were on the indictment. The prosecution set out to show the *pattern* of the murders. Each victim was a man. Each had been picked up in a pub. All were strangers to Nilsen. All, with the exception of Ockendon, had no permanent address. All had been strangled. Some were homosexuals or male prostitutes. Nilsen had had sexual connections with six of the bodies.

Nilsen's confession was read out to a shocked court. When the police had asked him about the ties which he used to strangle his victims Nilsen said he had started out with fifteen and only had one left at the time of his arrest. Asked how many bodies were under the floorboards at any one time he had replied flippantly, 'I'm not sure. I did not do a stock check.' He had told police he had taken on a 'quasi-God role' in killing.

The first prosecution witness was Douglas Stewart, twenty-nine. He was a married man, and stated that he was not a homosexual. He told of Nilsen's abortive attempt to strangle him.

On Tuesday 25 October two witnesses told of having been attacked by Nilsen. Paul Nobbs told of sex-play in bed with Nilsen, then waking up to find himself half-strangled. 'There were no whites to my eyes; they were all bloodshot. I had a sore throat and I felt very sick.' He said Nilsen had told him, 'God, you look bloody awful.'

Carl Stottor told of being picked up in a pub by Nilsen. Stottor had been feeling very depressed at the time, and told Nilsen he wished he were dead. Nilsen told him not to be silly – he should not throw his life away. They went to bed, and then 'I woke up feeling something around my neck. My head was hurting and I couldn't breathe properly. . . He was saying in a sort of whispering shouting voice: "Stay still! Stay still!" Then I passed out . . . I vaguely remember hearing water running . . . I was being carried. I knew I was in the water and he was trying to drown me. He kept pushing me into the water. The third time I came up I said: "No more, please, no more" and he pushed me under again. . . I passed out.' He woke up to find himself on the couch, the dog licking his face. Nilsen was solicitous and helped him to the tube station.

Defence counsel asked him, 'Was the defendant both calm and concerned before and after the "incident" as though he was unaware that he had done anything to harm you?' When the witness replied yes Mr Lawrence ruminated aloud, 'How odd that was. . .' and then sat down. Defence counsel established that the police only knew about the attempted murders because Nilsen had volunteered the information. Nilsen had spared Stottor's life when he had him at his mercy. It was an attempt to establish Nilsen's 'diminished responsibility'.

The document *Unscrambling Behaviour*, written by Nilsen at Hornsey Police Station, was read out in part:

> I guess I may be a creative psychopath who, when in a loss of rationality situation, lapses temporarily into a destructive psychopath. . . At the subconscious root lies a sense of total social isolation and a desperate search for sexual identity. . . God only knows what thoughts go through my mind when it's captive within a destructive binge. Maybe the cunning, stalking killer instinct is the only single concentration released from a mind which in that state knows no morality . . . There is no disputing the fact that I am a violent killer under certain circumstances. . . It amazes me that I have no tears for the victims. I have no tears for myself. . .

His personal letter to Mr Jay had read: 'My remorse is of a deep and personal kind which will eat away at me for the rest of my life. . . I have slain my own dragon as surely as the Press and the letter of the law will slay me.'

Mr Jay agreed with defence counsel that Nilsen had been totally co-operative, and had given his confession in a matter-of-fact manner – a confession which Mr Jay said he found 'horrific'. Under cross-examination DI Chambers agreed that the police had managed to trace fourteen men who had visited Nilsen's flat and come to no harm.

On Wednesday Mr Lawrence rose to open the defence case. He told the jury that he did not have to prove that Nilsen was insane – just that at the time of the murders he had been suffering from an abnormality of the mind. He called the first witness for the defence, psychiatrist Dr James MacKeith, who said that Nilsen suffered from a 'severe personality disorder' and at the time of killing was in a state known as 'disassociation', as if watching someone else do the deed.

Under cross-examination the doctor admitted that all a psychiatrist could know of a person's mental condition was *what that person told him*. There was the usual clash between the prosecution and psychiatrist which is endemic in these cases. The prosecution asserted that Nilsen was cunning, resourceful and had presence of mind. Mr Green said the fact that Nilsen had spared some of his victims proved that he could desist from killing when he wanted to; he had the power of *choice*. There was a shouting match between Mr Green and the witness, which ended with the doctor withdrawing his diagnosis that Nilsen had been suffering from diminished responsibility.

Dr Patrick Gallwey fared no better. He said Nilsen suffered from a 'false self syndrome', a theory developed by R.D. Laing from ideas postulated by Jean-Paul Sartre. It was simply another formulation of the 'Jekyll and Hyde' story. According to the doctor, this type of personality is fine when things are going well, but quickly falls apart under stress. The doctor went so far as to say, 'I don't see how he can have had malice aforethought when he had no feelings.' This brought a stern rebuke from the judge, who said he was trespassing on the law and should confine himself to medical matters.

The prosecution had stressed Nilsen's ability to make

choices. He *chose* to invite men to his flat. He *chose* to kill Barlow because he was a nuisance. Re-examination of Dr Gallwey by Mr Lawrence clarified the issue. The doctor said that Nilsen killed to save himself from going insane. The acts of murder pointed destruction outward instead of inward. Without the acts of murder his mind would have collapsed into psychosis. The doctor said that while Nilsen had known intellectually what he was doing, he had not known emotionally, and without emotion a man behaves like an automaton, a robot.

The prosecution psychiatrist was Dr Paul Bowden. He had seen Nilsen on sixteen occasions over an eight-month period and had determined that Nilsen was not sick. His report had stated 'I am unable to show that Dennis Nilsen had any abnormality of mind.' Mr Lawrence asked him, 'Were not his murders evidence of abnormal behaviour?' The doctor replied, 'Of course strangling people is not normal behaviour.' Mr Lawrence was able to trip him up on a number of points, establishing that the law and psychiatry do not mix. One deals in intangibles, the other in tangible evidence.

In his closing speech the prosecutor said, 'You are dealing with a defendant who liked killing people and derived satisfaction from the act itself. The defence says this man was simply out of his mind. The defence says he couldn't really help it. The Crown says, oh yes he could.'

For the defence Mr Lawrence opened by saying, 'Does not common speech oblige one to say of the perpetrator of these killings, he must be out of his mind?'

The judge spent four hours summing up the case to the jury, and his bias against Nilsen and psychiatry was evident. He said, 'There are evil people who do evil things. Committing murder is one of them. . . A mind can be evil without being abnormal.'

The jury retired on the morning of Thursday 3 November. At 4.30 p.m. the judge asked the jury if they could agree a verdict. The response was no, and the jury were sequestered in a hotel overnight. They resumed their deliberations at 10 a.m. the next day. At 11.25 a.m. the judge told them he was prepared to accept a majority verdict, and at 4.25 p.m. the jury returned. On every count the decision was a 10-2 majority verdict of guilty of murder, except for the attempted murder of Paul Nobbs when all twelve jurors agreed on guilty. The judge sentenced Nilsen to life imprisonment, with a recommendation that he should serve a minimum of twenty-five years.

Here, then, are the bare facts of the case. What remains are the disturbing reflections about motive. It so happens that years ago a Dr Brittain built up a portrait of the serial killer based on his experience of observing murderers for twenty years. That 'IdentiKit of a Killer' bears a striking resemblance to Nilsen. The doctor reports that this kind of killer is introspective and withdrawn. He engages in solitary pursuits. He is retiring, shy and uncommunicative. He rarely shows temper, and does not retaliate to violence. He feels different from other people, isolated. He is at his most dangerous when he suffers a loss of self-esteem, such as demotion at work or a failed relationship. He is arrogant, vain and narcissistic. Generally under thirty-five years of age. . . of high intelligence. Leads a complicated fantasy life. . . shows little or no remorse and is without pity for his victims. He plans his murders well and cunningly. . . is a plausible liar. The desire of having power over others is an essential part of his abnormality. . . Although these are essentially sexually motivated crimes, sexual intercourse or even orgasm does not always occur but sometimes the murderer masturbates beside his victim. Dr Brittain could almost have been describing Dennis Nilsen.

The police were accused by the tabloid press of 'blunders' in the Nilsen case. This is simply not true. The plain fact is that a man can go on quietly killing in a peaceful London suburb for years without detection, providing, like Nilsen, he preys on the dregs of society: those unfortunates who will not be missed.

Chapter Twelve

HENRY LEE LUCAS –
AMERICAN GOTHIC

Henry Lee Lucas was the man who finally made America aware of the menace of the serial killers in their midst. The FBI estimates that serial killers slaughtered some 5,000 Americans in 1983. The epidemic seems peculiarly American. Around the world, according to Interpol, no more than fifty serial killers have been identified over the past twenty years. Newspaper accounts of Lucas's claim to having murdered 360 people from coast to coast by virtually every known method: stabbing, shooting, strangulation, mutilation, decapitation and even crucifixion led to one top police official admitting that there could be as many as thirty-five such killers at large in America at any one time, with the numbers constantly increasing.

In September 1984 one-eyed vagrant Henry Lee Lucas led FBI officers on a gruesome nation-wide tour, showing sites where he had disposed of bodies. At that time 144 of his serial slayings had been verified, and Lucas, forty-eight, was named the worst mass-murderer in US history. Now under sentence of death in Texas, he is wanted by law officers in a dozen other states for questioning about unsolved sex murders.

It began in June 1983 when Reuben Moor, a preacher

who led a small fundamentalist sect called the House of Prayer in Stoneburg, Texas, reported to the police that one of his flock, Henry Lee Lucas, was in possession of a gun, and since Lucas was an ex-convict this amounted to a felony.

Police made a point of visiting Lucas, who was care-taker of the church camp-ground – known locally as the 'Chicken Shack', because that was what it had been before the owner gave it to the church. Lucas lived in the shack in conditions of squalor. A small man with long straggly hair and an unkempt beard, the fact that he had a glass eye and a downturned mouth made him look like a caricature of a horror movie character.

Police in the area had a full case-load of work. In the small town of Ringgold, just ten miles away from Stoneburg, the home of an eighty-year-old widow had burned to the ground in October 1982. It was felt lucky that Kate Rich, the widow, had not been in the house when it burned. No bones were found among the ashes, and it was assumed that she was away visiting relatives.

Then, two months later, two bird-watchers found her purse in a creek near Stoneburg. It contained her identification, but any cash it might have contained was missing. Sheriff W.F. Conway of Montague County now had the task of tracing Mrs Rich's relatives to ask if she was with them. Since all his queries had led nowhere, the sheriff had to assume that she had come to a bad end. He requested help from the Texas Rangers, who assigned their top homicide specialist, Investigator Phil Ryan, to the case.

Together the sheriff and Phil Ryan back-tracked on Kate Rich's movements and found no trace of her. Once again the ashes of her former home were searched, but revealed no trace of human remains. But by questioning people in the area they learned that a middle-aged drifter and a young girl whom he claimed as his wife had rented a trailer at Ringgold in the summer and had done odd jobs for the widow. The couple left the area after a few months, the man finding a job with the church, the girl moving on.

Now the two lawmen questioned the handyman, Henry Lee Lucas. He gave his age as forty-six, although he looked older. Originally from Tecumseh in Michigan, he had drifted across the USA for years, picking up odd jobs where he could. 'I guess I've got itchy feet,' he said. There seemed to be a sly humour in the man which both irritated and interested Phil Ryan.

Questioned about Kate Rich, he agreed that he and his 'wife' had been befriended by her and had done odd jobs for her. Sometimes she paid them cash, other times she invited them for a meal by way of repayment. He expressed regret at the news that she was missing, but said he had no information about her.

Then the lawmen asked him about his wife. Lucas said he didn't know much about her. She wasn't his official wife, she had just lived with him a while. She was about sixteen, a runaway from Florida, and went by the name of Becky, although he thought her real name was Frieda Powell. He had met her a year earlier at a camp-site in Austin, Texas, and she had begun travelling with him.

After a spell in Ringgold she had become homesick for Florida, so he took her to a nearby truck-shop where she could hitch a ride. 'She told me she would come back after she had seen her folks,' Lucas said. 'But I got a letter from her saying she had met a truck-driver in San Antonio and was going with him and wouldn't be back.'

With a philosophical shrug he added, 'I guess she's just like most stray cats. You feed them and they stay around awhile. Then they up and leave. . . She was a real nice girl.'

After ascertaining that Lucas did not have a gun, as reported, the lawmen left, by no means satisfied by his answers. They made a point of questioning every single one of Stoneburg's fifty-two residents. Not one had a bad word to say about Lucas. He was friendly, a hard worker and didn't drink. He could fix almost anything, from a broken tractor to a leaking roof. They all agreed that

Lucas had treated the young girl, Becky, like a daughter.

It was a standard routine police procedure that made Sheriff Conway send the name of Henry Lee Lucas to the National Crime Information Centre (NCIC). The reply stunned him. The file on Lucas was extensive. He had been convicted of stabbing his mother to death after raping her in Michigan in 1960, when he was aged twenty-three.

Detailed information on Lucas's background revealed that both his parents had been alcoholics, and from a young child onward Lucas had been beaten and abused by his mother, a Chippewa Indian who was also a prostitute. She had once hit him so hard with a piece of wood that the blow had caused brain damage. The father had lost both legs in a railway accident and had been subsequently thrown outdoors by his wife and left to freeze to death. It was like a bad parody of a country and western song. Then Lucas stabbed and raped his mother in the family home at Tecumseh, leaving her to die.

He was sentenced to forty years in prison, but unknown to the authorities he had committed his first murder at the age of fifteen, when a seventeen-year-old girl he met at a bus stop resisted his sexual advances and he strangled her.

After a short stay in prison, following several suicide attempts, Lucas had been confined to a mental hospital for six years, after which psychiatrists declared him well enough to rejoin society. He was released on parole in 1970, even though he had warned the hospital authorities that he would go on killing if released. Lucas promised, 'I'll leave you a present on the doorstep.' On the day he was released he killed a woman in Jackson, a few miles down the road, a murder which remained unsolved until his final confession.

For the next thirteen years Lucas followed a nomadic existence, living a killing-spree which was not directed but haphazard; he chose his victims at random and killed when he could. For the latter part of this murderous existence Lucas had been joined by another vagrant – Ottis Elwood Toole, an uncle of Frieda Powell – 'Becky' – whose own sexual preference was for children. He was a homosexual, and sometime lover of Lucas, Lucas himself being bisexual. The bizarre couple sometimes killed together, sometimes alone. This introduces an element of *folie à deux* – not uncommon, as we have seen – but just who was the dominant partner is vague.

A year after his release in 1970 Lucas was taken into custody for violating his parole by an attempted rape and kidnapping. His parole was revoked and he served four years in the state penitentiary before being released in 1975.

So the church handyman was a matricide and rapist – but all fifty-two residents of Stoneburg didn't have a bad word to say about him . . . The fact that Lucas had a record did not link him with the murder of Kate Rich – if indeed she had been murdered – and did not in itself prove him guilty of anything. But the investigators decided that they would very much like to meet the young girl, Becky, and get her version of events – if they could find her. If she had indeed gone to live with a trucker in Florida she might prove impossible to trace.

They questioned the residents of Stoneburg again, hoping for some clue, something which they hadn't been told before, and one woman revealed something of interest. She said Lucas had offered to sell her two of his 'wife's' rings, claiming that after she had left him she had returned the rings. That didn't seem like the behaviour of any sixteen-year-old girl.

The officers went back to the church site to question Lucas further, finding him with his suitcase packed and just about to leave. Asked what he was doing, Lucas said he had been in one place long enough and was moving on. Asked about the girl's whereabouts, Lucas said she could be anywhere. Faced with the fact that he tried to sell the girl's rings, Lucas said she had given them to him before she left, afraid she might get robbed while hitch-hiking.

There was nothing to hold Lucas on, yet if he left he could be impossible to find, and both officers felt that there was something sinister about the sardonic vagrant. Ryan asked Lucas if he had any objection to his looking in his suitcase. Lucas shrugged and gave permission. Ryan searched among clothing and then found a two-foot-long dagger which was razor-sharp. Questioned about it, Lucas said he kept it for self-protection while on his travels. 'There's a lot of mean people out there,' he chuckled. Now Ryan had something to hold him on: possession of an illegal and concealed weapon. He read Lucas his rights and took him to the county gaol in Montague.

Once in gaol Lucas – who had waived his right to have an attorney present – startled detectives by saying contemptuously: 'You guys aren't interested in that dagger. . . What you really want to know is about Kate Rich and my wife Becky.' He spoke in a harsh rasp, barely concealing an undercurrent of savage hate and bitterness.

'I'll tell you one thing,' he went on. 'You guys are up a creek without a paddle. You ain't ever going to know what happened to them – unless I tell you.' The officers listening didn't know it, but this was the culmination of years of drifting, killing at random. Lucas was finished. He was about to confess to hundreds of murders – but not from remorse. It was more from a wry recognition of futility and self-disgust. Lucas had reached a point of inner moral collapse.

A few hours of questioning went by, with Lucas making enigmatic remarks and offering tantalizing half-clues, playing mind-games with the detectives. Then, as if finally bored by it all, he said harshly, 'Hell. You won't ever find them. I'm tired of this. I'll show you where they are.'

He took the officers back to the church camp-ground where he had been living. At the rear of the building stood an old cast-iron stove. 'What's left of Kate Rich is in there,' he said. Sure enough, the stove was filled with charred bones. 'I chopped her up and burned her,' Lucas said patiently.

He was then asked about the whereabouts of Becky. He led the officers to an isolated field and said: 'Find her for yourself. She's in pieces all over here.' And sure enough the officers found the rotting chunks of a young woman's body.

Lucas was vague about his reason for killing Kate Rich, although he said he had taken the money from her purse. As for Becky, she had wanted to leave him, and that made him mad – after he had been so good to her. Police suspected another motive: that she might have had to be silenced because she knew too much about the disposal of Kate Rich.

It seemed routine enough, and the two laymen were satisfied. He had confessed to two murders, and was taken to court for a preliminary hearing on the charges before Judge Frank Doughit at Montague County Court. As the prosecutor read out the details of the complaint the judge noted the smirk on Lucas's face and reminded him sternly that he faced a very serious charge: murder, which was no laughing matter. 'I know that, your honour,' Lucas said. 'I've done it a hundred times.'

'What did you say?' the judge inquired.

'I've killed about a hundred women,' Lucas replied. "Maybe it's more than that, if I get to counting. I know it's not normal for a person to kill a woman because she won't have sex with him, but that's what I've done, lots of times.' He spoke with a kind of grim pride.

The judge demanded of the prosecutor, 'Is this man mentally competent to stand trial?' Before the prosecutor could answer Lucas said quickly, 'Judge, if you think I'm crazy, there's a hundred or more women out there who says different. Yes, I'd say I'm mentally competent – and I'm guilty. I'd just like to get this damn thing over with once and for all.'

The judge halted the hearing, pending further inquiries, and set bail at $1 million. When his court-appointed lawyer protested that the bail was too high Lucas laughed. Ignoring the pleas of his attorney to keep his mouth shut, Lucas said he wanted to get all his killings off his chest, and promised to confess them all to the police. 'I will finish what I have started,' he said from the witness chair. 'I will finish giving back the dead what I have taken.' The judge appointed three psychiatrists to examine Lucas and determine if he was competent to stand trial.

Back in the county gaol, Lucas began the long process of confession to murders which went back years, and had taken place in almost every state in the USA. 'Let me tell you about the last one,' he grinned. He told of having picked up a young woman hitch-hiking, then having cut off her head before having sex with her still-warm torso. 'It was messy, but I liked it,' he said. He went on, 'I like to have sex with women after they're dead because they don't holler, fight or nothing.'

One of the listening detectives suggested that he might be inventing murders in the hope of getting off on an insanity plea. Lucas was stung, and instantly retorted, 'You think I'm lying? O.K. You ask them down at Plainview if they found a body without a head. And then you ask them out in Scottsdale, Arizona, if they found a head and no body.' Lucas drew a rough sketch of the woman's features as he remembered them.

Checking revealed that the nude torso of a woman aged about twenty was found just outside Plainview, Texas, in December 1981. A wide search of the area failed to locate her head, and a post-mortem revealed that she had been decapitated while still alive, as there was aspirated blood in her lungs, indicating that she had gasped as her throat was being cut.

Ten months later a skull was found by campers in the desert near Scottsdale, Arizona. Detectives there had spent weeks looking for a body to go with the head, and had had a clay model made of the head as it might have looked in life, with photographs of it distributed to all police agencies. (Lucas's sketch showed an uncanny likeness.)

The skull was sent to Plainview eventually, where forensic anthropologists compared it to the torso's skeletal make-up. They determined that it was 'very probable' that the skull belonged to the body. The victim had been a white female aged about twenty years old, 5ft 2in tall, weighing just over 100 pounds. Just as Lucas had described her. . . The woman was never identified, and remains tagged as 'Jane Doe' to this day.

Because of the nature of Lucas's confessions – referring to murders in many different areas – other law officers had become involved in questioning him. Lucas confessed to Sheriff Jim Boutwell of Williamson County to the murder to a young unidentified female near Georgetown, Texas, in 1979. Lucas said she was a hitch-hiker he had picked up in Oklahoma City. The sheriff told reporters what Lucas had revealed: 'At a rest stop he had sex with her, then strangled her with his hands. He said he had sex with her again after she was dead.' Lucas told the sheriff that he kept the woman's body in the car with him as he drove into Texas, finally dumping it near Georgetown. The body had been discovered on Halloween Night, 1979. Although unsure of his victim's identity, Lucas thought her first name had been either 'Joanie' or 'Judy'. He gave details about the killing which only the police – and the killer – knew.

Lucas was to claim to have killed over a hundred women, starting when he was thirteen years old. It was a compulsion with him, he said. He described killing in a variety of ways, including shooting, stabbing and strangling, and disposed of the bodies in the same haphazard fashion, burying some, burning others. Often he carried pieces of their dismembered bodies with him in his car.

The details of the many murders he confessed to solved cases which had baffled Texas lawmen for years. One example was the murder by shooting of a young couple in 1978. Kevan Kay, nineteen, and his girl friend Rita Salazar, eighteen, had gone to see the movie *Midnight Cowboy* on the night of 5 November. While driving back to Georgetown afterwards their car ran out of petrol, so they had to hitch-hike. The body of Kevan Kay was found in Sheriff Boutwell's county on 6 November 1978, and that same day the body of Rita Salazar was found sixty miles away near Waco. Both bodies bore multiple gunshot wounds.

The teenagers had been given a lift by Lucas, who was accompanied by his new partner in murder, Ottis Elwood Toole. Toole was an uncle of 'Becky' Powell. All three had lived together for a time in Jacksonville, Florida, and had travelled together all over the country. Lucas had met Toole in 1976 at Jacksonville at a mission which catered for down-and-outs. The two men had become friends, and lovers. Lucas moved in with Toole's family, and it was there that he first met Frieda 'Becky' Powell, who was then aged twelve. He spent a lot of time with the girl, fixing her bicycle and talking with her, until gradually she became dependent on him.

After he had recounted details of half a dozen murders in Texas alone, Lucas called a halt to the questioning, saying, 'Give me a pad and pencil and I'll collect my thoughts. I can't remember all of them right away.'

While he sat in his cell listing the details and places of his 'kills' police in the various areas he had mentioned checked out his story. Some of the bodies had already been found, and now others were recovered from graves which he had indicated.

There was a twelve-year-old girl from Denton, Texas, whose nude corpse was found in a gravel pit. The mutilated corpse of another unidentified woman had been found in a culvert near Georgetown, Texas. A woman had been smothered to death in her home near Odessa,

Texas, and Lucas recalled in detail how the pillow had burst open, allowing feathers to pour out. In Fort Bend, Texas, a 22-year-old woman had been found stabbed to death under a railway bridge. Lucas remembered that she had worn black panties with 'Tuesday' embroidered on them.

He had listed ten murders on his pad which he had committed in Florida. When he handed the pad back to detectives he commented, 'I know there was more than that, but it may take a while to remember.'

All the murders he had listed had remained unsolved, and he had given precise details which only the killer could have known. When asked about particular murders in various states Lucas would frown thoughtfully and then reply, 'Yes, that's one of mine,' or 'No, I didn't do that. You have to realize I'm not the only guy out there killing women.'

Eventually he had detailed a hundred murders he had committed from New York State to California, and from Washington state to Florida. He had murdered his way across the USA, from coast to coast. Now he told detectives triumphantly, 'See, I wasn't kidding when I said I had killed a hundred. There are more, but some of them I can't remember exactly where, or what I did with them.'

In the months which followed, the nation read with morbid fascination as his confession to murders reached a total of 360 killings. He would often retract a confession only to repeat it, obviously unsure of his memory, and this led to doubts about his entire story. But the recovery of several bodies from sites indicated by him proved that it was not all fantasy.

Most of his victims were woman and young children, whom he had raped, tortured and murdered. He claimed that he had crucified some victims and 'filleted others like fish'.

Asked about his motives, he said, 'I was bitter at the world. . . I had nothing but pure hatred. Killing someone is just like walking outdoors. If I wanted a victim, I'd just go and get one.'

The curious aspect of the Lucas case is his teaming up in the latter years with Ottis Elwood Toole, whose own sexual preferences were for children. When Lucas named Toole as his accomplice in some of the killings it added a whole new dimension to the investigation. Sheriff Boutwell went to Jacksonville in October 1983 to question Toole, who had been taken into custody. As a result of his inquiries a grand jury indicted Toole for capital murder – committing murder during the course of another felony, murder, in the case of Kevan Kay. He was also indicted for the aggravated kidnapping and murder of Rita Salazar. Ballistics tests showed that the same .22 pistol had been used to kill both victims.

The probe into the Lucas-Toole connection implicated them in five other murders in Texas counties. Charges were brought against them for two killings in Odessa. On 11 August 1983 Lucas was indicted for the strangulation murder of Beverly Joyce Luttrell, forty-six, whose nude body was discovered at her home on 13 March 1981. She had been strangled with a phone cord.

Toole was indicted on 9 November 1983 for the bludgeon murder of 'Happy' Howry, sixty-six, an Odessa shoe-salesman whose body was found on a vacant lot in Big Spring, Texas, fifty miles from Odessa.

Lucas, meanwhile, was still talking, and based on his information officers took him on a trip to Conroe, forty miles north of Houston. There he indicated three sites where he had disposed of women. Lucas made a written confession to Conroe police officers detailing the killings of Glorie Stephan, twenty-eight, whose body was found near Magnolia, Texas, on 2 October 1981; an unidentified woman whose burning body was discovered in the area on 16 April 1983; and Laura J. Donez, sixteen, a Houston student whose body was found on 17 March 1983. Although the bodies had been located before Lucas identified the sites, again he gave details which could only have been known to the actual killer. He was subsequently indicted for the kidnapping, sexual assault and murder of these women.

The police kept scribbling down new cases as Lucas kept talking. On 17 September 1983 he was indicted by a grand jury in Fort Bend County, Texas, for the stabbing death of Deion Marie Wilkinson, twenty-two, of Houston.

By now everyone was getting in on the act. Louisiana authorities brought charges of murder and kidnapping against Lucas and Toole for the abduction and shooting to death of college student Kathy Whorton, nineteen, on 4 April 1981. And authorities in six different areas of Texas filed charges of first-degree murder against Lucas, with requests that he be held for them after he had gone to trial for the murders of Kate Rich and Frieda Powell.

Lucas was still revealing details of murders he had committed when it came time for him to face his first trial for murder, that of Kate Rich. The three psychiatrists appointed to examine him reported that he was competent to stand trial. Just before he appeared in court Lucas made a crude attempt at suicide in the county gaol at Montague by cutting his wrists with a broken light-bulb. He was found bleeding in his cell by deputies, taken to the local hospital for first aid, and returned to his cell. Lucas told the doctor who bandaged his wrists, 'I ain't going to no trial! I told them that – and if they'd let me alone it would all be over now.'

On 30 September 1982 the trial of Henry Lee Lucas for the murder of Kate Rich began, with his lawyer telling the court that he intended pleading his client innocent on the grounds of insanity. Lucas shouted his objections angrily: 'I ain't innocent – and I ain't insane! You've had all kinds of shrinks poking around inside my skull, and they've said I'm not crazy. So if you think I'm crazy, *you're* crazy.' Lucas pleaded guilty to murder, adding that he had killed a total of 157 women, including his mother.

He had told Sheriff Conway: 'See, I told you that unless I told you about killing Kate Rich and Becky, you'd never have known what happened to them. They never found out about any of the others either until I told them.'

Judge Douthwit consulted with prosecution and defence lawyers, asking if they were willing to agree to the guilty plea and pointing out that it would save the state time and money, since Lucas was adamant about his guilt. It was agreed that the guilty pleas should be accepted, and the judge sentenced Lucas to seventy-five years in prison, which he explained would keep him safely confined for far longer than a mere life sentence.

In October 1983 Lucas again stood trial, this time for the murder of his common-law wife Frieda 'Becky' Powell. On 9 November he was found guilty and returned to prison. But he was not to rest behind bars for long. There were six Texas murder charges to face, Florida had eight murder charges which they wanted to prosecute, and several other states had murder charges pending against Lucas. Several prosecutors have vowed to continue prosecuting Lucas until he receives the death penalty.

One prosecutor said, 'One thing is for sure. He'll never get out of prison alive. He's forty-six years old now, and there are enough murder charges pending against him to last a couple of lifetimes.'

After Lucas's first murder conviction one detective, asked about the 157 victims, said, 'I don't know the total. He has given us information which has shed light on killings that have gone unsolved for years, and shown us graves with bodies in them, when the victims were only reported as being missing. He didn't keep an accurate count of his killings, so the figure might be even higher than the 157 he claims. . . He doesn't remember, or maybe never knew, the names of all his victims. But he can tell you the colour of the underwear they had on, and locations of where he left his victims in almost every state of the nation.'

Investigator Phil Ryan of the Texas Rangers was asked how it was possible for one man to commit so many murders without coming under suspicion. Ryan said the explanation was simple. 'He was a drifter. All he needed was cigarettes, an old banger of a car and gas. He never stayed in one place for more than a month. He worked at odd jobs, and if he ran out of money he'd sell his blood to blood banks. And most often he had no personal contact with his victims before he killed them.'

He went on: 'And he had no set *modus operandi*. He'd stab, shoot, strangle or smother his victims, then move on for the next kill. And he had no preference for age. He killed girls as young as twelve and women as old as eighty. If they refused him sex, he killed them.'

With Lucas behind bars, starting his 75-year sentence, it was left to Detective J.T. Terry of Jacksonville, Florida, to check out the Lucas-Toole link in his city. He was keenly aware that there had been a dozen or more murders around Jacksonville over a period of three years which bore the trademark of Lucas.

Detective Terry had been to Montague County to talk to Lucas about the background of 'Becky' Powell. He spent an entire day listening to Lucas brag about his murders, often referring to himself as the 'moonlight murderer'. Never in his career had the officer listened to such a tale of relentless blood-letting and murder-mania. It was hard to believe that the one-eyed vagrant sitting opposite him could have committed such atrocities. They were not the understandable killings of a human being; they were murders committed by someone who had severed his contract with society and was operating in the realm of the sub-human.

Lucas calmly told Detective Terry that he had probably killed eight women in Jacksonville, and Toole had helped him haul some of the bodies away. Lucas was not boasting: he gave detailed facts about each killing which had not been made public.

Afterwards Detective Terry told reporters, 'That was the most depressing day I ever spent with anybody. It was depressing to sit there and listen to him talk about murders – including the murder of his own mother – and just show no remorse at all. I asked him about one case, 'Why did you kill the woman?' He said, "Hell, she was *there*." Lucas's attitude was: 'If I saw a woman by herself, she was mine.' He didn't go around just looking for a woman, but if he was driving around and saw a woman alone, she belonged to him.'

Officer Terry had the task of piecing together the years in Jacksonville when Lucas had lived with Toole and Becky Powell. Back in Montague Lucas *had* expressed remorse about the killing of Becky: it was the only one of all his murders which preyed on his mind. He told Terry, 'She was the only woman I ever loved.' Terry asked him why, then, he had killed her. Lucas hung his head. 'I just had to,' he muttered.

People who had known Lucas and Becky in Jacksonville remembered them well, because the teenage girl and the scruffy drifter made such an incongruous pair. Lucas had been forty then, and was 5ft 9in tall and weighed around 150 pounds. He had matted dark-brown hair and a scum-covered glass eye. His clothing was always greasy and dirt-stained. By contrast, Becky – described as 'a sweet girl' – was a clean and well-dressed adolescent. Her elderly aunt lived in the house and took care of the girl.

Lucas's killings in Jacksonville were established in chronological order. His first murder had taken place on 27 November 1979, in the course of a robbery at a motel where he shot Elizabeth Dianne Knotts, thirty-one. Two weeks later Debra Lynn O'Quinn, eighteen, was stabbed to death in her home, although her skeletal remains were not discovered in a wood near Jacksonville until 10 December 1979.

During the course of 1980 Lucas took the lives of five more women. The first was on 5 January, when Jamie L. Collins, seventy-six, was beaten, stabbed to death and sexually assaulted in her home. On 27 March Jo Scheffer, forty-five, was also beaten and stabbed to death. Her nude body was found in a day-care centre. Just under four months later Regina Azell Campbell, twenty-four, was strangled to death. Her body was found underneath a car on 12 July. Eight days later Tammy Keel Conners, nineteen, was found in a ravine near Jacksonville, and three days before Christmas Brenda Elaine Harden, twenty-eight, mother of two children, was found stabbed to death in her home.

The eighth Jacksonville victim – the killing was admitted by Lucas to Detective Terry in a videotaped statement – was that of Shirley Ogden, fifty-eight, a transient who lived just a few blocks away from the boarding house where Lucas, Toole and Becky were staying. Her body was found in an alley on 14 April 1981.

Then Becky's aunt, who had been a dominating influence over the trio, died of a heart attack in June 1981. Becky was placed in a state foster-home, but six months later Lucas and Toole engineered her escape from there, taking her back to Jacksonville to live with them.

Late in 1981 Lucas left Florida, taking Becky with him. From then until Lucas's arrest in June 1983 the couple drifted from state to state, travelling in junk cars and doing odd jobs along the way to earn money. And all this time Lucas was killing. . . Whether Becky knew about his grisly habits will never be known, but Lucas would not have exhibited any remorse. As he told Detective Terry, 'There's no need to feel sorry for them, because they're dead.'

Jacksonville police announced that they were closing the books on the eight killings to which Lucas had confessed: they were satisfied he had done them. His details were just too accurate. As medical examiner Dr Peter Lipkovic told reporters, 'In the case of 76-year-old Jamie L. Collins, Lucas described how he bludgeoned her in bed, dragged her into the living-room and cut her throat, then raped her and poured feathers from a ripped pillow over the body. The police never made it public that the body had been dragged from one room to another, or that pillow feathers were found at the crime scene. That's more than a coincidence. You can think of an active imagination, but this is a little too much.'

State Attorney Ed Austin said Florida would be unlikely to press for Lucas's extradition to face murder charges in view of the capital charges he faced in Texas. 'We'd have to look carefully about using taxpayer's money to bring him back here,' he said.

In mid-1983 a top-level conference in Los Angeles was attended by eighty officers from twenty states to compare information about cross-country killings admitted by Lucas and Toole. At the end of the three-day meeting a spokesman said that the pair had been linked to twenty-eight killings in ten states, and were looking at another sixty-nine murders. Lucas had told Detective Terry, 'We have killed someone in every state in the Union, except Alaska and Hawaii.'

Meanwhile Toole – now in prison in Florida serving a 20-year term for two arson convictions – came back into the headlines when Hollywood police announced on 2 October 1983 that he was guilty of the sensational murder of six-year-old Adam Walsh of Hollywood. Police Chief Sam Martin told reporters, 'Toole killed Adam Walsh by himself. We feel quite confident about that.'

The small boy vanished from a department store in Hollywood on 27 July 1981. His head was found floating in a nearby canal fifteen days later. The cause of death could not be established. This brutal murder so outraged public opinion that a crusade was launched to change the law to allow the FBI to be called in in cases of missing children, and for details of missing children to be put into the National Crime Centre computer. The parents lobbied Congress to enact such a law, and were eventually successful. When the law was passed the parents were at the White House to watch President Reagan sign the Missing Children's Act in October 1982. The case was dramatized in a TV feature called *Adam*, and the movie was screened just a week before Toole gave Hollywood police a signed confession to the murder.

Toole led officers to the site where he claimed to have buried the boy's body, but no trace of the missing torso was found. However, Chief Martin said, 'Certain statements this man has given us have convinced us that he was telling the truth. Toole told my detectives details that only the killer could know. We are satisfied with the answers we got.' He added that Toole told of driving to the Fort Lauderdale area for the sole purpose of abducting someone. Toole said he spotted Adam on the pavement outside the store and lured him into his car with promises of candy.

The Chief revealed that it had been Detective Terry who had elicited the confession from Toole, while talking to him at Duval County gaol at Jacksonville for about a month, as a result of information supplied by Lucas linking Toole to an arson murder.

As a result Toole had been indicted for the first-degree murder and arson in the death of Nicholas Sonneberg, sixty-four, of Jacksonville. Sonneberg died on 4 January 1982 when the boarding-house in which he lived was deliberately set on fire.

While interviewing Toole the man told Officer Terry that he 'knew something about the murder of a little boy in Fort Lauderdale'. Eventually he disclosed that Lucas had killed the boy. It was a crude attempt at revenge against Lucas, but it failed because Lucas had been in gaol in Delaware when the boy was murdered.

Detective Terry told Toole, 'I know Henry didn't do it because he was in gaol at the time. Did *you* kill that little boy?' Toole broke into tears and sobbed, 'Yes, I did.' It was after this admission that Hollywood detectives interrogated the suspect, and got a signed confession which, Chief Martin said, 'Made Charles Manson sound like Tom Sawyer and Huckleberry Finn.'

Chief Martin revealed that of all the killings to which he confessed, the killing of the Walsh boy seemed to be the only one which bothered him. 'He was remorseful about hurting this young boy,' Martin said, 'He broke down and cried when he talked about killing Adam.'

On 1 November 1983, Toole retracted his confession, his court-appointed lawyer telling a press conference, 'He denies having made that confession and he denies killing Adam Walsh.'

Chief Martin responded, 'We would be extremely surprised to have a homicide suspect not, somewhere down the line, deny his confession. That's just the way you play the game.'

Guilty or not, the press coverage of the Lucas-Toole killings made the American public uneasily aware of the serial killers in their midst. When psychologist Joel Norris began to study the case of Wayne Williams (found guilty of two child murders in Atlanta, Georgia but suspected of killing a further twenty-six), he became aware that there were at least six other less-publicized cases of serial killers in Georgia alone, and dozens more throughout America.

Norris subsequently wrote a book about the phenomenon of serial killers, noting that '. . . the majority of serial killers are physically and psychologically damaged people. Almost all of them had scars on their bodies, missing fingers, evidence of previous contusions and multiple abrasions on and around the head and neck area.' He pointed out that many serial killers had sustained head injuries – Earle Nelson being a typical example. Many had been abused children, lacking maternal affection. But it was the physical deformities which interested the psychiatrist most. He said, 'Oddly enough, many have obvious physical and congenital defects such as webbed fingers, attached ear lobes, elongated limbs and other abnormalities.' It sounds as if Norris is confirming some of Lombroso's theories.

Norris points out that the average serial killer – if that is not a contradiction in terms – wears a 'mask of sanity' to hide his perverse desires from the world. In fact, many such killers appear to be model citizens. John Gacy was a successful businessman who was photographed shaking hands with Mrs Jimmy Carter. Ted Bundy was active in politics. Wayne Williams ran his own advertising agency.

Although Norris concluded that a diagnostic test could be devised which would identify likely serial killers *before* they began to kill, he sounds a pessimistic note when he warns that demands for capital punishment are counter-productive. 'Perversely, he wishes for death, and the threat of the gas chamber, the electric chair or lethal injection is only an inducement to keep committing murders until he is caught and put to death. . . The serial killer can no more stop killing than a heroin addict can kick the habit.'

I would have thought that was a very good argument for putting serial killers down like mad dogs.

Chapter Thirteen

COLIN PITCHFORK:
A KILLER TRAPPED BY SCIENCE

The intrinsic interest of the Pitchfork case lies not in his murders – of two schoolgirls – but in the manner of his detection and arrest. The 'Enderby Murders' became an international text-book case which made legal and medical history, and marks as great a turning-point in the fight against crime as did the discovery of fingerprinting in 1901.

In November 1983 Lynda Mann, fifteen, set out from her home, The Coppice, in Narborough near Leicester, to visit a friend in the nearby village of Enderby, taking a short-cut through a footpath known as Black Pad. She never arrived at her destination, and the following morning her body was found lying near the footpath. She had been strangled with her own scarf and raped. A lengthy police investigation led nowhere, but as is routine in these cases, the rapist's semen stains were preserved. For many years now it has been possible to type a person's blood group from their semen or saliva.

The police came to a dead-end in the Enderby Murder, but of one thing they were certain: they were hunting the most dangerous rogue male in any society, the sex killer, and equally certain was the chilling fact that he would strike again.

When he did it was three years later, in July 1986, and this time the victim was Dawn Ashworth, another fifteen-year-old schoolgirl who lived in Enderby. She failed to return home from visiting the home of a friend. Her body lay undiscovered for three days, hidden near another lonely footpath. The semi-naked body bore horrific marks of violence. Dawn had been battered to death and brutally raped. The multiple injuries to her head, face and genitals showed that she had fought for her life. Her body was discovered at a spot less than a mile from where Lynda Mann's body had been found.

Police were now certain that the killer responsible for the Enderby murders was a local man. Obviously the lust-crazed killer was concentrating on his neighbours, picking off their daughters like pigeons. When a seventeen-year-old youth was seen loitering near the murder site he was arrested and charged with the murder of Dawn Ashworth. The huge police murder investigation team heaved a sigh of relief, thinking their task was over.

However, the senior officer in charge of the inquiry was not satisfied, and was aware that at nearby Leicester University a unique scientific breakthrough had been made, with experiments still continuing. Dr Alec Jeffreys, a biologist working there, had stumbled across a method of 'genetic fingerprinting'. The police decided to ask Dr Jeffreys to check their suspect's DNA code against the semen stains from the victim.

For those whose knowledge of biology is a little rusty, a word or two of explanation might not go amiss. 'Genetic fingerprinting' belongs to the field of serology, that branch of medicine which investigates blood and other body fluids. Scientists had long been able to test for blood-grouping, but in the mid-1950s it was discovered that skin cells possess blood characteristics and can be tested exactly like blood itself.

As early as 1911 it was known that human beings individually are made up of about a hundred million million cells, each consisting of a protein surrounding a nucleus, the nucleus consisting of a substance called nucleic acid. In 1911 the biochemist P. Levene discovered that there are two types of nucleic acid, RNA or DNA, according to whether they contain ribose or deoxyribose. When the cell nucleus is stained with a dye it displays the chromosomes: thread-like objects. Every cell has forty-six chromosomes: twenty-three from the father's sperm and twenty-three from the mother's egg, and the chromosomes are made up of DNA. . .

By the 1940s it was realised that DNA was the magic building-block of life, the substance which prints out the secret code which determines if we are to be born with red hair or brown, brown eyes or blue – in fact, the very blueprint for everything which we are to become. If you are left-handed it is because your DNA gene code dictated that you should be so. The instructions are very precise.

But exactly how does DNA issue its instructions? Scientists knew it had to be a code, similar to a series of dots and dashes. Every code is unique to each individual (rather like the bar-code seen on groceries), which is why no two individuals are exactly alike, save for identical twins, who share the same DNA code. Since the code determines the characteristics of a human being, in a sense we are all 'programmed' before birth. In the cloistered world of the scientists the race was on to 'crack' the code.

Crick and Watson solved the problem in the early 1950s, winning the Nobel Prize in the process. They demonstrated that DNA consists of a structure resembling two interlocking spirals – the double helix. This is made up of four types of chemicals in different permutations, adenine, guanine, cytosine and thymine – these are the magic ingredients. Any permutation of these – for example GGGTTCACAA – determines the characteristics of any human being, just as the letters of the alphabet determine a word or sentence. Since all Shakespeare's work is composed of just variations of twenty-six letters, it is not unreasonable to imagine a human being made up from a combination of four different chemicals.

So the amount of chemicals in each group and the order in which they appear determines the eventual characteristics of every human being. That was the important aspect of Crick and Watson's discovery: that the DNA code comes in short bursts or sequences rather like a morse code message. No two people receive exactly the same message. It was an interesting discovery without much practical application but it began the process of understanding the secrets of life, with the possibility that by artificially interfering with the spiral and introducing predetermined amounts of material one could alter the code for an individual and cure an inherited disease or weakness.

When each cell splits in two – as every cell in our bodies does eventually – the two spirals separate and each attracts to itself the various molecules of the four chemicals which make it a duplicate of the original helix. It is important to remember that long sections of the DNA code are the same for every human being, since we all have two arms and two legs, two eyes and one nose etc. But certain stretches of the three-foot-long DNA code show dramatic differences (except in the case of identical twins) – and these are called the 'hypervariable regions', and consist of short sequences of code repeated over and over again like a morse SOS.

The reason for this excursion into science is simply to demonstrate that no discovery comes about by accident: all progress comes about and builds on what has gone before. So it was that in September 1984 Dr Alec Jeffreys devised a completely new method of 'typing' an individual: the 'DNA Fingerprint', as it became popularly known. The discovery came about almost by accident, but could not have occurred without the pioneering work which had gone before, particularly in this century. Dr Jeffreys was studying the gene coding for myoglobin proteins, which carry oxygen to the muscles. In the course of this work he discovered a building block made up of repeated sequences within the DNA, each ten or fifteen sections long. Like any curious scientist, he was keen to 'read' the secret message.

He isolated two of these blocks and mass-produced them by cloning, then made them radioactive with an isotope so that he could 'track' them. When he introduced his treated blocks to other material (such as human blood) he would be able to follow the progress of his blocks as they 'homed in' on similar blocks to themselves – remembering that like attracts like.

Basically, what Dr Jeffreys did was to isolate the DNA from the proteins which surround the nucleus. Then he chopped the DNA material into tiny pieces, using an enzyme as a catalyst, then he sorted the chopped-up material into various sizes on to a base made of gel electrophoresis. This produced bands, which he stuck to a nylon membrane, before adding his radioactive 'probes'. He placed a radioactive-sensitive film over the membrane, and it registered marks where each probe had combined specifically with the highly variable DNA. This produced a unique 'autograph' – unique for every individual on earth.

By having the probes in gel form imprinted on X-ray film Dr Jeffreys was able to produce long columns of dark and light patches, each of different lengths and distances apart. It was just like a bar-code marking. With identical twins, a blood sample from each displayed as a 'genetic fingerprint' and placed side by side will show the light and dark patches in exactly matching positions. With other individuals, no two columns or bands will be the same. The odds against them matching are said to be four million to one and upward.

Dr Jeffreys then obtained blood samples from members of a family and sought to discover if he could prove the relationship. He did – to great excitement in his lab. The tests showed beyond doubt that all the bands of the children derived from the mother or father, and the same applied to the parents and *their* parents.

The first use of Dr Jeffreys's discovery was in paternity cases, where his test could prove beyond doubt that a particular man fathered a particular child. As a result of an early test the Home Office was forced to admit a Ghanaian boy into this country. Dr Jeffreys was able to patent his process and license it to ICI eventually.

The police first made use of Dr Jeffreys's technique in November 1987. In June of that year a burglar broke into a house in Avonmouth, Bristol, and raped a 45-year-old disabled woman, stealing some of her jewellery in the process. Later a man named Robert Melias was arrested for burglary, and the rape victim picked him out on an identity parade. Semen stains from the clothing of the raped woman were subjected to Dr Jeffreys's, 'bar-code' test, and matched exactly with the print of Melias's blood. On 13 November 1987 Melias was sentenced to eight years for rape and five years for robbery. The DNA fingerprint had secured its first conviction.

However, the next use police made of it had even more interesting implications. When the police suspect in the Enderby murders had his genetic fingerprint taken at Leicester University Dr Jeffreys was requested to carry out the test, and the result was that he was able to prove conclusively that the youth was not the killer-rapist. The bar-code obtained from his blood samples were in a completely different order to those found in the semen of the rapist, and he was released. He was an innocent man caught up in the nightmare of a murder hunt, who but for science would probably have been an innocent man languishing for years in a prison cell, his life ruined.

For the police the result was bad news, since it meant than an inquiry which had been brought to a halt by the arrest of a suspect had to be restarted in the autumn of 1986. It seemed as if all the months of work had been for nothing. But the reverse was true. The implication of Dr Jeffreys' revolutionary new test was that not only could it be a valuable and precise weapon, able to determine a suspect's guilt, but *it could also prove his innocence.*

The senior officer in charge of the Enderby murders inquiry now made a brave decision. Certain that the killer was a local man living in the small area around Narborough and Enderby – including the village of Little Thorpe – he decided to have the police visit all the young men in this area and request they give blood samples. Every man in the right age bracket was written to and consent obtained. It was a massive task involving more than 5000 analyses. The result was disappointing. All the men had been tested, but the killer was not among them.

Then came the first break in the case. A bakery-worker having a drink in a Leicester pub boasted of having 'helped out' a friend by offering the police his blood sample in place of that of his friend, who lived in the village of Little Thorpe. The conversation was reported to the police and a twenty-three-year-old man was quickly picked up and questioned. He admitted having acted as a 'stand-in' for his friend and fellow bakery-worker, Colin Pitchfork, twenty-seven, who lived at Little Thorpe.

A quick search of police records revealed that Pitchfork had two convictions for indecent exposure before he married in 1981 at the age of twenty-one.

It transpired that when the police made their request for blood samples Pitchfork panicked and begged several of his workmates to impersonate him, explaining that with his record for 'flashing' he would be an obvious suspect, and was afraid that the police would 'fit him up'. He offered one man £200 and another £500 and finally persuaded the second man to forge Pitchfork's passport signature and learn details of his family by heart. The deception was successful. The man, who lived in Leicester, offered a blood sample and identified himself as Colin Pitchfork.

Pitchfork was now arrested and a blood sample taken from him. It was rushed to Dr Jeffreys's lab, where his 'bar-code' proved to be identical with that of the DNA samples from the rapist-killer. Faced with this proof, Pitchfork admitted both murders.

He said that on both occasions he had been out looking for a girl to whom he could expose himself, and on both occasions the realization that the girl was alone and there were no witnesses led to rape and murder.

In the case of Lynda Mann he had taken his wife to night-school and committed the rape-murder before picking her up again.

On 27 January 1987 Pitchfork appeared in the dock at Leicester Crown Court, where he pleaded guilty to both murders and admitted two additional indecent assaults. Mr Brian Escott-Cox QC, prosecuting, told the court that of over five thousand people invited to take the test, only two did not come forward. One had a genuine reason, and the other had been Pitchfork. Of the stand-in deception he said, 'It worked. The other man went in and carried it off on January 22nd last year.'

Sentencing Pitchfork to life for both murders, with ten years concurrently for the rapes, three years for the indecent assaults and three years for conspiracy to pervert the course of justice, Mr Justice Otton said that if it had not been for genetic fingerprinting Pitchfork might still be at large. He said of the test, 'In this case it not only led to the apprehension of the correct murderer, but also ensured that suspicion was removed from an innocent man.' Pitchfork's 'stand-in' was given an eighteen months suspended sentence.

The American author Joseph Wambaugh came to Britain to write a book about the Pitchfork case, amazed that no English writer had seen the potential of genetic fingerprinting. He had read about the 'Enderby Murders' in American newspapers. His best-selling book *The Blooding* (an obvious reference to the mass blood-testing of the males of Enderby) is a gripping account of the Pitchfork case, and both tribute and testimony to a piece of scientific history.

The first American conviction by means of the DNA fingerprint took place in November 1987, when a brutal rapist and robber in Florida was trapped by the semen he had left in one of his victims. Only one of his victims could pick him out on an identity parade, and proving the suspect's guilt was not going to be easy.

The prosecutor had read about the Pitchfork case, and knew that the Lifecodes Laboratory of New York were offering the new DNA technology under licence. The suspect's blood was of a group belonging to 30 per cent of all American males, so the DNA fingerprinting seemed the only conclusive way of proving the man's guilt. The lab tested the semen, together with a blood sample from the accused. The result was that both were identical and had come from the same man.

In September 1987 Tommie Lee Andrews, twenty-four, was found guilty and gaoled for twenty-two years – the first man in the USA to be convicted by the genetic fingerprint. Tried on further rape charges with additional DNA evidence being submitted, Andrews received additional gaol terms totalling over a hundred years.

Chapter Fourteen

THE STOCKWELL STRANGLER

It began in the spring of 1986 and was to last four terrifying months. Old people began dying. . . nothing strange in that; in most cases death was expected. But these elderly men and women had been murdered and sexually assaulted. The killer had tucked up his victims so neatly after he had satisfied his perverse desires, pulling the sheet modestly up to their necks, that at first it was assumed they had died in their sleep. The victims all lived alone or in old people's homes, and ranged in age from sixty-seven to ninety-four. It needed hardly any pressure to strangle such frail people and in most cases the slight bruising to the neck was almost invisible. Four of the victims lived in the Stockwell district of London – hence the killer's nickname.

In each case someone had entered their bedrooms through windows, leaving no sign of forced-entry, and had killed using a one-handed grip, placing his other hand over their mouths. He left no signs of disturbance at his death-sites. He was like a wraith, drifting through the night to steal lives.

The first victim was Miss Eileen Emms, seventy-eight, who was found dead in her basement flat in West Hill Road, Wandsworth, on 10 April by her home-help. A doctor certified that death was due to natural causes, and Miss Emms was due to be cremated before it was realized that she had been murdered.

It was the second victim who alerted the police to something odd. Mrs Janet Cockett, sixty-seven, of Warwick House on the Overton Road estate, Stockwell, was found dead in bed on 9 June. Her nightdress had been torn off, but lay neatly folded on a chair. Palm-prints of a stranger were found in the flat, and another factor which was to become common to most of the murders was that photographs of relatives were turned to the wall. The killer did not like to be observed. . . .

If the police had begun to suspect that they might have a madman on the loose, an attempted killing on 27 June confirmed their fears beyond doubt. Retired engineer Mr Fred Prentice, seventy-three, was attacked in his bed at an old people's home in Clapham. An intruder got into his room and jumped on his bed, pinning him down.

The man began pinching his neck, and said, 'Kill!' Mr Prentice could never forget his face – he had glaring eyes and an evil grin. It was as if he was playing a cruel game with the old man, one which gave him a secret amusement. Finally Mr Prentice managed to free his mouth long enough to shout, and also pressed the alarm buzzer by his bed. The would-be killer banged his head into the wall and then fled.

The following night – 28 June – as if being thwarted had left him frustrated, the killer committed a double-murder. He broke into Somerville Hastings House, an old people's home in Stockwell Park Road, Stockwell. The victims were found in adjoining rooms. Valentine Gleim, eighty-four, was a former lieutenant-colonel in the British Army. Zbigniew Strabrawa, ninety-four, had been formerly a judge in his native Poland, and had worked for British Intelligence during the war. Both men died in quick succession. Another feature was noted by police to add to the killer's distinctive pattern – the victims were sodomized.

Now the police launched a hunt in earnest, with special night surveillance mounted on old people's homes. Forensic experts worked non-stop, gathering what information they could. Mr Prentice had given the police a sketchy description of the man they were seeking. He was aged twenty-eight to thirty, 5ft 8in tall, with short dark hair and a tanned or reddened face. The skill with which the unknown killer had gained access to flats and bedrooms led police to suspect that he was a professional burglar who might well have passed through their hands in the past. If so, his details would be in the Criminal Records Office at Scotland Yard.

Meanwhile the killings continued. The fifth victim was Mr William Carmen, eighty-two. He was found dead in bed by his daughter at his flat on the Marquess Estate, Islington. He had been sodomized, and photographs in his flat had been turned to the wall. He had been killed between 6 and 9 July.

By now the murder team hunting the Stockwell Strangler (as the Press had dubbed him) consisted of over a hundred detectives working from four murder incident rooms. Detective Chief Superintendent Ken Thompson, who co-ordinated the hunt, told a press conference held on 22 July that police were studying 'the probability' that one mass-killer was preying on elderly people. He warned elderly people, especially those living in South London, to be especially vigilant. Extra police patrols had been ordered in the danger areas. Pressed to state if the killings had all been done by one man, Mr Thompson said, 'Certainly, if all the offences are by the same person, he must be caught before he strikes again. This man is extremely dangerous.' Mr Thompson also revealed that Scotland Yard had called in a psychologist to study the murders and produce a profile of the likely killer. All the data on the murders was being fed into the super-computer HOLMES.

Because so many of the murders had taken place in old people's homes, police naturally had to investigate the possibility that a council employee might be responsible – someone who knew where the victims lived, knew they lived alone, and had means of access. However, Camden

Council refused to give the police details of present or former employees, and twenty-four members of NUPE – half the staff at one home – refused to have their fingerprints taken. The police angrily accused the council of hindering their hunt for the killer; the council strongly denied any obstruction. Murders or no, civil rights had to be protected.

The sixth victim had provided the police with very useful clues. Mr William Downes, seventy-four, a virtual recluse, was found on 9 July by his son at his bedsit in Stockwell. The son had arrived to prepare breakfast for his father. He found him dead, lying naked in bed with the sheets pulled up to his chin. He had facial injuries, and had been sexually assaulted. On the garden gate and a wall, police found impressions of a palm-print. They were getting close; they could sense it, as hunters do.

The seventh and final victim was disabled Mrs Florence Tisdall, eighty. She was found murdered at her home in Fulham on 23 July. She had spent the day watching the wedding of the Duke and Duchess of York on television before meeting her death at the hands of a sex-fiend. Mrs. Tisdall too had been sexually abused. Police also found valuable clues at this murder scene. Within three days of this killing police arrested the murderer.

They had known his identity before the last killing – they had matched those palm-prints. After two days of painstaking checks through more than four million records, police had come up with a name, and were confident they had made a major break-through. They spent all weekend combing his usual haunts for him, but he was not to be found. So police waited at his local DHSS office in Southwark for him to arrive on 28 July to sign for his dole money.

The short, thin figure of Kenneth Erskine duly arrived and police arrested him, driving him to Clapham police station. Erskine sat giggling in the back of the car. The evidence to connect him with all the killings consisted of a *pattern*, and those palm-prints at the homes of two of the victims. Mr Prentice subsequently picked out Erskine from an identity parade.

The police found it difficult, if not impossible, to question the killer about his bizarre sexual appetite. They had his record – pages of it – as an incompetent burglar who had served time for his offences. But they had no idea where he had been living for the past few months. And they found great difficulty in getting any answers to their questions. Erskine would grin and giggle when details of the murders were put to him, and he unnerved his questioners by engaging in continual masturbation during interviews. Detective Superintendent Bryan Jackson, who led the team of questioners, found his most experienced men baffled by their prisoner.

The police took the unusual decision to publish a photograph of Erskine in the national press before his trial, in the hope that it might bring forward witnesses who could fill in the missing pieces of the jigsaw. The photograph duly appeared in all the dailies on 12 August, with an appeal for anyone who knew the man in the picture to contact the police, who wanted to trace property stolen from the home of the victims, and to check Erskine's lodgings to check for possible forensic evidence. Police still did not know where Erskine had lived.

The appeal worked. A young businesswoman came forward who had come face to face with Erskine on Putney Bridge shortly after the murder of Mrs Tisdall. The woman was struck by his horrific grin, and had no trouble picking him out from an identity parade.

Erskine appeared at the magistrate's court in Battersea to be charged with the murders of Mrs Cockett and William Downes. He stood barefoot in the dock, grinning, and was formally remanded in custody. Police knew at this stage that he had killed seven people, but they suspected there might be many more, whose deaths had been attributed to natural causes. During his four-month killing spree there were at least four other cases of old people who died in similar circumstances to his victims. They included Wilfred Parkes, eighty-one, who died at his Stockwell council flat, and Trevor Thomas, seventy-five, found dead in the bath at his Clapham home.

The police were also delving into Erskine's past for clues. They discovered that while in gaol in 1982 for burglary he spent his time painting a gallery of old people lying in bed with gags stuffed in their mouths, knives sticking in them, or burned to death. Other drawings showed headless figures with blood spurting from their necks. He pinned these drawings up above his bed, and alarmed doctors at the prison pleaded with the authorities not to release him. But he had to be released once his sentence was completed. To be detained one day longer would have infringed his civil liberties. Fellow-prisoners were traced who spoke of Erskine boasting to them of killing old people. Yet he had been released upon society like a bomb waiting to explode.

From Erskine himself police could gather little. He was a giggling, deranged drifter who had a mental age of ten, who had moved around London from squat to squat, supplementing his dole money with the proceeds from burglaries. He may have been mentally retarded, but he had the cunning of a fox. He had two bank accounts into which he paid hundreds of pounds gained from crime.

Psychiatrists called in to examine him were as baffled as the police. Dr Gisli Gudjohnsson of London University said later, 'He was giggling, smiling and looking out of the window when serious matters were being discussed. He had serious difficulty distinguishing reality from fantasy.'

All that was known of Erskine's background was that as a child he had attended schools for maladjusted children in and around London, ever since his mother and his Antiguan father decided they did not want him living with them in their Shepherd's Bush home. When he was sixteen they had disowned him, and ever since the retarded and difficult youth had lived rough.

On 13 August Erskine was charged with an additional three murders and one attempted murder. Erskine always appeared in court without shoes – sometimes without socks – grinning in the dock as the charges were put.

The trial of Kenneth Erskine began at the Old Bailey on Tuesday, 12 January 1988. The thin, short figure of Erskine, wearing a blue denim jacket, stood grinning in the dock, unaware of his surroundings or of what was being said about him by prosecuting counsel. He pleaded not guilty to the seven counts of murder, speaking in a barely audible whisper.

Mr James Crespi QC, prosecuting, told the jury that the 'appallingly wanton' murders of seven pensioners in London between April and July 1986 were marked by such striking similarities that they could only have been the work of the same man. 'They were committed by a killer who likes killing, and that man was Kenneth Erskine,' Mr Crespi said. Telling of the deaths of the seven victims, Mr Crespi said that five of them had been sodomized immediately before or after their deaths. All died from manual strangulation. Mr Crespi said that after Erskine had murdered and finished 'playing with' his victims, he placed their naked bodies in their beds and tucked the sheets tidily up to their necks.

So peaceful and normal did the scene appear that in two of the cases it was not immediately recognized that the old people had died by violent means. In none of the cases was there any sign of forced entry to the premises.

Mr Crespi said the murder toll could have been eight had not the killer panicked and fled while attacking Mr Frederick Prentice. Mr Prentice was ambushed by an intruder in the early hours of 27 June. 'Mr Prentice told him to get out of the room and the man put his fingers to his lips as a gesture to be quiet. He then jumped on Mr Prentice, putting one knee on each of his hands to immobilize him, and his hands around his neck with his thumbs over his windpipe, pressing with a pumping action. He appeared to be playing with his victim and uttered only one word throughout: 'Kill'.

Mr Crespi told how Mr Prentice had picked Erskine out from an identity parade, and thumb and palm-prints found at the homes of Mrs Cockett and Mr Downes, and shoe-prints at the homes of Prentice, Gleim and Stabrawa, linked Erskine to the murders. Mr Crespi admitted that there was only indirect evidence linking Erskine to three of the murders and the attempted murder, but said a pattern was visible through all the counts. The common features were that all the victims were elderly people living alone; they were attacked by an intruder who left no signs of forced entry, and almost all late at night or in the early hours of the morning. In each case the intruder made his entry through a window. All the victims were killed by one-handed strangulation while the other hand was held over the mouth. All the victims were found in bed, and five of them had been sodomized.

Mr Crespi went on, 'In all these cases the killing was wanton. It was not done for the kind of reason which would encourage a burglar under normal circumstances to kill. In our submission, putting all these things together, there is not only a pattern but a striking pattern.'

On the second day of the trial, after forensic evidence, the only surviving victim of the Stockwell Strangler went into the witness box to relive the night of the murderous attack on him. Mr Prentice described to the jury how he had been woken by an intruder and looked up to see a pair of 'black glaring eyes' staring at him. 'I could only see his head and his glaring eyes, and he grinned. He had a terrible grin on his face.' By the electric light from the corridor outside, Mr Prentice could see something of his attacker. 'I saw the figure and I shouted at him to get out. . . he jumped on top of me . . . he had his legs on top of me. I couldn't move my hands and arms because they were pinned. I could feel him pinching my neck and I was screaming. I thought I was finished. I could feel his hands around my neck. He would stop for three or four seconds and then start again. It went on three times and the last time he chucked my head against the wall and ran off.'

Six weeks later Mr Prentice, a severely disabled man who can only walk with crutches, picked Erskine out from a police identity parade. 'I know the man I saw that morning', Mr Prentice said, 'and I never want to see him again. He ruined my life. I have still got pain.' Replying to Mr Roy Amlot, defending, Mr Prentice said the light from the corridor was sufficient for him to see his attacker. 'I'm sure it was the man,' he said. 'I recognized him by his hair, the top of his face and his glaring eyes.' He denied having seen any press pictures of Erskine before attending the identity parade.

Miss Denise Keena, twenty-five, the young business-woman who had seen Erskine leaning over the rail of Putney Bridge, apparently being sick, told the jury about the encounter. It came on the evening of 23 July, the day when Mrs Florence Tisdall was found murdered at her home in Ranelagh Gardens, Fulham, a short walk from Putney Bridge.

When she was about eight feet away from Erskine, Miss Keena said, he looked over his shoulder at her and she saw his expression. 'It was a sort of terrible grin,' she said. 'He looked almost as if he was out of control. It was a horrible, awful, disgusting expression. All the muscles in his face were taut and all the tendons strained across the bone structure. He had wide and staring eyes. His mouth was open.' Miss Keena told the jury that she had to look away, because Erskine's expression shocked and scared her. She said that when she looked back at him 'He was walking as if in a daze or a trance.' She later picked Erskine out of an identity parade.

The following day Detective Chief Superintendent Bryan Jackson went into the witness box to tell about the arrest, interrogation and background of Erskine. He described him as being a loner, without family or friends, who lived off the proceeds of burglary. He had no visitors during his eighteen months in custody, apart from legal representatives and doctors. Erskine had made no admissions to the offences, except to say, 'I don't remember killing anyone. I may have done it without knowing it.'

The trial lasted an astonishing fifteen days, and for that time Erskine repeatedly grinned in the dock. On Friday 29 January 1988, after the final speeches by defence and prosecution counsel and the judge's summing up the jury retired, returning with guilty verdicts on all the counts. Briefly, Erskine appeared to be tearful as the judge addressed him.

Mr Justice Rose told him, 'I doubt whether the time will ever come when you can be safely at large. I have no doubt that the horrific nature and number of your crimes requires that I should recommend, taking your age into account, a prison sentence of forty years.' It was the longest sentence ever passed in a British murder trial. Erskine was given seven life sentences.

Chapter Fifteen

DUFFY: THE RAILWAY MURDERER

For the general public the case began with the disappearance of 'Television Bride' Anne Lock, twenty-nine, a secretary at London Weekend Television who vanished on Sunday 18 May 1986 after leaving the TV studios on the South Bank to catch a train home. She had been married for only four weeks, and had just returned from a honeymoon in the Seychelles.

She lived with her husband Laurence, twenty-six, a wealthy wholesale butcher, in a £160,000 home in Brookmans Park, a picturesque Hertfordshire village, and when she vanished the gutter-press descended on the husband like a flock of vultures, camping outside his home, and by thinly veiled insinuation and innuendo giving the impression that he was somehow involved in his wife's disappearance.

They made much of the fact that Laurence Lock was only too willing to talk to them. He dressed smartly, changing his suits often. He even wore after-shave: hardly the behaviour of an anxious husband, was the implied suggestion. In fact, Laurence Lock became the victim of ugly rumour.

His wife's bicycle was found at the railway station where she parked it – she would normally have cycled home. Large numbers of police searched the surrounding area, and found her diary and address book half a mile apart, both shredded. Police frogmen searched local lakes. Detectives questioned Laurence Lock. If he was initially a prime suspect, it was simply because police know that over 75 per cent of all murders are 'domestic', with the victim being related to the killer.

The husband's disjointed remarks to reporters, taken out of context, were made to sound sinister, even though his words were the result of heartache, misery and feelings of persecution.

The body of Anne Lock was found on 21 July 1986, lying in thick undergrowth at the side of a railway embankment by two railway workers who literally stumbled over the body. Forensic examination revealed that the body had been lying there for about ten weeks, a police spokesman saying, 'The body was very carefully hidden. It's clear that somebody put it in there and packaged it in the weeds and shrubbery.' Police stated that Anne Lock had been gagged, with her hands tied behind her back. Cause of death was suffocation. An attempt had been made to set fire to the body, and the badly decomposed remains could only be identified from dental records.

Detective Chief Superintendent Vincent McFadden, now in charge of the case, answered criticism that the body should have been found sooner. He said, 'Officers made a tremendous effort to find her body and searched over an enormous area, but the resources were limited. It is an exaggeration to say that the body was found only a "few yards" outside the search area. It was some considerable distance away.' He said that police thinking now was that Mrs Lock had been followed from Brookmans Park station and then waylaid by a man who probably forced her down a path for half a mile, and murdered her at a spot opposite Potter's Bar golf-course.

He then revealed that Anne Lock's murder was not the beginning of the case, but another in a series of rapes and murders by that most dangerous of criminals, the sexual serial murderer. Definite links had been established between the murder of Anne Lock and the murder of two girls in Surrey and East London in the previous eleven months. That feature – not revealed at the time – was a distinctive ligature used by the killer to throttle his victims. It was the killer's trademark – that and the fact that he always killed near railway lines. It was known that the killer of schoolgirl Maartje Tamboezer, found murdered in West Horsley, Surrey, in April 1986, had a minority blood group, established from his semen. All known sex-offenders who shared that blood group were being interviewed. Detectives were also checking fingerprints, and had already examined more than 90,000 on file.

Detective Chief Superintendent McFadden said, 'We are dealing with a very dangerous man who obviously has no compunction about killing.' Saying that the three killings might also be linked with rapes in the London area, McFadden went on, 'Although we are keeping an open mind on the type of man responsible, there is a distinct possibility that the killer could be someone with a knowledge of the railways – possibly a British Rail worker, or an ex-employee.' It was a remarkably prophetic profile of the killer.

At a press conference two days later at a special Incident Room at Hendon Police Cadet College in North London (where over 100 detectives spearheaded the hunt for the maniac killer) the last savage moments of Anne Lock were revealed. She had been threatened with a Stanley knife as she stepped off the train at Brookmans Park station, and dragged half a mile along a remote path by a man dubbed the Railway Killer. She was then tied up and gagged before the brutal attacker – who had already killed twice before – raped her and then left her to die of suffocation, the gag still in her mouth, the Stanley knife lying nearby.

The man detectives were hunting was, they believed, responsible for a series of rapes and killings dating back to

1984. The unknown killer had begun as a rapist, with his first solo attack taking place in November 1984 near Barnes Common in south west London. The next was in February 1985 at Hadley Wood station, two stops away from where Anne Lock met her killer. The last was in August 1985 next to the line at West Hampstead station, North London. Then the rapist turned to murder.

Alison Day, nineteen, was murdered in December 1985 after getting off a train at Hackney Wick station, East London. She was seized from behind and forced to walk into a rat-infested garage complex by the river Lea. After she was raped her body was dumped into the river.

His second victim, Maartje Tamboezer, fifteen, the pretty blonde daughter of a Dutch oil executive living in Britain, was raped and battered to death in woods near the railway line at Horsley in April 1986. She was forced to dismount from her bicycle by a length of cord strung across the path, and made to push her bike 150 yards across a field to the woods where she was ambushed. She too had been bound and gagged, and a crude attempt had been made to burn her body.

All the rapes followed similar patterns, and all the rapes and murders had been linked by forensic evidence and the unique method used to kill the victim. All details of sex attacks throughout the Home Counties were being fed into the National Crime Computer. The links between the crimes were emphasized by Detective Chief Inspector McFadden. He said, 'In all three killings there has been a tying of the hands and the use of a knife and all took place on a footpath near a railway line.'

One lucky girl had a narrow escape from the killer. She was ambushed at knife-point and sexually assaulted, but was saved by her mother, who called her name loudly. The attacker panicked and fled. From this encounter police were able to establish a description of the wanted man. Detectives said he was white, in his mid-twenties, with fair hair and an athletic build.

Four police forces were now engaged in the biggest

police operation in Britain since the hunt for the Yorkshire Ripper. The Metropolitan, Surrey, Hertfordshire and British Transport Police were involved in an operation code-named Operation Hart, which was to last many months, and was to cost over £3 million. The Home Office appointed Detective Chief Superintendent McFadden, head of Surrey CID, to liaise between the Forces and so avoid a repetition of the mistakes made in the Ripper inquiry. Operation Hart was set up by Scotland Yard in July 1985, primarily to investigate twenty-seven rapes which had taken place in the Metropolitan area. On 29 December 1985, with the murder of Alison Day, it had become a murder hunt.

One baffling feature which was to hamper the inquiry was the fact that in some of the rapes under investigation two men had taken part, in others just one. Yet all the rapes were linked forensically by that rare blood group. In other words, the man the police wanted sometimes raped alone, and sometimes with a companion. But when he turned to murder police knew that their quarry had stepped over a critical boundary. He had tasted blood, and would not stop killing until he was caught. Yet amazingly, the police had had the killer under lock and key at one stage. . . .

On 19 June 1985 Margaret Duffy left her husband because of his increasingly violent behaviour, walking out of the flat they had shared in Barlow Road, Kilburn, North London. On 28 August 1985 the husband attacked Mrs Duffy and her Hungarian-born boy-friend with a knife, wounding them. The following day John Francis Duffy appeared before West Hendon magistrates and was remanded in custody awaiting trial on charges of causing grievous bodily harm. There was also the possibility of rape charges by his estranged wife. He routinely appeared before the magistrates every couple of weeks or so to be further remanded in custody, but on 19 September he applied for bail to a judge in chambers. At Acton Crown Court, Recorder Peter Archer QC listened to the application, and despite strong police opposition and a suggestion that a rape charge was being considered, he granted bail. The result of that decision was to be horrendous.

While out on bail Duffy was to commit three murders and two rapes. Fourteen weeks after being granted bail, Duffy raped and garotted Alison Day. Three months later he murdered Maartje Tamboezer, and a month after that Anne Lock. His final rape victim was to be a fourteen-year-old Watford schoolgirl he attacked on 21 October 1987.

Yet Operation Hart had begun running in July 1985, and had police been able to take a closer look at John Duffy in the August following that knife attack they would instantly have recognized certain sinister patterns. John Duffy had been a British Rail carpenter, and after losing his job in 1982 he used his rail pass and his extensive knowledge of the railway network in the South-East to prey on women, beginning his 28-month reign of terror. In 1982 five women were raped in attacks by two men wearing balaclavas. The attacks were carried out at first by two men, and from 1984 on by just one. Between 1982 and October 1985 police connected 27 rapes, all close to railway lines in North London. It was when they made this link that Operation Hart was set up. Three years later these rapes were linked forensically to Duffy.

No rapes took place during 1983. That year John and Margaret Duffy were trying hard to have a child. But after tests a consultant told Duffy that his sperm-count was too low to enable him to father children. That knowledge seemed to drive Duffy berserk. Fuelled by feelings of sexual inadequacy, and fired by the pornographic videos and magazines to which he was addicted, he began raping again, and this time his wife was one of his victims. She began to complain about his behaviour towards her. He would tie her up against her will, and could only become sexually excited if she struggled and protested. And he once told her, 'I've just raped a girl because of you. It's all your fault.'

The small – 5ft 4in tall – pockmarked man began his career as a solo rapist. His earlier accomplice has never been traced, although police have strong suspicions as to his identity. Duffy's first solo rape was that of a 22-year-old from Manchester in June 1984 as she waited alone at West Hampstead station. Over the next 28 months his prey tended to be younger – a fourteen-year-old, a nurse of seventeen, an eighteen-year-old – before he turned to murder.

What drove Irish-born Duffy to kill? By a grim irony, it may have been police activity. In the wake of the case police have been accused of 'blunders', yet when on 2 December 1985 Duffy appeared at Hendon magistrate's court on the assault charge brought by his wife a detective-inspector investigating the latest rape in the series took Duffy's fifth rape victim to the court in the hope that she might recognize him as her attacker. The detective thought Duffy fitted the description given by the victim. Unfortunately, she failed to recognize him – but Duffy recognized her. His strong instinct for self-preservation sealed the fates of future victims. Realizing that the police were getting close to him, he resolved that any women he raped in the future would have to be killed. He could not risk leaving them alive to tell the tale. Just three weeks after that court-room confrontation, on 29 December, Duffy killed Alison Day.

Duffy's trademark in murder – apart from always choosing his victims close to railway lines or station – was his method of garotting his victims, using an item of the victim's clothing to make a noose around the neck, and then inserting a piece of wood to twist it tightly like a tourniquet. Alison Day and Maartje Tamboezer had been tied with their hands behind their backs, and after being raped had been strangled with the tourniquet method, using scarves or tights. In the case of Anne Lock her hands too had been tied behind her back, and one of her long socks had been pulled off and tied around her face. At attempt had been made to apply a tourniquet with the other sock, and as in the case of the Dutch schoolgirl, her body had been set alight. In the rape case Duffy had shown that he enjoyed torturing and humiliating his victims. There was a *pattern* linking the rapes and murders, and the detection of crimes relies heavily on finding patterns.

Operation Hart built up an empire of files and dossiers from the flood of information which poured in. By 18 May 1986, when Anne Lock was murdered, the best part of a year had gone by. On 17 May, the day before Anne Lock vanished, Duffy was arrested 'on suspicion' by a police constable. He was loitering near a railway station, and was found to be in possession of a wicked-looking knife. He explained that as a student of Zen Budo, a rare form of Japanese martial arts which combined ju-jitsu and weapons training, he needed the knife for practice. All this was perfectly true. Duffy was a student at a Kilburn martial arts centre, and over a period of eighteen months had been taught nerve-pinches and strangleholds, as well as weapons training with sticks, knives and swords. He was allowed to walk free. . . .

However, Duffy's name was now on the 'suspect' list, which contained the names of some two thousand sex-offenders who shared the same minority blood group. He was a 'fourth division' suspect, number 1,594 on that list. That list, incidentally, had begun life with 4,900 names, but detectives had honed it down to 1,999.

On 17 July 1986 Detective Constables Andrew Kelly and Peter Code of the Metropolitan Police interviewed Duffy in the presence of his solicitor. It was a routine interview. Duffy was on the suspect list because of the attack on his wife and her lover, but both detectives instantly recognized his likeness to the official identity picture of the killer, and were not satisfied with his evasive answers. Four hours after that interview Duffy got a friend who was also a martial arts student to beat him up and slash his chest with a razor. He then had himself admitted to the Friern Barnet Hospital suffering from alleged 'hysterical amnesia', claiming to have lost his memory.

The following day, detectives Kelly and Code reported to Superintendent Ken Worker, their boss and the officer in charge of the Met inquiry, telling him that they thought Duffy was dangerous.

On 6 August Superintendent Worker tried to interview Duffy, but hospital doctors refused to allow him to question their patient, saying that it might jeopardize his recovery. (Duffy was watching a cricket match in the hospital grounds at this time.) The Metropolitan officially lost interest in Duffy at that point, although they did become aware of his release from hospital in mid-August. A brief attempt was made to trace him, but he had vanished from his usual haunts and could not be located. He was still regarded as being very much a 'fourth division' suspect, and for four months he roamed about London undetected, raping a schoolgirl on 21 October. During those four months, for six weekends in August and September, police watched every British Rail station in the Home Counties, without success.

It was at this point in the huge inquiry that a real-life 'Sherlock Holmes' made his important contribution to the investigation. In July 1986 Scotland Yard called in a Surrey University professor to help detectives by producing a 'profile' of the killer-rapist. Professor David Canter was a leading psychologist, and he sat quietly in an office going over witnesses' statements and seemingly banal and unimportant details to produce his profile. When the profile was matched on the computer with the 1,999 suspects on file, the computer threw up just one name: John Francis Duffy. The profile subsequently proved to be accurate on thirteen out of seventeen points, with the professor even predicting the district in which the killer lived. Now his revolutionary technique will be used in detective training colleges.

Surrey police agreed to target Duffy for surveillance, but it was well into October before they began making fresh inquiries into his background and life-style. By 8 November Duffy was officially under surveillance, but he proved to be a difficult man to follow. He was adept at spotting tails and shaking them off. The break-through came when Detective Superintendent John Hurst, head of Guildford CID, detailed a small team of detectives to focus on just one of the twenty-seven rapes under investigation. The work of that team also threw up just one name: John Francis Duffy.

On 23 November 1986 Surrey CID arrested Duffy, and his trail of terror had come to an end. A search of his Kilburn home produced overwhelming evidence of his guilt. Officers found martial arts equipment, pornographic and violent videos and magazines, and a 'rape kit' which included a bunch of more than thirty keys. Duffy claimed he could not remember what the keys were for, but the police were convinced that many of the keys had belonged to his victims, women too frightened to report that they had been raped, and that Duffy kept the keys as 'trophies'. Police also found a copy of the *Anarchist's Cookbook* in his flat, which lists ways to incapacitate, silence, and if necessary kill. The book emphasized the vital need to have escape routes, and Duffy's railway knowledge provided just that.

Duffy was the most intractable prisoner detectives had ever had to interview. He fixed his questioners with a 'laser-beam stare' and was never intimidated, and never spoke. He was to plead not guilty to all the murder and rape charges, simply because he would gain additional pleasure from watching his victims suffer as they testified in the witness box. They would be raped all over again, in open court.

The trial of John Francis Duffy, thirty, began at the Old Bailey on Monday 11 January 1988 before Mr Justice Farquharson, the judge allowing Duffy to be named 'in the public interest' even though rape was involved in the trial.

In fact, Duffy was tried for three murders and seven rapes, all of which took place near railway lines between June 1982 and October 1986. Mr Anthony Hooper QC, prosecuting, told the jury of six men and six women that Duffy 'drills his eyes into you like two laser beams. He is someone who looks at you very hard and directly. . . He is a shrewd and calculating man who knows exactly what he is doing.' The diminutive bearded man in the dock spoke only two words during the entire trial. They were 'Not Guilty' to all the charges.

The prosecution outlined Duffy's background, emphasizing the fact that an American book, *The Anarchist's Cookbook*, had been found in his possession. Mr Hooper read passages from this book, which he described as a guide to killing and subversive activity. The passages stressed the importance of finding an escape route because things could go wrong. 'Duffy is a man who knew how to escape through woods and fields,' Mr Hooper said. A martial arts video had also been found in Duffy's home. It was called *The Jaws of Danger*. Mr Hooper said, 'Duffy liked horror videos and Bruce Lee, but this was a very violent video with a number of deaths by strangulation. . . And it made it clear he had an interest in killing and weapons.'

After his arrest, the court was told, Duffy claimed to have lost his memory. 'The amnesia started on the very day he had been interviewed by police in connection with the inquiries,' Mr Hooper said. 'That amnesia is a total sham. It is totally false, and if you accept that it is a total sham, you may think that provides deadly evidence against him.'

Mr Hooper said that although Duffy was only 5ft 4in tall, some people involved in the trial would say they thought he was taller, because of his abundant curly reddish hair. Mr Hooper said that in two of the three early rapes two men were involved. Duffy was one, the other remained unknown. The first victim, aged twenty-three, was raped in June 1984 after visiting an ex-boyfriend in

West Hampstead. She was at West Hampstead station when two men approached her on the deserted platform. One grabbed her round the neck. The other produced a knife and both forced her underneath a bridge where she was raped. The third victim was attacked by two men, one of them Duffy, after leaving a dance in North London on Live Aid Day. Two knives were held to her throat and she was raped.

Mr Hooper told the jury that the deliberate destruction of forensic evidence featured in the murders and the rapes. Rape victims were wiped with tissues, which were then burned. And attempts had been made to destroy the murder victims by fire. Mr Hooper warned the judge that they would have to look at some 'absolutely horrible' photographs which were "shocking in the extreme".

Turning to the three murders, Mr Hooper detailed them one by one. Alison Day, nineteen, was murdered while she was on her way to visit her boy-friend in Hackney Wick. Duffy attacked her at Hackney Wick station, strangled her and probably raped her before dumping her naked body in the river Lea. She was not found until nearly two weeks later, her sheepskin jacket being weighted down with granite blocks. She had been knocked about by her killer. Her wrists had been tied with a strip torn from her skirt, and she had been strangled with another piece of the skirt, 'and yet another piece was stuffed in her mouth'. A tourniquet around her neck had been applied with tremendous pressure. Her watch had stopped at 8.10 p.m..

The Dutch schoolgirl Maartje Tamboezer, fifteen, whose father was working in England at the time, was the second victim. She was at school in Surrey, and had gone for a cycle ride on 17 April 1986 along a path beside the railway line between Effingham and East Horsley. It was daylight, and the girl was forced to stop and dismount when she saw a nylon line had been strung across her path. She was forced to detour across fields and into a wood where Duffy was waiting. He raped her and knocked her unconscious. Her hands were tied in an unusual way, being placed together in a prayer position behind her back, and then nine feet of string was wound around her wrists and over her thumbs, making escape impossible. Duffy first tried to murder her by the tourniquet methods but the girl's leather belt he used broke as he twisted it tight with a piece of wood. 'So he tried again. This time he used a scarf. Again it was tightened with a piece of wood.' Duffy then set about destroying the evidence. He set fire to the body, specially burning the area around the crotch to destroy evidence of rape. He was well aware that blood types could be matched from sperm samples. Although the girl's bicycle was found leaning against a fence, her burned body was not found until the following morning by two men out hunting. Her watch had stopped at 5.35 p.m. After killing the girl, Duffy escaped on a train. A number of people saw him get on, said Mr Hooper.

The third murder was that of Anne Lock, thirty, who had been married on 18 April and returned from honeymoon on 8 May. It was a Sunday, 18 May 1986, when she left the television centre where she worked to return home, arriving at Brookmans Park station at about 10 p.m. She went to get her bicycle from the station cycle-shed, but found her way blocked by a bench which had been moved by Duffy. He made her park her still padlocked cycle against a fence, and forced her to walk in the opposite direction for about half a mile. Her hands were tied in the unusual 'prayer position', and one of her socks was stuffed into her mouth. The tourniquet method was not used to kill her because she died before that was necessary. Her body was set alight and she was left beside the railway track. She had probably been raped, but advanced decomposition left forensic scientists with no clues to work on. The attempted destruction of forensic evidence was a feature which linked all the cases on the charge sheet. The similarities in the rapes and killings amazed forensic scientists, Mr Hooper told the jury. One expert said that in sixteen years experience he had never come across such a case. The similarities included: the gagging of the murder victims by using pieces of their own clothing. They were tied up in an identical fashion. Attempts had been made to destroy evidence by burning the bodies or placing them in water. Traps had been used to force the victims to walk into ambushes. And petty thefts from all the victims was another linking feature.

The estranged wife of John Duffy went into the witness-box on the second day of the trial to tell about her husband's strange behaviour. Speaking in a low voice, barely glancing at her husband in the dock, she spoke about his strange moods, saying he could be a 'raving madman' at times. She told how he had once revealed that he had raped a girl. He said he had taken a personal stereo from her and gave it to me, saying, 'Where do you think I got that from?' ' Speaking about the breakdown of her marriage, she said, 'Things went from bad to worse and by April 1985 I could not stand him touching me. We were always arguing and fighting.' Asked about the sexual side of the marriage, Mrs Duffy replied, 'The marriage was just fighting all the time. He wanted sex almost every night and used to force himself on me. It started with verbal threats and then he used to hit me to make me have sex with him. He was too strong for me. . . I used to try and stop him but in the end I just gave in. He would come up and be really nice to me. He would sit beside me and then he would pull my hands back and tie me up by the wrists so that I could not move.' After demonstrating to the jury how she had been tied with a dressing-gown cord, Mrs Duffy added, 'I was frightened at first, but it used to calm him down, and I thought if I responded he would let me go . . . Once he stuffed a handkerchief down my throat after tricking me by saying I was to close my eyes and open my mouth as if I was going to get a piece of cake. Then he put the handkerchief in. I couldn't bear to look at him or touch him. He used to lie on top of me so I couldn't move. He would tie my hands . . . the more I protested the more he got aroused. . . On one occasion he was talking quite calmly for a change, and he told me he had raped a girl and that she had enjoyed it and asked him to come back for more. He said it was all my fault. He said that he took a personal stereo from her and then he gave it to me as a present.' Mrs Duffy said that in June 1985 she had left her husband. But when she returned to the house to collect mail her ordeal continued. 'He used to force me again to have intercourse. . . I thought he was going to kill me.' She told of how he had attacked her and her new boy-friend, punching them and battering them with a Kung Fu weapon.

Cross-examined by Mr David Farrington, defending, Mrs Duffy said her husband had attempted suicide during the first two years of their marriage, and had talked about suicide again in 1985, especially after he had been told that because of his low sperm-count he only had one chance in a hundred of ever fathering a child. She denied making love to him willingly four or five times after she had walked out on him. During heated exchanges with Mr Farrington she denied making up 'juicy stories' for the Press. She said her husband had raped her after she left him, adding that he had 'scary eyes. You could not stare at him. You had to look away.' As his wife testified, Duffy scribbled notes which he passed to his solicitor.

The new boy-friend of Mrs Duffy told of how Duffy had attacked him with a knife and a cosh. 'Duffy behaved like a madman. He hit me on the head. I had to have eight stitches. . .' A young girl who had travelled on a train on the same day that Maartje Tamboezer was murdered told of seeing a man with a 'weird, penetrating stare' boarding the train.

One of Duffy's few friends, a fellow martial arts student, told the jury of how he had been persuaded to slash Duffy across the chest and punch him in the face. He explained, 'He said the reason was that the police were fitting him up on a rape charge. He said he had to fake a loss of memory or he was in trouble. Although I was extremely frightened Duffy gave me a cut-throat razor and told me to slash him across the chest. I punched him once, but he told me to hit him again because it wasn't hard enough.' He went on, 'It was difficult to come to terms with what John was accused of. Because of my great friendship and feelings for him, I tried to protect him at first.'

He denied a defence suggestion that he had made up the story about the attack on Duffy to get the police off his own back, saying, "I reject that completely. I am on oath in this court and what I say is true." He said he regarded Duffy as an older brother. 'I would like to say I have never met a nicer man, and would do anything for him, more or less.'

Martial arts instructor David Archer told the jury that after Duffy suffered the razor attack he could still remember complicated moves he had been taught before the alleged attack.

The second of Duffy's rape victims, now nineteen, told the court of how Duffy had abducted her at knife-point from a deserted railway station. She said Duffy made her put her arm around him to make them look like a courting couple, but he was holding a knife to her throat. 'He said if I struggled or screamed he would slash my throat.' The girl, who had been aged seventeen at the time, said that after Duffy had dragged her into woods near Hadley Wood station, he cut off her underclothing with a knife before raping her. Then he made her hand over her purse. When the girl complained that she had no money for her fare home Duffy gave her back £1.

Another rape victim told of being seized at knife-point and dragged into a wood near a North London swimming pool. The rapist had his mongrel dog with him throughout the attack. 'I heard him call it Bruce,' she said.

Evidence was heard about the murders. Detective Sergeant Garry Fyffe said that Alison Day probably spent her last moments in a dank, rat-infested garage block. He said, 'It was a very unpleasant place – very dark and dank

– with ample evidence of rodents. Rubbish had been strewn about, and there was a smell of decomposing matter. It was partly flooded, with pools of stagnant water.' The granite blocks found in the victim's coat had come from that garage, he added.

Duffy's final rape victim testified – the fourteen-year-old schoolgirl who was raped while on her way home from school near Watford on 21 October 1986. Duffy forced her at knifepoint into nearby woods, cut her tights to tie her hands, and gagged and blindfolded her before raping her against a tree. She broke down in tears as she told of her horrifying ordeal, describing how Duffy had told her he had a knife as he put a hand over her mouth. The judge praised her courage in giving evidence.

On 25 February 1988 the jury found Duffy guilty of two rapes, those of the fourteen- and sixteen-year-olds. The older girl, now nineteen, was in court to see him convicted. Duffy stared blankly ahead as the verdict was announced, then he walked down to the cells with his hands in his pockets. The jury then retired again to consider the additional rape and murder charges. Earlier the judge had instructed the jury to find Duffy not guilty of the murder of Anne Lock. There was a complete lack of forensic evidence to link him to the crime.

Duffy was finally sentenced on 26 February 1988 by Mr Justice Farquharson, receiving seven life sentences for two murders and five rapes. The thirty-year-old killer stood impassive in the dock as the judge told him, 'The murders of Alison Day and Maartje Tamboezer are as appalling as anything I have come across. The wickedness and beastliness of the murders committed on those two very young girls hardly bears description. Quite apart from cutting short those two young lives, you have blighted the lives of all the families of these girls. You are obviously little more than a predatory animal.' Sentencing Duffy, the judge recommended that he should serve at least thirty years, but added, 'The horrific nature of your crimes means that thirty years is not necessarily the total you will serve. It may well be more. Take him down.' His Irish-born mother collapsed and sobbed in the public gallery, comforted by her husband and daughter.

The jury had returned unanimous verdicts on the two murders and five rapes. The judge, whose sixtieth birthday it was that day, discharged the jury from giving verdicts on five outstanding charges against Duffy, two of rape in July and August 1985, two of assault against his wife in August 1985 and one of wounding his wife's new boy-friend.

Duffy had looked almost harmless in the dock, wearing a brown sports jacket, jeans and a shirt and tie. He displayed no emotion – certainly no remorse – throughout the six-week trial, not even when the women he had raped recounted their ordeals, at times in tears. But Duffy was not harmless: he was a monster whose mind had been perverted by porn videos and horror movies – another graphic example of the link between pornography and sex crimes. Yet he had shown extreme cunning and intelligence, using his detailed knowledge of railway timetables in the South-East to stalk his victims, prowling deserted railway stations and preying on lone young women. At first he subjected them to degrading practices, but by the end of his 28-month reign of terror the martial arts expert had turned into a cold and calculating killer.

Detective Superintendent John Hurst, deputy head of Surrey CID, who interviewed Duffy after his arrest, said, 'In my twenty-two years experience with crime, I have never found a man so calculating and cunning. He is a cold-blooded calculating killer with a razor-sharp mind. He is very intelligent and alert. He gave me the impression of being able to react to any type of situation in which he found himself.' The head of Surrey CID, Detective Chief Superintendent Vincent McFadden, said after the trial that he was satisfied that everything was done as quickly as possible to bring Duffy to justice. This was after Press accusations that the police had 'blundered' in the investigation, with one newspaper listing 'Five Blunders' which had allowed Duffy to reign for so long.

Theodore Robert Bundy. Undoubtedly one of the most fiendish killers in American history

BURN, BUNDY, BURN!

Crowds cheer outside jail as mass killer dies in electric chair

Americans celebrate as mass sex killer goes to electric chair

Ted Bundy in court

Margaret Bowman and Lisa Levy (below) were two of Bundy's Florida victims

Mass murderer Denis Nilsen in Army uniform

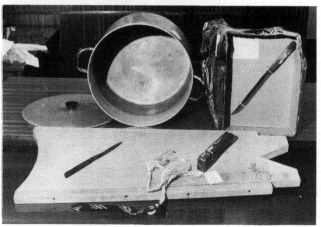

Nilsen's tools of murder

Police
digging for
body parts
in Nilsen's
garden

. Although the Anne Lock case was officially unsolved, Detective Chief Superintendent John Hurst said, "Duffy did kill Anne Lock. We are certain he killed her. He knows it and we know it. We couldn't provide the forensic evidence to convict, but the similarities between this murder and the other two are just so startling. We decided to charge him with only the cases where the evidence was strongest, although we are sure he carried out many other attacks. He got his bizarre kicks from the struggles and protests of his victims. We know he pleaded not guilty just so that some of them would have to suffer in the witness-box. His final victim, the fourteen-year-old schoolgirl, told me that he locked his eyes on her as she was giving evidence. The stare broke her up and she couldn't bear to go on. Every time he looked at her she broke out in a cold sweat. She was incredibly brave to carry on.' Mr Hurst added, 'I spent many hours with Duffy. His laser-beam stare frightened me, and I dread to think what it did to those poor women. Not once did he confess to the rapes or killings, but he told me how he would be quite happy to spend thirty years in jail.'

Alison Day's father, Kenneth, said bitterly, 'He should hang.' A leading martial arts instructor, Mr Frederick Adams, a prison officer, was scathing that a man like Duffy should have been taught deadly skills. He said, 'I am annoyed and concerned about private teachers because they are doing it for money. For £10 an hour they will teach almost anything, including garotting.' Anne Lock's husband said, 'I know people will still point a finger at me. . . '

It is difficult to build up a picture of Duffy as a human being. He refused to see a psychiatrist and never spoke during his trial.

Detective Chief Superintendent McFadden described Duffy as being one of the worst villains he had ever encountered, which speaks for itself. Defending the police against Press criticism of the handling of the inquiry, he said, 'What is important is that the police set the parameters and Duffy was in those parameters.' The sex killer is notoriously difficult to hunt down, and even at a cost of £3 million, the police are to be commended for putting this dangerous animal behind bars.

There can be no excuses for Duffy. Unlike say the Stockwell Strangler, who was driven by urges he could not control, the Railway Murderer, John Francis Duffy, was a cunning and intelligent killer who knew full well the consequences of his acts, and destroyed forensic evidence where he could to ensure his continued freedom.

Chapter Sixteen

PETER SUTCLIFFE:
THE YORKSHIRE RIPPER

5 July 1975. First attack: Keighley.

15 August 1975. Second victim survives attack: Halifax.

30 October 1975. Wilma McCann murdered: Leeds.

20 January 1976. Emily Jackson murdered: Leeds.

9 May 1976. Prostitute survives attack: Leeds.

6 February 1977. Irene Richardson murdered: Leeds.

23 April 1977. Patricia Atkinson murdered: Bradford – only victim killed indoors.

26 June 1977 Jayne MacDonald murdered: Leeds. George Oldfield, Assistant Chief Constable of West Yorkshire Police, takes over in charge of the Ripper investigation.

10 July 1977. Woman attacked in Bradford.

1 October 1977. Jean Jordan murdered: Manchester. Sutcliffe returns to body a week after murder in search of incriminating £5 note. Attempts to decapitate the corpse.

2 November 1977. Peter Sutcliffe interviewed by police for first time since 1969. This time about the £5 note.

8 November 1977. Peter Sutcliffe interviewed by police for second time – again about £5 note.

14 December 1977. Woman survives attack: Leeds.

21 January 1978. Yvonne Pearson murdered: Bradford.

31 January 1978. Helen Rytka murdered: Huddersfield.

8 March 1978. First Ripper letter sent to George Oldfield.

13 March 1978. Second Ripper letter sent to *Daily Mirror* in Manchester. Letter contains warning that Ripper will strike again in Manchester or Liverpool.

16 May 1978. Vera Millward murdered: Manchester.

13 August 1978. Peter Sutcliffe interviewed by police for third time in present investigation because his car has been seen so many times in Bradford and Leeds red-light districts.

23 November 1978. Peter Sutcliffe was interviewed again and the tyres of his car examined by police to see whether tracks match those found at the scene of Irene Richardson's murder. Sutcliffe had replaced the tyres and was therefore released.

8 March 1979. Third Ripper letter sent.

4 April 1979. Josephine Whitaker murdered: Halifax.

18 June 1979. The hoax tape is received by police.

26 June 1979. Police play Ripper tape to Press.

29 July 1979. Sutcliffe interviewed by police for fifth time.

2 September 1979. Barbara Leach murdered: Bradford.

23 October 1979. Sutcliffe again questioned about being seen in red-light districts.

January 1980. George Oldfield taken off Ripper investigation.

13 January 1980. Sutcliffe interviewed again by police about £5 note found on Jean Jordan's body.

30 January 1980. Sutcliffe questioned again about £5 note.

18 August 1980. Marguerite Walls murdered: Farsley, between Leeds and Bradford.

24 September 1980. Female doctor survives attack: Leeds.

5 November 1980. Woman survives attack: Huddersfield.

17 November 1980. Jacqueline Hill murdered: Leeds.

28 November 1980. Trevor Birdsall, friend of Peter Sutcliffe, sends anonymous letter to West Yorkshire police naming Sutcliffe as the Ripper.

29 November 1980. Birdsall goes to Bradford Police Station and names Sutcliffe as the Yorkshire Ripper.

2 January 1981. Sutcliffe arrested in Sheffield.

5 January 1981. Sutcliffe appears at Dewsbury Magistrate's Court.

22 May 1981. Sutcliffe sentenced at the Old Bailey to life with a recommendation that he serve at least 30 years. Sutcliffe was incarcerated in the top security wing at Parkhurst Prison. During his stay he was attacked by another prisoner who slashed his face with a broken jar. Three years later, in March, 1984, he was transferred to Broadmoor.

It is over ten years since Peter Sutcliffe, the man who terrorized Yorkshire for more than five years as the 'Yorkshire Ripper', was arrested in the company of a prostitute in Sheffield by Vice Squad officers. (Sutcliffe later admitted that he had intended to kill her.)

On 5 January 1981, Sutcliffe appeared at Dewsbury Magistrate's Court to be formally charged. A mob outside the building held up mock nooses and bayed for his blood. Your author was in that crowd, and the bloodthirsty unity of everyone around me was truly frightening. Had they managed to get their hands on Sutcliffe, they would have torn him to pieces.

On 22 May 1981, Sutcliffe was sentenced at the Old Bailey to life imprisonment for 13 murders and at least seven brutal attacks on women. The judge recommended that he should serve a minimum of 30 years.

The jury convicted him of murder rather than manslaughter, yet today Sutcliffe occupies a comfortably furnished room in Broadmoor, the secure hospital for the criminally insane, to which he was transferred in 1984.

But let us go back more than two decades to when a young bachelor named Peter Sutcliffe was involved in a 'rehearsal' for murder that would culminate in the horrendous reign of terror six years later.

If Jack the Ripper was operating today, given the advances in forensic science – fingerprinting, blood-grouping, the genetic 'fingerprinting' and modern police methods of communication, including the use of computers – would he have been caught? In the light of the Yorkshire Ripper case the answer must be no. For Peter Sutcliffe carried out a far worse reign of terror over a period of five and a half years – during which time he murdered 13 women and attempted to murder seven others. He was eventually caught by pure accident, one might say, despite the police.

Born in Bingley, Yorkshire, on 2 June 1946, Peter William Sutcliffe was a disappointing son for his father, John. John Sutcliffe was a dominating man. His wife, Kathleen, was a pretty woman and a staunch Catholic. Into such surroundings Peter made his appearance, the first of five children.

Peter was weak and sickly as a child. He was bullied at school, and because of that became secretive and solitary, often playing truant, hiding for hours in the loft.

Leaving school at fifteen, Peter became an apprentice fitter and at eighteen began body-building in an attempt to fit in with the Yorkshire macho image.

In 1964 he got a labouring job at Bingley Cemetery, and there he began to display his macabre sense of humour. He desecrated corpses, played practical jokes with skulls, and stole rings from the fingers of the dead, even to the extent of snipping off the fingers if the rings proved hard to remove.

In 1967, aged twenty-one, Sutcliffe was sacked from his grave-digging job for bad time-keeping. He met and began courting Sonia Szurma, a Czech girl who came from a rather better background. She had realistic expectations of qualifying as a schoolteacher. The courtship was to last seven stormy years.

Sonia must have been a little doubtful about Peter as a

suitable husband because she went out with somebody else. When Sutcliffe found out he was furious. He went with a prostitute in the area of Bradford to 'settle the score', as he put it later. But the prostitute cheated him out of £5, and when he tackled her in a pub about it, days later, she just laughed at him. He felt acutely humiliated, and later claimed that this incident gave rise to his hatred of whores.

In 1969 Sutcliffe carried out his first known attack – a rehearsal for murder. While out driving with his best drinking buddy, Trevor Birdsall, Sutcliffe stopped the car in Manningham and disappeared for a few minutes. He came back hurrying, and told Trevor he had hit a prostitute over the head with a brick-filled sock.

Both were questioned by police about the assault, but since the victim declined to press charges, they were simply cautioned and let go.

On 29 September 1969 Peter Sutcliffe was arrested for hiding behind a hedge clutching a hammer. His car had been parked nearby with its engine running. He appeared in court charged with 'going equipped for theft' and was fined £25. Incredibly, this early clue to the identity of the Yorkshire Ripper was never picked up.

On 10 August 1974 Peter and Sonia were finally married. Peter got his HGV driving licence and landed a well-paid job as a long-distance lorry-driver.

The pair lived with Sonia's parents till 1977, by which time they had saved up a deposit for their own house at Garden Lane, Heaton in Bradford.

The first murderous attack seems to have been in Keighley on 5 July 1975. Hammer blows to the head of the victim left her severely injured and nearly dead, but she recovered almost fully.

Sutcliffe was still going round with his friend Trevor Birdsall and they were at a pub together on 15 August 1975, when a 46-year-old office cleaner came in. Sutcliffe pointed her out as a prostitute, and said so to her face. The angry woman gave him a tongue-lashing and appeared to have won the point. But when Peter and Trevor were driving away from the pub, Peter spotted the woman walking along the road. He urged Trevor to stop the car, and got out. He was back, slightly breathless, in a few minutes.

This victim survived; the next would not be so lucky. Wilma McCann, twenty-eight, a mother of four, was found dead on a playing-field in Leeds, on 30 October 1975. The Ripper murders had begun!

The pathologist Professor Gee carried out the postmortem examination on Wilma McCann. He found no traces of semen in her vagina but got a positive reaction from the back of her trousers and panties. The killer had obviously ejaculated during the act of stabbing.

Detective Superintendent Dennis Hoban, head of the Leeds CID, was put in charge of the case. He had an impressive record, having solved more than 50 murders. He issued an internal memo to all divisions saying, 'The motive appears to be hatred of prostitutes.'

The next to die was Emily Monica Jackson, forty-two, from Morley. Last seen alive on Tuesday 20 January 1976, she was found dead next morning in the red-light district of Chapeltown, Leeds.

She was lying face downward with a coat thrown over her. Her legs had been spread apart and a piece of wood had been forced partly into her vagina. Her breasts were exposed and she had been killed with two hammer blows to the head. She had been stabbed some fifty times in the chest and stomach. Many of the wounds had been done with a large Philips screwdriver, which left a distinctive star-shaped imprint. The killer had also stamped on her body, leaving the imprint of a size 7 Dunlop boot on her thigh. Mrs. Jackson left three children.

Superintendent Hoban told the Press, 'There are links between this murder and that of Wilma McCann. Both women were prostitutes. In both cases the obvious deep-seated hatred of prostitutes manifested itself in the many stab wounds.'

A coloured prostitute was the next victim. She picked up a client in Roundhay, Leeds, on 9 May 1976. The man promptly hit her over the head with a hammer. Half-conscious, she saw her attacker masturbating close by. He pushed £5 into her hand, told her not to tell the police, then drove off. Her wounds required 52 stitches, but her accurate description of her attacker was dismissed because she had been classified as educationally sub-normal.

Months passed with police working furiously on the case. The dossier of information grew daily. Hundreds of people were interviewed, but where was the Ripper? Why had the attacks stopped? The year came to an end and fear on the streets lessened. Detectives wondered why the killings had stopped. What was the perpetrator doing during the last eight months? They were to find out in horrific fashion when in February 1977 the Ripper returned.

Irene Richardson, twenty-eight, was found dead in Soldier's Field, Roundhay, Leeds, by a jogger at 7.50 a.m. on Sunday 6 February 1977. She was lying face down, covered in blood. Her coat had been draped over her body to hide the mutilations. Cause of death was three blows to the head with a ball-pein hammer, stab wounds to her neck and throat and three ferocious slash wounds in the stomach which had caused her intestines to spill out. Curiously, her boots had been placed neatly between her thighs. The only clue to her killer was a tyre mark nearby.

Victim Patricia 'Tina' Atkinson, thirty-three, was another prostitute. She had the dubious distinction of becoming the only Ripper victim to be killed indoors. In her case, she was murdered in her own flat in Bradford. She was discovered dead on 24 April 1977, killed by four blows to the head and six chisel wounds in the abdomen. Her bra had been pushed up to expose her breasts and the killer had left the imprint of a size 7 Dunlop book on her bedsheet as well as a bloody handprint on her thigh.

On 26 June 1977 Jayne Michelle MacDonald, sixteen, went for a night out and vanished. She was found at 9.45 next morning, lying in an adventure playground close to Chapeltown Road, Leeds. She lay face down with her bra pushed up exposing her breasts. Cause of death was the blows to the head and stab wounds to the chest and back.

After this murder, the police told the Press, 'An innocent young woman has been slaughtered,' implying the horrifying attitude that they considered previous victims had not been innocent.

Assistant Chief Constable George Oldfield was now placed in overall command of the Ripper inquiry.

By now the Ripper's *modus operandi* was plain. He first hit his victims over the head then dragged them to the murder site. He always stabbed his victims after removing or lifting clothing; never through clothing. He liked to expose the breasts. He used an engineer's ball-pein hammer and a Philips screwdriver. But the Ripper often varied his instrument of killing, such as using a knife instead of a screwdriver, a rock instead of a hammer.

Professor Gee, who examined most of the victims, had come to recognize the Ripper's handiwork. Since five of the victims had been attacked in Leeds and one in Bradford, the evidence pointed to a local man as being the killer.

The tenth attack came on the night of Saturday 10 July 1977, in Bradford, when a 42-year-old woman was hit on the head with a hammer and stabbed four times in the chest and abdomen. However, the killer was disturbed and fled before he could finish her off. She was found at 8.30 the following morning, barely alive. In hospital a long slash from her breasts down to her navel was discovered. After delicate surgery, she survived. She was able to tell police that her attacker had been a white man of about 36, with shoulder-length hair. She said he drove a white Cortina. This description, however, was misleading, and she was no doubt confused by her ordeal.

The Ripper's tally was now five dead, three injured.

Intense police activity in the red-light areas of Leeds and Bradford forced Sutcliffe to cross the Pennines for his next victim.

Jean Jordan, 20, alias Royle, was a Manchester prostitute with two children. She was killed on the night of 1 October 1977 and her body lay undetected for a week in the Southern Cross Cemetery in Moss Side, Manchester. The cause of her death was established as being 11 blows to the head, 18 diagonal stab-wounds to the back and chest, with 10 horizontal wounds to the abdomen, each deep enough to reach the spine.

This murder presented the police with a very important clue. The killer had paid Jean Jordan for her personal attention with a brand-new fiver, serial number AW 51 121565. Sutcliffe, we now know, had become aware of the significance of that note, one of a consecutive series issued to only one bank, and distributed as wages to only 5,943 people. Sutcliffe was one of those people, and was interviewed twice about the £5 note; once on 2 November and again six days later.

However, the coincidence of his being one of the employees paid with notes in the suspect series, coupled to his prior arrest for being in possession of a hammer and being charged with going equipped for theft, was not recognized.

Seven or eight days after Jordan's murder, and prior to her body being found, Sutcliffe returned to where he had killed her, stripped her corpse and because he failed to find the incriminating £5 note, slashed at her in a frenzy. As he cut through her with a Stanley knife, the stench as her stomach blew open made him vomit. He tried to cut off her head as a means of disguising that she was a Ripper victim. To make doubly sure, he tried to burn her on a bonfire, which is where the owner of an allotment on an adjacent site discovered her.

Sutcliffe could not have been overly concerned by the police attention he had received because only weeks later he resumed his lethal activities when he returned to his old stalking-ground in Leeds. He attacked a mother of two, on Wednesday 14 December 1977. She survived after Sutcliffe was disturbed again, but suffered a blow to the head and heard her attacker shriek, 'You dirty prostitute!'

She had spoken with her would-be killer and was able to give police a description. She said he had called himself 'Dave', was a white man aged 25 to 28, and had a 'Jason King' moustache. This was a crucial clue, since Sutcliffe did indeed wear the distinctive moustache and beard made popular by a character in a TV series.

The first month of the year saw two murders within ten days.

Yvonne Ann Pearson, twenty-two, was murdered on the night of Saturday 21 January 1978, but her body was not found for some months. She had been hidden under an abandoned sofa on derelict land off Lumb Lane, Bradford. Stuffing from the sofa was found in her mouth. She was actually discovered on 26 March and it was obvious that once again the killer had gone back to her to commit further attacks on her corpse, and more importantly, to ensure that it *would* be found.

Sutcliffe, evidently obsessed with his Press coverage, must have been feeling neglected, because a copy of the *Daily Mirror* dated a month *after* her murder had been carefully placed under one of her arms.

Maggots in the original wounds, but not in the fresh wounds, also pointed to the Ripper's return. She had been hit on the head with a lump hammer.

Professor Gee thought it had been 'something like a large stone', and at first the police did not think it was a genuine Ripper killing. She had been jumped on with such force that her ribs had cracked. Once again, however, her bra had been pushed up, exposing the breasts.

Ten days later Helen Rytka, 18, a half-caste Jamaican, was found dead in Huddersfield on Tuesday January 31.

She had been hammered over the head and had several stab wounds to her abdomen. Her bra was pushed up. She was the only victim with whom the killer had sex. After her murder, the *Yorkshire Post* offered a large reward for the apprehension of the killer.

On 8 March 1978, Assistant Chief Constable George Oldfield received the first of three letters posted from Sunderland which were signed 'Jack the Ripper.' He took them seriously. His determination was so intense it tilted the investigation in the wrong direction.

In the spring of 1978, Detective Chief Superintendent Dennis Hoban died, to be replaced by James Hobson. However, whatever was happening within the police ranks was of no concern to Sutcliffe. The killing would continue.

Sutcliffe returned to Manchester to kill again. At 8.15 a.m. on Wednesday 17 May 1978, Vera Evelyn Millward, forty, alias Brown or Barton, and the mother of seven children, was found murdered in the car park behind Manchester's Royal Infirmary. She had been hit on the head three times with a hammer and had been stabbed so viciously that her intestines spilled out. She had also been stabbed in the right eye. Her shoes had been placed neatly on her body, and a tyre print was found close by.

In June 1978, West Yorkshire police circulated a confidential 18-page report entitled *Murders and Assaults upon Women in The North Of England* to other police forces. It detailed 16 attacks believed to be the work of the same man, and outlined his methods. One point which was stressed was that the killer might have a fetish about footwear.

Incredibly, on 13 August 1978, Sutcliffe was interviewed for the *fourth* time. Police had seen his car so often in the red-light districts that he was questioned, but not suspected. Towards the end of November that year, the tyres of his car were checked to see if they matched the tracks left at the scene of Irene Richardson's murder. Sutcliffe had by this time replaced the incriminating tyres, so he was not detained.

Almost a year went by before the next killing; a year in which police officers privately hoped that the Ripper had disappeared or committed suicide. Some speculated that he might have abandoned his 'hobby', but at 6.30 on the morning of 5 April 1979, the body of Josephine Anne Whitaker, a 19-year-old building society worker, was found dead at Savile Park in Halifax. She had been hit over the head and dragged to the killing-site, where 25 stab wounds to her breasts, stomach and vagina had been inflicted. Machine oil was found in her wounds, together with the familiar size 7 boot prints. One of her shoes had been placed carefully between her thighs.

George Oldfield received two more letters from the 'Ripper', and forensic tests on the saliva used to lick the envelopes showed that the writer had the rare blood group B, which is found in only 6 per cent of the population.

The police now had to reconsider the unsolved Preston murder of 23 November 1975. Joan Harrison, twenty-six, had been found dead in a lock-up garage. She had been dead for three days, lying face down, her body covered with her coat. The indications were that she had been battered about the head and then kicked savagely, although in her case there were no stab wounds. A bite-mark on her right breast revealed that the killer had a gap in his upper teeth. An anal smear test revealed that she had been sodomized, and the semen present was classified as blood group B. It tied in with the saliva on the envelopes and semen found in the vagina of Helen Rytka. But the Preston killer had been a group B secretor, and Sutcliffe, although he too was group B, was not a secretor. It was another blind alley for the police. Another lead to nowhere. More time wasted. The frustration within the Ripper Squad must have been pushing some members to breaking-point. Assistant Chief Constable George Oldfield's life had been taken over by the enquiry. He was giving everything. He has been criticized for letting the enquiry become an obsession with him, but what good detective doesn't become obsessed with the capture of a vicious killer he is hunting, knowing that until an arrest is made, he is free to murder again and again? Also, George Oldfield had taken over a badly initiated enquiry. The processing of information was being carried out by outmoded methods.

Statements and card indexes were piling up at murder headquarters – computers were not made available. If they had been, then surely Sutcliffe's name must have come to the top of any suspect list. Then for George Oldfield came the cruellest chapter of all; on 17 June 1979, the infamous hoax tape was sent to him. He played it to the Press, convinced that it was genuine.

To George Oldfield, the fake tape was some kind of holy grail. He believed in it, every word. Gone was the scepticism and detachment vital to every detective. He played the tape over and over, telling the Press, "It's a personal thing between me and him."

Because the man on the tape had a distinctly Geordie accent, the police now concentrated on suspects with Geordie accents. Sutcliffe had been interviewed by the Ripper police five times: on 2 November 1977 about the £5 note; on 8 November as a cross-check; on 13 August 1978 because his car had been spotted in the red-light areas of Bradford and Leeds; on 23 November 1978 when his car tyres were checked; and on 29 July 1979. On at least one of these occasions, Sutcliffe was actually wearing his size 7 Dunlop boots when interviewed, but police dismissed him as a likely suspect because he spoke with a high-pitched Yorkshire accent.

On 13 August 1979, George Oldfield suffered a heart attack, and Detective Superintendent Dick Holland was placed in temporary charge of the inquiry. It was he who, when asked by reporters if he was considering calling in Scotland Yard, retorted brusquely, 'Why should we? They haven't caught their own Ripper yet.' (A reference to the original Jack of 1888.)

In the summer of 1979 one of the hit records played on jukeboxes in the pubs of Bradford and Leeds was Donna Summer's *Bad Girls*. The lyrics, detailing the risks run by girls out alone at night, did nothing to deter local prostitutes from plying their trade, but to categorize Sutcliffe as a 'killer of prostitutes' is false anyway. Half of his victims were not. If he ever killed prostitutes, it was only because they were such easy prey.

Five times Sutcliffe had slipped through the police net. He was having the luck of the devil, and undoubtedly the hoax tape enabled him to go on killing longer.

On 2 September 1979 Barbara Leach, a twenty-year-old Leeds University student, was murdered in Bradford, being hit on the head and stabbed eight times in the abdomen. She was found in an alley, hidden under an old piece of carpet, on Sunday morning, by a constable. Her bra was pushed up.

A month after Leach's murder, Detective Chief Superintendent Jim Hobson stated in a Press interview, 'The Yorkshire Ripper has now made his point, after the murder of twelve women in five years, and should give himself up.'

By the end of 1979, a total of 259 officers, including 120 detectives, were working full-time on the Ripper inquiry, which had cost over £5 million and had led to 169,538 people being interviewed, 161,500 vehicles checked, 51,921 lines of inquiry followed and 23,052 house-to-house searches. Another statistic was that 25 children had been left motherless.

Dr. Stephen Shaw, a consultant psychiatrist at Stanley Royds Hospital, Wakefield, was asked to produce a psychological profile of the Ripper. He reported, 'The Ripper is an over-controlled aggressive psychopath, likely to be a young man. He is waging a crusade – a holy war – against prostitutes.'

Other, less scientific aides had offered their services to the police. Dozens of psychics from all over the world had come out with their personal visions of the Ripper. Most placed him in Sunderland and most were completely wrong. However, a South London woman, Mrs. Nella Jones, a psychic who had been used by Scotland Yard, was interviewed by the *Yorkshire Post* in October 1979. Her description of the Ripper was never actually published but she said that he was a long-distance lorry- driver, was called Peter, drove a cab with a name beginning with 'C' on its side (Clarks Transport) and lived in Bradford at number six in a street. Sutcliffe lived at 6 Garden Lane. Mrs. Jones also accurately predicted the date of the Ripper's next attack.

There was an illustration of how hopelessly off track the police had been led by the hoax Ripper tape with the Geordie accent. Private detective Jim Lyness, based in Oldham, who had been hired by the parents of the student murder victim to find her killer, was quickly able to report that the tape was a hoax and that the killer was 'a good-looking guy,' a driver living in Bradford. He based this on descriptions supplied by surviving victims.

On 29 July 1979, Detective Constable Laptew interviewed Sutcliffe at his home about his car having been seen in Lumb Lane for the thirty-sixth time in a month. Something about Sutcliffe aroused the detective's suspicions and he advised his superiors that the man should be seen urgently, as a prime suspect. That was after ten murders. His advice was not acted upon.

On 23 October 1979, less than a month after the murder of Barbara Leach, Sutcliffe was again interviewed about his car. Police had long since been recording the registration numbers of cars spotted in red-light areas. Sutcliffe explained that he had to travel through these areas to get to work. By now, Sutcliffe himself was having 'panic attacks' and often had to receive mouth-to-mouth resuscitation from his wife, Sonia.

In January 1980 George Oldfield was taken off the Ripper inquiry because of his poor health. That month, Sutcliffe was questioned twice more – on the 13th and

30th – about earlier statements over the newly minted £5 note.

On 18 August 1980 Sutcliffe killed again. His victim was Miss Marguerite Walls, forty-seven, an executive officer. She was found buried under grass cuttings close to a house in Farsley between Leeds and Bradford. The Ripper had changed his *modus operandi*, using a ligature to strangle her.

Mr. Hobson declared that this was *not* a Ripper murder.

The following month, on 24 September, a 34-year-old doctor from Singapore, who was studying at Leeds University was attacked by the Ripper, who tried to use a garotte on her. She survived, but only because Sutcliffe was frightened off by a passing patrol car.

Sutcliffe, after this bungled attack, must have been very frustrated, having been thwarted from plunging his knife into a female body, which for him led to ejaculation. On Bonfire Night, 1980, a sixteen-year-old girl was attacked with a hammer near her home in Huddersfield. She survived because the Ripper was disturbed, and was able to give the police a valuable description.

Not so fortunate was Jacqueline Hill, twenty, another Leeds University student who was found dead on Monday 17 November 1980. She had been hammered over the head and stabbed repeatedly with a Philips screwdriver. She had also been stabbed in the right eye.

Less than two weeks later, Trevor Birdsall, Sutcliffe's friend sent an anonymous letter to West Yorkshire police naming Peter Sutcliffe as the Ripper. Because his letter was not acted upon, on 29 November Birdsall went personally to Bradford Police H.Q. and there named Sutcliffe as the Ripper. He made a statement and was thanked courteously for his co-operation. But Sutcliffe was not arrested.

The situation at the beginning of 1981 was that after five and a half years, women in the major cities of the North were in a state verging on panic, and the police were no nearer to catching the Ripper. Thirteen women had been killed, another seven left with severe injuries. Five of the murders had been committed in Leeds, three in Bradford, two in Manchester and one in Halifax, Huddersfield and Farsley respectively. By an odd coincidence, four of the victims had been attacked close to hospitals. Despite the talk of a crusade against prostitutes, of the twenty women attacked, half had not been prostitutes. The cost of the Ripper investigation had exceeded £6,000,000, and the Ripper had been interviewed nine times.

On the evening of Friday, 2 January 1981, Sutcliffe drove to Sheffield in his brown Rover, registration FHY 400K. His usual killing-ground was swamped by police activity, so he hoped for kill in a fresh city.

He picked up a prostitute whom he intended for his 14th victim, and spoke to her about his wife's miscarriages and nagging. Giving his name as 'Dave', he explained he wasn't able to 'go with' his wife, as she wouldn't let him near her.

Two police officers on routine patrol spotted the Rover and recognized the passenger as a familiar prostitute. When they drove up expecting to make a vice arrest, a quick check on the computer with the car licence centre in Swansea revealed that the car had false number-plates. Sutcliffe was taken to the police station. Initially he was charged with theft.

Once at Dewsbury, however, he was questioned about the Ripper killings. Sheffield arresting officers had found a ball-pein hammer and a Philips screwdriver at the scene of his arrest and had flashed this information ahead to Dewsbury. Detective Sergeant Des O'Boyle, attached to the Ripper Squad, questioned Sutcliffe very closely, and his persistence eventually made Sutcliffe confess, 'I am the Yorkshire Ripper.' He had been in custody for 48 hours and took a further 16 hours to dictate his full confession.

Sutcliffe confessed to three attacks the police had not linked to the Ripper: the murder of Marguerite Walls, and the two Leeds attacks on the coloured girl and the woman doctor. He firmly denied the Joan Harrison killing in Preston, which appeared to indicate that two sex-killers had been operating independently, both killing women in the North of England, both with gaps between their front teeth, both with a footwear fetish and both with the rare blood group B.

Asked how he could remember his crimes in such detail, Sutcliffe said the victims 'are all in my brain, reminding me of the beast I am'. He admitted that he had intended killing the Sheffield prostitute but mentioned nothing of a crusade against prostitutes.

Sutcliffe's younger brother visited him in Leeds Prison, and asked why he had done the murders. Peter smiled as he replied, 'I were just cleaning up the streets, our kid. Just cleaning up the streets.'

When police searched Sutcliffe's lorry at Clarks Transport they found inside the cab a card which was hand-lettered with the legend, *'In this truck is a man whose latent genius, if unleashed, would rock the nation, whose dynamic energy would overpower those around him. Better let him sleep?'*

Sonia Sutcliffe was informed of Peter's capture marginally ahead of the Press. News that a man had been apprehended for the Ripper murders went out over television and radio.

Two sisters in Bingley were elated when they heard the news 'I'll take you for a slap-up meal to celebrate, after work,' one promised. She arrived at the factory to find her workmates clustering around a man who was reading out of the newspaper, '. . . Heaton. . . Lorry driver. . . married to a schoolteacher. . .' Suddenly, all her misgivings about her brother, Peter, came to a head and she collapsed on the factory floor.

Sutcliffe's father, too, heard by accident. He was on his tea break when a colleague came up to him with a newspaper and said that the man they'd got for the Ripper job was a Sutcliffe, asking jokingly if he was any relation. The photograph of his son's house in Heaton was prominent and recognizable. His works manager quickly drove him home.

The arrest of Peter Sutcliffe as the Yorkshire Ripper and his conviction for the five-year reign of terror he had inflicted upon the North of England was not the end of the affair. It did, however, mean the end of the longest murder hunt in British history, with over 30,000 statements taken, nearly 300,000 people interviewed, 200,000 cars checked, and some 700,000 man-hours having been worked at a cost to the taxpayers in excess of £6 million.

Police officers could relax, even celebrate – and prostitutes could again ply their trade without the fear of the Ripper hanging over them. But it was not the end of the story. It could not end there, leaving a huge void in the understanding of Sutcliffe's motives, or the politics of the law.

It is easy to criticize the police for their failings, but it must also be considered that random murders are notoriously difficult to solve, though in the case of the Yorkshire Ripper it must bluntly be said that the inquiry got off on the wrong track from the start, and once the ball had started rolling in the wrong direction its own momentum proved impossible to correct.

Let us begin with Sutcliffe's arrest, which took place in an atmosphere of cavalier disregard for facts and procedure which had characterized the entire investigation.

Senior police officers from West Yorkshire held Press conferences and appeared on television and clearly stressed that the police had caught the killer they had been hunting for so long. The two Sheffield officers were seen on TV reading a telegram of congratulations in West Yorkshire. The impression was given and fostered that the infamous murderer they had sought for so long was safely behind bars.

On 5 January 1981, smiling senior police officers sat at a television press conference watched by the nation. They gave details of Sutcliffe's arrest in Sheffield, saying that a man had been detained in West Yorkshire and was being questioned in relation to the Yorkshire Ripper murders. That was fair enough, but police now confirmed that the hunt for the Ripper was being scaled down.

In other words, before Sutcliffe had even been officially named, or had appeared before magistrates, the nation was told that the Ripper had been caught. Therefore, that Sutcliffe was guilty of the Ripper murders.

But the basic principle of law is that a man is innocent until proved guilty and that his guilt must be proved beyond reasonable doubt. It prejudiced the possibility of any fair trial.

Shortly after this, editors of newspapers were sent letters from the Solicitor-General (on behalf of the Attorney-General) expressing his concern about the publicity which had been given to the Yorkshire Ripper case following the arrest of Sutcliffe.

It was hardly the fault of newspaper editors, who simply reported the news.

What we *can* blame the newspapers for was the 'cheque-book journalism' that followed. Many witnesses were paid large sums by newspapers to tell their stories. Such practices should be made illegal for fear of perverting the course of justice.

Newspapers began paying out thousands of pounds for photographs or information about Sutcliffe and his family. One prostitute who'd survived meeting Sutcliffe was paid £4,000 by a newspaper to tell readers that Sutcliffe could not get an erection!

The Ripper killings became an industry.

Let us remember that Sutcliffe was arrested by accident. The Vice Squad officers were more interested in the prostitute than in Sutcliffe – until they spotted that the number plates on his Rover were false. This fact was quickly ascertained by a check with the national computer.

Sutcliffe was arrested for theft of the plates and was allowed to walk away from the car to relieve himself before being taken to the station. Once at Dewsbury police station, officers were ready to release him on bail until a woman officer with the Ripper Squad had second thoughts. She sent for a detective from the Ripper Squad to interrogate Sutcliffe in depth. He took 48 hours to break.

What caused him to break was the fact that one of the arresting officers in Sheffield, Sergeant Bob Ring, arrived back on duty on the Saturday night to learn (to his surprise) that Sutcliffe was still being questioned. Acting on a hunch, Sergeant Ring went back to the spot where Sutcliffe had relieved himself. There he found a ball-pein hammer and a knife – the tools of the Ripper.

Shortly before Sutcliffe's trial was due to take place, the defence did a deal with the Crown. Sutcliffe was prepared to plead guilty to 13 counts of manslaughter and seven counts of attempted manslaughter – but not murder. It was plea-bargaining, which has never been a feature of English law.

The Crown was prepared to accept this deal because all the psychiatrists were united in their opinion that Sutcliffe was a schizophrenic and therefore not responsible for his actions.

Had this deal been accepted, it would have meant a very short trial, with none of the fruitless labours of investigating officers being made public.

The trial judge, however, would not accept such a deal.

On 29 April 1981 the trial opened in Number One Court at the Old Bailey. Relatives of some of the victims sat at the back of the court. At a table sat the detectives in the case, and on that table were the exhibits: seven ball-pein hammers, a claw hammer, three carving knives, eight screwdrivers, a kitchen knife, a cobbler's knife and a length of rope.

These were instruments of death which had claimed 13 lives, and from which the relatives could hardly avert their eyes.

Sir Michael Havers and Harry Ognall QC represented the Crown, with James Chadwin QC and Sidney Levine the defence.

At 10.30 a.m. Sonia Sutcliffe arrived in court with her mother. Sutcliffe himself appeared in the dock at eleven o'clock, a slight figure with a curious high-pitched voice. He did not look like a demon. If anything his moustache and beard gave him the appearance of a benign foreign waiter. The charges took seven minutes to read out, and Sutcliffe stuttered 'not guilty' to all of them.

Sir Michael told the judge that the Crown accepted Sutcliffe's pleas, saying that he had four reports from psychiatrists who had interviewed the prisoner and who were agreed that he was not responsible for his actions. 'The general consensus of the doctors is that this is a case of diminished responsibility, the illness being paranoiac schizophrenia.'

The judge, Mr. Justice Boreham, responded, 'I have very grave anxieties about Sutcliffe and his pleas. I would like you to explain in far greater detail than usual any decisions that you are going to make about the acceptance of these pleas.'

Something extraordinary now took place. In criminal cases, if the defence wishes to plead insanity or state of mind as a defence, then the burden of proving that illness or state of mind falls on the defence. Now, however, the prosecution took up the burden for them, and argued on *behalf* of the prisoner!

For two hours Sir Michael spoke, trying to persuade the judge to accept the pleas. He put forward all the arguments in support of the diminished state of Sutcliffe's mind. The death of Sutcliffe's mother 'greatly distressed him.' (Sutcliffe had been killing for years before his mother's death.) Then the prosecution said, 'He is saying that he is under the direction of God and that he has a mission. . . to kill all prostitutes.' (Half of Sutcliffe's victims were not prostitutes.)

Sir Michael explained how Sutcliffe had heard the voice

CD1. CD2. Maxi-Cassette

After the phenomenal success of the No.1 single *Don't Speak*, NO DOUBT release their eagerly awaited follow up single JUST A GIRL. A huge radio hit in the U.S. when released last year, JUST A GIRL practically became an anthem.

Available in the UK as a fantastic package, JUST A GIRL is available on 2 Cds and Maxi-Cassette featuring live and previously unreleased tracks from their recent European tour.

NO DOUBT, Just A Girl - out June 23rd.

Look out for more live dates in the Autumn!!!!!

POSTAGE PAID

ROYAL MAIL

COVENTRY 617

70331

DAWN CHRISTY
132 ALIBON ROAD
DAGENHAM
ESSEX
RM10 8BY

UNIVERSAL

of God speaking to him from a tombstone in Bingley cemetery.

In 1968, argued the prosecutor, he had become convinced that Sonia was having an affair, and in 1969, to set the balance right or get his own back, he had picked up a prostitute in Manningham. She robbed him of his money. Later this prostitute had laughed at him in a pub, causing him humiliation.

In September 1969, while out driving with Trevor Birdsall, he stopped in the Manningham area and got out, leaving Birdsall in the passenger seat, while he went to attack a woman with a brick in a sock. When he got back into the car, he did not explain himself.

Sir Michael told the court how Sutcliffe was interviewed by the police but let off with a caution because the woman had not wished to press charges. Then in October 1969 Sutcliffe was arrested for hiding in a garden in Manningham with a hammer in his possession. He was fined £25 at Bradford magistrate's court for 'going equipped for theft'.

Next the trial judge listened to the evidence of the psychiatrists and their tales of Sutcliffe's 'mission to kill', and he remarked, 'The matter that troubles me is that all these opinions are based simply on what this defendant has told the doctors, nothing more.'

In other words, what the judge was saying, was that if Sutcliffe had lied to the doctors, then their opinions were worthless.

The judge went on to make the point that Sutcliffe had said nothing about his mission to kill to the police, and finally said sternly, 'It seems to me it would be more appropriate if this case were dealt with by a jury.'

The jury should be the judges of Sutcliffe's sanity, not the doctors!

The defence, who had not expected this, applied for an adjournment, and the trial proper began on Tuesday 5 May.

Sutcliffe appeared once more in the dock, twice

challenging jurors. Neither by speech nor action did he give any sign of mental illness, and then Sir Michael Havers, who had already argued one way, had now to argue the other way – without embarrassment.

He told the jury, 'You have to decide whether this man sought to pull the wool over the doctors' eyes. You have to decide whether, as a clever, callous murderer, he deliberately set out to create a cock and bull story to avoid conviction for murder.'

Sir Michael concentrated on 'discrepancies' between what Sutcliffe had told the police and what he'd later told the doctors. The Attorney-General gave away his own leaning towards double standards when he said of the victims, 'Some were prostitutes, some were women of easy virtue, but the last six attacks from 1979 to 1980 involved victims whose reputations were unblemished,' which suggested that the court regarded the last six murders as being more grave than the previous seven.

Confirming that the letters and tape from the 'Ripper' were hoaxes, the Attorney-General said, 'The harsh truth is that the author of the letters and tape has nothing to do with this case. Most regrettably, it became widely accepted by a number of senior officers that this man [the hoaxer] was in fact the Ripper and that he spoke with a Wearside accent. One of the things which affected the investigating officers was that if the suspects interviewed did not speak with a Sunderland accent, they tended to be eliminated.'

Peter Sutcliffe's confession, made to Dewsbury police over a period of many hours, was read out in court.

Of the first victim, Sutcliffe said:

'I asked her if she fancied it. She said 'Not on your life.' I followed her and hit her with a hammer. I intended to kill her, but I was disturbed.'

Of the second victim:

'I saw her in the Royal Oak. She annoyed me, probably in some minor way. I took her to be a prostitute. I hit her on the head and scratched her buttocks with a piece of hacksaw blade or maybe a knife. My intention was to kill her, but I was disturbed by a car coming down the road.'

Of his first actual murder victim, Wilma McCann, Sutcliffe said:

'She said, "Come on, get it over with." I said, "Don't worry, I will" and I hit her with the hammer. She made a lot of noise so I took my knife out of my pocket and stabbed her about four times.' (It was fifteen times.)

Asked by the police why he had stabbed so many of his victims in the heart, Sutcliffe said, 'You can kill them quicker that way.'

Of Emily Jackson he declared:

'I pushed a piece of wood against her vagina to show how disgusting she was.'

He also stabbed her fifty times with his screwdriver in the region of the womb. Of his first black victim – who survived his attack – he recalled:

"She went behind some trees for a pee and suggested that we start the ball rolling on the grass. I hit her once on the head with the hammer, but just couldn't bring myself to hit her again. (He had actually hit her over the head nine times.)

Of Irene Richardson: 'I used the hammer and a Stanley knife on her. As she was crouching down, urinating on the grass, I hit her on the head at least two or three times. I lifted up her clothes and slashed her abdomen and throat.'

Of Tina Atkinson:

'I heard her using foul language. It was obvious why I picked her up. No decent woman would have been using language like that at the top of her voice. When I had killed her I picked her up under the arms and lifted her up onto the bed.' He'd used the claw part of the hammer to hack at her body.

The details Sutcliffe had given in his confession were specific. After the usual stunning hammer blows to the head, he told police, he wiped his knife clean on Jayne MacDonald's back after stabbing her nineteen times. He told how he had returned to Jean Jordan's body six days after killing her in an attempt to cut her head off. Why? 'To make this murder more mysterious.'

He confirmed that he had used a walling hammer to smash Yvonne Pearson's skull into 17 fragments, then used stuffing from a settee and rammed it into her mouth to stop her moaning. But it had taken more hammer blows to shut her up for good, he told police.

His account of Helen Rytka's murder was even more pathetic, since this young half-caste girl had endured such a sad life prior to meeting Sutcliffe.

'She undid my trousers and seemed prepared to start sexual intercourse right away in the front seat of the car. It was very awkward for me to find a way to get her out of the car.'

Why was he so anxious to get her out of the car? 'Because it would have left evidence and would also have been very difficult.' Sutcliffe had had enough sense to realize that leaving forensic evidence of murder in the car would be dangerous for him.

'For about five minutes I was trying to decide which method to use to kill her. She was beginning to arouse me sexually. I got out of the car with the excuse that I needed to urinate and managed to persuade her to get out of the car so that we could have sex in the back. As she was getting in I realized that this was my chance, but my hammer caught on the edge of the car door frame and only gave her a light tap. She said, "There is no need for that, you don't even have to pay." I expected her to immediately shout for help. She was obviously scared and said, "What was that?" I said, "Just a small sample of one of these" and hit her on the head, hard. She just crumbled, making a loud moaning noise. I realized that what I had done was in full view of two taxi-drivers who had appeared and were talking nearby. I dragged her by the hair to the end of the woodyard. She stopped moaning, but was not dead. Her eyes were open and she held up her hands to ward off blows. I jumped on top of her and covered her mouth with my hand. It seemed like an eternity and she was still struggling. I told her that if she kept quiet she would be all right. As she had got me aroused a moment previous, I had no alternative but to go ahead with the act of sex as the only means of keeping her quiet. It didn't take long. She kept staring at me. She didn't put much into it.'

The taxi-drivers eventually drove off, and Helen took the chance to scramble to her feet and stagger towards the car. Sutcliffe, who had dropped his hammer, had to scramble on the ground for it before going after her.

'This was when I hit her two heavy blows to the back of the head. I dragged her to the front of the car and threw her belongings over the wall.

'She was obviously still alive. I took a knife from the car and stabbed her several times through the heart and lungs. I think it was the kitchen knife which I believe the police later retrieved from my home.' It was in fact found in the cutlery drawer in the Sutcliffes' pristine kitchen.

The Attorney-General now turned to the death of Josephine Whitaker, describing this as 'a respectable victim'. 'Now we come to another sad one,' he told the court, and holding up a giant Philips screwdriver, some two feet in length, Sir Michael continued, 'Sutcliffe told the police he used this on Josephine Whitaker and Barbara Leach. That was after he had used his hammer to shatter their skulls, leaving the tell-tale pattern of golf-ball size indentations in the scalp. He used the round head of the ball-pein hammer. He had used that screwdriver as a substitute penis, introducing it into the vagina many times.'

When asked about the murder of Barbara Leach, Sutcliffe had declared, 'It was forty-six weeks after the last one [Whitaker]. I was never urged to do it again until then.'

Sir Michael held up a length of cord which Sutcliffe had used to strangle Marguerite Walls and which was found on him at the time of his arrest. When the police asked him why he had changed his method of killing, Sutcliffe told them, 'Because the Press and the media had attached a stigma to me. I had been known for some time as the Yorkshire Ripper. I didn't like it. It didn't ring true. I had been on my way to Leeds to kill a prostitute when I saw Margo Walls. It was just unfortunate for her that she happened to be walking by. I don't like the method of strangulation. It takes them even longer to die.'

He explained the murderous attack on his 18th victim by saying, "She was walking slowly like a prostitute and I hit her on the head with a hammer. I didn't have any tools with me to finish her off so I used the rope." But she survived.

Why did he kill 16-year-old Jayne MacDonald? 'I attacked her because she was the first person I saw. I think something clicked because she had a straight skirt with a slit in it.'

The trial continued the next day, with more details from Peter Sutcliffe's 16-hour confession. 'The last I did was Jacqueline Hill at Headingley. I sat in the car. . . then I saw Miss Hill. I decided that she was a likely victim. I drove past her and parked up and waited for her to pass. I got out and followed. I took the hammer from my pocket and struck her on the head. I dragged her on to some waste ground. A car appeared and I threw myself on the ground, but the car passed by. She was moving about so I hit her again. I pulled most of her clothes off. I had a screwdriver with a yellow handle and I stabbed her in the lungs. Her eyes were wide open and she seemed to be looking at me with an accusing stare. This shook me up a bit so I stabbed her in the eye.'

Now came the medical evidence: a report from Dr. Hugo Milne, psychiatrist, who said, 'There is no suggestion that he is a sadistic sexual deviant. I am convinced that the killings were not sexual in any way.'

Trevor Birdsall went into the witness box and spoke of that early 'rehearsal', and of the night of the attack on the first victim.

'On the way home we passed through Halifax. Peter stopped the car and got out. I remember seeing a woman.

She was walking quickly and Peter went to the back of the car and disappeared. . .He was away ten to twenty minutes. When he came back he said he had been talking to a woman. The next evening I read about a brutal attack on a woman in that area. It crossed my mind that Peter might be connected with it.'

This was in August 1975.

It was not until 26 November 1980 that Birdsall was uncertain enough about his friend to send an anonymous letter to the police denouncing Sutcliffe as the Ripper. It was just after the murder of Jacqueline Hill. Worried by a lack of police response, he went to the police personally a few days later – and was courteously dismissed. It never came out at the trial why the police had failed to act on Birdsall's allegations, and nor has it since.

Detective Inspector John Boyle went into the witness box to tell about the most important interview of his life, when he was questioning Sutcliffe at Dewsbury on the night of 4 January, almost at the end of a 48-hour period of questioning.

Boyle asked Sutcliffe why he had dumped the hammer and knife following his arrest, to which Sutcliffe replied, 'I think you've been leading up to it.'

'Leading up to what?' Boyle asked.

'The Yorkshire Ripper.'

'What about him?'

'Well, it's me.'

Prison officers testified next. One had heard Sutcliffe say to a relative, 'I am going to do a long time in prison, thirty years or more, unless I can convince people in here I'm mad, and maybe then ten years in the loony bin.'

Another reported a conversation he'd had with Sutcliffe in which the latter said, 'I have been told by my psychiatrist that I will have to do no more than ten years to satisfy the public.'

A third testified, 'He was saying to me that the doctors considered him disturbed and he was quite amazed by it and smiling broadly and leaning back in his chair. He said to me, "I'm as normal as anyone."

On 11 May Sutcliffe went into the witness box and said, 'I have killed these thirteen women. I intended to kill the other seven,' before going on to tell of his religious mission from God to kill prostitutes, and of being 'selected' to kill. He had taken the hoax Ripper tape as proof that God was protecting him.

Yet the fact was that Sutcliffe, who claimed to view prostitutes as 'scum', had regularly paid them for sexual services. And Sutcliffe had told the police he felt an urge to kill *all* women.

Under cross-examination Sutcliffe was asked, 'Do you think you are mad?'

'No,' he replied.

'Do you think there is anything wrong with you mentally?'

'Nothing serious at all, no.'

The prosecution ended by claiming that Sutcliffe had shown self-control and cunning throughout his reign of terror. He had used the 'mission to kill prostitutes' story to fool the doctors.

Then it was the doctors' turn to be put on trial. They followed one another into the witness box to proclaim Sutcliffe's madness.

Dr Hugo Milne was forced to admit that Sutcliffe might well have lied to him, and that the murders showed very clear sexual components. The second doctor had seen Sutcliffe for an hour and could not be certain that he was not a liar. If he was a liar, 'then my diagnosis falls'.

A third doctor stated that he was either an incompetent psychiatrist or that Sutcliffe was a very competent actor.

A fourth doctor refused to agree that Sutcliffe, in inserting a two-foot-long screwdriver into a victim's vagina without tearing the tissues, was not deriving some sexual satisfaction from the act.

Attorney-General Sir Michael Havers summed up for the prosecution by urging the jury to consider whether Sutcliffe was 'bad or mad'.

The same point was made by the judge in his summing up.

The jury retired on 22 May, 1981.

Unable to agree a verdict after four hours, they were sent away again to reach a majority verdict. An hour later they returned, finding Sutcliffe guilty of 13 murders and 7 attempted murders. He was bad, not mad. The verdict meant that Sutcliffe had indeed fooled the doctors, in the jury's opinion.

Chapter Seventeen

HEIDNIK

The pornography of an age reflects its fears and fantasies, and modern pornography seems to be a perversion of the will-to-power. It may be argued the it is not too different from the writings of de Sade or Nietzsche – but they were unique in their age, and their evil philosophy is now commonplace. John Fowles's powerful novel *The Collector* is not pornography but literature. However, even literature can inspire devotees to act out the fictional fantasy. The novel is a study of a clinically obsessive man who wins the football pools and put his fantasy into action. He buys a house in an isolated spot, has the basement turned into a prison cell and then 'collects' a girl and keeps her prisoner in his private dungeon.

The pleasure he derives from his captive is compared to that felt by a fanatical butterfly collector with a rare specimen, but what is captured so strongly in the book is the sheer power-kick of having a woman completely submissive to the man's masculine and dominant will – rather like a sultan with his harem.

The book, which was a best-seller and turned into a film, seemed to capture something of the spirit of its age; a feeling that women should exist only to serve the whims of men, and in a sense the novel was a prophecy which was to be fulfilled in the USA in 1987 in a case which the Press called Philadelphia's 'House of Horror'.

Just before midnight on March 24 1987, black prostitute Josefina Rivera banged frantically on the door of her boy-friend's apartment in Philadelphia. He had not seen her for four months, since she had gone out on a November evening to 'turn a trick'. He was shocked to see how appallingly she had changed; she looked thin and haggard and had deep scars and sores around her ankles.

The boy-friend, Vincent Nelson, said later, "She came in rambling on, you know, talking real fast about this guy having three girls chained up in the basement of his house and she was held hostage for four months. She said he was beating them, raping them, had them eating dead people . . . a dog was in the yard chewing their bones. I just thought she was crazy. . ."

However, he and the girl went to the phone box and rang the emergency number for the police. Two officers arrived in a squad car and listened to her story. They were initially sceptical, thinking she was perhaps on drugs, but the scars around her ankles convinced them it was a story worth checking out.

She said she had been kidnapped on November 26 1986, by a bearded white man driving a Cadillac Coupé de Ville, who she described as well-dressed and wearing a Rolex watch. The house in which she claimed to have been held was just three blocks away. She said she had been tortured and sexually abused and had seen other women in the house being treated in a similar fashion. She had also witnessed the murder of her fellow-captives.

Police kept the house under observation while a warrant was obtained and a search-team of officers was assembled. The two-storey brick house was in a white working-class neighbourhood and had bars over its windows. On the outside was a placard reading United Church of the Ministers of God, and the house was guarded by two fierce dogs, a German Shepherd and a Doberman.

The address – 3520 North Marshall Street – seems destined to go down in the annals of murder with the same horrific impact as 10 Rillington Place.

Police forced entry into the house at 4.30 a.m. on March 25, and were confronted by a bearded white man, who raised his arms when he saw drawn guns. He said his name was Gary Michael Heidnik, forty-three.

He was taken into custody and removed to the Sex Crimes Unit at headquarters. He seemed to think the police had called about his late alimony payments . . .

In his basement police found two naked black women chained to a sewer pipe by their ankles. They were terrified at first, but when they realised it was the police they cried out in joy "Hosanna – we are free!" and kissed the officers' hands in gratitude.

Sergeant Frank McCloskey asked them, 'Is anyone here but you?' The two women, one eighteen and the other twenty-four, pointed to a board on the floor.

'She's there. She's in the hole.' Pushing the board aside, the officer discovered a pit in which crouched another naked black woman. She too was shackled, only her hands were cuffed behind her back. She was so weak she had to be lifted out of the hole – and immediately started screaming. 'It's all right,' the other two women assured her. 'It's the police. We're free.'

Still in shock, the woman who had been in the hole began raving 'He took my thirty dollars; get my money back!'

Police had to use bolt cutters to remove the shackles, and the women were rushed to hospital. All were extremely thin and weak, and covered with bruises. The police now searched the house, finding a stack of pornographic magazines all of which featured black women. On the stove was a blackened cooking pot, its interior covered in a thick crust.

An officer opened the fridge and was confronted by a human forearm. That did it. He ran outside and vomited.

Officers sent urgently for forensic experts from the medical examiner's office to assist them. Detective Lamont Anderson, at the scene, told reporters that 'other body parts' had been found in the house and it was believed that at least two women had been killed in the basement.

The following day, all the newspapers led with lurid headlines which tried to include the elements of murder, rape, bondage, torture and cannibalism. It was known from early on that Heidnik was a 'Bishop' in his own invented church and had extensive dealings with the stock exchange. He was worth in excess of half a million dollars and had a Rolls-Royce in the garage of his run-down home. Newspapers called him the. "Rolls-Royce Reverend" and stated that he was into "stocks and bondage'.

Other headlines declared: MAN HELD IN TORTURE KILLINGS; MADMAN'S SEX ORGY WITH CHAINED WOMEN; and WOMEN CHAINED IN HORROR DUNGEON.

While police continued to take cardboard boxes filled with human remains from the house, the four surviving captives were questioned in hospital and the grotesque and sickening details of their ordeal emerged. Three of them had been imprisoned for three months, tortured and raped daily by the white man, who kept them alive on a diet of dog food, bread and water.

They were kept shackled in the basement, being released from their manacles only for further sex and torture sessions upstairs.

Police were overcome to learn that at times the starving captives had been fed on human flesh which had been put through a food-processor and blended with the dog food. A dog had been seen chewing on a human leg . . .

One of the freed victims guided police to where another woman's body laid buried Survivor Lisa Thomas, nineteen, said she'd seen a woman she knew only as 'Sandy' fall while handcuffed to a chain from the ceiling and strike her head on a concrete floor. Sandy was later identified as Sandra Lindsay, twenty-four.

Miss Rivera, the woman who'd raised the alarm, told police that the white man had been boasting that he'd fed the boiled remains of 'Sandy' to herself and the other captives. Police also heard that Debbie Dudley, twenty-three, had been murdered by being placed in a pit filled with water and electrocuted by wires attached to her chains.

That pit had served another purpose; it was the 'hole' in which the captives were kept when being punished, as well as to prevent escape whenever the 'master' left the house. A wooden board would be placed over it, held down by a sack of sand.

Josefina Rivera had been the first captive, picked up on 26 November 1986, for sex. Heidnik had driven her to his house, where after sex, he'd begun to throttle her into submission. He handcuffed her and took her down into the basement, shackling her by the ankles. She had to watch him dig a pit in the concrete floor, and feared it was going to be her grave. He'd assured her that the hole was only for punishment if she misbehaved, confiding that he was only attracted to black women. His ambition was to have ten women captive in the cellar and to have children by them all. 'We'll all be one big happy family,' he'd promised.

He also told her that he had served four years in prison after being found guilty of the rape of a mentally retarded black woman by whom he wanted to have a child. It had been unfair, he said, because sex had been voluntary, and the daughter he'd had by the black woman had been put in a home.

'Society owes me a wife and family,' he'd told Josefina, before forcing her to perform oral sex on him.

Later that day, Josefina had managed to force open a boarded-over window and scream for help. Nobody came. Heidnik heard her and came down and beat her, then threw her into the pit. He left her alone, with a radio playing rock music at full volume to drown out any more cries for help.

On 29 November, three days later, Heidnik brought his second captive down into the basement. She was Sandra Lindsay. She had known Heidnik for years and had once been pregnant by him. He had been furious when he discovered she'd had an abortion. Heidnik forced her to write a letter to her mother saying she was all right, and later posted her letter from New York.

The basement was cold, lit only by a bare bulb. The floor was covered in litter. The routine each day was the same: beatings and forced sex, a prison diet of oatmeal and bread. Later Heidnik began giving them dog food from tins, which he spread on sandwiches.

One by one the other captives were brought down to the basement.

On 22 December, Lisa Thomas was accosted by a white man sitting in a Lincoln. She accepted his invitation to dinner and afterwards agreed to go home with him to watch video-tapes.

'I fell asleep and the next thing I know he was choking me and had handcuffed me,' she said. 'He took me down to the basement and put chains on my legs. He beat me with a wooden stick. There were two other women down there. They were chained too.'

Later, two more girls had been brought down to the basement and chained. On 1 January 1987, Deborah Dudley joined the others. Heidnik came to regret taking her because she was a stronger character and argued back, inciting the others to revolt. She had to be beaten frequently.

On 18 January Jacquelyn Askins, eighteen, was captured. Her ankles were so thin that she could not be shackled, so Heidnik used handcuffs.

By now, Heidnik was treating Josefina Rivera as a "trusty", allowing her out of the cellar to have meals with him and keep discipline among the other captives. She reported any talk of escape attempts. On March 23rd, Heidnik took Josefina out driving and together they picked up Agnes Adams, 24, another prostitute. She was necessary because by that time two of the other captives had died.

On February 7th, Sandra Lindsay died. She had been

suspended by her hands from the ceiling for a week as a punishment for attempting to escape from the hole and died from sheer exhaustion.

On March 18th, Heidnik filled the pit with water and made everyone except Josefina climb in. He gave them electric shocks from a bare wire. It touched Deborah Dudley's chains and she was killed instantly.

Heidnik disposed of Sandra by putting her body through a meat-grinder, and boiled her head in a pan on the stove. Nieghbours complained of the stench of cooking meat, but Heidnik told an investigating policeman that he had burnt his dinner. The officer did not bother to look in the saucepan on the stove. . .

Next came another refinement in cruelty. To make the girls deaf so that they would not hear any rescue attempt. Heidnik jabbed a screwdriver into their ears, twisting it around to rupture their ear-drums. Josefina was not subjected to this. She had by now gained Heidnik's trust by snitching on her fellow-captives and beating them on Heidnik's orders. She was often taken out to fast-food restaurants for meals, or for a ride in his Cadillac or Rolls-Royce.

She was with him when he buried Deborah Dudley in a New Jersey park on March 22nd, and when he stopped on the way back to buy a newspaper. "I want to check my stocks," he told her.

It was the action of a madman to check the stock-market prices after disposing of a murder victim.

On March 24th, 1987, Rivera had become so trusted that she persuaded Heidnik to let her see her family to put their minds at rest. She promised to return . . . Heidnik dropped her off at the same corner he had picked her up at four months previously, but she hurried immediately to Vincent Nelson's apartment and babbled out her astonishing story.

When arrested, Heidnik was found to have almost $2,000 on him, and numerous credit cards. There were documents for four cars, and a statement from the stockbrokers Merril Lynch, showing his account standing at $377,382.52. Within hours of his arrest on March 25th, Heidnik was attacked by disgusted fellow-prisoners who broke his nose. In isolation for his own protection, Heidnik attempted to hang himself in the shower on April 2nd. He was rescued unconscious, but alive.

Police continued to search Heidnik's house, dredging the sewers and tearing apart the walls in search of further bodies. They had already recovered parts of the dismembered body of a girl wrapped in plastic from the freezer and were seeking a third body.

Meanwhile, other detectives began investigating Heidnik's background. He was a wealthy, self-styled "Bishop", who insisted that police address him as "Reverend". He had a record of violence, having been charged the previous year with "spouse rape" by his Oriental wife, who had since left him. Police established that his *modus operandi* was to seduce women with a mixture of religion and kindness – then terrorise them with sadism.

Born in November, 1943, in Cleveland, Heidnik is the archetypal serial killer; the product of a broken home, whose parents had separated when he was two years old. His mother committed suicide in 1970 when she learned she had cancer, and Heidnik had not seen his father in 20 years.

Heidnik had a loveless childhood, which he spent in solitary fantasizing. He was also a bed-wetter, a fact which enraged his heavy-drinking father, who beat him often for it.

By now, Heidnik was an object of ridicule because of the shape of his head: classmates called him 'football head'. His head was slightly deformed following injuries after a fall from a tree. (A high proportion of serial killers have a history of head injuries.)

Following his son's arrest his father told the Press, 'I hope to hell they hang him, and you can quote me on that. I'll even pull the rope.'

Gary Heidnik's younger brother, 41-year-old Terry, gave an interesting insight into the Jekyll and Hyde character who had been labelled the 'Beast of Philadelphia' by explaining that he and Gary had been raised in a family atmosphere of violence and racism. It was an unhappy childhood.

When Heidnik left school he joined the army where he became a loan-shark and started making money. His childhood fantasies had always centred around money and on dreams of becoming a millionaire.

On 25 August 1962, he complained to an army doctor of headaches and dizzy spells and was diagnosed as being either schizoid or schizophrenic. On 23 January, 1963, he was given an honourable discharge and awarded a 100 per cent mental disability pension for life because his condition was considered to be service-related. He had served just fourteen months of his enlistment.

For over twenty years Heidnik lived on his pension, some $2,000 a month plus social security payments.

Having failed in an army career, Heidnik settled in Philadelphia. At first he tried to gain credits at the University of Pennsylvania in a number of subjects. He had an IQ of 130, 30 above average. His attempts in the 1960s to live first with his mother, then his father, were failures. His father did not want him in his life, so he drifted from job to job, the last one as a male nurse. He never lasted long.

In the years that followed he was admitted to mental hospitals at least 21 times, and attempted suicide on 13 occasions. In the spring of 1971 he founded his own church, registering it as a charity with himself as Bishop for life. He seems to have held genuine services with his flock, but his church's money-raising ventures included bingo and loan-sharking.

In 1975 Bishop Heidnik opened an account with Merrill Lynch in the name of his church, and began playing the stock-market – with remarkable success. By

1976 he was a wealthy man. In that same year came his first arrest, for carrying a firearm on a public street. He had let an apartment to a man, but when his tenant climbed in through a window one night, Heidnik fired at him with a revolver. The charge of assault with a deadly weapon was dropped, however.

In March, 1978, Heidnik became a father. A mentally retarded black woman bore his child. Her sister was in a mental institution and on 9 May Heidnik helped her escape and hid her at his home. He considered he was doing her a favour. When the police found her she was hidden in Heidnik's basement. There was a quantity of pornographic material in the house, and it was obvious that the girl had been grossly sexually abused. Since she had a venereal infection of the throat, oral sex was not hard to prove, and Heidnik was convicted of unlawful imprisonment and deviant sex.

In November, 1978, he was sentenced from there to seven years in the state penitentiary. He served four years, being released on parole on 12 April, 1983, aged forty.

Heidnik bought the house at 3520 North Marshall Street and became noted for his extraordinary sexual behaviour. Every night he seemed to have three-in-a-bed sex, always with black women, some drawn from his congregation.

Deciding he wanted an Oriental wife, he got one through a matrimonial agency, and Filipino girl Betty Disto flew from Manila to Philadelphia to join him. They were married within three days. A week later she came home from shopping to find him in bed with three women. Heidnik tried to assure her that this was a normal custom for American males, but after being subjected to forced sodomy she left him in January, 1986. The court ordered him to pay her $135 a week.

In November of that same year Heidnik began stocking his harem, first kidnapping Josefina Rivera. . .

Gary Heidnik's trial began on 20 June, 1988, in Philadelphia City Hall, room 653 before a woman judge,

Lynn M. Abraham. It was obvious from the outset that the defence tactic would be to claim insanity; however, Assistant District Attorney Charles Gallagher made it plain that he would seek the death penalty.

Defence counsel was Charles Peruto, a flamboyant lawyer with a good record of acquittals, but in this case he knew he would be fighting a losing battle.

It took a long time to choose a jury. The defence, for some reason, sought an all-white jury. The prosecutor told this jury that Heidnik had murdered, raped, kidnapped and assaulted six young women aged between 18 and 25.

'Gary Heidnik took these women home with him,' Gallagher said. 'He plied them with food and in some cases sex. He assaulted them. He choked them. He handcuffed them and took them to his basement where he put shackles on their ankles. He starved them. He tortured them. He repeatedly had sex with them.'

He added that Heidnik had killed two of them, one of whom he dismembered, cooked and fed to the others.

'The evidence will show that from the eve of Thanksgiving, 1986, up to March twenty-fifth, 1987, the defendant committed repeated and sadistic malicious acts. He did them in a methodical and systematic way. He knew exactly what he was doing, and he knew it was wrong. He took advantage of underprivileged people.'

When defence counsel rose, the judge reminded him that he need not make an opening statement; that his client was innocent until proved guilty.

Peruto retorted, 'My client is not innocent. He is very, very guilty.' He said his client had indeed done all the things he had been accused of, but added that while the prosecutor had promised to construct a trail of evidence leading right to Heidnik's door, he didn't want to stop there. He wanted to take the jury through that door and show the man inside.

'There's no mystery here,' he went on. 'This is not a whodunnit. If all we had to decide here was who did it and what was done, it would be easy. You're not here to determine if Gary Heidnik is going to walk out of here a free man. He's never going to see the light of day. He will be put behind bars or in some mental institution. Any person who puts dog food and human remains in a food processor, calls it a gourmet meal and feeds it to others is out to lunch!'

Peruto said the defence would be one of insanity, telling the jury that he would be calling expert witnesses to testify to that fact.

'Understand two things,' he intoned to the jury. 'One; Gary Heidnik didn't want anybody to die. Two; because of his mental illness, he couldn't tell right from wrong.'

Witnesses were called one by one. Josefina Rivera was asked what the women had done to pass the time in the basement.

'Nothing too much . . . outside of just having sex and staying in the hole. Three times we were down in the hole and we ran out of air. We couldn't breathe. We started screaming and hollering and Gary came down and beat us . . . We didn't take any baths or wash our hair. . . Music was going twenty-four hours a day.'

In telling of the death of Sandra Lindsay. Josefina said, 'He carried her body upstairs and we heard an electric saw. Then we smelt a terrible odour. He smelled of it and so did the food he brought us.'

She said that Heidnik had stopped beating her in January because he was beginning to feel he could trust her. But he was having problems with Debbie Dudley. 'He always had trouble with Debbie, Debbie always fought back.'

Not long after Lindsay died, Heidnik took Debbie upstairs. 'In about five minutes she came back. She was very quiet.' Josefina said she asked her what had happened, and Debbie told her, 'He showed me Sandra's head cooking in a pot. Her ribs were cooking in a roasting pan in the stove and her legs and arms were in the freezer. He told me if I didn't start listening to him, that would happen to me . . .' Six weeks later, Debbie Dudley was dead.

The black woman's shocking testimony continued, clear in the silence of the court. 'Everybody went on punishment in early March. We were eating dog food mixed with body parts.'

She was asked if she knew where Heidnik had got his ideas from, and replied brightly, 'Yes, he got them from watching movies and TV. He got the idea of feeding us parts of Sandy's body from *Eating Raoul,* and his ideas on punishment from *Mutiny on the Bounty.* He also saw *The World of Susie Wong* and said he liked the way Oriental women were. That's why he picked a Filipino wife.'

Lisa Thomas was the next witness. The day after he'd first shackled her, Heidnik seemed to have a touch of compassion and fitted a longer chain between her ankles. 'Why did he do that?' Gallagher asked.

'So I could open my legs wider to have sex,' she replied.

'Did he beat you too?'

'Yes, almost from the first moment. He hit me five times with a thick brown stick. . . He told me to beat Sandy regularly; he'd get his kicks from seeing us beat each other. . . Then he'd get on top of me and make me suck his penis.'

Jacquelyn Askins was the youngest of the witnesses, still only nineteen when she took the stand. She looked frightened to death as she described the sex-parties Heidnik forced her to join in from her basement cell. 'I'd suck his penis and another girl would suck his balls. Then he'd have sex with one girl and I'd lie next to him so I could catch his juice.' She told of the frequent beatings she endured, and of having to eat dog-food sandwiches.

The remaining witnesses were policemen and doctors. Detectives told of what they found in Heidnik's house.

Dr. Robert Catherman, who'd performed the autopsy on Dudley, confirmed that she'd died of electrocution. 'It was an almost classic example of electrothermal injury.' he said. The irony of this was that if found guilty, Heidnik would die in exactly the same way as his victim.

Dr. Paul Hoyer had examined the body parts removed from Heidnik's freezer. He testified that he had found a bone covered in dog hairs in the yard. It was from an upper left arm and matched the other frozen limbs in the freezer. They included several ribs, a number of tooth fragments and one whole tooth. Positive identification of the remains came from a wrist found in the freezer. Lindsay had injured her wrist a year earlier and her X-ray was on file. 'The overall size and shape matched, plus the pattern matched. There is a pattern in bone and each pattern is unique. By comparing this we were able to say that this was Sandra Lindsay.'

The prosecution rested its case.

A psychiatrist called by the defence, Dr. Clancy McKenzie, argued that there existed within Heidnik's head an adult mind and a mind only 17 months old. It was the infantile part of the mind that kidnapped and raped women. Heidnik was a schizophrenic, he declared firmly.

The judge was openly sceptical of this explanation and ruled that the defence could not call in evidence Heidnik's twenty-year history of mental illness, or even produce the records from various doctors in evidence. It was a blow which sunk the defence.

A broker from Merrill Lynch said that 'Bishop' Heidnik had opened an account with a cheque for $1,500. Over the next seven years, Heidnik had bought shares over the telephone and his original stake increased to over half a million dollars.

District Attorney Gallagher asked the witness, 'What kind of investor was he?'

'A very astute investor,' was the broker's reply.

In his closing speech for the defence, Peruto told the jury, 'What was Gary Heidnik's purpose? His purpose was to raise ten kids, not to kill anybody. Third-degree murder in reckless disregard for human life. This is a classic case of third degree.'

He said of Heidnik's captives that one was retarded and three were prostitutes.

'As sick as it is, these were his chosen people. These were the girls he wanted to reproduce with. Is that sane? It's a case of Dr. Jekyll and Mr. Heidnik. Isn't it more likely that he's more insane than not? What kind of mentality does it take to have human flesh in front of you; a human being, and to cut through that body? To cut through flesh? To cut through bone and to take some of those body parts and wrap them up and put them in the freezer? And then to cook some and feed it to the others? Who was he trying to impress with that delusion?'

Peruto demanded a verdict of not guilty by reason of insanity.

District Attorney Gallagher countered by saying that Heidnik had planned each of the abductions, killed in a cold premeditated fashion and disposed of Sandra Lindsay's body by dismembering it and cooking those parts that could have led to her identification – the head and hands.

'Just because someone does bizarre acts, the law doesn't recognise them as insane. . . What he did was pre-meditated, deliberate murder,' he declared.

On 1 July, 1988, the jury found Heidnik guilty in the first degree on all counts in the indictment. Under Pennsylvania law, the jury that returns a guilty verdict for first-degree murder must also decide the penalty, and they have two choices: Life in prison, or death in the electric chair. The jury returned the following day with a decision of death.

Peruto was angry, insisting that the jury had acted emotionally, not intellectually.

He asked Judge Abraham to issue an order to prison officials to make sure Heidnik was kept in isolation. 'If he is put in the general population, the jury's wishes will be carried out immediately,' he warned.

Judge Abraham said, 'If your client is going to commit suicide, he's going to do it. Prison officials don't want

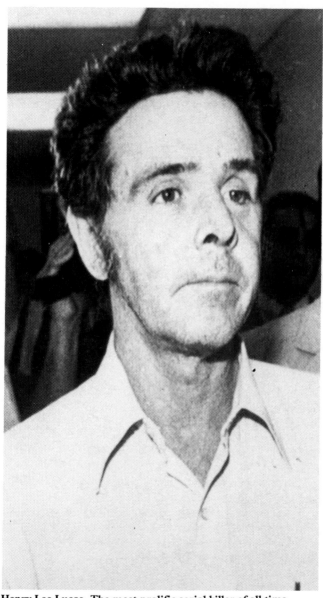

Henry Lee Lucas. The most prolific serial killer of all time

Colin Pitchfork. A murder case that made legal history

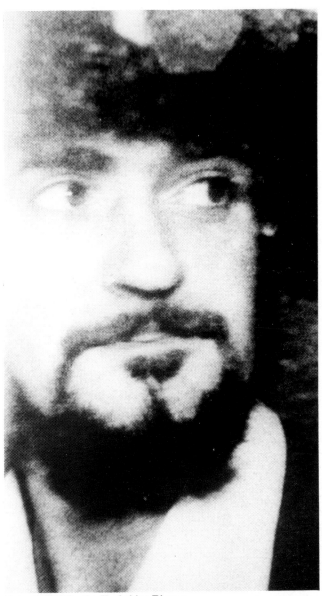

Peter Sutcliffe, the Yorkshire Ripper

Gary Heidnik. Tortured women to death in his dungeon of horror

that, but neither do they want prisoners killing other prisoners. I don't have the authority to order him held in isolation, but I will suggest they carefully watch him for suicide and carefully house him.'

She then immediately sentenced Heidnik to death for the murder of Sandra Lindsay, setting a date three months ahead for sentencing on the Dudley killing. A reporter telephoned Heidnik's father with the news and asked for his reaction. The father replied, 'I'm not interested. I don't care. It don't bother me a bit.'

Gary Heidnik now sits on Death Row in the state correctional institution at Pittsburgh. He is simply prisoner number F1398. He eats alone, showers alone, and is watched at all times lest he tries to cheat the executioner.

He was attacked by other prisoners on the way to prison and was severely beaten, but it was little compared to what he did to his victims.

Sheer horror at his activities should not preclude our objectivity in seeking the truth. And the truth must be that Heidnik has been as mad as a hatter for years. Twenty-one times in mental institutions, twenty-one times released.

Psychiatry is not an exact science and experts are always disagreeing, but Heidnik's insanity is plain to see. No civilised nation executes madmen.

Heidnik will have to wait years for his execution if it ever comes. In the meantime he is safely caged, as he caged his harmless victims. While he is there we should study him, learn from him, try to enter the icy madness of his mind and see if we ourselves are reflected there.

How many others like him are there out there?

Chapter Eighteen

CONCLUSIONS

1 THE SERIAL KILLER IN FILM, BOOK, AND REAL LIFE

With the astonishing success of films like *The Silence of the Lambs* and novels like *American Psycho*, and other films and books of the same ilk – including the 1989 film *Henry: Portrait of a Serial Killer*, which is based on the career of Henry Lee Lucas – the public have demonstrated an almost insatiable desire to learn more about the phenomenon of the serial killer, who more often than not is a sex killer. It is a comment on human nature that we make celebrities of such creatures, because in making them celebrities – i.e., unlike normal people – we miss out on an important truth: they are so *ordinary*.

Before we study the case in detail, it might be instructive to examine something of the new genre. *The Silence of the Lambs* was based on the fine novel by Thomas Harris, and features the work of the FBI's Behavioural Science Unit in Virginia. (It is the first time the FBI have allowed film-makers access to the Unit.) The FBI were the first police force to study the serial killer, and in fact the very term 'serial killer' was coined in the 1970s by FBI agent Robert Ressler, who chose the name because such killers, operating in an episodic manner, reminded him of the film serials he had watched as a child.

Ed Gein, the grisly psychotic killer of 1957, had formed the basis of the novel and film *Psycho*. For the first time such violent anti-heroes were given the limelight. There have been many imitators since, including the *Friday the Thirteenth* films.

In films, we had *Psycho* in 1960; *Homicidal,* with Jean Arless as a female serial killer in 1961; *Paranoiac* starring Oliver Reed, 1963; *In Cold Blood,* based on Capote's novel, in 1967; *The Boston Strangler,* starring Tony Curtis, in 1968; *The Honeymoon Killers* in 1970; *Texas Chainsaw Massacre* in 1974. Meanwhile in real life, with life imitating art, we had Ed Gein in 1957; Charles Manson, 1969; Edmund Kemper, 1973; David Berkowitz, 1976-77; Ted Bundy, 1978; Henry Lee Lucas, executed in 1979; Peter Sutcliffe, convicted 1981; and the Green River killer in Seattle, as well as the Zodiac Killer, New York, 1990, both as yet uncaught.

The Silence of the Lambs is the best of the films dealing with serial killers because it is so firmly based on reality. The device of having the killer lure his victims with his arm in a fake plaster cast was taken from Ted Bundy's ploy.

The plot is stomach-churning. FBI agent Clarice Starling (Jodie Foster) has to catch 'Buffalo Bill', a killer of five women who flays his victims and wears their skins. She is sent to interview Dr Hannibal Lecter in prison. Lecter is nicknamed Hannibal the Cannibal, because of his penchant for eating his victims. Played with realistic malevolence by Anthony Hopkins, Lecter is a psychiatrist who is also a genius. In exchange for the agent feeding him bits of her own life, Lecter supplies clues to the identity of Buffalo Bill. But, of course, there is a twist . . .

The agent tries to understand how a brilliant man like Lecter could have killed nine people, and asks him what happened to change him. 'Nothing happened to me, Officer Starling. I happened. You can't reduce me to a set of influences . . . A census-taker tried to quantify me once. I ate his liver with some beans. Go back to school, little Starling.'

But there is a passage where Lecter tries to explain himself. 'You created me,' he says. 'All that talk about breaking away from the timid compromises of bourgeois morality, all those grand liberal gestures – all that sex wherever you looked – I am the monstrous result.' And he has a point.

Norman Mailer in his essay *The White Negro* advised us to 'liberate the psychopath within oneself'. The 1960s were a period when everyone was advised to 'turn on' to drugs and sex, and morality was rejected as being 'old-fashioned'. There was nothing new in this either; the Marquis de Sade had advocated the same beliefs two hundred years ago in such books as *Philosophy in the Bedroom,* arguing with passionate logic that everyone ought to be able to do his own thing – in his case it was torturing women.

The critics agree that de Sade was a genius. Friedrick Nietzsche, the German philosopher of the last century, was certainly a genius. Nietzsche urged his followers to go *Beyond Good and Evil* (the title of one of his books). Two of his disciples, Leopold and Loeb, who believed in the Nietzschean philosophy of the 'Superman' – the man of the future who is above the rules which govern ordinary men and makes his own mortality, – and who were reading Nietzsche at University, decided to put his philosophy into practice, and in 1925 in Chicago kidnapped and killed little Bobby Franks to demonstrate their 'superiority'. Needless to say, they were quickly caught because they were not supermen but inept criminals. And genius or not, Nietzsche died insane.

But is Hannibal the Cannibal a genius? In the film he is portrayed as a caged panther with the mind of a computer. When he blames us for creating him, the truth is that he has dared to explore the forbidden zones; he has gone beyond good and evil into a realm where we dare not follow. This is exemplified in the sneering remark Richard Ramirez, the 'Night-Stalker', made to the court in Los Angeles which recently sentenced him for the murder of twelve people. 'You maggots make me sick. I am beyond your experience.' There is massive vanity here, a contempt for the rest of us who lack the courage to go where he has been, into the ultimate reality. But to learn what he has learned, to go where he has been, has its price. You have to become insane. . .

The recent motif seen in many killers of this type was best exemplified in the case of Eugene Chantrelle, hanged in 1878 for the murder of his wife. While in the condemned cell he growled at one warden, 'Would that I could but plant a fuse in the centre of this earth, that I could blow it to pieces, and with it, the whole of humanity. I hate them.' This curious sense of resentment is seen in so many killers. Henry Lee Lucas explained his killing-spree by saying, 'I was bitter at the world.'

It seems that criminals of this type suffer from ego-frustration, a desire to be recognised, a frustrated craving for esteem – when of course what they lack is self-esteem. Angry at being unrecognized, such killers decide to destroy the world – and themselves. Their crimes are one long suicide note, acts of revenge against what they view as a basically uncaring and insane world.

The statement 'You maggots' is reminiscent of the journal entries made by Ian Brady. He too had read de Sade avidly, and constructed a warped personal philosophy in which other people were 'morons, maggots, cabbages. . . not deserving to live'. Charles Manson made the same challenge to us when he said:, 'The children who come at you with knives – they are *your* children – you taught them. . . ' In other words, society is to blame. The greedy, uncaring lax society. This society is captured in *American Psycho,* the gruesome novel by Bret Easton Ellis. The main character – and killer – is Patrick Bateman, a young Wall Street broker who spends his evenings watching hard-core porn or killing people. Mainly women, but even men, children and dogs. Using a power drill on the face of a girl, casually gouging the eyes out of a tramp, leaving bodies in his wake like dandruff. It is his idea of fun. Just as consumer items have become disposable, then in his society people have become disposable too.

But curiously, it is a very moral book, and the author gives us a clue to the personality of serial killers when he tells us: 'There wasn't a clean, identifiable emotion within me, except for greed, and possibly total disgust. I had all the characteristics of a human being – flesh, blood, skin, hair – but my depersonalization was so intense, had gone so deep, that the normal ability to feel compassion had been eradicated. . . I was simply imitating reality, a rough resemblance of a human being, with only a dim corner of my mind working.'

Since women are victimized in the novel, it has led to women's groups in America ceremoniously burning the book in public, and the author has received death threats. But the ultimate question is, what do such novels tell us about ourselves?

It is not too far removed from reality. In the 1980s Leonard Lake killed twenty-five women in the San Francisco area, video-taping their deaths. His isolated bungalow was a torture chamber equipped with chains and shackles. It was not enough to kill his victims; he has to keep them prisoner for days on end to torture them.

Henry: Portrait of a Serial Killer, by director John McNaughton, is a film about a few days in the wake of Henry, a killer in Chicago, who kills people to make himself feel better. (It is based on the real-life killer, Henry Lee Lucas.) He introduces his friend Otis to this hobby, and they video-tape themselves torturing and killing their victims, then go home and have a beer in front of the television. After the first joint killing, Henry asks Otis, 'Feel better now?' It is no surprise to learn that at the first public screening, 15 per cent of the audience walked out in disgust.

Of course, the reality of the serial killer – and they currently account for 500 murders a year in the USA – is that he is so *ordinary*. Christopher Wilder, millionaire killer of eight women, was described by those who knew him as 'just an easy-going quiet guy'. Ted Bundy was a clever law student who happened to kill twenty-three women; Dennis Nilsen, killer of fourteen boys in London, worked for the Manpower Services Commission. Peter Sutcliffe was a lorry-driver. All of them lacked the seductive glamour of the killer on the big screen. The very names given to these demons are so ordinary. Gary, Frank, Harry, Henry, Jack. Names of the man next door. . . As Sutcliffe showed, your neighbour might even be *married* to him.

Perhaps giving publicity to such demons is counter-productive; perhaps they do not deserve to be glamorized. But the fact is, ever since Bram Stoker published *Dracula* a century ago, people like to be frightened. We do well to be frightened by the real-life cases, but perhaps we can learn from studying them.

Of one thing we can be certain. Although the serial killer is a headline-grabber associated with the USA, he exists here in Britain, as Sutcliffe and Nilsen demonstrated. And even as you read these words, somewhere in this country a serial killer is going about his secret work, unsuspected by the neighbours. . .

2 HOW THEY CATCH THE SERIAL KILLER: THE MIND-HUNTERS

With the beginning of the 1980s the USA suffered a dramatic leap in the nation's murder statistics. There were 20,000 cases in 1980, jumping to 23,000 in 1981. There was a kind of hysteria fostered by the media, to such effect that on 21 June 1984 President Reagan set up the National Centre for the Analysis of Violent Crime (NCAVC) at the FBI Academy in Quantico, Virginia. He described the Centre as a tool in the fight against 'stranger murderers', as serial killers were then called.

America, because of its vast size, has special problems in countering the serial killer, who can travel the nation state by state, leaving bodies in his wake with virtually no risk of detection. Each city has its own police force, and once the killer has moved on they have no hope of tracing him. He becomes the problem of another police force somewhere else.

To counter his ability to kill and travel nation-wide, only a nation-wide police force could hope to combat him: thus the FBI, the only force who can operate anywhere in the USA, was given the task. They used every scientific aid to help detect and track such killers. NCAVC was a product of the FBI's Behavioural Science Unit at Quantico. They set it up, devised its programme, trained the staff.

The FBI Academy itself stands in 600 acres of woodland, surrounded by stout defences and with armed guards checking traffic in and out. The NCAVC is situated in a huge concrete bunker sixty-feet below the Academy. There are no windows, just strip lighting and the glow from countless VDU consoles. The head of NCAVC is 45-year-old John Douglas.

He tells of how he joined the FBI aged twenty-five, straight out of the US Air Force. 'About 1964 I became interested in violent crime, the psychology, the whys of their behaviour. After many of the arrests I was doing, I got into talking about their personal lives, why they got into violent crime.' As a result of his curiosity, he is now the leading expert on the serial killer, and worked on the filming of *The Silence of the Lambs*. He coached Jodie Foster for her role, and says of the film: 'The movie is really accurate. I am not easily scared, but it's a scary movie. Hopkins does a hell of a job as Dr Lecter. The film has given a lot of publicity to the unit. Most people don't even know it exists.'

In 1979 Douglas and his team began going into prisons and questioning notorious serial killers about their motives, asking them to fill in a 57-page questionnaire containing thousands of questions. Most of the 35 killers selected co-operated. Men like Charles Manson and David 'Son of Sam' Berkowitz, Juan Corona, and Richard Speck. They had never been asked such questions before. How did they select their victims? Where did they take them? Did they talk to the victims? What did they do to them? Did they follow the press coverage of their killings, and if so, how did it affect their behaviour?

Going into a prison cell and talking to a man like Emil Kemper, six feet nine inches tall and built like a tank, is not without its risks. Douglas explains, 'For them, being a murderer gives them status, and what better status than to kill an FBI agent?' The men on Death Row have nothing to lose, and are not handcuffed. Before going in to interview them, the FBI agent has to sign a disclaimer stating that he is 'not negotiable'; meaning that if he is taken hostage, no deals can be struck for his release.

Kemper killed his grandparents when he was fourteen; in his twenties he killed college girls before decapitating his mother. Kemper told the agent who went in alone to question him, 'The rooms are soundproofed here. Nobody can hear your screams. By the time you press that button I'll tear you apart.' The agent had to bluff his way out of that situation!

Under the leadership of Douglas, NCAVC developed the concept of 'psychological profiling' (PROP) which has had remarkable results. It was first used in Britain in 1987 to trap Duffy, the Railway Murderer. What it attempts to do is to build up a psychological portrait of the killer from clues left behind at the murder scene. For example, if a body is dumped in a remote area, with difficult terrain, that might suggest that the killer drives a Jeep-type vehicle, and is likely to be a macho-type person.

A typical case is cited by Douglas. In 1979 schoolteacher Francine Evelson was found mutilated and very dead on top of her apartment block in New York. On the very roof itself. Douglas explains, 'The killer used a surprise "blitz" type of attack to render her unconscious, breaking her jaw and nose. He carried her up to the top floor to the roof of her apartments. He spent hours up there mutilating her body. What's strange is that he spent so much time up there that he had to defecate on the steps, and he covered it over! Somehow *that* was repulsive to him.'

Douglas had been called in to help by the New York Police. After examining the scene he told them, 'The killer is a white male, in his mid to late twenties, and lives in the apartment block or works there.' He also said that the killer was unmarried and would have a collection of detective or pornography magazines. He said that the killer had already been interviewed, and in fact had probably been overly co-operative.

It was an educated guess. Most serial killers tend to select their victims from their own racial group. Most are in their mid-twenties. And the fact that the killer spent so much time on the roof was proof that he felt safe there. He *knew* the roof intimately. The killer turned out to be the janitor of the building, Carmine Calabro, who fitted the profile exactly. Detectives, amazed at the success of the profile, asked Douglas jokingly why he hadn't given them the suspect's phone number too.

Douglas explained his thinking on the case. 'He was too comfortable up there on the roof. He spent way too much time up there. Sometimes the killer will insinuate himself into the police investigation so they can keep track of how well it is going, and so they can relive the details. I felt he wouldn't be married.'

Douglas elaborated further on his techniques. 'First I try and put myself in the mind of the victim – what she was experiencing, what happened to her and so on. Then the same with the subject. Because I've interviewed so many of them, I know why they're doing certain things. It takes a certain breed of man to do this.'

Does it take a certain breed of man to catch them? Douglas is modest. 'Sometimes with me, depending on the case, I can do it, and sometimes I can't. It's just not right.'

Every police force in the USA sends details of their homicides to the FBI Academy. There they are examined and analysed. If the case in question remains unsolved, the FBI can request video photographs to be sent to them. Teams of officers examine the scene-of-crime photographs, looking for psychological clues in the case. From long experience and from studying the clues they have developed the ability to predict the likely murderer, his probable age, colour, the car he is most likely to drive, and the probable area where he lives. It is back to the world of Sherlock Holmes, in a sense.

The FBI officers have become 'mind-hunters', and from talking to real killers have developed a unique insight into the mind of the killer. They discovered, incidentally, that all these people had one thing in common: all were intelligent, but all had been abused and rejected as children, and had reacted by retreating into a world of fantasy.

The result of the NCAVC programme is that we now have cops who can think like killers, and by getting inside their heads, predict their next move. They learn to interpret the perverse fantasies which fuel the serial killer, and given the background to the murders, the 'mind-hunters' can predict which sadistic fantasy is being enacted, predict where and when the killer will strike next, get into his mind and figure out why he does what he does, and try to imagine what his post-crime behaviour will be like. Will he be boastful or remorseful? Either way, the killer's own fantasy can be used against him to trap him. (For example, if he is remorseful, the killer may well turn up at the victim's funeral.)

But for these specialist 'mind-hunters' there is an obvious danger: they might come to identify too much with the insane killers they chase. This was the thinking beyond the taunt which Dr Lecter throws at the FBI agent responsible for his capture in the film *The Silence of the Lambs*. 'The reason you caught me is we're just alike.'

Douglas has no fears for his own sanity but admits, 'Sometimes you just have to get away from the investigation to get by yourself. And even then you may think about it, or dream about it.' It is dangerous work.

Douglas became involved in the Green River case in Seattle in the early 1980s, when he was thirty-nine. The case was – and – remains – the worst unsolved serial murder case in history, with a total of forty-nine women victims. Douglas went out to lecture the task force, and next day was found in his motel room with a high fever and partial paralysis. The stress had got to him.

Over the years psychologists have developed what they term the *Diagnostical Statistical Manual,* which is a guide to the classification of almost every type of madman .But not the serial killer. He is not in that book, because he is by definition unclassifiable. 'You don't learn this stuff in college or from a book,' Douglas explains. And Ted Bundy himself said, 'If anybody's looking for pat answers, forget it. If there were, the psychiatrists would have cleared this up years ago.'

Douglas says that psychiatrists are of little use to the police, since they refuse to look at autopsy photographs or visit the scene of the crime, fearing that this may force them to come up with preconceived ideas about the man responsible. But as Douglas says, 'Unless they look at those reports, they won't know who is sitting in the chair in front of them.'

The 'mind-hunters' have developed their own manual on the serial killer. The typical killer is white, male, works alone, and will begin killing in his mid-twenties, but can go on killing into old age, depending on how organized he is. Henry Lee Lucas boasted of having killed 360 people in his bloody career, and was middle-aged when arrested.

The motivation for his acts is not sex, even if a sexual element is present, such as rape or sex after death. 'What they really want is to control the victim for a period of time, manipulate, dominate, have overall control for hours if not days. They want to see the fear come across the victims' eyes, they want to hear them begging for their life. That's the turn-on.'

Most serial killers tend to pick a specific *type*. Most of Bundy's victims had long hair and were remarkably similar in appearance. They may have a preference for blondes or brunettes, slim girls or plump ones, but in most cases opportunity is everything. They spot a woman on her own and she is a 'target'. The victim just happens to be in the wrong place at the wrong time.

Douglas calls serial killers the 'sportsmen' of murderers, because the thrill is in the hunt as much as the kill. He cites the case of Chris Hanson, forty-two, a baker who killed 187 prostitutes. 'He was a big hunter and had a plane. He would pick them up, cuff them, fly them off to some backwood, let them out, strip them, and tell them to run. He'd give them a head start and then he'd hunt them down like an animal.'

Although most serial killers don't fit into neat psychological patterns – like Norman Bates in *Psycho* – research has shown that most have a background of childhood bed-wetting, cruelty to animals and arson. Often they are bright, but under-achievers. Most have suffered abuse as a child, either physically or mentally. In one survey, 43 per cent of the subjects interviewed were sexually abused in childhood, 70 per cent felt sexually incompetent, and a large percentage used pornography.

The FBI has divided serial killers into two types. There is the 'loner' killer who is withdrawn and anti-social. He will commit 'cowardly' murders, knocking the women unconscious first. He leaves behind a 'disorganized' crime scene, often with fingerprints and no attempt to hide the evidence of his crime. The victim will have come from close to where he lives, and he will tend to have a menial job.

The other type appears to have a good social front, maintaining normal relationships with friends and women, and seemingly quite normal. He is organized, mobile, creative, and can quickly adapt to any situation and is not given to panic. He is more likely to select a certain type of victim, and often teases the police with messages, taunting them because he feels much more powerful then they are themselves.

This is the type which attracts the media attention, the creative kind of killer. His very apparent normality is the reason why he fascinates the public. He could be the guy next door. Often he is. Gary Gilmore got thousands of letters, fan mail and proposals of marriage. David Berkowitz, 'Son of Sam', who terrorized New York during 1976-77, wrote several taunting letters to a New York columnist. Following his capture, the public paid pilgrimages to his house, cutting up bits of carpet to take away as souvenirs. They had made him into an instant legend.

The killer craves publicity: the public is only too ready to grant it. They are fascinated by cops and robbers TV shows, for example, just as the killers are. Most serial killers are would-be cops; men who tried to join the force but were rejected, or who work as security guards with tin badges, like Kenneth Bianchi, the 'Hillside Strangler.' Gerald Schaffer was a real policeman. Douglas says, 'He picked up hitchhikers, took them to a remote spot, and hanged them up by their necks. He was all screwed up, he would feed them beer, he'd want to see them urinate, defecate. Then he'd hang them and have sex with them afterwards. And you should see this guy: he looked like he sang in the choir. He looked really normal. Yet he may have killed up to two dozen.'

Normal-looking guys. Creative and organized. No wonder Americans are fascinated by the type: they could be anybody, and anyone can be a victim. It is a very democratic process.

The latest news is that two women – which is very rare – are being sought as serial killers in the USA. They operate together, hitching lifts with male motorists and then killing them after sex. . . Do you drive? Be careful who you pick up. . . Thanks to the advances in police procedure, they have a better chance of catching your killer, but it won't give you back your life. . .

3. INSIDE THE MIND OF THE SEX KILLER

This entire book has been an attempt to look inside the soul of the sex criminal, and now it is perhaps appropriate to ask ourselves what we have learned about the inner workings of his mind. At first glance the answer might seem to be: not very much. But in fact we now know a great deal, and we owe that knowledge to the pioneering work of the FBI's "Mind-Hunters", and before them to such people as Dr James Brussel, and even fiction writers like G.K.Chesterton, who was pointing the way forward in his Father Brown stories.

In *The Secret of Father Brown*, a curious American asks him how he had been able to solve so many murders. Had he used occult means? What was his secret? Father Brown replies, 'You see, it was I who killed all those people. . . I murdered them all myself. . . I had planned out each of the crimes very carefully, I had thought out exactly how a thing like that could be done and in what style or state of mind a man could really do it. And when I was quite sure that I felt exactly like the murderer myself, of course I knew who he was.'

Father Brown describes his technique as being 'a religious exercise' recommended to him by a friend of the Pope. But in fact Chesterton was in 1927 describing how a detective could get inside the mind of a killer and by thinking like him, capture him. Such ideas were quickly followed up in real life.

Dr James Brussel was formerly the Assistant Commissioner of Mental Hygiene for the State of New York and psychiatric consultant to various police forces. It comes as no surprise to learn that he once worked for the CIA. The Press have described him as the 'Sherlock Holmes of the couch', and his fascinating account of the criminal cases in which he has been involved, *Casebook of a Criminal Psychiatrist* (1968), certainly bears this out.

The police first consulted Dr Brussel about the case of the 'Mad Bomber' who planted twenty-eight explosive devices around New York City over a sixteen-year period, beginning in 1940. With the bombs came letters blaming 'Con Edison', the company which supplies the city with its electricity. In December 1956 a bomb planted in the back of a cinema seat injured six people, forcing the police to mount a major hunt for the bomber.

Inspector Howard Finney of the New York Police Crime Laboratory visited Dr Brussel, giving him copies of the letters from the bomber and the files on the case. After studying the documents for some time, Dr Brussel told the detective, 'It's a man. Paranoiac. He's middle-aged – forty-five to fifty. Well-proportioned in build. He's single, a loner, perhaps living with an older female relative. He is very tidy, neat and clean-shaven. Well-educated but of foreign extraction. He's a Slav. Probably lives in Bridgeport, Connecticut. (It has a large Polish community.) He has had a bad disease – possibly heart trouble. When you catch him he'll be wearing a double-breasted suit. Buttoned.'

When arrested at his home in Bridgeport, Connecticut, George Metesky, the 'Mad Bomber', was found to be well-proportioned, aged fifty-one years, of Polish extraction, unmarried, living in a house with two older sisters, and was wearing a double-breasted suit. Buttoned.

Why had Dr Brussel's profile been so accurate? Because it was based on solid deductive reasoning, experience, and playing the averages. Paranoia takes a long time to develop – say ten years before that first bomb in 1940 – which meant he had started to become ill in 1930, making him middle-aged in 1956. Paranoiacs tend to feel intellectually superior, are neat and obsessive, tidy to a fault. Hence the neat lettering on the notes and the double-breasted suit. The words in the notes were those of an educated man, but had no American slang and read as if they had been translated into English. The wildly Victorian 'dastardly deeds' in one note hinted at a foreigner. Why a Slav? Because historically bombs have been favoured in Central Europe. Well-proportioned? Because research had shown that 85 per cent of paronoiacs have an athletic build. Why a paranoiac? Because they are the champion grudge-holders Why single? Because of all the neatly printed capital letters in the notes, only the

'W' was odd: it was shaped like two U's joined together – the shape of a woman's breasts. This suggested that the Mad Bomber had sexual problems... It all sounds far-fetched, but it actually worked, and Dr Brussel went on to solve many other cases using the same techniques. And, of course, the FBI's 'psychological profiling' owes much to his pioneering approach.

We can sum up the data gained to date by saying that the typical sex killer is usually young – under thirty-five – and fantasises about killing long before he actually turns to murder. He tends to be a quiet, withdrawn person – witness Sutcliffe and Denis Nilsen – and in most cases kills not for sexual needs, but to service power needs.

There is usually some history of early abnormal behaviour, graphically seen in the case of Kürten and in Patrick Byrne's peeping-tom activities. There may be bed-wetting, arson, cruelty to animals. There is usually some trace of necrophilia present in the killings, and more often than not a latent homosexual streak in the killer. Most have rich fantasy lives.

Currently there is great disquiet about cannibal cases, following the arrest of Jeffrey Dahmer in Milwaukee in August 1991, and his subsequent confession to seventeen cannibal murders. There is even a cannibal killer loose in the Soviet Union, Nikolai Dzhumagallev, nicknamed "Metal Fang", who has butchered dozens of women, serving their barbecued flesh to unsuspecting neighbours. The psychologist Joel Norris has written four books on three hundred separate serial killers, and claims that about one in three experiments with cannibalism, often saving portions of their victims as a talisman. Christie, of course, saved pubic hairs. . .

Does it help to try to see what these killers have in common? They do not look alike, for example, or even have the same domestic situations. Albert deSalvo was young and good-looking and committed 13 murders and 1300 sex crimes and his wife complained that he was sexually insatiable. Ted Bundy had an active sex life, and Norman Collins dated two or three times a week. Paul Knowles was an attractive man who had normal relations with many women. They were intelligent, dominant men who wore what Norris calls a 'mask of sanity'.

On the other hand, Dennis Nilsen was miserably alone, as was Henry Lee Lucas, apart from his 'Becky' whom he had to kill when she threatened to leave him. In other words, we cannot detect sex-killers by their appearance, domestic situations or day-to-day behaviour. *Nor should we expect to*. The sexual impulse is primarily a mental process like murder, it begins inside the head. It is a closed, secret interior universe.

We only get the chance to look inside the head of a sex killer after he has been caught, and only then, with the benefit of hindsight, will some of his early behaviour take on significance and reveal a *pattern*. That is the value of compiling cases like these: every new case provides us with that much more data, so that we can begin profiling the sex killer as a type, and hopefully we may quickly identify him.

We are now in a position to make some statements about the nature of sex killers, even though in most cases they are merely broad generalizations. It is a fact that sex killing is a specifically male activity motivated by a lust for power, or as a means of expressing intense anger. Adler would seem to have been nearer the mark than Freud in this respect.

Generally, the sex killer will belong to one of three broad types, characteristics of which may overlap in some cases. First we have the 'biological' killer, whose crimes are triggered by a physical defect of some sort. A surprising number of such killers have a history of head injuries in early youth. Albert deSalvo might be considered to have been born with an over-active sex-drive, perhaps an organic brain defect.

The second type of killer are those predisposed psychologically to kill. Perhaps there was a trauma in early childhood, or the child grew up in an all-female environment, or was rejected by females. He is more likely to be motivated by a power-needs complex, and to kill compulsively over and over again to release some internal psychic pressure. Both Bundy and Sutcliffe were of this type.

The third type might be termed the sociological, for want of a better word. They are 'made' killers, born into a grim environment, the typical deprived-child syndrome. This type may feel that he has been cheated, that life owes him more, that he is being brutalized by his job, marriage, or life in general. He would welcome imprisonment, since prison imposes a structure on life and gives meaning and order to existence. Hence Heirens's note: 'For heaven's sake catch me before I kill again.' To such a miserably alienated person only the act of murder can bring a sense of being alive to his torpid sense of reality. To him murder is therapeutic: murder as psychodrama.

Norris warns us that demands for capital punishment are counter-productive because 'Perversely, he wishes for death, and the threat of the gas-chamber and the electric chair or lethal injection is only an inducement to keep committing murders until he is caught and put to death. . . The serial killer can no more stop killing than a heroin addict can kick the habit.'

And so finally, what use is all this information to us? The answer must be a frank: none on a practical level. It may be possible in the future to devise a diagnostic test to detect serial killers *before* they begin to kill. But not yet.

However, the situation is not as bleak as it appears, and there is good reason to feel optimistic about the future. Technical advances alone will help to make the detection of sex killers that much easier.

But the most exciting and promising developments have been in the field of behavioural science. The detective is no longer expected merely to sleuth; he must also be a psychologist. The new type of 'psychological detectives' will prove to be far more successful than the old type of man-hunters. You simply cannot hope to catch a sexual serial killer by the same means that you would employ to catch a bicycle thief. You need to become a mind-hunter. And in a very real sense, every reader of this book has now become just that. . .

SEX CRIMES:
A CENTURY OF SEX KILLERS.
Brian Marriner.
Select Bibliography

Angellella, Michael. *Trail Of Blood – The Albert Fish Story* (Bobbs–Merrill, New York, 1979).

Berg, Karl. *The Sadist* (Heinemann, 1945).

Bolitho, William. *Murder For Profit* (Dobson, 1926).

Burn, Gordon. *Somebody's Husband, Somebody's Son* (Heinemann, 1984).

Camps, Francis. E. *Medical And Scientific Investigations in the Christie Case* (Medical Publications, 1953).

De River, J. Paul. *The Sexual Criminal* (Charles C. Thomas, Illinios 1949).

Duke, Thomas. S. *Celebrated Criminal Cases of America* (James. H. Barry, San Francisco, 1910).

Englade, Ken. *Cellar of Horror* (St. Martin's Press, New York, 1988).

Frank, Gerold. *The Boston Strangler* (Jonathan Cape, 1966).

Fromm, Erich. *The Anatomy of Human Destructiveness* (Jonathan Cape, 1974).

Gaute, J.H.H. and Robin Odell. *The Murderers' Who's Who* (Harrap, 1979, 1986).

Green, Jonathan. *The Directory of Infamy* (Mills & Boon, 1980).

Griffiths, Major Arthur. *Mysteries of Police and Crime* (Cassell, 1899).

Kennedy, Ludovic. *Ten Rillington Place* (Gollancz, 1961).

Larsen, Richard. W. *Bundy: The Deliberate Stranger* (Prentice Hall, Cliffs. USA, 1980).

Leyton, Elliot. *Hunting Humans* (Penguin, 1989)

Linedecker, Clifford. *Thrill Killers* (Futura, 1990).

Lucas, Norman. *The Sex Killers* (W.H. Allen, 1974).

Lunde, Donald. T. *Murder And Madness* (W.W.Norton, New York, 1979).

Masters, Brian. *Killing For Company* (Jonathan Cape, 1985).

Nash, Jay. Robert. *Murder, America* (New York, 1973; Harrap, 1981).

Norris, Joel. *Serial Killers* (Arrow, 1990).

Notable British Trials. (A series of 83 titles. Pub James Hodge.)

Rule, Ann. *The Stranger Beside Me.* (W.W. Norton, New York, 1980).

Sifakis, Carl. *The Encylopaedia of American Crime* (Facts On File, New York, 1982).

Simpson, Keith. *Forty Years of Murder* (Harrap, 1978; Granada, 1980).

Smith, Sydney. *Mostly Murder* (Harrap, 1959).

Sodermann, H. *Auf der Spur des Verbrechen* (Köln–Berlin, 1924).

Williams, Emlyn. *Beyond Belief* (Hamish Hamilton, 1967).

Wilson, Colin. *A Casebook of Murder* (Leslie Frewin, 1969).

Wilson, Colin. *Origins of The Sexual Impulse* (Arthur Barker, 1963).

Wilson, Colin, and Donald Seaman. *The Serial Killers* (W.H. Allen, 1990).

Yallop. David. A. *Deliver Us From Evil* (Macdonald Futura, 1981).

Also: grateful thanks to *True Detective* magazine for access to their files covering the last forty years.

Index

Fatal Attraction:
When Love Turns To Murder

Twenty incredible stories make up this enthralling volume of murder at its most passionate. It will root you to the spot. Compulsive reading for all fans of the true crime genre.

£3.99

A Date With The Hangman
T.J. Leech

This is an outstanding volume of British murder cases, uncanny and strange. The killers are an odd mix – robbers and rapists, cop-killers and con-men, jealous lovers, paedophiles, madmen and ruthless women. But all had one thing in common. . . a date with the hangman.

£3.99

All books in the True Crime Library are available at your local bookshop or newsagent or can be ordered from the publisher. Please send the cover price plus: 60p for the first book plus 30p per copy for each additional book ordered to a maximum charge of £2.40. Send to: Forum Press, P.O. Box 158, London, SE20 7QA.